The Spaghetti Western Digest
Issue Two

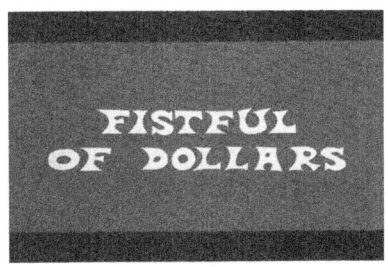

Copyright © 2020 Michael Hauss. M.H. Books.
All rights reserved.

The Spaghetti Western Digest: Issue Two. Fall 2020

The Spaghetti Western Digest includes photos, posters, lobby cards, screenshots, and other items, including drawings and illustrations for the purpose of criticism and documentation. All copyrights held by production companies, artists, authors, and/or any copyright holders.

Nothing within The Spaghetti Western Digest can be copied, transmitted, or shared. Only small quotes from this work can be reproduced in critical reviews. For permission requests, please contact the editor.

ISBN: 9798686321779

The Spaghetti Western Digest
Issue Two...

Contributors: Tom Betts, Dennis Capicik, Eugenio Ercolani, Steve Fenton, Steve Mason, Tony Nash, Anthony Thorne, Van Roberts
Cover: Tim Paxton
Editor: Michael Hauss

Contents

Tom Betts Editorializin' about the Holy Land	4
Roberto Curti Interview	7
Tom Betts on the Truth behind the Death of Peter Lee Lawrence	15
Eugenio Ercolani: The Cinema of Giulio Petroni	17
Petroni, a Family Business by Eugenio Erconlani	21
Steve Mason on A Man called Noon	29
By George! It's An Interview with Daniel Camargo	42
The Specialist: Eureka! Blu-Ray Review... Tony Nash	50
Van Roberts Aims for the Heart	54
Goodbye Maestro by Tom Betts	75
Any Gun Can Play: Interview with Kevin Grant	78
Van Roberts' Day of Anger	82
Steve Mason Reviews: Wild East Productions: Thou Shall not Kill and The Beast	102
Retro Interview from WAi: Glenn Saxson- Conducted by Rene Hogguer	109
Tom Betts- 1966: The Year Django became Unchained	119
Euro- Westerns 1919- 1961; Anthony Thorne	123
The Noir and the West: Tony Nash	148
Cover Review: Killer Kid: Dennis Capicik	158
The Ballad of Django: Dennis Capicik	163
A Man Called Sergio Martino: An Interview	166
The Western Films Of Alberto De Martino: Michael Hauss	169
Steve Fenton Reviews....	212
Afterword	245

VISITS TO THE HOLY LAND... PART ONE

In 2003 and 2005, I was fortunate to be able to visit Spain and many of the filming locations of the Sergio Leone westerns. My good friend Don Bruce and his companion Marla Johnson had been going over to Almeria, Spain, usually twice a year, for six years to search for the filming locations of the Leone films in hopes of writing a book with the proceeds being donated to the SAG Actors Home in Woodland Hills, California. He had been over there so often he bought a condo in San Jose, Andalusia, Spain, and when not there, he rented it out. The managers of the condo were a British couple who also had a teenage son, so language was not a problem and any time they had a problem communicating with any of the Spaniards they would come in contact with, who didn't speak English, they would call John or his son, and they'd translate or talk to whomever they were and get the information needed.

I flew into Madrid and then down to Almeria. I had a four-hour layover in Madrid, so Aldo Sambrell came to the airport, and we hung out together and had a couple of cervezas. I then boarded a prop plane and flew down to Almeria. Walking down the stairs and across the runway to the baggage claim in Almeria, I felt like Clint Eastwood must have seen and felt much the same way. Don and Marla were there to pick me up, and we drove to their two-story, two-bedroom condo in San Jose. Before getting there, they stopped at the Hotel Cortillo el Sotillo- as we drove up the driveway, I immediately recognized it as the small house from "Fistful of Dollars," where Marisol was kept captive. Walking in, I was amazed to find it looking much like what I had seen in the film. The same fireplace and shelves, recently painted and chairs, sofas, and lamps all around because it was now the lobby of a hotel. After our stop, we drove to their condo two miles or so away. They told me the jet lag would soon catch up with me, and I would basically just pass out. That's exactly what I did watching TV and drinking another beer I was cutting *zzzzzz*s within the hour.

The next morning I awoke and had a cup of coffee and a breakfast pastry, and then Don made sandwiches, and we packed a cooler drove to the nearest petrol station and filled up. We then drove to Los Albaricoques, Cabo de Gata, Almería, Andalucía. The famous village featured in "**For a Few Dollars More**," and we walked all around the village- Saw the bullet holes still left from the barber chair scene. We also saw the ring where the final duel was staged, at that time still in partial disrepair.

I couldn't believe I was walking down the same streets that Clint, Lee, Gian, and Sergio had tread some 40 years before and having it look like it was almost yesterday. We saw very few people in any of the villages we visited. They were inhabited, but we had them almost all to ourselves. We visited the San Antonio Mission location and walked up on the roof, which was used as the roof of the jail in "For a Few Dollars More." We visited the village of Cabo de Gata, where Shorty Larson was hanged and laid down on the same cistern that Clint did when his job was interrupted by Tuco.

On and on we would go from mid-morning till around 8 p.m. We'd stop for lunch and have the great sandwiches Don made along with drinks and chips and fruit. I remember the first day we ate on the steps of a church in Guadix right across from where the ramp that the three revolutionaries were executed in "Duck You Sucker." Don took pictures of us and the surrounding area and then posted them on John Nudge's Spaghetti Western website jokingly asking where did you have lunch today?

Since it really didn't get completely dark until around 10 p.m., we had plenty of time to get back to the condo and fix us a light dinner and watch the BBC cable channel or DVDs. Once we were watching "The Wind and the Lion," and they showed a watchtower in the film that I could look right out the front picture window of the condo and see the same one perched atop a hill on the other side of the bay his condo overlooked.

On the other side of the hill behind Don's was the windmill seen in "**A Pistol for Ringo**," Cortijo del Romeral which was used as the main house in the same film and "The Big Gundown" past the windmill was the beach from "Hannie Caulder" and a little further the location of the ruined fort seen in the opening of "Shalako."

The places we visited and the people we met were for me, like visiting the Holy Land, and I felt as if I were walking on sacred ground. Hopefully, if Mike continues his series of books on Spaghetti westerns I can fill you in with greater detail on all the locations we visited and then a return trip in 2005 and even more locations and a birthday I celebrated at the Hotel Cortillo el Sotillo with several of my European friends who I still am in contact with today.

- Tom Betts

Left: Arrow Video release of A Pistol for Ringo/The Return of Ringo
Right: Grindhouse Releasing: The Big Gundown. original art © Mario De Berardinis (MOS)

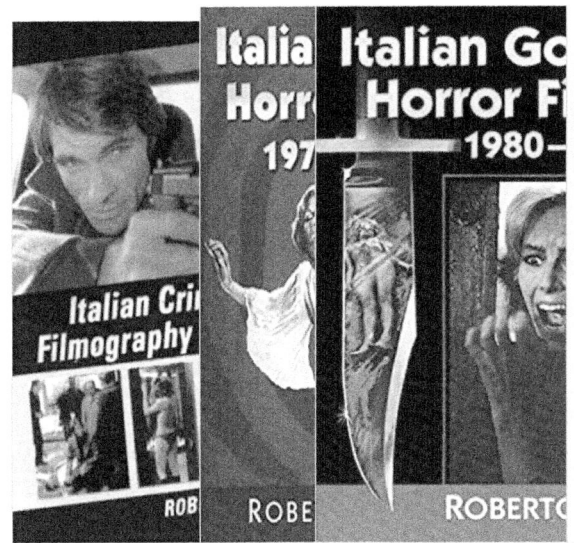

ROBERTO CURTI INTERVIEW

S.W. Thank you for allowing us here at The Spaghetti Western Digest to interview you! Let us start with how you became interested in film. And how you became a film historian.
RC: Thank you for your interest! Well, I grew up watching films. My father loves cinema (and still collects DVDs at the venerable age of 87!). He was a big Western fan and took me to second and third run venues to watch old movies (I was born in 1971, and back in the late 1970s it was the rule). As a kid my favorites were Westerns, and even nowadays some of my favorite films are Westerns. Stagecoach – I don't know how many times I saw it! –, **The Searchers**, **She Wore a Yellow Ribbon**, **3:10 To Yuma**... I remember watching **Vera Cruz** on a big screen when I was just a small kid, Delmer Daves' **Drum Beat** starring Alan Ladd, in a small theater at a matinee... And of course I loved sci-fi and monster movies. De Laurentiis' remake of **King Kong** in a packed venue was an amazing experience. Watching 2001 on the big screen (another third-run matinee) literally blew me away.

Likewise, in the late 1970s-early 1980s you could watch tons and tons of old films on Italian TV. I kept watching all the films I could catch. I remember staying up late at night to see Les Diaboliques, and that became a favorite too. Late night TV offered lots of great retrospectives: Ingmar Bergman, John Huston, the Marx Brothers, Preston Sturges, Roger Corman's Poe cycle, Akira Kurosawa... but also plenty of genre films, gialli, spy films, sci-fi, erotic comedies—you name it.

Then I started recording and collecting films. Perhaps that's why I'm still partial to old, barely watchable VHS copies. And I started raiding video shops, buying old VHS originals that were given away for a few bucks, old movies that nobody rented anymore such as... Bava's **Reazione a catena**. Over weekends some friends and I gathered at another friend's house and binge-watched movie marathons on his video recorder—he put the VCR and the couch, we brought the drinks and the movies. This meant horror movie marathons but also weird pairings, such as **Santa Sangre** and **Salò**, or **The House by the Cemetery** and **Fellini-Satyricon**.

Anyway, watching and collecting movies was not enough. I started reading lots of books (a personal favorite being Lindsay Anderson's monography on John Ford), magazines, interviews, and discovering things. I remember taking the train from my hometown to Milan just to buy Phil Hardy's *Aurum Film Encyclopedia–Horror* and *Obsession: The Films of Jess Franco* which I had noticed the day before in a bookshop but hadn't enough money to buy (a condition common to many university students, I guess).

However, I did not study cinema at school. You can say I'm self-taught. I have a degree in Law, and my thesis was on the Italian cinema law system in post-war years. I started writing about movies in the mid-1990s, small 'zines, the local newspaper, etc.. By the end of the Nineties I became acquainted with the people at *Nocturno magazine*, and around the same time I became a contributor to *Il Mereghetti*, Italy's best-selling film dictionary (the 2021 edition is coming out this Fall). In 2000 Davide Pulici and I interviewed director Corrado Farina in Milan, and the ensuing booklet (attached to Nocturno magazine as part on a series of interview books on filmmakers) was possibly my first "book". In 2003 Tommaso La Selva and I co-wrote *Sex and Violence – Percorsi nel cinema estremo* (a critical history of "extreme" cinema from the early days to the present) which became a sort of cult book in Italy, so much so that it was republished again in 2007 and then 2015, in revised and expanded editions. Several more books followed, including a monography on Kubrick's **The Killing**, one on religion in American horror cinema called *Demoni e dei* and a two-volume history of Italian film censorship co-written with Alessio Di Rocco, *Visioni proibite*.

In 2010 I approached U.S. publisher McFarland & co. with a proposal for a book on Italian crime films, which became *Italian Crime Filmography*, 1968-1980. This began my series of English language books on Italian cinema. I like writing about the films produced in my country because it allows me to explore its history and the evolution of mores and popular culture. My idea is to offer readers – at least, I hope so – a new perspective on films and filmmakers they already know, allowing them to discover and savor those works in the historical and cultural context during which they were made. And, to me, it is also a way to learn more about the past and reflect about it, to better understand the present. Another fascinating part of this job is wading through archive material (such as early drafts of scripts, production papers, censorship documents) which open a different and more detailed perspective of how a certain film was born. For instance, for my book on Mario Bava's **Blood and Black Lace**, I discovered an early draft of the script which features some striking differences with the finished film.

S.W. To you, is there anything specific that can be pointed at as the instigator behind the explosion of Popular Italian Cinema?
R.C. There were various factors, less artistic than economic I'd say, and mostly related to the state of the film industry in the post-WW2 years, as the harshness of Neorealism—which depicted post-War Italian life with an explicit rawness that censors didn't like a bit—gave way to comedies and tear-jerking melodramas. American productions were setting their eyes on Cinecittà and coming to Rome because it was cheaper to film there, thus allowing the Italian film industry to fortify again after an economic crisis of the mid-1950s and giving work to a whole series of technicians, craftsmen and assorted people related to the film business in one way or the other. The growing reliance on the coproduction system allowed producers stronger revenues but in turn pushed them to rely on films which would be palatable to foreign audiences as well. And of course **Le fatiche di Ercole** becoming sort of a hit overseas opened the way to overseas markets and started the big sword-and-sandal thread of the late 1950s. Something similar appeared a few years later with the horror film, with **La Maschera del demonio** being the detonator for the Gothic trend, with Sergio Leone's first Western and later with Argento's debut giving way to the giallo frenzy of the early 1970s, and on and on ...

SW. You wrote an excellent book on Riccardo Freda entitled Ricardo Freda: The Life and Works of Riccardo Freda. Can you talk a bit about the man and his legacy?
RC. Thank you! Freda was a maverick figure of sorts in Italian cinema. Today he is mainly known to foreign cinephiles for his horror films, and we can safely say he was the initiator of the genre in Italy with **I vampiri**, which was a movie ahead of its time (so much so that it was heavily tampered with during the making, and the result is quite different from Freda's original idea, but that's another story...). But I feel that, even though it includes outstanding films such as **The Horrible Dr. Hichcock** and **The Ghost**, his later output in the horror genre is neither representative of his status in Italian cinema nor of his technical proficiency. Freda made films such as **Iguana with a Tongue of Fire** or **Tragic Cere-**

mony (to name a couple that are widely available on home video) without any commitment to those projects, merely to keep working at a time when he was marginalized by the film industry (in the early-to-mid 1960s he even spent a few years in France, where he directed one of his best films, **Roger La Honte**) and struggling to keep up with the public's changing tastes. But he had been a predecessor in his quest for an Italian popular cinema that would be aesthetically relevant and narratively engrossing. When in 1946 he made **Aquila nera** (a remake of the silent classic **The Eagle**, starring Rudolph Valentino and based on Pushkin's novel, starring Rossano Brazzi) he was the first to direct action sequences worthy of that name: previously, Italian adventure films and swashbuckers were static, boring dramas shot in studio with actors riding rocking horses. Nobody knew how to shoot an action sequence. In the 1940s and 1950s Freda was perhaps the only Italian director who believed it was possible to make films that would rival Hollywood cinema, and he made several exceptional adventure films, swashbucklers and sword-and-sandal epics which display outstanding technique and a taste for spectacle that are still relevant nowadays.

Still, he had a dark side in him which made even his more spectacular films somewhat darker. One of his best works is a version of **Les miserables** which is definitely gloomy in parts, not to mention 1948's **Il cavaliere misterioso**, starring Vittorio Gassman as Casanova, which sports a surprising Gothic mood. His best film, in my view, is **Beatrice Cenci** (1956), based on a true story later remade by Lucio Fulci: it is a gripping drama about love, death and incest, with outstanding camerawork, photography and music, and was hailed as a masterpiece by French critics, who first celebrated Freda as an auteur. But in Italy it was booed as cheap melodrama and had little commercial success, causing Freda – who was never an "easy" director – to deviate toward another type of cinema. In the late 1940s and early 1950s he had been one of Italy's most successful directors at the box-office, and had even worked with the prestigious Lux Film, but he quickly adapted to low-budget, hit-and-run productions. He was adamant that he did it only for the money—he could save another director's film by shooting an action sequence that his colleague could not handle, and he could do it in record time, for he was fast as lightning (and used to boast about his proverbial quickness in wrapping shoots behind schedule). Many fellow filmmakers were adamant that Freda was a master of technique. Yves Boisset, who was his a.d. on a couple of films, said he was a much better director than Vittorio De Sica. And Bertrand Tavernier compared **Beatrice Cenci** to Visconti...

S.W. What was Freda's feelings on the Italian western genre, a genre it must be noted that he only made one film in, that being Death at Orwell Rock- Freda also wrote the film along with Luigi Maini. Was Freda connected to any other westerns in any capacity?
RC. He adored John Ford. The climactic sequence in **Aquila nera** (1946), with the Russian cavalry attacking the villain's castle, was clearly inspired by the one in Stagecoach, and shot with incredible audacity on Freda's part, for he had at his disposal the heavy and old Debrie cameras. He filmed the scene with four cameras, one providing a lateral traveling shot of the riders from a jeep driving at full speed. Moreover, Jean Valjean's escape sequence in **I miserabili** has a bit of Western in it (he escapes on a horse's back and the guards chase at full speed). And his version of **Romeo and Juliet**, shot in Spain around the same time as Leone was working on **Per un pugno di dollari**, looks almost like a Western in parts. But, as can be expected, his remarks on Italian Western were scathing. "To make a Western, one needs the Grand Canyon…" he once said. Remember, Freda had perhaps the sharpest tongue in Italian cinema. He made lots of enemies, and publicly dissed fellow filmmakers such as Rossellini, Antonioni, Fellini (he loathed Neorealism, incidentally). His only Western is not without merits, and I think its elaborate plot recalls those feuilletons Freda loved (interestingly, he claimed to have taken inspiration partly from Mérimée's Carmen, which provided the source for Luigi Bazzoni's **L'uomo, l'orgoglio, la vendetta** aka **Pride and Vengeance**, made around the same time). At some point, he was involved in a Western project starring Steve Reeves, with whom he got along very well during the making of **Agi Murad il diavolo bianco** (1959)—Freda getting along well with an actor was a rare occurrence, incidentally! He claimed that Reeves brought him a novel which he wanted to adapt, the story of a veterinarian who becomes an avenger but who never uses a gun. But the project came to nothing. Reeves then attempted to have Freda direct **Vivo per la tua morte**, aka **A Long Ride to Hell** (1968) but Camillo Bazzoni eventually made it.

S.W. You also wrote a magnificent book on Tonino Valerii called Tonino Valerii: The Films. Can you give our readers some background on Valerii, the man, the filmmaker? And his early association with Sergio Leone.

RC. Thank you for your appreciation! Tonino Valerii was first and foremost a friend. I met him through Tommaso La Selva (who wrote an excellent interview booklet on him, published by Nocturno in 2000 in the same series I mentioned above) and was immediately struck by his friendly and open attitude. Tonino had an interesting background, for unlike many other genre filmmakers he had been a CSC alumn (CSC being the cinema school in Rome, which many prestigious directors attended), and he was a cinephile too. He came from the province (the Abruzzo region) to Rome to follow his dream, and sometimes his Southern accent turned up again every now and then. It made him seem more vulnerable and genuine. He was easy-going but temperamental sometimes, well-read and full of amusing anecdotes, but you could tell that he had many regrets and some unhealed scars about his career. I always thought of him as a one-of-a-kind figure, a director who made genre movies (and could do any genre, for he proved his skills with the giallo, the crime-action film, the war film...) but could have been an auteur, had he followed another path, and some of his unmade projects lead to that direction. His association with Sergio Leone marked his future as a filmmaker, for better or worse. He worked at Arrigo Colombo and Giorgio Papi's Jolly Film, and followed the making of **Per un pugno di dollari** (including the decisive casting of Clint Eastwood, in which he claimed having a small part...). Leone took him in sympathy and Tonino became his assistant on **Per qualche dollaro in più**, and it was he who suggested the Genesi cousins that they hire Valerii as assistant director for a Western directed by Ricardo Blasco which never got made but which which led to Valerii scripting and directing **Taste of Killing**. And, finally, it was Leone who called him to direct **My Name Is Nobody,** which would be a blessing and a curse for Valerii.

SW. Valerii's first film directing was Taste of Killing, which is an excellent western and was quite a triumph for the first-time director. Can you tell us the critics and Valerii's opinion of the film?
RC. I agree with you, it's an above-average Western, and critics noticed it when it was released, for it got surprisingly good reviews at a time where most Westerns were panned. Even though it has some Leone-style touches, it features some original and intriguing elements. Tonino told me he spent a lot of time studying the shots, the camerawork, the locations, and his script is very detailed in this respect. He had good memories of the film, not the least because he had just got married when he made it and he and his wife Rita went on their honeymoon in Spain, which allowed him for some location scouting as well. By the way, there's a weird story about the actor who was originally to play the lead in the film. Valerii cast a young unexperienced American actor who arrived in Rome "stuffed with amphetamines", in Tonino's words, and was immediately taken to a clinic where he stayed for a few weeks. Valerii had to find a replacement overnight and cast Craig Hill. Sometime after the book was published, I got in touch with a man named Vincent Flaherty—whose name had never turned up neither in Valerii's recollections nor in ministerial papers or any other source—who claimed to be the actor originally cast to play Lanky Fellow. Some details of Flaherty's recollection matched Valerii's version, but overall his story was bizarre to say the least. He denied that he was high with drugs when he landed in Rome, and claimed that he was drugged, kidnapped and kept segregated in a private clinic called Villa Belvedere as part of a scam on the part of the producer to collect an insurance settlement. I won't comment further on this, but since Flaherty's story has since surfaced on his Facebook page and even on his Wikipedia entry (which he has obviously compiled himself) I thought it would be just fair to mention it.

SW. Valerii's next film is the masterpiece Day of Anger. Can you tell us how the film came about? What was Valerii's working relationship with the leads in this film Giuliano Gemma and Lee Van Cleef, and were both actors the first choices for the roles they eventually authored?
RC. The film was scripted by Ernesto Gastaldi, who expanded an idea from an aspiring screenwriter named Renzo Genta. Perhaps Gastaldi was influenced by the American Western **Black Patch** (1957), written by Leo Gordon, with which the film has some similarities. It surely had very little to do with the novel it appears to be based on in the credits (Der tod Ritt Dienstags by Ron Barker, a.k.a Rolf Becker). Gastaldi and Valerii were adamant that it was just a coproduction scam, the film being co-financed by a German company. Actually, Gemma was not the first choice for the lead. Valerii thought of Lou Castel, who had made a great impression on him in Marco Bellocchio's debut **Fists in the Pocket.** He thought Castel would be perfect for a tormented character such as Scott Mary. But the producers thought Castel was not a very commercial name, so Valerii accepted to cast Gemma—who was already a big name in Italy after his Ringo films—in the lead. Gemma told me Valerii approached him one day in the street, while he was riding his bike. Apparently, he had gotten in touch Gemma's agent, who didn't bother to alert the actor.

Valerii and Gemma became very good friends, and worked together again in the future, also on TV, in the crime series **Caccia al ladro d'autore**. As for Van Cleef, he and Valerii had a good relationship, but the actor's drinking problem led to some unpleasant episodes on the set. As Gemma himself put it. "Lee Van Cleef was an adorable man, but only up to a certain time of the day. Then, unfortunately, he started to drink..."

SW. Valerii's directed three westerns in a row. His third being A Bullet for the President. To me, the film from an American's perspective is two-fold: First that the film is a violent reimaging of the American West- And secondly, then Valerii has enough gumption to reimage American history. An obvious political western that is bold and daring but maybe just a bit too ahead of its times. Quentin Tarantino has received nothing but praise for his reimaging history. Was the film Valerii's way of commenting on the violent nature of the United States and a jab at its involvement in Vietnam?

RC. I agree with you, the film was daring in taking inspiration from the JFK's murder and transporting it into the Wild West. Some Italian filmmakers had done something similar in their Western adaptations of novels or plays (such as with **Quella sporca storia nel West**, which sets Hamlet in a post-Civil war scenario), but never so boldly. It was indeed a political movie, at the time the Italian Western dealt with contemporary issues (see the films scripted by Franco Solinas which refer to Third World liberation movements, etc.), and indeed its view of violence as part of a country's history was influenced by what Italy was going through over the same period, with bombings and political plots which would lead the country to its blackest decade, the 1970s, marked by terrorist attacks and the Red Brigades kidnapping and killing ex-prime minister Aldo Moro in 1978.

But I think the film is rather different from its peers, and perhaps more nuanced, in the way it meditates on the clash between idealism (with Giuliano Gemma's character Bill Willer portraying a somewhat naïve hero, who believes in social justice and in the ultimate triumph of truth) and pragmatism, embodied by the ambiguous Bill McDonald (Warren Vanders). In the end, Willer realizes he can't change the world with his own hands (and his gun), and there need to be people like McDonald, who "get their hands dirty" with politics (and therefore compromise), to quote Jean-Paul Sartre.

In the film, the president (played by Van Johnson) is an idealist who gives a speech where he says: "Some people look at things and ask 'Why?', I dream of things to come and ask, 'Why not?'" It is a line which recalls Martin Luther King's famous "I have a dream" speech. In the Italian version a character replies to it with a chilling, cynical line: "You don't make politics with dreams." I think this halo of disillusionment is part of the film's power, and that's why—despite some budgetary issues which forced Valerii to tone down his vision—it has aged better than some of its peers.

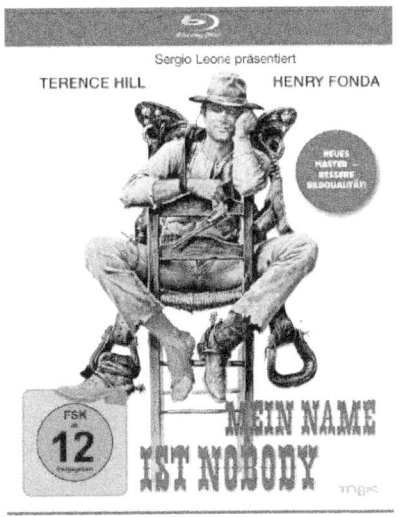

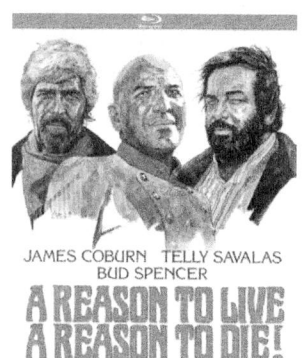  

Page 11: Left to Right: Spanish release of Lanky Fellow; German release of My Name is Nobody
Page 12: Left to Right: Blu-rays releases- A Reason to Live A reason to Die; Day of Anger: Price of Power

SW. After two films outside the western genre in A Girl Named Jules and My Dear Killer, Valerii returned to the western genre with the ultimately unfulfilling A Reason to Live, A Reason to Die in 1972. While there's no denying the film is well crafted, it just lacks that something. What're your thoughts on this film? Also, can you give us a bit of background on the film?

RC. I think the return to the Western was a return to safe waters after the underwhelming box-office performance of those two films (even though **My Dear Killer** is one of Valerii's very best works in my opinion). Undoubtedly **A Reason to Live**... is flawed. There are two different souls in it, and they don't gel well. Bud Spencer is a distracting presence, at odds with the overall mortuary tone. Perhaps the film suffers from too many diverse elements and influences. Besides the obvious nods to **Dirty Dozen**, Valerii claimed he and Gastaldi took inspiration from Augusto Genina's 1940 war movie L'assedio dell'Alcazar, as well as from Gordon Douglas's **Only the Valiant** (1951), and there are indeed elements of both films in the plot. Moreover, other parts—the scene of the village celebrating the end of the Civil War—recall Leone's cinema and are perhaps an attempt at a wider scale epic which is somewhat lost in the bigger picture. I think the more interesting reference is the one to Kurosawa's **Seven Samurai** (the sequence about the farmers who kill travelers)—by the way, an unmade project Gastaldi and Valerii worked together was a Western remake of Masaki Kobayashi's **Harakiri** (1962), proving once again the bond between the Italian Western and Japanese cinema.

Anyway, back to **A Reason to Live**...: Valerii told me he would have cast Eli Wallach instead of Bud Spencer, and this would have given the character a different edge. One cannot deny that the film would have been better without Spencer's customary antics (including an infamous raspberry after he breaks out of jail in a scene). Still, it was Spencer's name that drew audiences to see the film, and as you're probably aware in Germany (where Spencer was incredibly popular) **A Reason To Live**... was actually re-edited as a comedy Western as Der Dicke und das Warzenschwein, with a new dubbing and the most violent bits cut out... and even a different ending! Moreover, Valerii never got along with James Coburn. He told me it had been the only actor he had had problems with on the set (whereas he got along wonderfully with Bud Spencer; when I interviewed Spencer, he almost got moved at the memory of that film and of his relationship with Tonino).

SW. Tonino Valerii's final western would be the classic My Name is Nobody, from 1973, which starred Henry Fonda and Terence Hill. Much has been said about the involvement of Sergio Leone in the making of the film- including that he directed it or at least portions, can you help clarify this issue for us.

RC. I'll try to make it as brief as I can, but it's a long and troubled story. That film was Tonino Valerii's biggest hit, but it basically ruined his career—and destroyed him psychologically. It was a work for hire, of course, and Tonino came aboard after Leone fired Michele Lupo just a couple of weeks before filming began. Gastaldi and Benito Stefanelli suggested Valerii as the right man for the job. But it soon became clear that Leone and Valerii had different ideas on the film and on the character of Nobody. Valerii claimed that to Leone the film "was all about putting to death the Trinity character" whereas he wanted to portray Nobody as some sort of Peter Pan. Without going into deep on how this clash of visions affects the film, it is obvious that shooting was going to be difficult for Valerii. Moreover, he didn't get along with d.o.p. Armando Nannuzzi and with production manager Piero Lazzari. Both were replaced, with Giuseppe Ruzzolini and Claudio Mancini, respectively. Having known him in person, I can confirm that Tonino was a stubborn type, and certainly not a malleable one. He would have it his own way. And perhaps this made Leone nervous.

The crew moved to Spain and there were severe schedule issues. A crate of costumes got lost and the production was forced to a halt. But Henry Fonda had to finish his scenes in a hurry because he would start shooting Ash Wednesday soon. So, Leone offered to help Tonino and direct a second unit. Valerii accepted. According to Valerii, Leone shot the following scenes: Nobody getting drunk in the saloon (but not the footage of Pero Lulli taking the money nor the close-up of shattered glasses); much of the sequence at the fair (from the apple-stealing bit to the pies thrown at the black men's faces); the public urinal scene (which Valerii always dismissed as unnecessarily vulgar); and parts of the battle against the Wild Bunch (but not the whole sequence, as some claim).

But there was more. Before moving to Spain, Leone showed up in New Orleans, for the shooting of one of the last scenes in the States, the final duel between Nobody and Jack Beauregard, and stayed there for five days. There were photographers, who asked him to pose behind the camera for a photo shoot. Leone asked Tonino permission and Tonino obliged. And, as Sergio Donati told me, that was a big mistake, for those pictures were published in magazines all around the world… "and inevitably, from that moment on, everyone, in and outside the movie business, started saying: 'Yeah, actually the real director of the film was Leone, who saved it from the disaster of an incapable director.'"

Professionally, to Tonino this meant that: a) Many people in the film business started thinking he was a hack, despite the fact films such as **My Dear Killer** and **Go Gorilla Go** show that Valerii could direct better than most of his peers (or take a look at 1977's **Sahara Cross**, another flawed film which nevertheless features remarkable, elaborate long takes shot with a Steadicam, which Valerii was the very first Italian director to employ); b) With the film industry rapidly falling into another deep crisis in the mid-to-late 1970s and producers resorting to lower budgets, few would employ Valerii (who had directed an expensive film such as **My Name Is Nobody** and was therefore considered a costly filmmaker) and relied on less demanding directors. To Valerii, this meant several projects to be shelved and several years of forced inactivity; c) And this is the worst part, Valerii developed a long-standing depression and personal grudge against Leone. Every time – and I mean it – I touched the subject of his relationship with Leone, Tonino couldn't help but cry. The pain, the humiliation, the bitterness was too much for him.

Over the years Leone increasingly emphasized his own contribution to the film, while minimizing Valerii's, and sometimes contradicting what he himself had claimed on previous occasions. The situation became even worse in 1995. Six years after Sergio Leone's death, a monography on him came out in Italy, which included a never-before-published interview where he claimed he shot most of the film ... including some scenes (such as the barber shop opening) which would have been impossible for him to shoot, since he was in Rome during most of the U.S. shoot. This made Valerii mad. The author of that book never bothered to ask Valerii (or Ernesto Gastaldi, for that matter) his version of the facts, neither did other film historians. This led to more arguments, more anger, more frustration.

At least in Italy, it has now become common knowledge that Leone was the director of **My Name Is Nobody**, and even Terence Hill, when asked on TV what it was like to be directed by Leone (which did happen in those aforementioned scenes) has never made it clear that there was another director who actually shot most of the film.

Among Valerii's Westerns, **My Name Is Nobody** it is the one with the most references to Leone's oeuvre. But this is understandable since this was Leone wanted and this is what Ernesto Gastaldi gave him when he wrote the script. It is certainly not Valerii's best film, but for better or worse it is his film, not Leone's.

SW. I must add that your books on Italian Gothic Horror films, Italian Crime Films 1968-1980, and numerous others are some of the best written on Italian popular cinema (Most available on Amazon). So, what's next for Roberto Curti?

I have just finished a book on Elio Petri, in my opinion one of the greatest Italian filmmakers ever. He made only a dozen films, but almost all of them are outstanding, including Investigation on a **Citizen Above Suspicion** (which won the Oscar for Best Foreign Film). Franco Nero labeled him as "the Italian Stanley Kubrick" and Ennio Morricone called him "an extraordinary director ahead of his times." It took years to research and write, and I'm very pleased with the result. I hope readers will be, too.

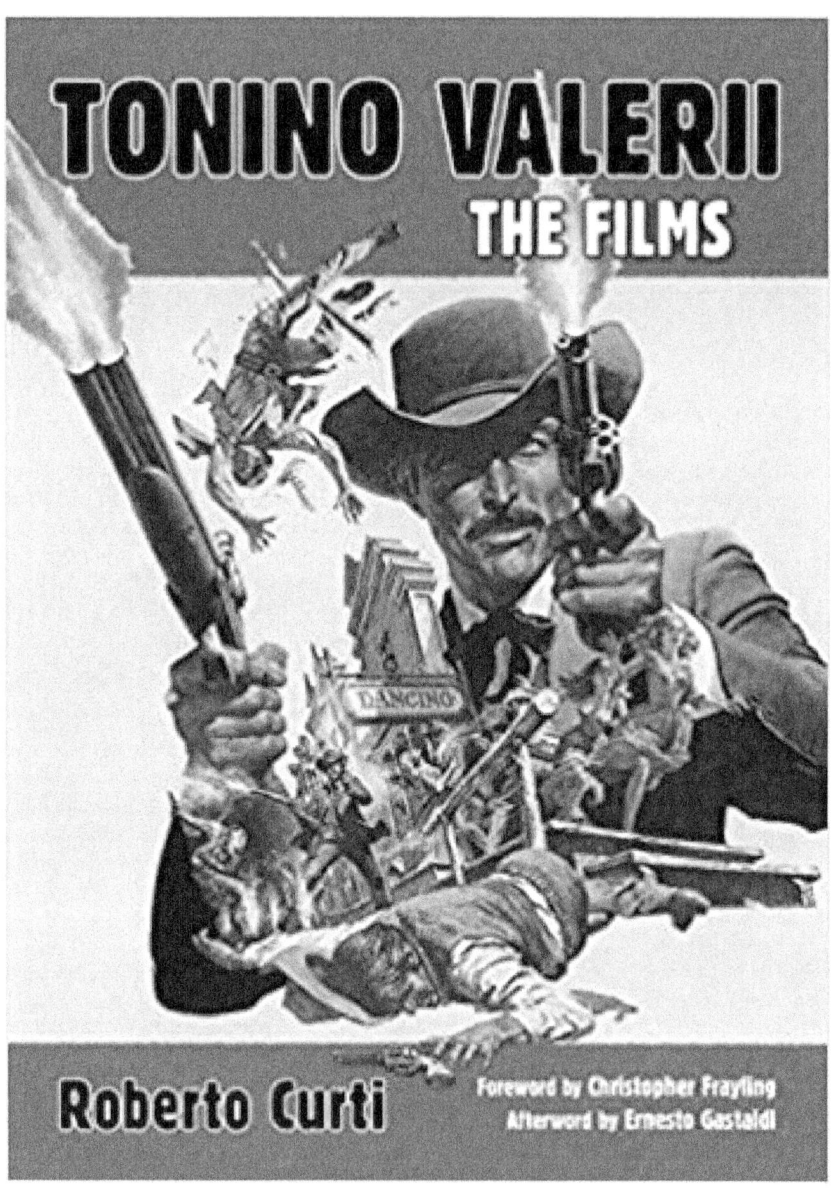

THE MYSTERIOUS DEATH OF PETER LEE LAWRENCE

One of the main stars of the Spaghetti western phenomenon was a young actor named Peter Lee Lawrence. Looking even younger than his actual age he was able to play roles the other actors had either outgrown or looked unconvincing in. On the other hand he often looked too young to play a hardened gunfighter.

Lawrence was born Karl Hyrenbach (not Hirenbach) on February 21, 1944 in Lindau-Bodensee, Germany. He was part of a large family with three brothers and two sisters. He spent most of his youth in Nice, France. Sometime in his late teens he had a relationship with a girl and a son Karl Hyrenbach was born in 1965.

In 1960 while still a student, his cinematic career began with small parts in fotonovelas. In 1965 at the age of 21 he had his first credited role in **"For a Few Dollars More"** appearing in a flashback sequence as Colonel Mortimer's (Lee Van Cleef) brother-in-law.

Peter Lee Lawrence and Cristina Galbo

1966 found Peter starring in his first film a western called "**Dove si spara di più**" (The Fury of Johnny Kid aka The Ultimate Gunfighter) under the alias Arthur Grant. It was on this film that he first met actress and flamenco dancer Cristina Galbó who played the role of Giulietta Campos. The takeoff of Shakespeare's Romeo and Juliet was prophetic for the young couple would meet again off the set in 1968 and would marry on July 30, 1969. On May 4, 1970 Cristina gifted Peter with the birth of a son David M. Hyrenbach, who today is a professor of Oceanography at Hawaii Pacific University.

Peter's career blossomed and he became one of the stars of the new Spaghetti western genre appearing in 19 of his total of 29 films, from 1965 until 1972. Sometime in 1972 Peter began suffering from headaches. After the completion of a film called "**Boton de Ancla**' he was admitted to the Foundation Jimenez Diaz Hospital in Madrid, where he was operated on by Dr. Sixto Obrador. The surgery was a success, but the report confirmed their worst fears. It was glioblastoma (the most aggressive type of cancer that begins within the brain).

In an attempt to use all their resources, Peter and Cristina moved to Zurich, where, under the auspices of Professor Wolfgang Horst, Karl began both chemo and radium treatments. Realizing how serious his illness was, they decided to do things they had always wanted to do but never got around to. They had the privilege of living in Tahiti for several months, and having lots of time to spend with family and friends, and to enjoy the peace of their home in Rome, and going back to Zurich for check-ups.

On February 12, 1974 Karl had a routine check-up with Professor Horst. The results were good, which kept their hopes up. But on March 25, Karl was admitted to the Villa Stuart Clinic in Rome with severe stomach pains. He died on Saturday, April 20th 1974, at ten past three in the morning. He was only thirty years of age.

Cristina, their son David and all who knew him say among the defining traits of his personality, were his dedication to the people he loved, and his anti-conformist attitude, which he maintained against anything he considered unjust. He was very sociable and a polyglot to boot, who used short-wave radio to connect with people's struggles around the world. But his real passion was scuba diving and everything related to the sea. With his sophisticated equipment and his underwater cameras, he used to spend hours and hours enjoying and exploring the seabed. David's dedication to the sea must be genetic.

Cristina states that; "I will merely add that those of us who spent the sixteen months of his illness with Karl can attest to his dignity, courage and desire to live and fight with the spirit he always showed. I will never forget he used to say "Don't you worry Pichuqui, I will get over this because I have so many reasons to do so". After Peter's passing Cristina eventually moved to the United States and became a flamenco instructor at a university in San Diego, California.

Left: David Hyrenbach
Below: Peter Lee Lawrence and Cristina Galbo appearing together in The Fury of Johnny Kid

A Brief Introduction to the Cinema of Giulio Petroni

When Giulio Petroni (21 September 1917, Rome–31 January 2010, Rome) left Italy in 1945 with his wife and limited resources, he left behind him a broken country. "I had lost weight and was unrecognizable, going, as I was, towards possibly nothing more than a glimmer of hope." This is how he described his state while crossing the ocean towards what was then called Ceylon, now Sri Lanka: "I didn't know how and when I was going to return to Italy." However, the new geopolitical logic of the Cold War made it possible for Italy to be perceived as a "hinge country" between Western Europe and the Mediterranean, and from a fragile democracy, threatened by the proximity of the Soviet-controlled Iron Curtain, Italy became, from an American prospective, a potential ally for the Free World. Therefore, its past as an enemy was put aside and the country was granted the financial help provided by the Marshall Plan. Specifically, the European Recovery Plan was an economic reconstruction program that the United States would fund, placing itself in continuity with aid provided since 1943 to the war-affected populations. There was some opposition against this from left-wing political and trade union movements, the main accusation being that the US was trying to colonize Europe. Beyond any ideological conviction, it is impossible to deny that the humanitarian motivation hid an anti-Soviet political agenda. However, just two years after the approval of the Plan, Europe showed signs of a rapid economic revival. The completion of the Plan, in 1952, which might have stopped this recovery, coincided with the culmination of the Korean War (1950–1953), creating a strong demand for metal and other manufactured products. This, combined with a large and cheap labor force, laid the foundations for spectacular economic growth. Petroni, with new contacts and a new reputation, would move back to Italy in the fifties, right in the midst of this slow but unstoppable mutation in the financial and social life of the country. He found a stronger Italy and a film industry that could not have been imagined before his departure. By the time Petroni directed his first film, the industry had blossomed.

However, during his years in exotic lands he never completely lost touch with his country. After having conquered the trust of local politicians, he began to forge what would become the foundation of

Sri Lanka's Government Film Unit. Petroni sent for technicians and experts from Italy to teach locals the grammar of filmmaking. In the space of a few years he had become a figure of relevance in the country which had let him in and an appreciated documentarian back in his homeland.

Putting aside his excursus as a journalist and his prolific activity as a documentarian and an assistant director, and dwelling exclusively on his activities as a film director, it is fairly easy to identify very distinct phases in the career of Petroni. The first is represented by comedy, which officially begins in 1959 with La cento chilometri (The One Hundred Kilometers) and is composed of four films. Petroni's debut, though dated, has, over the years, acquired a somewhat historical value, being a snapshot of a specific cultural and social atmosphere, in no small part thanks to a cast populated by familiar faces: the famed singer Fred Buscaglione, the star Massimo Girotti, and a long list of popular character actors and TV personalities such as Carlo Giuffre, Gigi Reder, Gianrico Tedeschi, Riccardo Garrone, Marisa Merlini, and Mario Carotenuto (who will appear in other two times films by Petroni), among others. The film was a success, partly due to a much-discussed, censorious intervention regarding the shapely legs of a teenage Paola Pitagora. Petroni then directs, chronologically: **I piaceri dello scapolo** (The Pleasures of a Bachelor, 1960), **Una domenica d'estate** (Always on Sunday, 1962), and **I soliti rapinatori a Milano** (The Usual Thieves from Milan, 1963). This last film marks the end of the first chapter of his directing career. The following one will give him fame and prestige, inextricably tying his name to the Italian West. Petroni's Western filmography unravels itself in five titles: **Da uomo a uomo** (Death Rides a Horse, 1967), **...e per tetto un cielo di stelle** (A Sky Full of Stars for a Roof a.k.a. And for a Roof a Sky Full of Stars, 1968), **Tepepa** (a.k.a. Blood and Guns, 1968), **La notte dei serpenti** (Nest of Vipers a.k.a. Night of the Serpent, 1969), and finally **La vita a volte è molto dura vero Provvidenza?** (Life Is Tough, Eh Providence? a.k.a. Sometimes Life Is Hard—Right, Providence?, 1972).

On **Death Rides a Horse** much has been said. It was praised and paid homage to by Quentin Tarantino, who borrows from it various stylistic and narrative elements in shaping the structure of his **Kill Bill** (2003–2004) saga. It was one of Italy's most successful Westerns worldwide, including in the States, where it was picked up by United Artists. Lee Van Cleef, who gives one of his best performances, is placed at the center of a rich cast that includes John Philip Law, Luigi Pistilli, Josè Torres, Anthony Dawson, and Mario Brega. It also marks the beginning of the long-lasting

Page 17: Giulio Petroni (sitting at the centre) with all the members of the Film Unit he founded in Sri Lanka.
Above: Page 18: Luke Askew and still photographer Divo Cavicchioli on the set of Nest of Vipers. Giulio Petroni is in the background, behind the camera.

collaboration between the Roman director and Ennio Morricone, who, for the occasion, composes a vibrant and dark soundtrack that perfectly fits what many consider the quintessential Italian "vengeance Western". This theme—that of vengeance—returns in another extremely successful film directed by Petroni, **Tepepa**, which, together with Damiano Damiani's **Quien sabe?** (A Bullet for the General, 1967), is the purest and most representative example of so-called "revolutionary Westerns". Tomas Milian, in a role clearly inspired by the figure of Ernesto "Che" del Serna Guevara, leads his fellow peons through the violence and disappointments of a revolutionary uprising at the start of 20th century Mexico. Like Damiani before him, Petroni too had difficulties considering his film a Western, as he himself explained: "Tepepa is much more of a historical film. It has none of the iconography of Italian Westerns, or American ones for that matter: no gunfights, no saloons and no Americans or cowboys. John Steiner's character is called "Yankee" but simply because the Mexicans in the film don't make any distinction between Americans and British. There is dust and there are horses but that's it. Attention was paid to infuse the film with the right scenography and costumes. Contrary to my previous Westerns, here I tried to make sure the film was visually realistic and as close as possible to historical reality, something that was not normally necessary in Westerns, Italian ones I mean, because our West was not an actual historical period. It's a parallel dimension which has more to do with literature, comic books, and cinema itself. It's an abstract West, not a realistic one. Mind you, this is what made Italian Westerns successful. So, Tepepa, in this sense, cannot be labeled a Western, though on the other hand it is too metaphorical and symbolic, too over-stylized and bigger than life to be considered a historical film. So, I guess it lives in an in-between territory. Though I don't mind people calling it a Western. I understand why they do, but it's incomplete as a definition." The film stirs up much attention upon its release, starting with the cast which, besides Milian—at a peak in his popularity—also features Orson Welles as the antagonist. Between these two columns of his filmography, Petroni directs another Western, a strange and atypical one graced with a poetic, nearly bucolic title: **A Sky Full of Stars for a Roof** with Giuliano Gemma and Mario Adorf. The relationship between the two protagonists anticipates many of the elements that will be utilized in subsequent Giuseppe Colizzi Westerns, that will ultimately help create the Bud Spencer and Terence Hill couple. If Gemma plays a character not dissimilar to the ones of his previous films—the romantic scoundrel, the irresponsible but loveable troublemaker—it is Adorf's character that represents a new input, and more importantly, the contraposition of the two opposing yet compatible personalities. It is difficult not to observe and analyze Adorf's behavior without comparing it to what Bud Spencer was just on the brink of becoming: strong though naïve, capable of violence but ultimately childlike and idealistic, and prone to simple pleasures, Adorf is the barely controllable arm of Gemma's brain. What makes Petroni's second effort in the genre such a peculiar one is not solely tied to the comedy within it, but to the contradictory results these comedic elements create when put together, with the sudden peaks of drama and violence the film encompasses. In fact, the film has one of the more spectacular and violent beginnings in Petroni's West. However, the podium for the most cynical and violent film must be left free for what has yet to come after this successful triptych. Fierce and tense, **Nest of Vipers** is a forgotten Western. Petroni has always considered it a minor effort within his body of work and has often refused to talk about it. But the film, over the years, has found a niche of admirers, such as Spanish critic Carlos Aguilar who, for example, considers it one of his favorite Westerns, comparing the redemptive parable within it to "Lord Jim". Not dissimilar in tone to other darker themed Westerns of the late sixties, such as the subsequent **E Dio disse a Caino** (And God Said to Cain, 1970), **Nest of Vipers** feels the influence of the new and growing giallo genre. So, it shouldn't come as a surprise to discover that someone like Lorenzo Gicca Palli helped Petroni write the script. Gicca Palli, in fact, must have firmly believed in the combination of these two genres, so much so that shortly after he will direct **Il venditore di morte** (Price of Death a.k.a. Last Gunfight, 1971), a film which is as much a Western as it is a giallo. This is confirmed by Petroni himself: "Palli was definitely the one more interested in developing the mystery part of the film, which I would tone down. I was interested in making a different kind of Western, visually speaking, but concentrating more on the characters and in the redemption factor, the arc the character has to live through. Before dying out or before becoming innocuous and purely comedic, there were attempts to find new interpretations of the genre. The fusion with giallo was probably one of those attempts. It was certainly something Palli had in mind." To conclude the cycle, we find **Life Is Tough, Eh Providence?** with Milian, Gregg Palmer, and Janet Agren, which Petroni directs with great detachment. "By the early seventies it was blatant to me that Westerns were dying. I was not the creator of the genre, of course, but I had helped it become what it was and I didn't want to participate in the inevitable vulgarization that had begun. I refused many projects around that time. Westerns need money but most importantly they need space and faces. Producers are not forward-looking; they only see what is happening in the present

Giulio Petroni and Magda Konopka on the set of Nest of Vipers.

and what was happening was that people would go and see any Western that was thrown at them. So, all of a sudden, a fleet of improvised actors, usually stuntmen, with unlikely faces, were upgraded to leading men as the budgets got slimmer and slimmer. For all my Westerns I was fortunate enough to have big producers and the right amount of time to be able to give the epic breath the films required. I wasn't willing to help destroy the genre that, I can't say I loved, but that had given me a lot. Providence is a film I did for financial reasons. I needed the money, but it was still dignified enough. I mean, it had a good cast and a reasonable budget." The huge success of the film, which spawned a 1973 sequel directed by Alberto De Martino, also anticipates the current of over-the-top, grotesque Western comedies derivative of Enzo Barboni's Trinity movies: **Il bianco, il giallo, il nero** (The White, the Yellow, and the Black a.k.a. Shoot First... Ask Questions Later a.k.a. Ring Around the Horse's Tail, 1975) by Sergio Corbucci and **Cipolla Colt** (Cry, Onion! a.k.a. The Smell of Onion, 1975) by Enzo G. Castellari. In five films, Petroni looks at Westerns from five completely different points of view, creating what he called a short circuit: "I intentionally looked for different projects, mainly because I wanted to try new things and explore the genre as much as I could, but actually this didn't pay in terms of visibility because people thought they were all made by different directors."

Despite the fact that his Westerns are so different from each other, there is a very strong thematic unity: the polarizing element around which the story rotates—revenge and stolen innocence. Interesting, in this respect, is the role of children in his films: the opening sequence of **Death Rides a Horse**, in which the child—who will later become John Phillip Law—witnesses the cruel extermination of his family; Nest of Vipers, in which Askew is forced to live with the remorse of having killed his own son while drunk; and then of course, Tepepa, where the last one to dirty his hands with blood is little Paquito. Even Adorf and Palmer are, in their respective films, perhaps nothing more than children too grown-up for their context. The figure of the child is always surrounded by violence or contaminated by it.

-Eugenio Ercolani

Giulio and Silvia Petroni on the set of Tepepa.

The following interview is interspersed with comments and statements by Giulio Petroni, taken from the interview published in Darkening the Italian Screen by Eugenio Ercolani and published by McFarland Publishing (2019).

Petroni: A Family Business
Interview with Silvia Petroni (and Giulio Petroni)
by Eugenio Ercolani

"Everybody seems to have a confused expression when I tell them I used to work in films as a script supervisor. They've heard the term, but most people don't know exactly what it means, what it stands to indicate. A script supervisor has many responsibilities, but let's start by saying that the role is part of the directing department. First of all, he or she must check and make sure the director is covering each scene in such a way that he will be able to edit it later on in the best possible way. So, you have to keep track of every shot, angle, and camera lens and also how much film is being used because the script supervisor is the communicating bridge between the set and the editor who receives and starts organizing the dailies. That said, he or she must also make sure there is consistency and continuity within each scene. As most people know films are not made in chronological order, like indicated by the script, so I would also have to make sure everything coincided and was coherent—make up, costumes, set design, props, hairdos… everything. Keep in mind that all this I've been describing has been made much easier over the years by technology; script supervising in the seventies was a whole different matter. Now you've got monitors and can rewatch a scene a thousand times if you believe it's necessary. When I was working you had to rely only on your eyes, a stopwatch, with which you would time each shot, and a polaroid camera. That is it!" These are the words of Elena Silvia Petroni (1947, Colombo, Sri Lanka, at times credited as Sylvia). Although her career in the Italian cinema industry was relatively brief—spanning little more than a decade— sadly it is probably more intense and prolific than the careers of those beginning where she began now are likely to be. With roughly forty films and a long list of shorts and TV spots forming her filmography, why interview, you may be asking yourself, such an unknown figure, in what is, for many at least, an equally unknown role? In the mind of the person writing, it is important, now more than ever, to collect as many testimonies of that silent and often ignored army of technicians and crew members that were really the heart and soul of what was one of the most prolific and powerful film industries the world has ever known. Not motivated by ego and the consequent desire to shape and guide the readers perception of themselves, it is only from these people you can really hope to extract an honest and truthful depiction of the filmmaking process and the world surrounding it. Petroni, as most professionals of the time, seems to have worked transversally with profoundly different directors and for a diverse number of production companies pertaining to different substrata of the filmic hierarchy: from everything-goes, low-budget exploitation products to powerhouse Festival favorites; from independent films distributed regionally to big international co-productions, Petroni has cut through all levels of the cinematic milieu. "There was so much work at the time: something that nowadays is difficult to imagine. As soon as my job on a film was done I had several scripts and projects to choose from. The workflow was incredible; it would just go on and on. I probably should have, in hindsight, been more selective but most of us weren't, you just wanted to keep the momentum going and often you would choose a project on the basis of who was working on it and the people you knew more so than on the artistic value of it." Among the directors Silvia Petroni has worked alongside, worth mentioning are Fernando Di Leo ("he is, I think, the director I have worked most with"), Romolo Guerrieri ("he was very kind and soft-spoken on set and would ask me what I would think of his work on a scene, which is very rare for a director to do"), Luciano Emmer ("he would go batshit crazy at times, shout, kick stuff on set, but would always do so with a twinkle in his eye. I had a feeling he liked pushing peoples' buttons to see how far he could go with them"), Paul Morrissey ("he was one with Andy Warhol but he would make sure he always kept control of the set; he was very protective of his decision-making power on set"), Mario Amendola ("he felt ancient to me. He was really quite old when I encountered his path and I kind of feel his heart wasn't really in it anymore"), Franco Lo Cascio, a well-known and prolific AD-turned-director who would later on in the eighties become one of the most important and popular Italian porn moguls, under the pseudonym Luca Damiano ("there was nothing about Franco that would have made you think he would have chosen that path. I worked with him when he was a 1st assistant director and then when he directed his first non-pornographic films, and in the first position mentioned he was one of the best in the business"), Marco Ferreri ("it was a big deal to be working with him and the film was star-studded: you had Vittorio Gassman, Ugo Tognazzi, Claudia Cardinale. One of the most embarrassing episodes of my career happened on that film. There was a segment in which Cardinale wore a necklace that from one scene to the next simply disappeared. We only realized once principal photography was over and I was so embarrassed I wanted to dig a hole and vanish in it. We had to shoot the whole sequence again which meant more money and time for the producers. It was the costume and props department's fault but, ultimately, I was the one responsible and I should have done a better job. Every time I think back that damn necklace becomes bigger and bigger in my mind"). As some might have realized from the surname, she is also the daughter of writer/director Giulio Petroni, one of the most influential shapers of the Italian Western landscape, and the two have shared four sets together. It couldn't be but from her father that this interview begins.

Page 22: Silvia Petroni, Paolo Pietrangeli, Joe Dallessandro, Dalila Di Lazzaro and Arno Juerging on the set of Any Warhol's Frankenstein.

Page 23: Silvia Petroni and Arno Juerging on the set of Frankenstein, directed by Paul Morrisey.

* All photos used in the Petroni pieces courtesy of Eugenio Ercolani.

Despite being Italian, you were born in Ceylon, now known as Sri Lanka. Why is that?
During World War II, my father was in the Resistance. He collaborated with the Allies and was parachuted several times over enemy lines. My mother too was arrested by the Nazis and put into prison for distributing anti-German leaflets and for helping a Jewish architect to escape. After 8 September 1943, one of my father's brothers, commander of a submarine stationed in Shanghai, headed for Ceylon, and surrendered to the British. Subsequently, he was nominated consul for Italy in Ceylon, and it was he who encouraged them to join him there and since my parents, like so many others, had lost everything, they decided to go. Moreover, my father had lost another brother he was very close to, a lieutenant commander, who had refused to fight alongside the Germans and whose battleship was consequently bombed by the Nazis killing almost everyone on board. So it was that my parents boarded a cargo ship and sailed for the Orient. The situation in Ceylon, however, was not easy, but in time my father managed to create from scratch the Government Film Unit of Ceylon. He was a good documentarian and made several documentaries, some of which won prizes around the world. A few years later, he was expelled from the country for his political ideas. By this time my parents were separated and when Giulio returned to Italy, my mother decided to stay in Ceylon. I was born shortly after. I remained in Ceylon apart from brief periods in Egypt and Switzerland because of my stepfather's work. Then he was transferred to London. I was around seven at the time and for me London is still home. Growing up, I had a secret passion for the theatre. I say "secret" because I never told anyone about it. I was an extremely withdrawn child and there was no one I felt comfortable talking to. When I was fifteen, my stepfather was transferred to Italy, but I remained in London to complete my education.

Giulio Petroni: Between 1945 and the following year, I had nothing to lose. The war had taken its toll on me. When I look at the few photos of that period, I realize how hard life had been. I was so thin and looked so much older than my age. Remember I had participated actively in the Resistance. I had killed and seen many of my fellow partisans die. I had nothing to lose. What my life had been before the war seemed like a distant memory, somebody else's life, and one that had no importance anymore. I was married at the time; Italy was in ruins and the world seemed much bigger then than it does now. I don't like talking about that period but, anyway... where can I start? Well, one moment is as good as another. I guess things really changed with... Manlio, my brother. I was in Rome training as a pilot when I stopped getting news from him. Communications were interrupted. I fled to Naples without saying anything to anyone. I had to know what had happened to him. When I reached Naples, it was chaos. What went down in history as the "Four days of Naples" had just begun. There was a huge insurrection against the German occupation. There were bodies in the streets. I contributed and helped out as well as I could. It was only when the Americans arrived from the south of Italy that I discovered what had happened to my brother. He was a captain in the navy, and the last time I talked to him he had told me that he'd received orders to take the Battleship Roma to an Allied-controlled port. This was after Italy had declared the armistice with the Allies. But things were done badly and in a hurry. The details of the armistice were fuzzy, to say the least. All the Italian top brass fled from Rome together with the monarchy leaving Italian armies scattered around Europe with no precise orders. Do you know what Operation Achse is? It's what the Germans put into action when they found out about the armistice. History books define the operation as an attempt to invade and occupy Italy, but the orders were really to kill, destroy, annihilate as many Italians as possible. From 1943, Italian was a dangerous thing to be. Everything began with the bombardment of the Battleship Roma. Manlio was on that ship, in the middle of the Mediterranean Sea, going to surrender to the Allies when Luftwaffe planes attacked, but because of the nebulous orders regarding the armistice the ship was late in responding to the attack. Many men died: 1,352 to be precise. Manlio died a few days later in Majorca. He had severe burns on his face and body and died slowly and painfully. I was distraught and determined to do something, so I went to the Americans. They trained me as a paratrooper and dropped me behind enemy lines in Piedmont which was controlled by German forces. My mission was to take dispatches to members of the Resistance and then find my way back to Rome and repeat. Three times I was dropped. After my last mission I stayed with the partisans till the end of the war. But all this means nothing. Italy has forgotten the names and faces of the fallen.

My other brother, Attilio, also a high-ranking officer in the Navy, after having been in China for some time became consul in Ceylon. He asked me to join him there, so I embarked on this adventure with Lidia, who was my wife at the time. As I said, I had no reason to say no. Attilio described the place as a land of opportunity. It was a very long trip, days. No planes of course. Days and days on a ship. When I arrived there, I had limited economic resources, and though I had picked up some English working for the American Secret Service, it was by no means sufficient. Anyway, my brother had made friends in the diplomatic and political spheres and introduced me to a few people. You must keep in mind that at that time the government was trying to gain independence, which it did soon later thanks to Prime Minister Don Stephen Senanayake. The political atmosphere was very left wing and I was still a member of the Communist Party and had been the head of one of the movement's most important headquarters in Rome. So, I managed to convince the local government to put me in charge of what was to become the Government Film Unit. Ceylon had no cinema; everything that was screened there was imported from India. You can say I invented cinema for them. Once things got rolling, I brought technicians and equipment from Italy to teach a team of locals I had put together the grammar of cinema. We made them independent. Under my direction we produced newsreels, documentaries—some of which I directed and had positive feedback here in Europe, like **Capitol Hill** (1951), that was selected for the Edinburgh Festival. Plus, we would give technical and logistical support to foreign productions that would come to shoot there. For example, in the case of **Outcast of the Islands** (1952) by Carol Reed, based on Conrad's novel, I provided assistance through my Film Unit. Those were great years. I remember long dinners with Arthur C. Clarke who had a house there...

How did you get into films?
I started working in cinema by pure chance. I was on holiday in Rome on one of those very rare encounters with my father. I hardly knew him, and he certainly didn't know me. At the time he had just started

working on **Tepepa** at Cinecittà. My ignorance regarding films was total. The only films I had seen in London were mostly British films like **Tom Jones, Darling, Alfie,** etc. I knew my father was a film director, but I had no idea what that implied. I don't know whether there's anybody who is going to read what I'm saying, but if there is, I hope to be forgiven for my hazy recollections. Anyhow, I do remember Cinecittà. It was a lively, bustling, crazy place full of busy people carrying stuff around, building, painting, fixing, and the theatres were filled with lights hanging from everywhere, coils of electrical cables strewn on the ground, cameras big and small, actors, extras, and people shouting, but funnily enough, in spite of the chaos, everyone seemed to know what they were about. I met so many actors and directors whom I later discovered to be famous like, for example, Eduardo De Filippo, Marcello Mastroianni, Anthony Quinn, Raquel Welch, Terrence Hill, and many more. It's sad to think what Cinecittà has now become. I particularly remember Cinecittà's canteen. We would all queue together, no matter who you were, and then find a seat in this huge hangar-like structure. Some bigger name directors, stars, or producers, if they had the time, would maybe go back to their hotels or eat outside Cinecittà in some restaurant, but you could and would find anybody. I remember once having a long conversation with Henry Fonda, who was left alone and had nobody who spoke in English to chat with. I was particularly stricken by his complete lack of unpretentiousness; he just enjoyed talking about small things: his walk the previous evening in the centre of Rome with his wife. He asked me a lot of questions about why I spoke English so well. Anyway, going back to **Tepepa**, my first film, at the time it was bewildering for me. I felt intimidated. My father introduced me to his script supervisor and said, "Stay with her and try to learn something." And that is what I did. I remained glued to her. Her name was Anna Maria Montanari and I believe she was one of the best script supervisors at the time. She was kind and patient with me, and I am very grateful to her. Then from Cinecittà we went to Almeria, in Spain. After about a week into shooting, Anna Maria announced that Gillo Pontecorvo wanted her to work on his film, **Queimada** (Burn!, 1969). That came as a surprise, at least to me. The question now was who was going to take her place. The production manager, Gianni Minervini, came up with a "brilliant" idea. "What about Silvia?" I instantly said no but he insisted. Since no member of the crew spoke English, except for my father, and since Orson Welles was expected in Spain shortly, he probably thought I might come in handy. Anyway, that was the start of my career as a script supervisor.

Tell me a little about Orson Welles.
Everyone feared Orson Welles' arrival on set, expecting him to be difficult. In fact, he was rather surly with some members of the crew, but he had an excellent rapport with my father and he was kind to me. The other actors on the film were Tomas Milian, John Steiner, and Luciano Casamonica (a young gypsy boy who had been singled out in Rome for the role of the child, Paquito). I have to admit that Giulio was remarkable with actors in general. He was patient and listened to their suggestions and to be sure, Tomas Milian always had a lot to suggest! He was a good actor but to me he seemed very self-conscious and extremely insecure. Moreover, his relationship with Orson Welles was a disaster. Orson seemed to have very little consideration for him and would call him "the little Cuban". As for John Steiner, he was kind and reassuring and followed Giulio's directions without a problem. Orson Welles and Giulio got on splendidly and seemed to understand one another both on the set and away from it. They would often hang out together even once the day's work was done. Welles in the evening would drink heavily and always had a twinkle in his eye and a wicked sense of humour, but it all came down to how he perceived you. If you rubbed him the wrong way he would dig in to you but without ever raising his voice.

Giulio Petroni: Cuomo managed to get in touch with him through some agencies. When I met Welles I told him that the idea of directing **Citizen Kane** *was quite intimidating, but, with a grin on his face, he just said, "Don't be silly." When I made* **Tepepa** *I was no longer that young, and this was a relief for him because he couldn't stand newbies. Needless to say, he was preceded by his reputation as an unmanageable, grouchy man—which he actually was, but not with me. Welles and I spent many nights talking over a bottle of whiskey. He liked drinking. He would often talk about Rita Hayworth… I suppose he never got over her. He never interfered with my work or role on set—maybe a suggestion once or twice… and he was always perfectly right. Unfortunately, Tomas Milian became his target. He would call him "the tiny Cuban".*

Tell me something more about Milian.
He was a powerhouse of ideas and keeping up with him was not easy. I worked with him twice. Once, of course on Tepepa, and then on **Liberi, armati, pericolosi** (Young, Violent, Dangerous a.k.a. Young, Violent, and Desperate, 1976) directed by Romolo Guerrieri. On the latter film I found not necessarily more

mature but a definitely more relaxed Milian. Generally though he was very insecure. I know my father often had to really make an effort to keep on track.

Giulio Petroni: A good actor but sometimes a bit hard to manage. He was a powerhouse of ideas; therefore, he had this tendency of going a bit overboard. When we were working on **La vita, a volte, è molto dura, vero Provvidenza?** *(Life Is Tough, Eh Providence? a.k.a. Sometimes Life Is Hard—Right, Providence?, 1972), he would come to me with these odd suggestions and I had to contain him. For example, in that film, the yoga thing was his idea. He was very self-doubting as well. On the one hand he would be a very dominant presence on set but on the other he was very self-conscious and insecure. Welles was after him and I think he felt very much under pressure. He especially had problems with his physical appearance. He felt ugly and would constantly be comparing himself to other men. This is one of the reasons he felt the need to seduce everybody. Tomas hated, in a pathological way, the idea of being unnoticed or unappreciated.*

Orson Welles, Giulio Petroni and Tomas Milian on the set of Tepepa.

You also worked on Giulio Petroni's subsequent Western.
Yes, I did; I also worked on a film called **Nest of Vipers** directed by Giulio but in all honesty I don't remember much. The actors were Luke Askew, and Chelo Alonso in the role of the prostitute. It was filmed in Rome and Almeria. Divo Cavicchioli was the set photographer. He was quite a character and an excellent photographer. Most of the time he seemed to be snoozing somewhere on the set and then he would suddenly jump up and be extraordinarily active, taking a quantity of photos, mostly with his Hasselbladder, and then retreat once more. He was partial to drugs and there was quite a bit going around on that film. Divo always spoke enthusiastically of Cartagena, the freedom he felt over there and of his intention of retiring there, which he eventually did. Askew I think felt a little overwhelmed by the experience. I believe it was his first role as an absolute protagonist and I think he felt the responsibilities of being the lead. I remember a big Italian newspaper dedicating a lot of space to Askew's arrival with his wife at Rome's biggest airport.

Giulio Petroni: In all my films my social and political consciousness can be found looming in some corner. I'm an atheist and have always been one. It's in my blood. My great-grandfather was the last person to be condemned to death by the Church. He spent nearly twenty years in the Vatican prisons. I remember during the premiere of the film, a man got up from his seat and started repeatedly making the sign of the cross, shaking his head like an epileptic, in the scene when Luke Askew says, "I don't have imaginary friends" after he'd been asked if he believed in God. If it hadn't been a Western, so unworthy of attention, that scene would have probably been cut. I was the one who chose Askew as I chose everybody in the film. The production company sent me to Los Angeles asking me to come back with someone new. I picked him through a big casting agency in the heart of Hollywood. He'd had a role in **Easy Rider** (1969) and before that he had been in **Cool Hand Luke** (1967). I chose him mainly because I thought he would be credible in a Western context, but also because of his modern face. I wanted somebody that would have been credible as a hippy. And I didn't regret it: just like all American actors, he was punctual and meticulous. They all were, regardless of their artistic abilities. I had no problems with Askew. He smoked a lot of weed but, after Milian on **Tepepa**, I was used to that sort of thing. Milian had just discovered cocaine. I had a good relationship with everybody on that film. Chelo Alonso was a bit of a diva but nothing I couldn't handle. **Nest of Vipers** was my seventh film, so I had built a trustworthy team. Divo Cavicchioli came back after Tepepa as a set photographer. Pistilli, Minervini, Luciano Casamonica, Magda Konopka… I had good people on that film.

Let's keep talking about westerns, what can you tell me about Padella Calibro 38 (Panhandle 38, 1972) by Antonio Secchi?

That was the first and I think only film directed by Antonio Secchi, who until then had been a director of photography. Secchi directed it as a cinematographer would—with detached professionalism. He would pay absolutely no attention to the acting or narrative. The actors were Keenan Wynn and Scott Holden, William Holden's son. They said Keenan Wynn drank heavily but I never noticed. He would turn up on the set punctually, ready for work. He was versatile and charming. I don't remember much about Scott Holden, I'm afraid. What I can tell you though is that Wynn had problems dealing with Delia Boccardo. She was shy and quite emotional and would often forget her lines or be late on set.

You worked quite a few times with Fernando Di Leo.

I worked on several films directed by Fernando Di Leo. It was a pleasure working with him. He would arrive every morning knowing exactly what he wanted. He would give instructions and disappear until everything was ready. He was quick at making decisions and never wasted time. With Di Leo we never worked overtime, which was a rarity in those days. However, he didn't seem to be particularly demanding as far as the acting was concerned. His directions to the actors was telegraphic. I have at times wondered whether Di Leo believed in the films he directed because sometimes he appeared to be detached, although you can't really argue with the results. I do think he had more of a writer's predisposition than a director's one and in fact the scripts, even of his lesser films, are rock solid. Working with Fernando gave me the opportunity of meeting many big American actors like Jack Palance, Richard Conte, and Henry Silva, but the person I found myself better with is Lee J. Cobb, an adorable man who would talk about his wife back in the States—he missed her dearly and was always calm and warm with everyone.

Finally, going back to Westerns: Ah sì? E io lo dico a Zzzzorro! (Mark of Zorro a.k.a. Who's Afraid of Zorro? a.k.a. They Call Him Zorro... Is He?).

That is a film directed by Franco Lo Cascio starring George Hilton and Lionel Stander. I had worked with Lo Cascio before when he was a 1st AD. He was good at his job and I liked working with him. This was his first film as director and his mother, who had been a famous assistant director working with the likes of Luchino Visconti, was his 1st AD. I lost touch with him after this film but some years later I learnt that his interests lay elsewhere and that he was directing porn films. I don't what went wrong, but I didn't see that coming. However, going back to his film, it was filmed in a 15th century castle overlooking the lake of Bracciano. Lionel Stander was an interesting person. I remember that in between takes he would sit in his chair and read avidly, oblivious to what was going on around him. One day I asked him what he was reading: it was Charles Dickens.

If you want to know more about Italian Westerns, Giulio Petroni and generally about the Italian film world and its genre cinema, make sure to pick Eugenio Ercolani's book Darkening the Italian Screen (McFarland, 2019), available on paperback and e-book.

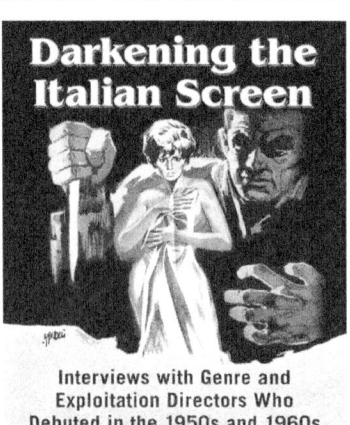

Upper: Giulio Petroni and Gabriella Giorgelli on the set of Life is Tough, EhProvidence? starring Tomas Milian.

Middle: Silvia Petroni, Fernando Di Leo and Jack Palance on the set of Rulers of the City.

Bottom: Darkening the Italian Screen written by Eugenio Ercolani, available through Amazon.

**All photos used in Eugenio Ercolani's Petroni articles used courtesy of Eugenio Ercolani.

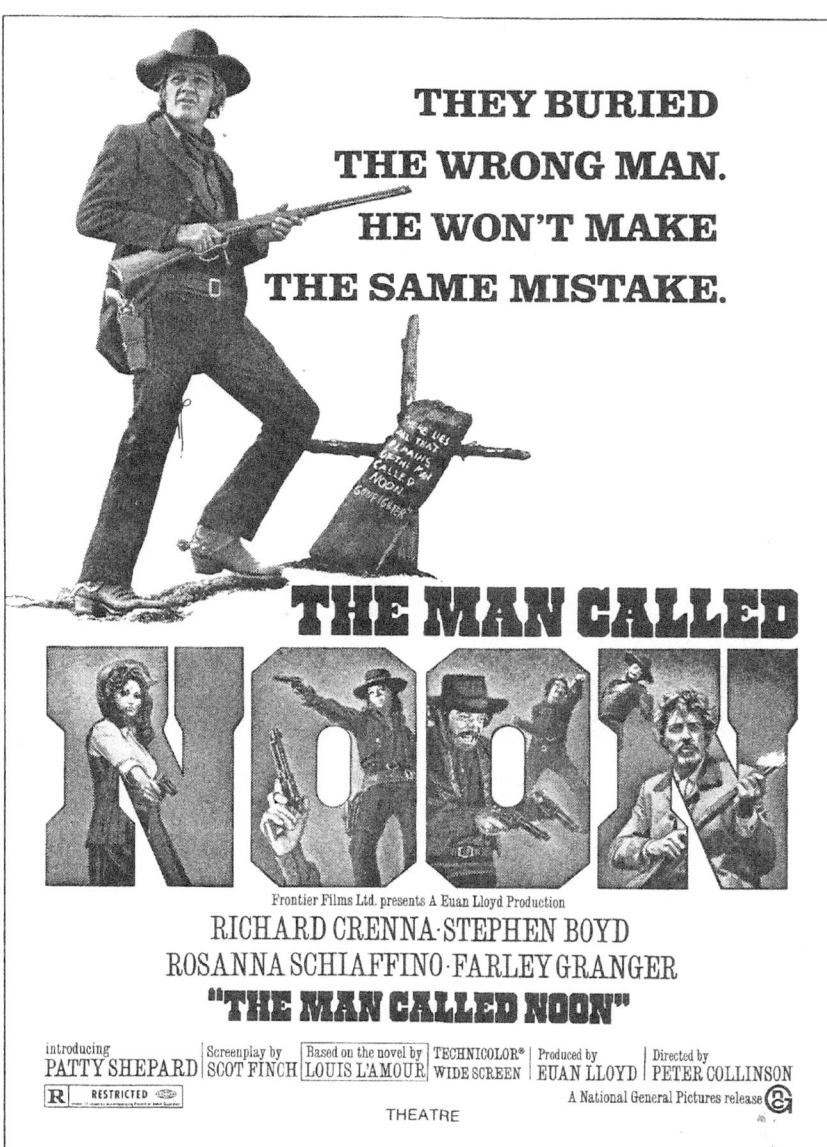

The Man Called Noon
(And musings on Peter Collinson and the Louis L'Amour European Westerns)

Steve Mason

Louis L'Amour (March 22, 1908 – June 10, 1988) is without question one of the pre-eminent and best-known authors of Western American fiction, with 89 novels and 14 short-story collections to his credit. Commencing with the Republic Pictures production of the **Wells Fargo Gunmaster** (United States, 1951), a 60-minute oater featuring Allan "Rocky" Lane and his stallion "Black Jack," over forty of L'Amour's stories and novels have been adapted for cinema and television. Four of these adaptations have been filmed in Europe, or Spain, specifically: **Kid Rodelo** (United States, Spain, 1966), **Shalako** (United Kingdom, Germany, United States, 1968), **Catlow** (United Kingdom, United States, 1971) and **The Man Called Noon** (Un hombre llamado Noon, United Kingdom, Italy, Spain, 1973).

The first of the L'Amour-Eurowestern cycle, **Kid Rodelo**, starred Don Murray, Janet Leigh and Broderick Crawford. The film is a standard B-Western and largely indistinguishable in style and form from its American counterparts of the 50's and 60's aside from the Spanish desert locales and the bit-parts from a handful of actors recognizable to genre fans including Jose Nieto, Fernando Hilbeck, and Luis Barboo. Filmed in black-and-white, the decision to produce the film in Spain was likely a cost-saving measure. The director, Richard Carlson, is much better known for his work as an actor. With over fifty roles to his credit, two of his most-notable leads include **It Came From Outer Space** (United States, 1953) and **Creature From the Black Lagoon** (United States, 1954). Most of Carlson's directorial output was for television serials, although he had also previously helmed another L'Amour adaptation, **Four Guns to the Border** (United States, 1954). A review by the New York Times (February 23, 1966) said of **Kid Rodelo**: "A spokesman for Paramount testifies that this silly shivaree was filmed in Spain, which seems to be a tiring way to do it, since it all could have been turned out just as badly in Hollywood's Television City."

British producer Euan Lloyd, best known for his international action films including **The Wild Geese** (Switzerland, United Kingdom, 1978) and **The Sea Wolves** (Switzerland, United Kingdom, United States, 1980), was introduced to the books of Louis L'Amour by his friend Alan Ladd. Lloyd initially intended to produce five L'Amour adaptations through "Frontier Productions," which he co-founded with actor Stephen Boyd. The first, and most-ambitious, of these productions was **Shalako** (United Kingdom, West Germany, United States, 1968), starring Sean Connery (while on hiatus as James Bond) and directed by the well-established American director Edward Dmytryk whose impressive credentials included **The Caine Mutiny** (United States, 1954), **Raintree County** (United States, 1957), **The Young Lions** (United States, 1958), **The Carpetbaggers** (Unites States, 1954), and **Anzio** (United States, Italy, 1968). Unfortunately, **Shalako** would enjoy none of the success of these films, especially in the financial sense, and the $5-million film (Connery's salary alone was $1-million) failed miserably at the box-office. Part of the blame was attributed to the complete lack of on-screen chemistry between the superstar leads, Connery and Brigitte Bardot. As Ed Andreychuk notes in his book "Louis L'Amour on Film and Television," the sexual chemistry between "despicable" secondary characters played by Honor Blackman and Stephen Boyd far exceeds that of the Connery-Bardot pairing. A corny theme-song ("Shalako! Shalako! He rode wild country down New Mexico"), badly outdated even by 1968 standards, sets the tone for the remainder of the film which bears little resemblance to traditional Euro-westerns aside from the filming locales. In all fairness, the film is visually impressive at points and features some good action set-pieces, though the film fails as a whole. As Roger Ebert aptly summed it up in his November 12, 1968 review: "Shalako is a disappointment… Strangely enough, the long-awaited meeting between Connery and Miss Bardot is a flop… Considering the resources they brought to their roles, we might have expected more. The same can be said for the movie." In retrospect, it's a pity that Connery chose this project over staying on as 007 for **On Her Majesty's Secret Service** (United Kingdom, 1969), as I tend to agree with many others that Connery in the lead could have elevated the Bond film to a classic, and perhaps the best film of the series.

Undeterred by the tepid reception of **Shalako**, Lloyd pressed on with a second L'Amour adaptation, **Catlow** (United Kingdom, United States, 1971), a (relatively) modest production which succeeds largely because of its light and humorous approach and lack of bombast that was largely the undoing of Shalako. Starring Yul Brynner, with Richard Crenna as a U.S. Marshal and Leonard Nimoy as a nasty bounty hunter. The film is reasonably enjoyable, though both Brynner and female-lead Daliah Lavi ham it up a bit much for my liking. The director Sam Wanamaker, is (also) better-known as an actor, typically in supporting roles including **Taras Bulba** (Yugoslavia, United States, 1962) **The Spy Who Came in From the Cold** (United Kingdom, 1965), **Billy Jack Goes to Washington** (United States, 1977), **Raw Deal** (United states, Netherlands, 1985) and two Peter Collinson-directed films: **The Spiral Staircase** (U.K., 1975) and **The Sell-Out** (United Kingdom, Italy, Israel, 1976). His work as director consisted of occasional gigs for a number of popular American television series including **The Defenders**, **Columbo** and **Hart to Hart**, while his best-known theatrical film, as director, is probably **Sinbad and the Eye of the Tiger** (United Kingdom, United States, 1977). Among the familiar Almeria locales, the McBain Ranch set from Once Upon a time in the West (C'era una volt il West, Italy, United States, 1968) is re-purposed, and a few Spaghetti Western regulars turn up in supporting roles, including Angel Del Pozo and Dan Van Husen.

Actor/Screenwriter Scot Finch, who had adapted both **Shalako** and **Catlow,** also wrote the screenplay for **Noon**. The storyline is complex. Probably a bit too complex for its own good as far as action/adventure films go. The film opens with a failed attempt on the life of Crenna's character (Jonas Mandarin/"Ruble Noon") wherein he takes a blow to the head that erases most of his memory. With the help of a mysterious stranger (J.B Rimes, played by Stephen Boyd), Noon escapes his pursuers and holes up with a group of outlaws (posing as ranchers) at the isolated Rafter D Ranch. The ranch was recently inherited by Fan Davidge, the young and attractive daughter of the previous owner, however, it now functions more as a hideout for bandits who hold Davidge while attempting to locate a cache of gold rumored to be hidden somewhere on the expansive spread. Noon begins to piece together his memory and comes to learn that he was in fact a wealthy arms dealer named Jonas Mandarin. Following the murder of his wife and child by outlaws, Mandarin went undercover as the notorious vigilante/hired gun "Ruble Noon," known and feared for killing off low-lifes and criminals with ruthless efficiency. Noon seems to have some previous knowledge of the expansive Rafter D Ranch, and he eventually pieces together some clues that lead he and Rimes to the Town of El Paso. The final act boils down to a showdown between the disparate group of "bad guys", united primarily for the purpose of stealing the hidden gold, in a battle with the "good guys," who are trying to see that the gold remains with its rightful owner, Fan Davidge.

The "Good Guys" (and their portrayers):

Jonas Mandarin/"Ruble Noon" (Richard Crenna) – The film's hero and protagonist. Tall, rugged and with a naturally world-weary appearance, Crenna fits the part well. Known more as a supporting actor through his extensive film and television career, **The Sand Pebbles** (United States, 1966) and **Wait Until Dark** (Unites States, 1967) were two of his more notable roles. He's best-remembered by the current generation of filmgoers as Rambo's former commanding officer, Colonel Sam Trautman, in the popular Sylvester Stallone franchise.

J.B. Rimes (Stephen Boyd) – Rimes is an enigmatic character. His efforts to assist Noon are, apparently, partly altruistic and partly self-serving ($). A likeable character, he communicates largely through quips and one-liners. Boyd is best-remembered for his turn as "Massala" in **Ben Hur** (United States, 1959).

Fan Davidge (Rosanna Schiaffino) – Fan is the inheritor of the Rafter D Ranch, and a captive of the nasty element that has taken control of it after her father's passing. She also takes an immediate liking to Noon, of course, thereby providing the film's romantic subplot. The lovely Schiaffino was an Italian actress in the Sophia Loren mold (literally and figuratively). Her best-known film is probably **Arrivaderci, Baby!** (United Kingdom, 1966), a comedy wherein she costarred with Tony Curtis.

Arch Henneker (Jose Jaspe) – Henneker is Fan Davidge's elderly ranch foreman, having worked the ranch for her father. He is loyal to Fan but wary of Noon. Spanish actor Jose Jaspe appeared in several other Spaghetti Westerns over his lengthy career, usually in bit parts.

The Brakeman (Ricardo Palacios) – A "good guy" by association. He's well-familiar with "Ruble Noon" as he works the route that services an isolated railway station that is apparently used only by Noon. He also appears to be the only character personally familiar with Noon: "You've gotten to where you can kill a man and not even remember it?" Palacios, of course, has an extensive Spaghetti Western resume. I'll always best-recall him as the bartender in **For a Few Dollars More** (Per qualche dollar in piu, Italy, Spain, West Germany, 1965) who, with just an upwards glance, gives up the location of "Guy Calloway" to Lee Van Cleef's "Colonel Mortimer".

The "Bad Guys" (and their portrayers):

Peg Cullane (Patty Shepard) – Looking great in the all-black outfit she dons in the film's final act, Cullane is a femme fatale of the highest order. She eggs on her co-conspirators: "Unless one of you big heroes makes a move nobody's going to get a cent…" Played by American model-turned –actress Patty Shepard, who is best-remembered for her work in European horror films and giallos.

Ben Janish (Angel Del Pozo) – The man who tries (and fails) to kill Noon in the film's opening. Janish is described as the head honcho of the outlaws, though he has only one line of dialogue in the film and appears to be just "one of the gang," for all intents and purposes. The character is considerably more fleshed-out in the book. Angel Del Pozo has amassed a long-list of roles, including the European Westerns **The Big Gundown** (La resa de conti, Italy, Spain, 1966) and **Face to Face**, Faccia a Faccia, Italy, Spain, 1967). [1]

Judge Niland (Farley Granger) – Niland is introduced in the film as a mild-mannered intellectual, spending his spare time pondering over chess strategy while delivering a monologue to Noon (and the audience) which helps to tie up many of the plot's loose ends. He's every bit as nasty as his partner Peg Cullane, we later discover, and doesn't hesitate to shoot his own compatriots as punishment for perceived cowardice. Farley Granger is probably best-remembered for his co-lead (with Robert Walker) in Alfred Hitchcock's **Strangers on a Train** (United States, 1951).

Kissling (Aldo Sambrell) – Despite being a minor character, Kissling actually has a character arc, of sorts, in the film. Aldo Sambrell needs no introduction to readers of this journal, of course.

Christobal (Julian Ugarte) – Cristobal specializes in extracting information from people with the help of his very large and very sharp buck knife. Julian Ugarte made his biggest impression in giallos and European crime films of the 1970's, often playing creeps and psychos.

The cast of villains are rounded out by a few familiar faces: Dave Cherry (Jose Canalejas), Lang (Charley Bravo) and Ford (Fernando Hilbeck) . [2]

Top to Bottom:
Title Card
Richard Crenna and Stephen Boyd
Patty Shepard
Rosanna Schiaffino
Farley Granger

Peter Collinson directed seventeen feature films in his brief career, from 1967 to 1980. He was born in 1936 in Lincolnshire, England, to show-business parents but was neglected by both upon their separation and spent the majority of his upbringing in a foster home, Actor's Orphanage in Chertsey, Surrey, where he wrote and acted in many plays. [3] Legendary actor Noel Coward was serving as president of the orphanage at the time and took the young Collinson under his wing, to the extent of taking in Peter as his godson and eventually steering him towards work in directing plays post-graduation. After a brief stint (3 years) directing television dramas, Collinson's feature film career started strongly with **The Penthouse** (Great Britain, 1967) and **Up the Junction** (Great Britain, 1968), both starring a young Suzy Kendall, and both critical and commercial successes. [4] He followed with a very-good (anti) war film starring David Hemmings, **The Long Day's Dying** (Great Britain, 1968), and the hugely-popular comedy/heist film, **The Italian Job** (Great Britain, 1969), starring Michael Caine. Over his career, Collinson directed films of various genres and over a wide-ranging list of international locales (See filmography at end). His final two films, **The House on Garibaldi Street** (United States, 1979) and **The Earthling** (Australia, United States, 1980) were both good films, especially compared to most of the middling efforts he directed in the mid/late70's. Unfortunately, Collinson's late-career resurgence was short-lived as he was diagnosed with an aggressive form of cancer immediately after completion of **The Earthling** and passed a mere twelve weeks later, on December 16, 1980, at the age of 44.

Collinson has been described by co-workers as being of the "the ends justifies any means" school of inspiring actors and crew (a la Sam Peckinpah and William Friedkin). "He had a filthy temper, but it lasted seconds, then he was back to the happy chap we all loved dearly…" recalled actor Frank Jarvis (**The Italian Job**). [5] During the filming of **The Earthling**, even the (then) 10-year old Ricky Shroder came under Collinson's ire, to the extent that co-star William Holden interceded and stuck up for the young actor and helped him with the rather demanding role of a child coping with the sudden loss both parents. Shroder later named his first child "Holden" in William's honor. Aldo Sambrell had a Colinson anecdote of his own: (While filming **The Man Called Noon**) "I made the mistake of finding the girlfriend of the director – Peter Colinson – attractive. He cornered me, but I told that guy, 'I was only talking to her, and she gave me the cold shoulder anyway, so don't worry about it. I'm not going after her. So maybe he thought my moustache was going to appeal to her, so he made me shave my moustache off and disguised his reason as 'Oh, you'll look so much better without it.' I think he was a little bit out of his mind, to put it nicely." [6] Regardless of his personal quirks, however, numerous actors and actresses would choose to appear in a number of Collinson's films, most notably John Philip Law, Oliver Reed, William Holden and Susan George.

A constant amongst all of Collinson's films is solid visual presentation, even though he worked with a number of different cinematographers through his career. His visual style is typically evidenced by a liberal use of dolly/tracking shots and the use of creative shot framing. Even in regard to some of his lesser efforts, it is not fair to say that any of Collinson's films looks bad. Roger Ebert, in his review for The Penthouse noted: [7] "By the evidence, the movie was photographed by the hardest working cameraman in history. He sneaks up on his shots from every angle except through the floor, and swoops, dips, whirls and zig-zags, meanwhile moving in and out of focus so dramatically you'd think he was Andy Warhol with skill." **The Man Called Noon** boasts some great cinematography, as well, by John Cabrera. The film's visual presentation is often called out as its strongest point in most contemporary reviews.

Left: Peter Collinson and wife Lisa Shane aka Hazel Collinson

Right: German Lobby Card

Luis Bacalov's score to Noon is one of his best. The main theme is similar in style to that from **The Grand Duel** (Il grande duello, Italy, West Germany, France, 1972) with operatic vocals. The most unique element of the score, however, is the use of indigenous South-American pan flute at several points. Perhaps Bacalov was harkening to his Argentinian roots? A cue of "traditional" western music also up in a couple of spots to denote a dynamic action occurring, somewhat in the style of Elmer Bernstein's theme to **The Magnificent Seven** (United States, 1960).

The stunts in the film were coordinated by Bob Simmons, who was the long-time (1962-1985) stunt coordinator for the James Bond films. A number of rough-looking horse-and-rider falls turn up in the climax. A couple of fights, utilizing the actors and not stuntmen, are also well-choreographed. Simmons also served as the associate producer of the film. "Women-in-peril" was a recurring theme in Collinson's films, leading some critics to label him as a "misogynist". Noon doesn't jibe with this attempt to pigeon-hole Collinson, however. The two female leads in Noon arguably turnout to be the strongest and most determined characters in the film. Further, the "big showdown" is not, in my opinion, Noon vs. Janish but rather Peg Cullane vs. Fan Davidge at the film's finale. "You wouldn't shoot a woman... You haven't got the guts…" says Cullane to an injured and helpless Rimes during the melee. "No, but I would… I'd shoot you and enjoy it, murderous bitch..." answers Davidge in a climax that makes a nod to **Johnny Guitar** (United States, 1954).

The film was rated "R" by the Motion picture Association of America upon release, due certainly to the violent nature of most of the killings. The gun-deaths are mostly prolonged affairs, punctuated with a number of bloody squibs and victims that stagger around and "hang on" long enough to feel them all. One character is pinned to a wall with a pitchfork (then shot) while another is crushed by a large boulder. The only (relatively) clean deaths are those who take a bullet followed by a fatal plunge.

Western films had largely been reduced to parodies, comedies and revisionist stories by 1973. **The Man Called Noon**, a "straightforward" western, was released with scant promotion, due largely to the fact that the distributor, National General Pictures (1951-1974), was in the process of folding. Noon, was in fact one of their final film distributed. Critics, at the time, were generally receptive, though un-enthusiastic, about the film. The New York Times (September 25, 2973) noted "Peter Collinson's brisk direction," and described the film as "…fairly successful in maintaining some mystery." Variety (July 18, 1973) stated "Collinson's helming is effective especially when transmitting charged atmosphere." Smaller-circulation newspapers provided some of the most-positive reviews: [8] "Three actors in the film give the best performances of their respective careers: Richard Crenna, Stephen Boyd and Farley Granger," (The El Paso Prospector, July 19, 1973). "It's a good rowdy shoot-em up fun. Crenna is suitably strong and mysterious in the great tradition of Western heroes, and Steve Boyd is something of a surprise in the role of his badman friend who has a sense of humor," (The Danville Register, April 11, 1973).

For many years, the most easily-accessible (quality) print of **NOON**, in the US, would turn up on Ted Turner's "TNT" cable TV channel. The film must have received decent ratings when shown because it turned up quite a lot in the 90's and 2000's on the national network. The numerous VHS and DVD releases over the years (mostly public domain) have ranged in quality from fair, at best, to completely unwatchable. Thankfully, a British (Region 0) DVD was released in 2010 on the Odeon Label and Kino-Lorber released the film on a high-quality DVD (Region 1) and Blu-Ray in 2016.

In a 1967 interview with Roger Ebert, [9] Collinson stated "I'm not one of those directors with his life-span all mapped out, and a deep ponderous philosophy to put into my films. All I want to do is make movies as well as they can be made. Period. No philosophy." This statement is evident in **The Man Called Noon**, which succeeds because it plays it straight, and because it's a beautifully –presented film.

Peter Collinson filmography:
1. **The Penthouse** (Great Britain, 1967) - Essentially a play-on-film wherein a young Suzy Kendall and her sugar-daddy are held captive in a high-rise apartment penthouse by a pair of odd-ball thugs. The film, directed by a then-28-year old Collinson, was a modest hit in both Britain and the US. "'**The Penthouse**', quite simply, is a pretty good shocker," summarized Roger Ebert in his November 14, 1967 review.

2. **Up the Junction** (Great Britain, 1968) – Suzy Kendall plays a rich Chelsea girl who renounces her family wealth and opts to take a blue-collar job. She begins hanging out with her co-worker girlfriends, all working-class Londoners, and gets a full taste "working-class" life, for better or for worse. The film is a fascinating take on late-60's British lifestyle and youth culture. Based on the novel by Nell Dunn and deftly punctuated by a really-good Manfred Mann soundtrack. Arguably Collinson's best film.

3. **Long Day's Dying** (Great Britain, 1968) – A bit uneven, though highly original, WWII film with some very tense sequences. The film effectively employs the technique of voice-over dialogue to "hear" what the characters are thinking (without speaking). Similar in spirit to Sam Peckinpah's brilliant **Cross of Iron** (United Kingdom, West Germany, 1977), though heavier on the introspective dialogue and lighter on the action.

4. **The Italian Job** (Great Britain, 1969) – A big hit with an enduring following, the film is certainly Collinson's best-remembered effort. A big-budget Hollywood remake, in 2003, starring Mark Wahlberg in the Michael Caine role was also a big success at the box office. A fun watch but a bit dated. If Austin Powers were an actual person, this would have been his favorite film. 10

5. **You Can't Win 'Em All** (United Kingdom, Unites States, 1970) Gene Corman (brother of Roger) produced this US-British co-production for Columbia pictures. Set during the 1922 Turkish Civil War, the actioner starring Charles Bronson and Tony Curtis has faded into well-deserved obscurity. Summarized New York Times critic Roger Greenspun (July 25, 1970): "But for that sweet sense of male companionship that in one form or another has sustained the best of the genre from Ford through Peckinpah, the film discovers no resources. It is therefore aimless in its energies, lost in its landscapes, and hopelessly wasteful of its ancient conventions."

6. **Fright** (United Kingdom, 1971) A few good scares highlight this shocker wherein a recently-escaped lunatic returns to the home of his former wife and child and proceeds to terrorize the babysitter (Susan George). Reportedly the first of the now clichéd "babysitter-in-peril" genre, for what that's worth. Solid but unspectacular.

7. **Straight on Till Morning** (United Kingdom, 1972) A small-town girl (Rita Tushingham) moves to London and makes the mistake of shacking-up with an attractive, but badly un-hinged, young man (Shane Briant) in this well-made but unpleasant psychological thriller. A Hammer Studios production.

8. **Innocent Bystanders** (United Kingdom, Spain, Turkey, 1972) – A pretty bland attempt at a 007-type international thriller. Starring Stanley Baker, Geraldine Chaplin (daughter of Charles), Donald Pleasance and Dana Andrews.

9. **The Man Called Noon** (Un hombre llamado Noon, United Kingdom, Italy, Spain, 1973) The lone western in Collinson's resume.

10. **Open Season** (Spain, Switzerland, United States, United Kingdom, 1974) A variation on The Most Dangerous Game (United States, 1932); Peter Fonda, John Philip Law and Richard Lynch play Vietnam vets who liven-up their annual hunting trip by kidnapping people, turning them loose at their isolated ranch, and hunting them for sport. William Holden plays a small, but pivotal, role. Not as entertaining as the premise suggests. The cast seems to be split between playing it straight and playing it like a parody. Set entirely in the US, but filmed partly in New Mexico and partly in Spain.

11. **Ten Little Indians** (Italy, West Germany, France, Spain, united Kingdom, Iran, 1974) A reasonably-good take on the Agatha Christie novel of the same name; Filmed in Spain and Iran, the film sports an impressive cast including Oliver Reed, Richard Attenborough, Elke Sommer and Orson Welles (bit-part). According to IMDB.com, the original cut was several minutes longer and included a sub-plot involving Teresa Gimpera and Rik Battaglia as spies, and though their names still appear in the credits they do not appear in the film. This "lost" segment was retained, however, in the Spanish print and includes music by Bruno Nicolai (temporary cue?), whereas the remainder of the film is scored by Carlo Rustichelli.

12. **The Spiral Staircase** (United Kingdom, 1975) A tedious remake of the 1946 Robert Siodmak classic psychological thriller; Stars Jacqueline Bissett, Christopher Plummer and John Philip Law.

13. **The Sell-Out** (United Kingdom, Italy, Israel, 1976) Oliver Reed and Richard Widmark star in this draggy espionage thriller. Filmed in Israel, Reed's always-welcome presence and a good chase scene in the final act elevate the film to watch-ability.

14. **Target of an Assassin** (South Africa, 1977) A thoroughly average action/espionage effort, filmed in South Africa; Scripted by Scot Finch, Anthony Quinn's character reads a Louis L'Amour paperback to pass his spare time.

15. **Tomorrow Never Comes** (Canada, United Kingdom, 1978) – A storyline that starts out like **Falling Down** (France, United States, United Kingdom, 1993) and evolves into **Dog Day Afternoon** (United States, 1975). Stephen McHattie plays a man who snaps and Oliver Reed plays a police chief working his final day on the job who has to deal with him. Not a very good film, despite an interesting cast that also includes Susan George, Donald Pleasance, Raymond Burr and Paul Koslo.

16. **The House on Garibaldi Street** (United States, 1979) Produced by the American ABC television network, this riveting docudrama details the covert 1960 capture and extradition of Nazi war criminal Adolf Eichmann from Argentina to Israel. Starring Topol and Martin Balsam and filmed in Spain. Ricardo Palacios appears in a small (but key) role. The storyline is presentation is highly similar to **Argo** (United States, United Kingdom, 2012). A very-good film.

17. **The Earthling** (Australia, United States, 1980) A thoughtful and eloquent film; William Holden stars as a terminally ill man traveling to his childhood home in the isolated Australian outback to pass his final days in solitude. Along the way he is forced into a friendship with a young American boy (Ricky Shroder) who suddenly finds himself orphaned and alone when his parents are killed in an accident. A somewhat far-fetched premise, overcome by the excellent acting and Collinson's solid direction.

A Man Called Noon
Left: French Program
Right: Still- Stephen Boyd

Random Notes:

The production crew of **The Man Called Noon** was primarily Spanish.
Spaghetti Western locations location expert John Crummett provides the following information:
- The Tucumcari train station used in **For a Few Dollars More** serves as Noon's "personal" station here.
- The McBain house and surrounding area from **ONCE UPON A TIME IN THE WEST** has a prominent role (As the "Rafter D" - SM)

- Other locations include the "Widow's Ranch" area from **THE BIG GUNDOWN** and many other sw's including **THE HILLS RUN RED**, with its green valley and vast expanse of rocks; the Bank of El Paso town from **FOR A FEW DOLLARS MORE** shown rundown and in disrepair before being restored years later as a tourist attraction ; the town Clint rode into near the beginning of **FOR A FEW DOLLARS MORE**; the numerous trails and hills Clint and Lee rode up and down in the "Dollar" movies; the ramblas that have appeared in almost every spaghetti ever made. The train, tracks and train stations used in many a sw including **ONCE UPON A TIME IN THE WEST** and **FOR AFEW DOLLARS MORE**. And, last but not least the massive El Condor fort that was also used in Jimmy Coburn's **A REASON TO LIVE A REASON TO DIE**.

The plot device of a protagonist piecing together his lost memory while also attempting to solve a crime is a somewhat familiar one. It's been employed in a number of mainstream films including **Memento** (United States, 2000), **The Bourne Identity** (United States, Germany, Czech Republic, 2002), and **Unknown** (United Kingdom, France, Germany, United states, 2011). The Euro-Westerns **Man Who Cried For Revenge** (Il suo nome gridava vendetta, Italy, 1968) and **Twice a Judas** (Due volte Giuda, Italy, Spain, 1968) also fall under this category.

Actor Bruce M. Fischer (un-credited) plays a thug that makes the mistake of picking a fight with Noon, and takes a beating in the process. Fischer's character "Wolf" in **Escape from Alcatraz** (United States, 1979) made the same mistake with Clint Eastwood's character, "Frank Morris."
Richard Crenna would, in the 90's, narrate two Louis L'Amour "books on cassette." ("*Survival*" and "*Showdown Trail*")

A popular Chicago-based blues/rock band goes under the name "Man Called Noon," after the book and film, according to the group's front-man, Anthony Giamichael. For more info: https://www.facebook.com/mancallednoon

1. Angel Del Pozo is the last of the main cast members still living as of the writing of this article. Currently 85 years-old, his lengthy film career would make for a great interview.
2. I'll always associate Hilbeck with the zombie "Guthrie" in Jorge Grau's **Let Sleeping Corpses Lie** (Non si deve profanare il sonno dei morti, Spain, Italy, 1974)
3. BFI Online: http://www.screenonline.org.uk/people/id/862751/index.html
4. **Up the Junction** was in fact the highest-grossing British film of 1968 –(TVGuide.com)
5. From the DVD bonus material documentary directed by Lancelot Narayan & Matthew Field - 2002 Paramount Pictures: "A Great Idea / The Self Preservation Society / Get A Bloomin' Move On"
6. "*The Westerners.*" McFarland, mcfarlandbooks.com/product/the-westerners/.
7. The Chicago Sun – Times, November 14, 1967
8. The Stephen Boyd blog: https://stephenboydplog.com/tag/louis-lamour/
9. https://www.rogerebert.com/interviews/interview-with-peter-collinson
10. The Austin Powers character (Mike Myers) drives a Cooper Mini as his vehicle of choice in the popular New Line Cinema series, most-likely as a nod to The Italian Job which features the vehicles prominently.

Turn to page 210 for more rare photos from the set of A Man Called Noon

Der Mann aus El Paso

Der Mann aus El Paso

Der Mann aus El Paso

Der Mann aus El Paso

Frontier Films Ltd. zeigt eine Euan Lloyd Produktion
RICHARD CRENNA · STEPHEN BOYD
ROSANNA SCHIAFFINO · FARLEY GRANGER
Der Mann aus El Paso
Produktion: EUAN LLOYD Regie: PETER COLLINSON
Im Verleih der Warner Columbia

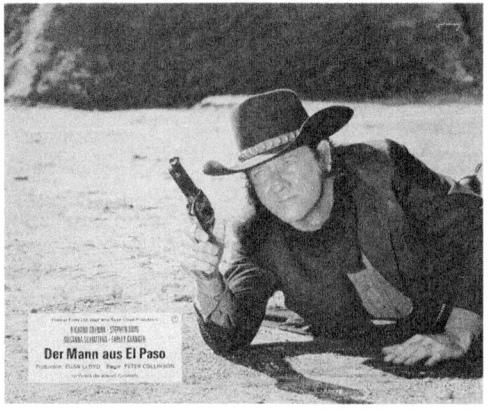

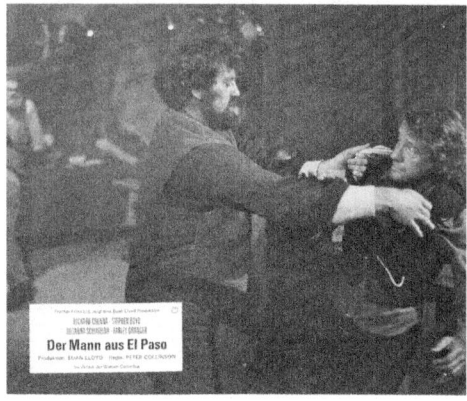

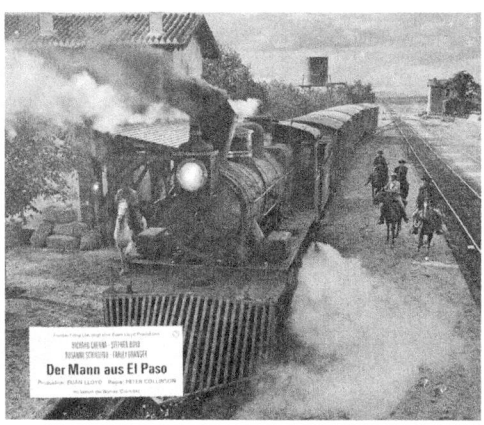

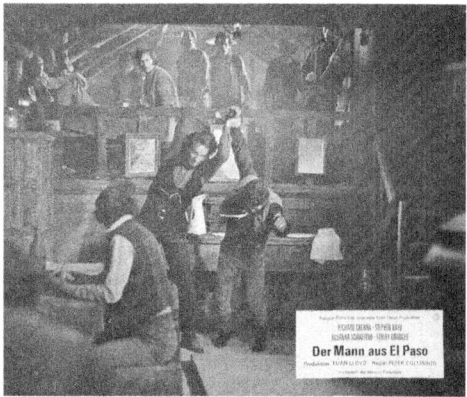

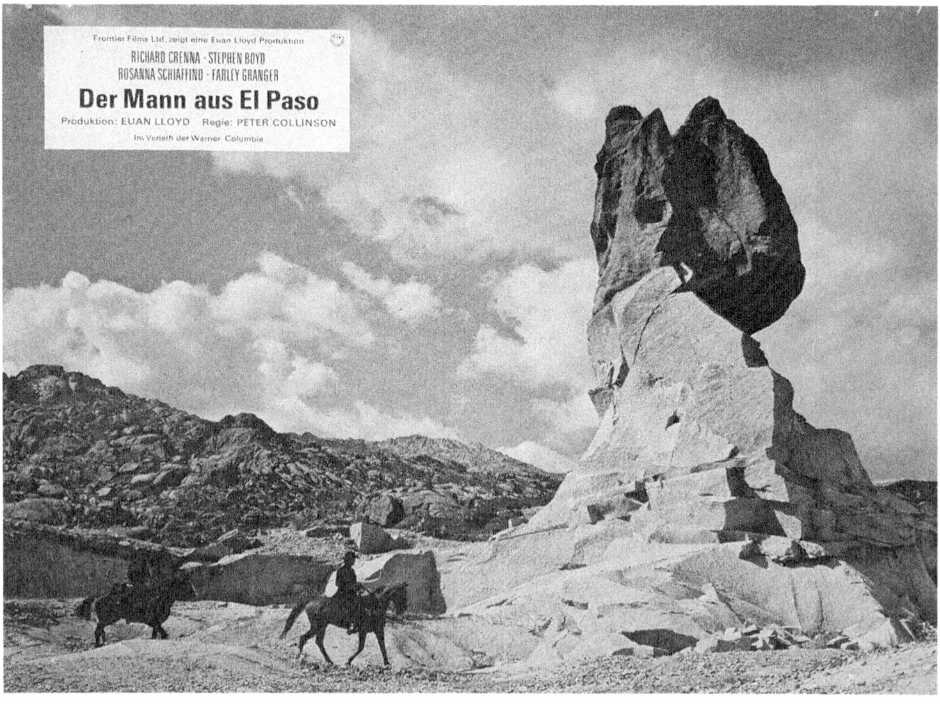

Page 39: Behind the scenes during the filming of A Man Called Noon. Left to right, Top to bottom: Peter Collinson; Patty Shepard and Farley Granger; Richard Crenna; Stephen Boyd; Peter Collinson and Richard Crenna; Peter Collinson and Richard Crenna.

Page 40- 41: German Lobby Cards.

*Thanks to Mike Siegel for the use of his rare photos and Steve Mason for his great bartering skills! (-Editor- M.H.)

By George! It's an Interview with Daniel Camargo!

"It is very important, specially for an actor, to have luck, luck and luck, and to be prepared."
George Hilton

S.W.. Tells us what is happening with your brilliant documentary George Hilton – The World Belongs to the Daring?
D.C. First of all, thank you for such nice words regarding my work. It has been a really though journey which I would have never been able to do if it was not for the support of so many people in several countries, specially my dear wife Rosa. After a nice run in the festival circuit, I was in search for a distribution or a sales agent until the COVID19 pandemic stopped everything.

To make movies you got to be crazy. It is a very difficult enterprise, even more when you are producing it yourself. Although, I had the support of George Hilton's family and friends, some institutions, festivals and companies that supposed to be interested in keeping the history of Italian film alive did not care about my project at all. A notorious Italian film historian refused to be interviewed because, according to him, it seemed an amateur project. Is it because the popular cinema that Hilton did – which in Italy is known as B-movies – has no historical value whatsoever? Ok if people do not like them, if people consider it a lesser kind of film when compared to other well know directors and actors but weren't the non-Leone westerns and non-Argento gialli a significant part, at least economically, of the Italian cinema? Or maybe the problem was that a Brazilian had to come to Italy to talk about Italian culture through the life of one of its more recognizable leading actors of the 60's and 70's? You have seen the film and liked it, so I imagine the problem was not quality. One thing the pandemic did not stop was problems concerning copyright showing up. Nevertheless, some films were reasonably easy to find its owners, some are still a mystery like in a giallo. For example, until now I have not been able to locate the owner of the great "A Bullet for Sandoval". I wrote to the people who has been somehow involved with it or released it in home video through the years and most of them would not even reply me. Some people will not help you, just like that. This same exhausting detective work has been done to all Hilton' films in Italy, Spain and Argentina. Some owners, like both Hallelujah's, which would not be the same to all territories, I could locate after the documentary was already running in the festivals and they asked me a prohibitive amount of money. Ok, people are totally entitled to make money out of their possessions, we all have to make a living. But I am an independent producer and I can't afford what documentaries directors like Matt Tyrnauer and Asif Kapadia can.

So, I have to get by as I can and every time I face a Sophie's Choice, should a license a scene or hire a lawyer? Unfortunately, the Fair Use (a legal doctrine that promotes freedom of expression by permitting the unlicensed use of copyright-protected works in certain circumstances) is not the same in all countries and if I do not have all formal authorizations no distributor or sales agent will take my movie. Couldn't I crowdfund to raise the money? Yes, I could, but successful crowdfunding is an art and takes a real lot of time and strategy, believe it or not. And when you are doing everything yourself, your subject is plus 80 years old and you are trying to make a living in a new country you have just arrived, time is something you don't have. So, what is happening right now to "**George Hilton – The World Belongs to the Daring**" is that I am re-cutting the movie to avoid legal problems. I will lose some precious images, but I will replace them with brand new material, among them a recent interview with Franco Nero who brings new lights to "The Brute and the Beast". You mentioned my documentary is brilliant (thanks again) so in honor to you and to everyone who believed in me and in my work, I will do everything in my power to keep it still brilliant, if not better!

S.W. How did you become interested in film in general? And what led you to your passion in Italian westerns.
D.C. Since I was 5, I wanted to work in films. I did not know what a producer or a director was, but I knew I wanted to tell stories using moving images. I would devour films and in early 80's Niterói, a beautiful city just by the side of Rio de Janeiro where I was born, late TV shows would be the source of the most obscure and vintage ones. These flicks would impress me more than the regular contemporary Hollywood stuff. Of course I have liked "**Raiders of the Lost Ark**", but I was much more pleased with Vincent Prince breaking eggs with the power of his mind over Boris Karloff's head in Roger Corman's "**The Raven**" or Peter Cushing masterfully changing his hands position holding the candle sticks while dispatching Christopher Lee back to hell in Hammer's "**Horror of Dracula**". I was not only having the time of my life; I was beginning to put names on those people faces so, years later, when I was in my mid 10's and VHS would allow me, I could pursue what other films these actors and directors have done. It was a real treasure hunt on the renting vídeo stores and without realizing, I was comparing genres, aesthetics, and narrative styles. I was in such a hunger for knowledge that I went after books about cinema that were not available in Portuguese. I had to recur to Italian, German, French, English, Spanish dictionaries, once there was no Google Translator.

But still before the VHS era, I have seen a tv commercial of a film that would be shown in a couple of days. I was mesmerized by it, a weird mixture of cowboys, a robot sheriff and a beautiful blonde woman (Sandra Milo). I cannot say if 1967 **Bang Bang Kid** was my first European western because I already knew the codes and mythology of the genre, but it was the first one I have full conscience and expectation. Then came two films that changed my perspective on western films, like showing very different faces of the same coin: John Ford's "**Stagecoach**" and Ferdinando Baldi's "**Carambola's Philosophy: In the Right Pocket**". I was more overwhelmed by Ford's movie, but what called my attention in Baldi's one is that there were flies flying over Paul Smith and Antonio Cantafora's horses. Carambola's location were dirtiest, people were unshaved and there was this tongue-in-cheek air, while Ford's film had a more solemn aura, besides the wonderful cinematography, Monument Valley locations and everything else that makes it what it is. I came to learn that such films as Carambola were known as "bangue-bangue à italiana" (bangue is a Brazilian Portuguese onomatopoeic for bang – from a shooting gun). For my surprise, there was a daily tv show that aired westerns of that kind with a few Winnetou once in a while. I could see all those characteristics used in very different a pattern of the movies starring John Wayne, Gary Cooper and James Stewart. A little later I have watched Ralph Nelson's 1972 "**The Wrath of God**" and I realized that American cinema had borrowed enormously from the "made in Italy" westerns.

These "faroestes espaguete" (faroeste: Brazilian corruption of the words far west; espaguete: spaghetti) were very popular not only in Brazil but in whole Latin America. So much that Terence Hill, Bud Spencer and Giuliano Gemma were idols and regarding the last one, Giorgio Ferroni's 1965 "**Blood for a Silver Dollar**", which I came to see much later, was synonym for Italian western and they were despised by the Brazilian intelligentsia. But who cared about the critics? We loved the film and its congeners and when we heard the Brazilian title of Ferroni's film, "**O Dólar Furado**" (translation: dollar with a hole) we would be transported to an exciting new world.

Like everywhere else, the western has always been a fascinating subject to us Brazilians. Our own cinema took a lot from it, as it can be seen on our cangaceiro (famous Northeastern Brazilian outlaws from the late 19's and early 20's) movies and in our "Feijoada Westerns" (feijoada is a famous Brazilian dish made with black beans and a variety of salted pork) a small cycle of films whose main name was director and star Tony Vieira, who actually brought the action from the American ambiance with cowboys and everything to western villages build in Brazil. The world-famous José Mojica Marins, before making a mark on horror films with his Coffin Joe character, started his career with his 1958 "**A Sina do Aventureiro**", a mix of Mexican melodrama and western. Even Glauber Rocha took western elements to the arthouse circuit, as it can be seen in his 1969 "**Antonio das Mortes**". Although, Rocha has always declared himself a John Ford aficionado, when you see the extreme close-ups in his movies, there's Sergio Leone all over them.

S.W. How did the documentary on George Hilton come about? What was its genesis?
D.C. It was a succession of events driven by the will of some great people who knew that George Hilton deserved a more thorough recognition. Pablo de Arteaga Hill, a Hilton's cousin who lives in Brazil, warned an important Brazilian film critic that George Hilton was coming to Brazil for a visit. Since his health was not good, he told it Ovadia Saadia an important PR and mutual friend of ours. Ovadia didn't think twice and gave me a call. It was something amazing and I had to do something about it. First thing that came to my mind was my friendship to Anthony Steffen. My author and film historian friend Fábio Vellozo and myself had met Steffen and we wanted to do a documentary or book about him. But we took a lot of time and he passed away before he could see the book we did on him (written with Rodrigo Pereira and Fabio Vellozo). Since I don't know when I will have the opportunity to meet George Hilton again, it is now or never, I thought.

As I have been working in movies and tv since 1997, I immediately thought of making a film. I got in touch with Pablo who is one of the kindest persons in the world. He mentioned my idea to Hilton, and he said "nah, too much trouble. I came here to rest." Hats off to Hilton's companion, the sweet Argentinian Gabriela Reston, who was able to convince him to give me a chance. Fábio Vellozo works at the Cinemateca do MAM, the film museum, research center and temple of cinema of Rio de Janeiro, he was able to book a date for us to show "**The Strange Vice of Mrs. Wardh**" to be followed by a Q&A session with Hilton himself. Now all I have to do was setting everything else in the nick of time. I got in touch with the specialized press and went after support of institutions that would probably be interested in the event, after all it would be presenting a remarkable period of Italian film history through the eyes of Uruguay's most famous actor. For various reasons, no one could do a thing. I managed to hire a small crew, book a hotel for George and Gabriela and Pablo and his wife, make all arrangements for their food and transportation and find a nice location for the interview. All I had to do now was relax and wait for the following week. But I couldn't. I decided to drive 6 hours from Rio de Janeiro to São Paulo, where Pablo lives, introduce myself personally because although George has always been very sympathetic, he was a formal person. Going there would serve to break the ice and it has been one of the wisest choices of my directing career. The weekend at Pablo's was amazing and spending this time with George made everything easier. Since I wanted to do it fast, I thought of following the same style directors and producers Jake Paltrow and Noah Baumbach adopted for their 2015 documentary "**De Palma**". I read somewhere they had De Palma for one week and accomplished circa of 30 hours of interview footage while I would have about 6 hours to do all I could of a subject 6 years older than theirs. And what a trouper George Hilton was. All his colleagues would say the same thing. I interviewed him for about 4 hours, he then went back to the hotel and 2 hours later he was there for screening of **Mrs. Wardh** and 2 hours more for the Q&A. He was charming and professional the whole time and I managed to cover a great deal of his life and career, but some personal matters he was not comfortable to address. George went back to Italy and I started editing. As I was watching the footage, I realized the film I wanted to make was not only about Hilton's life and career, but about that fantastic moment of the Italian cinema when the country came close to the United States in number of films released. In order to do that properly I needed more interviews and my documentary became a film with scenes shot in four countries (Brazil, Italy, Uruguay and Argentina) and interviews, thanks to George, with noteworthy names of the Italian cinema such as Sergio Martino, Enzo G. Castellari, Gianni Garko, Michele Massimo Tarantini, Luigi Cozzi and producer Manolo Bolognini just to name a few, besides Hilton's family and friends who were all very supportive.. I also had the gentile permission from Michele de Angelis to use some great interviews with Luciano Martino and the one and only Edwige Fenech.

S.W. Can you tell us a bit about George's life in Brazil, and his eventual relocation to Italy?

D.C. By George's life and career, you have a fascinating panorama of life in such countries and the struggle of a man who went after his dreams with nothing but courage. I still did not have a titled I liked, but when I heard George's motto, "The World Belongs to the Daring", I got the name of the documentary and its soul. George Hilton real name was Jorge Hill Acosta y Lara and he was the first born of a rich and influential family from Montevideo. From an early age he would be fascinated with movies, specially, American ones. When he met Tyrone Power, who was on a vacation tour in Latin America right after the Second World War, George could see that those big names on the screen were as real as him. The 1936 MGM "**Camille**", starring Greta Garbo and another of his idols, Robert Taylor, made a big impression on him and he realized that an actor was what he wanted to be. His family, specially his father, was profoundly against it because it was still seen as a bad reputation profession. Even so, George would not give up and joined a theater group. Nevertheless, an intuitive actor with no formal education, he has learned the craft by doing and got to work in a famous company. But the young man was not satisfied with playing in theater and radio serials and with his family rejection, so he went to Argentina, where cinema and tv was way ahead of the other Latin American countries.

Buenos Aires was a very cosmopolitan place, like a piece of Europe in South America, with plenty of opportunities to a handsome young man like George. But timing couldn't have been worst. He arrived the same day of the Massacre of Plaza de Mayo, in which 30 Argentina Navy and Air Force aircrafts bombed the most famous square of Buenos Aires. It was the first step in a coup d'état attempt against President Juan Perón, Evita's husband. It targeted the adjacent Casa Rosada, the official seat of government, when a large crowd was expressing support for Perón. I was able to spend a couple of nights and film the hotel that hosted George during this period and he vividly remembered the sound of passing planes, machine guns, screams and explosions. He was by himself right in the middle of the action and barely escaped from being one of its 364 victims. He didn't have much money and as soon as things calmed down, he became friends with the doorman of the most important tv channel in Argentina. This guy had connections and George auditioned for a famous live anthology drama series. He got the role and his career skyrocketed. Argentine cinema in the 1950s was of a high standard with directors like Fernando Ayala, Leopoldo Torre Nilsson, Narciso Ibáñez Menta and Hugo Fregonese.

Page 42: Poster for George Hilton: The World Belongs to the Daring; George Hilton, Gianni Garko and Daniel Camargo

Page 45: Daniel, George, Enzo Castellari; Sergio Martino, George, Daniel; Still from Ruthless Four

It did not take too long to George to be in front of film cameras, each time with bigger roles. Instinctively and by observation, he has learned how to adapt his theatre acting to the small and bigger screen. George was fascinated with Montgomery Clift, who could express so much with the slightest moments, so he would always police himself not to exaggerate.

His fame got even bigger thanks to the photonovels (or photo-comics or photo-romances) which were extremely popular in Latin America. His image and voice were everywhere, George was what would be later called a multimedia artist, although not well paid like his counterparts in Hollywood. The press loved him, and he would be often romantically linked to his female costars, even when it was not true. A romantic relationship would be the turning point not only to George's career, but his life. He met and fell in love with this beautiful Argentinian woman. But George was living, so far, his best years and he was not prepared and did not want any serious commitment. Unfortunately, the lady didn't see it the same way and became jealousy obsessed with him, sometimes with outbursts of violence. It was so serious that George told her, one day, he was going to buy some cigarettes and went straight to the airport. He didn't have much money and asked for the farthest one-way flight he could afford. It was to Milan, Italy.

S.W. Can you talk about George Hilton, the man? Including your first meeting with him.
D.C. George Hilton was a very sympathetic and down-to-earth man. He had worked hard his whole life and now could relax. He lived by himself in a nice apartment north of Rome and enjoyed life with his friends. It was his girlfriend Gabriela who suggested him to enter Facebook. He was not into computer things, but agreed and all of a sudden, he was filled with friend requests from all over the world. George recognized his career but was amazed that he was still loved by so many people, many of them who were not even alive when he was making films. From that came invitations to film festivals, conventions and even work proposals. He was very selective but once he accepted, it was a hit. People loved his stories and his admirers would show an impressive knowledge of his career. Some in an annoying way, but he was always a gentleman. When I finally met him, I could witness his kindness and gallantry but ours was still a professional relationship. On our first interview, he had some ready answers that were great, but I wanted to go a little deeper, making him reanalyze passages and moments of his life. I asked things that apparently no one has and he, although cautious, was revealing himself in a whole different manner. But he was in his early 80's, so by the end he was tired and there would still be the screening and Q&A. He rested for a while and there he was brand new for our other appointments. When Fábio Vellozo conducted the Q&A with his encyclopedic knowledge of Italian cinema, George realized he was in good hands and I was serious in doing a work he would be proud. But some subjects as the suicide of his first daughter was still off limits. When I told him, months later that the film had become bigger, that I wanted to interview more people and follow his steps in Uruguay, Argentina and Italy, our professional relationship slowly developed into friendship.

A.I.P still: The Brute and the Beast, USA.
German Wild Pearl release of A Bullet for Sandoval- DVD. Audio- German/English.

S.W. The film The Brute and the Beast made George Hilton a star, what was his feeling on the film and its notorious director, Lucio Fulci?

D.C. Since in Italy they could not pronounce Jorge, Hilton changed it to George. He had adopted the Hilton back in Argentina, once his father did not want the Hill surname associated to George's profession. He had a name but no work. Somehow George always happened to be in the right place at the right time, which was an evening at Via Veneto when he had just arrived in Rome. If you wanted to be seen, Via Veneto was the place to be because in the 60's the street was the centre of "**la dolce vita**" with its elegant bars and restaurants frequented by Hollywood stars and jet set personalities. George was hanging around and entered the Café de Paris where he got acquainted to Lea Massari and a group of actors. He hardly spoke Italian, but they were fond of him and wanted to help the foreign colleague. From that gathering George got a place to live and an agent and his career in the new country started moving. Among his early roles was the protagonist one in the cheap but fun "**The Masked Men Against the Pirates**" and a small part in the James Bond spoof "**The Amazing Doctor G**", a once more successful vehicle of the popular comic duo of Franco and Ciccio.

Enters a woman who not only came to be another turning point in his life, but his wife: the adorable Maria Teresa Tarantini. Marisa believed in George and knowing his career back in Argentina, she encouraged him to pursue better roles. And that's how the audition for "**The Brute and the Beast**" came on. He auditioned with dozens of actors and got the role of the drunken brother of Franco Nero, who had become a household name due to "**Django**". What "**Django**" was to Nero, "**The Brute and the Beast**" would be to Hilton. The film was a hit, and George stole the film. Even Michelangelo Antonioni considered casting him for one of his films.

Both Franco Nero and George Hilton had problems with director Lucio Fulci. He would yell, throw the script on the floor, the kind of abusive attitude Hilton would not take, and they would often argue. Even so Hilton recognized Fulci's talent and considered "**The Brute and the Beast**" one of his best films and roles. Too bad it was their only collaboration.

S.W. George Hilton mostly played comedic, unmotivated, or exceedingly sly characters in his numerous westerns, making his dramatic turn in the film A Bullet for Sandoval a revelation, what was his thoughts on the film.

D.C. Among his westerns, George hold three of them in a higher regard: the aforementioned "**The Brute and the Beast**," the majority Spanish production "**A Bullet for Sandoval**" and the Italian "**The Ruthless Four**". Three dramatic roles that go against the ones that are normally associated to him in which George demonstrates his versatility when given a well written script and good direction. He could say only good things about Giuliano Carnimeo, the director whom he worked most, but Carnimeo, with help of his usual cinematographer Stelvio Massi, was more concerned with visuals. **Sandoval's** Julio Buchs and **Ruthless'** Giorgio Capitani, on the other hand, would give a special attention to acting instead. And their work showed up on the screen, since their casts made credible two tales about moral degradation of people, in "**The Ruthless Four**" motivated by greed, in "**A Bullet for Sandoval**" by intolerance. It's a shame the available versions of "**A Bullet for Sandoval**" are severely edited, but it's still powerful.

Both **Sandoval** and **Ruthless** had great production values like a good use of Almería locations and a notable international cast. George had great memories of working with Ernest Borgnine on Sandoval (their first scene together is superb) and with Van Heflin, Gilbert Roland and Klaus Kinski on Ruthless. As a sponge, George would absorb their way of acting and put it into his own. Their (except for Kinski) Hollywood professionalism impressed George, but also their simplicity and absence of prima donna excesses. He could say the same thing about Carroll Baker, whom he considered an exemplary actress. Those stellar names would bring prestige to Italian films and would bring some extra money to actors who were not so much in demand anymore in the United States.

S.W. Were the westerns with comedic overtures the choice of George? Or was it because of being typecast?

D.C. George had a tremendous sense of irony and when allowed, it worked quite well. Every time he says "Hey gentlemen" in "**The Brute and the Beast**" it brings fun and lightness to the cruelty and drama present in Fernando Di Leo's original story and screenplay. Still in Uruguay, he had performed classic comedies of George Bernard Shaw and Claude-André Puget on stage. From that George has learned not only how to act, but to react to situations which is essential to comedy. George had the timing and was at ease in the genre, as it can be seen in films like Michele Massimo Tarantino's 1977 "**Taxi Girl**", Giorgio Capitani's 1981 "**Teste di quoio**" and Sergio Martino's 1982 "**Don't Play with Tigers**". Back in the golden period of the Italian western, Enzo G. Castellari, who George admired, was aware of his comic flair and had no doubt in casting him to spoof Clint Eastwood's notorious Stranger from Leone' films in his 1967 "**Any Gun Can Play**" whose Italian original title, "**Vado... l'ammazzo e torno**" became mythological. To start a trend in Italian films, all you need to have was a success. Since Castellari's hit the jackpot, other westerns with comic tones would follow as 1968 Mario Caiano's "**Train for Durango**", starring Anthony Steffen (he thought to much of himself, would say George off camera) and Sergio Sollima's "**Run, Man, Run**", with Tomas Milian (the best [actor] of us, would say George on camera) culminating with Enzo Barboni's 1970 international blockbuster "**They Call Me Trinity**".

But yes, there was a typecasting among de Italian western stars. Producers were not willing to take chances, so if their budgets permitted and the role was of a suffering avenger, Anthony Steffen would be their first choice; if it was a wronged good boy, it was a job for Giuliano Gemma; an astute mysterious gunslinger full of tricks, they would call Gianni Garko; the few words man with a job to do, Franco Nero. Of course, all of them did a variety of roles, but once their screen persona had been established, they would take the ones that they knew audiences would be satisfied. In that way, George would tend to roles as Halleluja and Tressette/Tricky Dicky. With the title character of Giuliano Carnimeo's 1970 "**Sartana's Here... Trade Your Pistol for a Coffin**" it was a little different. The film had another title and Hilton's character was something else, but due to the success two years before of "**If You Meet Sartana... Pray for Your Death**", the producers renamed the film and George's character in order to maximize their profits. Distributors too would do that all the time, that's how George ended up playing Santana, Django, Trinity and even Johnny Guitar, depending on the country.

S.W. George Hilton is best remembered for his fantastic appearances in Giallo films, which fit his personality and acting strengths. What is George's acting legacy is?
D.C. I believe George's acting legacy is the entertaining and thrilling moments he provided us in each of his performances. It is there, in every printed frame of his films. George has been a brave legionary of Italian cinema, once he participated in almost all of its popular genres: westerns, war movies, spies, gialli, malicious comedies, crime, post-apocalypse, you name it. Maybe had he arrived a few years earlier we could add gothic horror and peplum to his filmography, although his first Italian film was a pirate one and his part was supposed to be played by a Steve Reeves type – George got the role because he convinced the producer he was famous in South America, which was true. Anyway, his films are all there, I was more concerned in immortalizing in my documentary another legacy of George: his testimony of a golden moment of aa Italian film history, giving voice to whom was actual part of it.

S.W. George Hilton died July 28, 2019, what were the emotions that you felt when you heard the news?
D.C. I was aware from his falling health from the beginning, late 2018. He did not smoke, drank very little and was very well. But when you are 85 years old, you look great one day, not so much the next. He had a heart condition and once it took its toll, his health declined rapidly. I had just moved to Milan and got married and every time we could, me and my wife would pay him a visit. I showed him a rough cut of the documentary and he gave me his approval. He realized it was his legacy too. My wife was pregnant of our first son and I told him, in secret, we might name the baby Giorgio. When we were leaving, he joined his forces and spoke out: "give my name to the little boy". My wife whispered to me, "how did he know?" He then blinked to me and smiled, just like Halleluja would have. In that second, all our conversations, all interviews, all films, everything came to my mind. A man who went against all odds after his dream, who achieved stardom in two countries but was hit by fate twice, the second time in the most devastating way. The suicide of his daughter, which he managed to address on camera later, almost destroyed him. No father can stand something like this and remains the same. He managed to stand up again and carry on. He had to, for his other daughter, Georgia, who was of incredible support to the documentary, was the center of his life. After a tough 7 months period of illness, in which George was brave and a gentleman the whole time, it was time to rest now. Less than 20 days after the documentary premiere in a festival in Milan, he was gone.

I felt a natural and egotistical sadness, but then, I felt comforted that he was not suffering any longer. I was that I could pay him a homage still in life.

S.W.. Tells us about how George Hilton: The World Belongs to the Daring has fared upon its festival runs. What is next for Daniel Camargo?

D.C. The film was well received in all festivals it has been selected. It's premiere has been in the Festival Internazionale di Cinema Brasiliano Agenda Brasil with screenings in Milan, Torino and Rome. The latter was something magical, in the open air at the prestigious Casa Del Cinema, in Villa Borghese, with Sergio Martino, Michele Massimo Tarantino, Ruggero Deodato and full attendance of fans, George's family and friends. It has also been screened in Sitges, Salento, Montevideo and it was the opening film of the 2019 edition of the Almería Western Film Festival, which has been unforgettable too. Stepping on the Spanish sand and sets where film history has been made is really exciting and I felt honored in receiving the Leone in Memoriam award in name of Georgia Hill. But as I said first, there's still job to do, but I am already planning a new documentary regarding film history, this time involving a famous fashion designer and also some fiction projects. I hope I have better conditions to make them, but if there's one more thing I have learnt from George Hilton is to never give up.

George and Daniel after the wrapping up of filming in Rio de Janeiro, 2017

Eureka! Classics UK Edition
The Specialists

- Tony Nash

The Specialists (Gli Specialisti/Le Specialiste/The Specialist) (1969)

Cast: Johnny Hallyday, Gastone Moschin, Françoise Fabian, Mario Adorf, Sylvie Fennec, Angela Luce, Serge Marquand, and Gino Pernice
Written by: Sergio Corbucci & Sabatino Ciufinni
Directed by: Sergio Corbucci

Blu Ray: Eureka! Classics, UK, Region B, Rating Certificate 15

Sergio Corbucci, who already made his name in the Italian Western with the classics **Django** and **The Great Silence** (Il Grande Silenzio), decided to see if lightning would strike again with **The Specialists** (Gli Specialisti). The result is a slightly trippy Western that's not as downbeat as **The Great Silence**, and not as brutal as **Django**, but is still an entertaining film. Going more towards an investigative type of plot-line, Corbucci has his Anti-Hero Hud Dixon going back to his old hometown of Blackstone to discover who has killed his brother and made him the patsy for an armed robbery of the local bank. Hud soon finds himself not only dealing with his two prime suspects, an eccentric Mexican bandit he shares an uneasy friendship with, and a corrupt lady banker whom Hud was able to resist the exotic charms of. He must also contend with an overly idealistic Sheriff, who is in way over his head, a group of rowdy young vagabonds who may want revenge for being treated like dirt by the town, all of which will eventually lead to an explosion of violence.

The film itself is relatively straightforward in plot and action. And Corbucci's favorite themes are here, including a hero at the crossroads between giving life another try or disappearing forever into the shadows. A community teetering between full decadence and salvation, and the hero facing an injury he must use to his advantage to succeed are on display- a little more subtle and not as focal as usual, still makes the impact the director was looking for. Surprisingly, Corbucci seemed more intent on bashing the Counter Culture Movement, especially the rising Hippie Culture, and Pacifism of the period with the film. Whether this was out of jealously to the Movement or some clash with Corbucci's viewpoints is unknown, but that the film seems to both support and rejects various liberal views make finding the direction the filmmaker intended to take viewers into a little more complicated.

Eureka! Entertainment's release of the film on Blu Ray was a co-production with the French company TF1, and TF1's 4K restoration was used for the Eureka! Edition. The film's original 2:35 aspect ratio is preserved for the release, the large widescreen format looking very vast and expansive when viewed on anamorphic screens. The TF1 and Eureka! image transfer looks crisp with deep and vibrant colors and contrasts between light and dark. The scenes shot in the mountains of Northern Italy are breathtaking- Every rock, river, and blade of grass looks crisp and clean as if the viewer is riding along the prairie, going between the town of Blackstone, the rural farm regions, and the cemetery. The blues come off as very blue, the reds as very red, and the greens as very green, the only possible downside being that the nighttime scenes can be a little too dark. The Technicolor and Techniscope camera images and coloring are the best looking on screen, and the quality looks even better when restored to how it originally looked. With the exception of the scene at the climax where the truth is revealed, the entire film looks practically brand new as if the original negative had just been completed with minimal signs of age and scratches. The one scene towards the end where Hud is looking to get the drop on El Diablo and his gang seems lighter compared to the vibrant colors of other scenes, but this doesn't take away from the overall quality of the restoration.

Three audio options are available on Eureka! **The Specialists** Blu Ray: the original Italian, the French version, and the English dub. The English dub is incomplete; however, Eureka! flashes a message when that options selected that an English dub was created for the cut version that premiered in the UK in 1973. But no official English track was recorded when the film was originally in post-production. The only known full English audio was damaged severely over the years, and several spots don't exist, which are replaced by the French dub with subtitles. Also, the English dub appears to have been made from a translation of the French track. The existing English dub isn't completely crisp and clear, but is still listenable to, and has some pops, but nothing excessive. The French audio and the original Italian audio are equally clear and crisp, with only slight hisses during some music cues.

The original Italian audio is the best of the bunch as it retains everything from Corbucci and Ciufinni's screenplay and is completely uncut. The French audio lacks much of the dialogue heard in the background of most scenes. Some dialogue is changed as well, particularly in the opening scene of the stagecoach passengers and hippies being held up by Diablo's gang, the head bandit in the Italian original tells the hippies the stagecoach people can pay for their survival while they must fight over a measly silver dollar so one of them can live, and in the French version, he appears uninterested in toying with the passengers and focuses solely on humiliating the hippies. Only excess dialogue and background voices are eliminated from the French audio, the dialogue and story are pretty much the same, the only difference being that the French translation seems to lack the explicit vulgarities and swears of the original Italian, opting for words that were sill offensive to an extent, but not frowned upon as much by the censors. Both subtitle tracks for the film are consistent and easy to follow. The track translated from the Italian audio suffering some occasional misspelling and run on, but nothing too intrusive to ruin the pacing.

Gastone Moschin was the only actor to loop his voice for the post-production dubbing for the Italian version. In contrast, Johnny Hallyday, Françoise Fabian, Sylvie Fennec, and Serge Marquand looped their voices for the French version. Mario Adorf, who was multi-lingual, had to be dubbed for both the Italian and French tracks due to his thick Swiss-German accent. Sergio Graziani, an Italian actor and voice dubber, noted for supplying the voices for genre greats Franco Nero, Gianni Garko, George Hilton, & Klaus Kinski, helps Hallyday enter into the genre with ease, as if he always belonged there, and completes the personification of the character of Hud. Ironically, to suit performers Hallyday, Fabian, Fennec, and Marquand, the cast members who could speak French would deliver their lines in that language. This process did lead to a debate of whether the film should be categorized as an Italian Western with French cast members, or a French Western made by Italians and shot in Italy.

Filmmaker and Spaghetti Western fan Alex Cox provides a full-length audio commentary for the film discussing how **The Specialists** came to be made. Cox provides some backstories on the film; info on the cast and crew; Corbucci's style and his favorite and recurring themes, etc. However, Cox speaks with very little enthusiasm in his commentary, save for his exasperation with the hippie characters. While he has gone on record saying he's an admirer of Corbucci, particularly with **The Great Silence**, Cox seems to be just going through the paces and sometimes sounds like he's very confused by some of Corbucci's choices and ideas with the film.

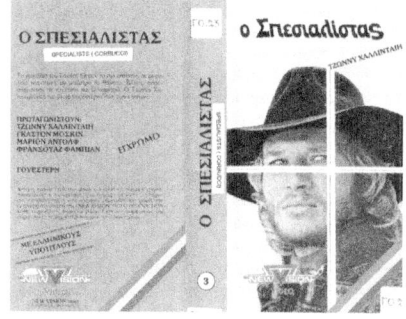

Left: Top to Bottom: Johnny Hallyday; Francoise Fabian; Johnny Hallyday
Right: Top to Bottom: Gastone Moschin; Mario Adorf; Greek Vhs of The Specialiast

Also available on the disc is an interview with SW Historian Austin Fisher who discusses the unusual place **The Specialists** fell into when first released to the Italian public and critics in 1969, which he notes was the peak year for creativity within the genre. He states that while the film was received favorably by fans, the critics, especially those in the UK, felt the film wasn't original enough and was merely playing on already existing tropes, styles, themes, and plots, and that the genre was on its way out. He goes on to say that these were misconceptions by said critics, who didn't understand the Italian film industry standard of running with ideas using innovation until the public lost interest in the fad, and that while this could be repetitive, didn't lead to the complete scene for scene copying.

Also included is a booklet that delves into the film's production history as well as the little-known period of French Westerns, and little hints about French characters and culture used in the SW genre itself. SW historian Howard Hughes pens both articles.

For those fans miffed about the English track not being complete, Eureka! included both a slideshow presentation and a PDF download of the complete, unused English language dialogue script.

The extras wind up with the French and Italian language theatrical trailers.

While slightly hindered by mixed messages regarding the kind of revolutionary stance to take during the turbulent Counter Culture age, and a probable too ambiguous ending, **The Specialists** is an enjoyable film that's worthy of viewing by any SW fan.

Van Roberts' Aims For the Heart!

INTRODUCTION

The supreme irony of Sergio Leone's "**A Fistful of Dollars**" (Per un pugno di dollari, 1964) is the debt of gratitude Leone may owe fellow Spaghetti western filmmaker Enzo Barboni. As it turns out, Stelvio Massi and Barboni saw Akira Kurosawa's "**Yojimbo**" (Yôjimbô, 1961) before Leone, and Barboni urged him to see it. According to his chief biographer Sir Christopher Frayling, Leone was captivated by the violent samurai saga about an avaricious bodyguard who pits two rival merchant clans against each other in a small village so he can profit from their enmity. Perhaps Leone would have seen "**Yojimbo**" even without Barboni's recommendation. Perhaps he would have seen it out of sheer curiosity. Meantime, we may only speculate about how much the future director of "**They Call me Trinity**" (Lo chiamavano Trinità..., 1971) influenced Leone. The worst-case scenario is, had Leone never seen "**Yojimbo**," would he have kept on making peplums?[1]

Eventually, Barboni made his directorial debut with the Spaghetti western "**The Unholy Four**" (Ciakmull - L'uomo della vendetta, 1970), a serious, existential, shoot'em up sans comic relief in the Leone tradition. Later, Barboni discovered he preferred gags over gunplay. After he helmed "**They Call Me Trinity**" and then the smash hit sequel "**Trinity is Still My Name**" (Continuavano a chiamarlo Trinità, 1971), Barboni realized he had a gift for comedy and never stopped clowning. Interestingly, Barboni's success prompted Leone to throw down the gauntlet and produce his own western spoof with actor Terence Hill as the protagonist. Ultimately, however, Sergio Leone's "**My Name is Nobody**" (Il mio nome è Nessuno, 1973), which was directed by Tonino Valerii, failed to surpass Barboni's "**Trinity is Still My Name**" at the box office.[2]

This nostalgic reminiscence of Sergio Leone's "**A Fistful of Dollars**" and the film's historic impact is neither comprehensive nor definitive. For example, the obvious issue about the plagiarism suit Kurosawa brought against Leone isn't dealt with here. Space simply doesn't permit coverage of every facet about this seminal western in scrupulous detail. Erudite Spaghetti western specialists, among them Sir Christopher Frayling, Robert C. Cumbow, Kevin Grant, Howard Hughes, Bert Fridlund, Oreste De Fornari, Terence Denman, James L. Neibaur, and Alex Cox have contributed a cornucopia of scholarship about this Spaghetti western which this writer supports without reservation. Virtually every Spaghetti western scholar worth his salt agrees "**A Fistful of Dollars**" launched the subgenre. Instead of writing a bibliographical essay about the plethora of scholarship on "**Fistful**," which richly deserves one, all allusions to enlighten and entertain readers have been kept to a minimum. Although it doesn't qualify as the greatest Spaghetti western ever made, "**Fistful**" ranks as the most influential. Now, "**Fistful**" is neither my favorite Spaghetti western nor Leone's best. Nevertheless, like the epicenter of an earthquake, "**Fistful**" shook the venerable Hollywood western formula down to its roots and sired the Spaghetti western. Adopting his nonchalant hipshot stance in a poncho, The Man with No Name or Joe as he is sometimes called, emerges rather like Botticelli's painting of Venus arising, except the Clint Eastwood figure stands in a Dante's inferno of a desert with the pugnacious Baxters and Rojos on either side brandishing firearms. Primarily, the aim here is to account for the significance of "Fistful" as the most influential Spaghetti western, and explain that Leone defied several conventions inherent in the traditional Hollywood western. All of my interpretations are drawn strictly from the spectacle and the storyline of "**A Fistful of Dollars**." Ultimately, these ruminations and their historical basis may serve to enrich the reader's appreciation of this groundbreaking horse opera. This scrutiny of "**Fistful**" covers a number of thematic tropes which the Italians altered to forge the unique essence of the Spaghetti western. First, embryonic as it was, "**Fistful**" established the ABCs of Spaghetti Westerns. One advertising campaign for the English-language release of the film prophesied that "this is the first motion picture of its kind and it won't be the last." [3] Ironically, this proved to be a case of truth in advertising. Although Europeans had been producing westerns in Spain before Leone, nobody made anything as sensational. Second, in the course of tweaking its hybrid source materials, "**Fistful**" synthesized not only the spectacle of Hollywood westerns, but also specifically the storyline of Akira Kurosawa's legendary samurai saga "**Yojimbo**" (1964). While he established the rituals of Spaghetti westerns, Leone remained indebted to Hollywood western filmmakers, such as John Ford, Raoul Walsh, Henry King, Anthony Mann, John Sturges, Robert Aldrich, Gordon Douglas, and Samuel Fuller for style and Kurosawa's "**Yojimbo**" for content. A comparison of "**Fistful**" with the other four Leone westerns reveals "**Fistful**" lacked the artistry and sophistication of "**For A Few Dollars More**" (Per qualche dollaro in più, 1965), "**The Good, the Bad, and the Ugly**" (Il buono, il brutto, il cattivo, 1966), "**Once Upon a Time in the West**" (C'era una volta il West, 1968), and "**Duck, You Sucker**" (Giù la testa, 1971). Ennio Morricone spoke candidly to The Guardian newspaper about "**Fistful**" as well as his own orchestral score. "It's the worst film Leone made and the worst score I did. There are other films I wrote music for that had a bigger success. "**The Mission**" (1986), "**Once Upon a Time in America**" (1984), and "**The Good, the Bad and the Ugly**" are all much better."[4]

In his superlative study *Once Upon A Time: The Films of Sergio Leone*, Robert C. Cumbow quantified the monumental impact of "**Fistful**" on the Spaghetti western. "Of the more than 300 'spaghetti westerns' released between 1964 and 1975, a mere fraction were distributed outside of Italy, fewer still in the United States, and none enjoyed as much attention and exhibition as the five films directed by Sergio Leone."[5] The surprise success of "**A Fistful of Dollars**" qualifies it alone as the most influential Spaghetti western. Howard Hughes writes in *Once Upon A Time in the Italian West*, notes the "runaway" popularity of "**Fistful**" inspired "a slew of imitations and rip-offs in the period 1965-67." Hughes ranks Sergio Corbucci's "**Django**" (1966), Carlo Lizzani's "**The Hills Run Red**" (Un fiume di dollari, 1966), and Giulio Questi's "**Django, Kill**!" (Se sei vivo spara, 1967) as the best of the bunch.[6]

Eventually, according to Hughes, Spaghetti western fever spread beyond Europe, and Hollywood film producers collaborated with Italians to make the "Stranger" trilogy: Luigi Vanzi's "**A Stranger in Town**" (Un dollaro tra i denti, 1967), "**The Stranger Returns**" (Un uomo, un cavallo, una pistola, 1967), and "**The Silent Stranger,**" (Lo straniero di silenzio, 1968).[7] Shamelessly derivative but prodigiously profitable, "The Stranger" franchise cast unknown actor Tony Anthony as the eponymous protagonist. Swathed in a serape, he constituted a poor man's Clint Eastwood. Like the Man with No Name, The Stranger got beaten up by a psychotic Mexican villain who wielded a machine gun. Had "Fistful" not been successful, it is reasonable to assume Leone might never have made "**For A Few Dollars More**," etc.

The triumph of this westernized "**Yojimbo**" remake triggered the Spaghetti western craze, catapulted Clint Eastwood to eternal stardom, and crowned Sergio Leone as a visionary directorial genius. Spaghetti westerns would thrive until the late 1970s. Lucio Fulci's "**Silver Saddle**" (Sella d'argento, 1978) would be the last authentic Spaghetti western. Thus, the genre endured for 14 years from 1964 to 1978.[8] One of Sergio Leone's assistants Tonino Valerii would rise to prominence in the genre, while Leone's second-unit director Franco Giraldi went on to helm "**Seven Guns for the MacGregors**" (7 pistole per i MacGregor, 1966), "**Sugar Colt**" (1966), "**Up the MacGregors**" (7 donne per i Mac Gregor, 1967), and "**A Minute to Pray, A Second to Die**" (Un minuto per pregare, un istante per morire, 1968). One of Leone's supporting actors, Aldo Sambrell, who lurks on the periphery of "**Fistful**" as an anonymous villain, would become one of the most prolific Hispanic adversaries in forty Spaghetti westerns!

The production history of "**A Fistful of Dollars**" yields a wealth of trivia about the humble origins of Leone's film. Once Jolly Film decided to produce it, they conserved costs. Leone found himself sharing the same sets but an alternate shooting schedule with Mario Caiano's Italian western "**Bullets Don't Argue**" (Le pistole non discutono, 1964), because the producers saw little potential in Leone's film. They had higher hopes for Caiano's oater starring Canadian actor Rod Cameron. According to Frayling, the salary Arrigo Columbo and Giorgio Papi paid Cameron eclipsed the salaries for everybody in "Fistful!" After "**Bullets**," Cameron made only two more Euro-westerns "**Bullets and the Flesh**" (Il piombo e la carne, 1964) and then "**Winnetou and Old Firehand**" (Winnetou und sein Freund Old Firehand, West German, 1966). Columbo and Papi must have been genuinely shocked when

Upper: U.S. Still from A Fistful of Dollars from a re-release of this film from 1969 (June 6, 1969). The film was also re-released to theaters in Italy in August of 1968

Lower: Dutch program of A Fistful of Dollars. The film was originally released in the scandinaviancountries Sweden and Denmark in 1966 and Norway in 1967

"**Fistful**" topped "**Bullets**" at the box office. Frayling has written other incredible stories about the budgetary problems Leone encountered on "**Fistful**."9 Amazingly, despite the dire circumstances and a gauntlet of other woes, Leone managed to achieve more with less and establish himself as Italy's foremost commercial filmmaker.

Before Leone reimagined the Continental western, Europeans had been making frontier yarns since the dawn of the medium. Appropriately, Leone's father Vincenzo Leone helmed the first Italian western, the silent film "**Indian Vampire**" (La Vampira Indiana, 1913) starring Leone's mother as the Red Indian. Carl Koch produced "**A Lady from the West**" (Una Signora dell'Ovest, 1942) with Rossano Brazzi. Giorgio Ferroni followed in Koch's tracks with "**The Kid from the West**" (Il Fanciullo del West, 1943). Later, Ferroni adopted the alias Calvin Jackson Padget. He directed Giuliano Gemma in "**Blood for a Silver Dollar**" (Un dollaro bucato, 1965), "**For a Few Extra Dollars**" (Per pochi dollari ancora, 1966), "**Wanted**" (1967), and then Anthony Steffen in "**Two Pistols and a Coward**" (Il pistolero segnato da Dio,1968).9 Mario Amendola's "**Terror of Oklahoma**" (Il terrore dell'Oklahoma, 1959) was another early Italian western. Later, Amendola contributed to the screenplay of Sergio Corbucci's "**The Grand Silence**" (Il grande silenzio, 1968), one of the foremost Spaghetti westerns.10

Meanwhile, other filmmakers made noteworthy Continental westerns in Spain, such as Joaquín Luis Romero Marchent's "**Zorro, the Avenger**" (La venganza del Zorro, 1962) and "**The Shadow of Zorro**" (L'ombra di Zorro, 1962), and this trend reflected the rising popularity of European westerns. Michael Carreras, son of James Carreras, who helped found Hammer Pictures, the gothic British horror studio, helmed "**The Savage Guns**" (Tierra brutal, 1962) with Richard Basehart and Alex Nicol for Metro-Goldwyn-Mayer.11

Bestselling German author Karl May's novels served as the basis for a popular, long-running West German western film franchise. The Germans produced the first Winnetou western in 1962. These popular films paired a Native American chieftain Winnetou (Pierre Brice) with a savvy white scout. Imagine Tonto as a tribal chief and the Lone Ranger as the sagacious frontier scout, and you'll have an idea what May's narratives involved.

These Spanish/Italian/German co-productions largely replicated the traditional Hollywood western with its moral imperatives.

Upper: USA MGM/UA video cassette release of A Fistful of Dollars. Copywrite 1984

Lower: Excellent Italian GDM Music CD release of A Fistful of Dollars from 2006

Former "Tarzan" star Lex Barker appeared in the first five Karl May adaptations: Harald Reinl's "**The Treasure of the Silver Lake**" (Der Schatz im Silbersee, 1962) and "**Winnetou**" (Winnetou - 1. Teil, 1963), Hugo Fregonese's "**Old Shatterhand**" (1964), Reinl's "**Winnetou: The Red Gentleman**" (Winnetou - 2. Teil, 1964), and "**Winnetou: The Last Shot**" (Winnetou - 3. Teil, 1965). Later, British actor Stewart Granger took over the role of the venerable frontier scout Old Surehand in three more adaptations of May's western novels: Alfred Vohrer's "**Among Vultures**" (Unter Geiern, 1964), Harald Philipp's "**The Oil Prince**" (Der Ölprinz, 1965), and Alfred Vohrer's "**Old Surehand**" (1966).[12]

Oreste De Fornari has published many Leone quotes in his referential tome All About Sergio Leone: "But one thing I must make clear: many people think I am the father of the Italian Western. It's not true. Before me twenty-five [Italian] Westerns had been made." Leone would add with modesty, ". . . and so let's say that "**A Fistful of Dollars**" was the twenty-sixth Italian western." Most of those early Italian westerns, including Richard Blasco's "**Gunfight at Red Sands**" (Duello nel Texas, 1963), did not impress him. Said Leone, "It was the sort of film where an actor fell to the floor before the pistol-butt actually made contact with his head."[13] Despite his lack of enthusiasm for Blasco's film, Leone didn't realize at the time that one of his future collaborators—the incomparable Ennio Morricone— would score all his westerns. Morricone wasn't excited about his own orchestral work at the time when he met Leone. Nevertheless, "Gunfight at Red Sands" bears the distinction of having an end credits ballad "*A Gringo Like Me*" that epitomizes the basics of the Spaghetti western. "Keep your hand on your gun," warbles vocalist Peter Tevis, "don't you trust anyone. There's just one kind of a man that you can trust—that's a dead man or a gringo like me."

Not surprisingly, having borrowed heavily from the superb Akira Kurosawa and Ryûzô Kikushima screenplay of "**Yojimbo**," "**A Fistful of Dollars**" qualifies as a concise, literate, larger-than-life, cat and mouse western, bristling with suspense, surprises, and shootouts. Several scribes, both credited and uncredited, including Víctor Andrés Catena of "**Kill Django... Kill First**" (Uccidi Django... uccidi per primo!!!, 1971), Jaime Comas Gil of "**Danger! Death Ray**" (1967), and Leone penned the screenplay. Fernando Di Leo of "**Navajo Joe**" (1966), Duccio Tessari of "**A Pistol for Ringo**" (Una pistola per Ringo, 1965), and Tonino Valerii of "**Day of Anger**" (I giorni dell'ira, 1967) received no credit for their contributions. Sergio Leone, Adriano Bolzoni of "**Minnesota Clay**," and Víctor Andrés Catena developed the story. Meantime, Mark Lowell of "**High School Hellcats**" (1958) wrote the English-language dialogue. How much each individual writer contributed as well as what was used is wholly a matter of conjecture. With no advertising budget when it premiered in Florence, Italy, in 1964, and only word of mouth to generate interest, this remarkable 99-minute western found its audience and has weathered the passage of time splendidly, boasting stalwart casting, gripping performances, spectacular scenery, complex plotting, and quotable dialogue.[14]

A cursory analysis of the best scenes illustrates the enduring legacy of Leone's first western. Mind you, there isn't a single scene that either doesn't stand up to scrutiny or fails to entertain no matter the number of times I have watched it. Ideally, "**Red River**" director Howard Hawks once said a good movie should boast five memorable scenes, and there are more than five in "**Fistful**."[15]

Once the Man with No Name has made his entrance, these scenes are (1) the showdown with the Baxter gunmen in San Miguel, (2) Ramón's Rio Bravo River massacre, (3) the cemetery gunfight between the Rojos and the Baxters, (4) Joe's ghastly beating at the hands of Ramón and his henchmen, and (5), the audacious finale between Ramón and Joe in San Miguel. The content of these scenes underlines the differences between "Fistful" and the traditional Hollywood western. Moreover, before scrutinizing these five scenes, let us see what made the Spaghetti western seem dystopian. Generally, when the word dystopian crops up in literary criticism, it is usually associated with science fiction films. Nevertheless, the use of the term dystopian accurately describes the changes that the Spaghetti westerns of Sergio Leone brought about and is a useful way to distinguish them from traditional Hollywood westerns. In his book *The Western*, David Lusted writes "Italian Westerns break away stylistically from the romantic American western in action and tone. They shift attention from the sexual hysteria of Western melodramas to a dystopia of male action. Action in Italian Westerns is emphatic and brutal, an 'opera of violence' and a 'ballet of the dead' from which few are spared."[16]

Throughout this reappraisal, the influence of Sergio Leone hovers over the subgenre and shows how "**Fistful**" jump-started the Spaghetti western. Leone's cinematographer Massimo Dallamano used the widescreen format Techniscope to give "**Fistful**" a unique look, just as Ennio Morricone's orchestral music played a crucial part of its success, too. According to Tonino Valerii, Dallamano understood that the widescreen Techniscope format yielded "a new kind of close-up, a sort of very close-up, which would frame the face from the chin to the bottom part of the forehead, in order not to lose too many of the small details and features . . ." [17] Indeed, these unique close-ups became a trademark of Leone's films, even after Tonino Delli Colli replaced Dallamano for "**The Good, the Bad, and the Ugly**" and "**Once Upon A Time in the West.**" Later, Giuseppe Ruzzolini replicated these unusual close-ups in "**Duck, You Sucker**" and "**My Name is Nobody**," too.

Leone has Ennio Morricone to thank for a unique orchestral score. Afterward, Morricone would score all Leone's movies. Hugh Wilson's "**Rustler's Rhapsody**" (1985) commented on the vast difference between the music of Spaghetti westerns with traditional Hollywood western film music. In this cheeky parody of American and Spaghetti westerns, lensed on location in Spain, an American cowboy actor confides in a Spanish cowboy actor that Spaghetti western scores always sounded better than their American counterparts! Howard Hughes applauds Morricone's contribution: "Of all the film's accomplishments, the most innovative was the soundtrack and Ennio Morricone's groundbreaking composition is still popular today."[18]

For the record, I savor every second of "**A Fistful of Dollars**" with the same reverence that admirers of "**Casablanca**" (1942) impart to the landmark Humphrey Bogart and Ingrid Bergman film. Since I have embarked on this subject, I have watched "**Fistful**" many more times for reference. Although I have singled out specific scenes at the exclusion of others to bolster my argument why mine deserves greater attention, I don't think a single scene can be excised without tarnishing the artistry of Leone's efforts. Conversely, adding superfluous scenes, such as ABC-TV did when they hired "**The Shooting**" director Monte Hellman to helm a prologue, had to be the most atrocious idea ever imagined. ABC-TV executives behaved as if they were censors with the notorious Production Code Administration that ruled Hollywood with a tyrannical iron fist from 1933 to 1968. This new abominable idea changes everything about The Man with No Name and his motivation for riding into San Miguel. Noted character actor Harry Dean Stanton was cast in this prologue as a prison warden who releases No Name—insert an extreme close-up of Clint Eastwood—from prison, so he can clean up San Miguel. Anybody who saw "**Fistful**" between the time of its domestic release in 1967 and its prime-time television premiere must have been—or at least should have been--appalled by this blasphemous contrivance. "**Fistful**" is a cynical western and our hero—I argue he is a hero rather than an anti-hero—is largely without morality.[19]

The disparity between the traditional Hollywood western and the dystopian Spaghetti western boils down to three primary factors. First, the Spaghetti western clashes with the traditional Hollywood western because of the changes in the hero's use of violence. Second, the physical setting of the Hollywood western exerted a redemptive effect on its characters, whereas little of what could be classified as redemptive can be found in San Miguel. Third, until Leone made his masterpiece "**Once Upon a Time in the West**," the place of women in most Spaghetti westerns was restricted largely to the periphery of the action. Briefly, in "Fistful," the female character Marisol, who has been taken hostage by Ramón, manages to escape thanks to the intervention of the Man with No Name. Sadly, Consuelo Baxter doesn't share Marisol's fate. Ramón's younger brother Esteban Rojo guns her down in cold blood after she stares in horror at the slain bodies of her husband John and her son Antonio. Rarely did a traditional Hollywood western either kill a woman in an act of premeditated murder or abruptly send her packing halfway through the narrative.

Each cinematic generation has produced a new western hero. Broncho Billy Anderson, Tom Mix, Ken Maynard, and William S. Hart were some who dominated silent movies. Gary Cooper rode tall in the saddle from Victor Fleming's "**The Virginian**" (1929) to Delmar Daves' "**The Hanging Tree**" (1959). Actually, before he ascended to stardom, Cooper got his start in Hollywood as an uncredited wrangler and stunt rider. John Wayne sprang to stardom in John Ford's milestone western "**Stagecoach**" (1939) after toiling for almost a decade as a B-movie cowboy hero following the abortive failure of Raoul Walsh's widescreen western "**The Big Trail**" (1930). Everybody else on a horse rode in Wayne's shadow. Some carved out sterling careers for themselves on horseback, such as Joel McCrea, Randolph Scott, George Montgomery, Audie Murphy, and Rory Calhoun, but the Duke ruled the range. Clint Eastwood emerged during Wayne's twilight years in the early 1960s. Nobody has replaced Eastwood since "**Fistful**" as the top stud.

Not surprisingly, Eastwood had grown dissatisfied with his clean-scrubbed image as cattle-drive ramrod Rowdy Yates on CBS-TV's "**Rawhide**" (1959-1965). He needed little incentive to toughen up his image for Leone. Initially, publicists christened the Eastwood character as the Man with No Name, despite the fact that one character, the coffin maker Piripero, repeatedly addresses him as Joe. The Rojos variously refer to him as either 'Americano' or 'gringo.' Joe never reveals his name, and Silvanito never questions him about his identity.[20]

Primarily, Eastwood shunned most things that a John Wayne hero would do. He had no qualms about resorting to gunplay. He taunts his adversaries deliberately in "**Fistful**." Furthermore, he is no objections about shooting an opponent in the back, as he does at the small house. Above all else, the Sergio Leone western hero served himself first and others second. One of the few exceptions to this rule appeared in the subplot about the beleaguered family trials of Marisol, Julio, and little Jésus. By comparison, John Wayne in Burt Kennedy's "**The Train Robbers**" (1973) refuses to instigate a gunfight when he hears an infant cry and dreads the prospect a stray bullet may silence the child. Spaghetti western heroes shared little of this sensitivity as "**Fistful**" shows.

Furthermore, the Spaghetti western heroes were far less obsessed about either personal hygiene or sartorial elegance. Beards replaced clean-shaven jaws. Comparatively, as in Sam Wood's "**Ambush**" (1950), the hero wore a beard just long enough to shave it off. Traditional Hollywood heroes patronized both barbershops as well as bath houses. Sometimes, Spaghetti western characters couldn't wait to bail out of the barber chair to shoot somebody, as in the opening scene of "**For a Few Dollars More**." The Spaghetti western hero cavorted about in wrinkled, often slept-in, threadbare apparel. When Lee Van Cleef made his Spaghetti western debut as Colonel Douglas Mortimer in "**For A Few Dollars More**," he adopted a more formal wardrobe which reflected his social standing in the hierarchy of characters. Although he never eclipsed Eastwood, Venetian actor Mario Girotti, who later anglicized his name to Terence Hill, parlayed a comic career out of Spaghetti western parodies. Such was Hill's success in these comic westerns that he became a household name in America. Barboni's "**Trinity**" movies appeared when Spaghetti westerns degenerated into poking fun at themselves. If anything, Trinity and his breed were sharpshooters whose apparel was even more threadbare and who refused to make an honest living. Interestingly, before he landed his "Trinity" break, Hill had been one of Eastwood's imitators. Moreover, he followed in another Eastwood imitator's footsteps—Franco Nero—when he starred in Ferdinando Baldi's "**Django, Prepare a Coffin**" (Preparati la bara!, 1968). About the same time that he played in "**Django**," Hill co-starred with Bud Spencer in Giuseppe Colizzi's trilogy of Spaghetti westerns "**God Forgives... I Don't!**" (Dio perdona... Io no!, 1967), "**Ace High**" (I quattro dell'Ave Maria, 1968), and "**Boot Hill**" (La collina degli stivali, 1969).

Examine any post "**Fistful**" western that adheres to the formula, and the hero is liable to be labeled an anti-hero. Mind you, over the years, the typical Hollywood western hero has evolved, particularly in regard to his treatment of Native Americans. The landmark movie that rejected the credo that "the only good Indian was a dead one" was Delmer Daves' "**Broken Arrow**" (1950) with James Stewart. Mind you, anti-Native American epics continued to be released. Nevertheless, most westerns as well as their protagonists had grown more sympathetic to the plight of the Native American. Predictably, while the hero got toughened up around the edges in Spaghetti westerns, the villain waxed even more wicked, as Ramón Rojo demonstrated with his sadistic disposition for murder. Leone confined his westerns to the southwestern border between the United States and Mexico. Mexicans largely replaced Native Americans as the villains.

The protagonist or hero is often a privileged character. Privileged here refers to the extent of the protagonist's knowledge about what is happening around them. Leone and his scenarists orchestrated many of the scenes in "Fistful," so somebody was watching events as they played out. For example, Joe watches the turmoil at the small house when Jésus visits his mother and suffers the fury of Chico's wrath. Afterward, once he has killed a quartet of Baxter gunmen, Joe eavesdrops on Don Miguel's conversation with Esteban about him. Similarly, Silvanito and Joe witness the Rio Bravo massacre without being spotted. Later, they observe the hostage negotiation when the Baxters swap Marisol for their son Antonio. Our hero watches the Rojos as they slaughter the Baxters after he has escaped from the Rojo's storehouse.. Evidently, the only time the Man with No Name isn't watching an event is when he creates an event.

In this instance, after he pits the Rojos against the Baxters at the graveyard, he hangs around San Miguel to search the Rojo's storehouse for the stolen Mexican cavalry gold. Interestingly, all of Joe's surveillance activities constitute the edge he enjoys over the Rojos. Earlier, when he met Don Miguel for the first time, No Name complimented the eldest Rojo about being "well informed" concerning the whereabouts of the Mexican cavalry. Don Miguel explains the value of vigilance, "In these parts, a man's life often depends on a mere scrap of information." Later, the Man with No Name is able to fool the Rojos, until they learn more about his clandestine movements.

Sergio Leone violated a cardinal rule in his westerns that alarmed movie producers. Women didn't play primary roles in his westerns! He would only recognize women later when he made "**Once Upon A Time in the West**," and Jill McBain served as a primary character in that film. He curtailed woman's roles in "**The Good, the Bad, and the Ugly**" as well as "**Duck, You Sucker**." Consequently, Clint Eastwood had no love interest in the trilogy. Hollywood producers rarely made a western where the hero didn't tangle his spurs up in a petticoat for a romantic relationship with a woman. Often, the traditional Hollywood hero had the option to choose between the moral woman and the immoral woman. Occasionally, the woman wore the pants in westerns, such as either Nicholas Ray's "**Johnny Guitar**" (1954) or Samuel Fuller's "**40 Guns**" (1957). Dorothy Page toplined three Grand National westerns back in the late 1930s as the gun-toting heroine of Samuel Diege's B-movie trilogy: "T**he Singing Cowgirl**" (1938), "**Water Rustlers**" (1939), and "**Ride 'em, Cowgirl**" (1939). Later, Roger Corman's "**Gunslinger**" (1956) saw Beverly Garland take over her husband's post as the town marshal to track down his murderers. The women in "**Fistful**" lurk largely on the periphery. Marisol escapes the captivity of Ramón, while Esteban shows no qualms about murdering Consuelo Baxter.[21]

Essentially, Spaghetti westerns placed a higher value on material goods, particularly wealth. Westerns that followed the Leone formula often depicted the dangers of greed, and many westerns inserted the word 'dollar' in their titles. After "**For a Few Dollars More**" reaped a box office bonanza, bounty hunters became popular heroes—the most reviled character in the traditional Hollywood western—and more movies about bounty hunters proliferated. When John Ford—the most celebrated American director of traditional westerns--forged the Hollywood western in his own image before and after World War II, he celebrated the renewal power of the West.

People migrated westward, lured by the spirit of opportunity. The frontier was presented as a land of redemption, and Ford's heroes and heroines sought to turn the wilderness into an Eden. Ford's westerns celebrated the community spirit of pioneers cooperating with each other to create something of lasting value. Ford staged a dance in "**My Darling Clementine**" (1946) in a half-built church, with Wyatt Earp (Henry Fonda) dancing with the eponymous heroine Clementine Carter (Cathy Downs), while musicians played musical instruments and pioneers sang Christian hymns.[22] While a spirit of opportunity lured the pioneers into a promised land in Ford's westerns, it was the sirens of economic prosperity that drew pioneers into the dystopian west of Sergio Leone. Leone's Spaghetti westerns had no such dances and no churches that were built by the willing participants of the community. Moreover, the west in Leone's films is not a paradise, but rather a purgatory. The same opportunities settlers sought in Ford's westerns didn't occur in Leone's westerns. Indeed, the land bristles with opportunity, but only of a monetary nature. Families in "**Fistful**" are a parody of those in Ford's westerns. Indeed, families are an endangered species in Spaghetti westerns. Leone turned the values of traditional Hollywood westerns inside out and rechristened them. The same communal values that brought the settlers together in "**My Darling Clementine**" doesn't exist in "**Fistful**." Indeed, Leone often ridiculed religion. Examples abound in "Fistful." No sooner has the Man with No Name entered Silvanito's cantina than he picks up a Christian wreath from atop a pile of other miscellaneous objects on a shrouded billiards table. Momentarily, he holds it up for inspection, framing himself in its oval wreath, and then he tosses it aside in an act of rejection. Christian values have no place in Spaghetti westerns. Clearly, this wreath symbolized not only Jesus's crucifixion but also his rebirth. Ironically, it suggests that Joe's future is framed by similar events, but with little of the Christian symbolism. Another example is the parody of the Last Supper at the Rojo hacienda as Ramón's henchmen wallow in a drunken orgy. The messianic hero in "**Fistful**" is an inversion of the Christian hero. Many commentators have written about No Name entering San Miguel on a mule like Jesus, getting crucified as he swings from a crosspole after his mule stampedes out from under him in front of Silvanito's cantina, and then metaphorically dies after Ramón and company literally beat in within an inch of his life. Our hero manages to crawl into one of Piripero's coffins and convalesce in a cave until he recuperates enough to challenge Ramón. No Name isn't so much an endorsement of a Christian hero as an inversion of it. [23]

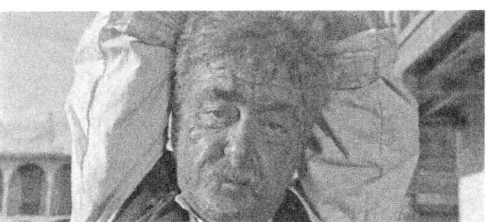

Top to Bottom: Clint Eastwood; Marianne Koch; Gian Maria Volonte; Sieghart Rupp; Jose Calvo; Joseph Egger

Igino Lardani's catchy pop-art animated title credits prepare spectators for what to expect from "**Fistful**" with Ennio Morricone's atmospheric orchestral score enhancing the rotoscoped scenes of riding and shooting from the film. Essentially, rotoscoping is an animation technique that enables animators to sketch over live-action footage, frame by frame, to create a cartoon-like effect. The images of horsemen galloping and gunmen whirling as bullets perforate them and they fall were taken from the original film and converted to resemble cartoon footage. The result is a colorful montage of the same scenes repeated in a loop, as if it were a trailer. More often than not the image is bathed in flashing colors of black and blood red, with circles within circles eventually enclosing a single horseman until the credits fade out in glaring sunlight to show a rider trotting through the wilderness.

Leone sows the Spaghetti western's seeds of dystopia at the outset. The initial live-action scene in "**A Fistful of Dollars**" captures your attention with its wanton cruelty. Somewhere below the Mexican border, an armed, unshaven, poncho-clad American rides up on a mule and helps himself to a dipper of water from a well. Two whitewashed adobe houses stand nearby, and the front doors of each building are mirror images. Iron grilles mask those windows. The landscape surrounding these two houses is bleak and barren. Joe (Clint Eastwood) quenches his thirst when a dark-haired, pint-sized, five-year old boy, Jésus (Nino del Arco), emerges from the house on his right. Circling around from behind his house, as if he were sneaking out the back way, Jésus crosses over to the other house on his left. The urchin looks around and then enters the house. He climbs under the grille and in through the front window. Moments later, harsh abusive voices bellow within the house. The child cries hysterically. The next thing we see is the ousted munchkin driven out the front door. He falls down and before he can arise, a gargantuan Mexican in a colossal sombrero comes stomping up behind him. Chico (Mario Brega) and another vaquero treat the adolescent like a leper. Chico boots him in the rear to propel him forward. Brandishing their revolvers, they blast away at the child's heels to hasten his departure. The bawling tyke dashes toward his dad, Julio (Daniel Martin), who has emerged from the front door of the opposite house. Chico assaults Julio, knocks him down, and kicks him. The Man with No Name watches this scene unfold with a conspicuous lack of expression. Eventually, Chico notices him. Joe glances back at the house the child had entered and exchanges glances with a beautiful woman, Marisol (Marianne Koch), stands at a window. Women in "**Fistful**" don't so much constitute objects of love as much as they do hostages. Despite his cynical demeanor and desire for money, the Man with No Name performs one of the standard-issue duties of the traditional Hollywood hero, he saves the damsel-in-distress!

Chico's abusive behavior toward little Jésus would have prompted a traditional Hollywood western hero to intervene. In the words of a quintessential John Wayne hero, he would make what wasn't his business into his business. No self-respecting traditional Hollywood hero would have left the five-year old and his defenseless father in the lurch. The Man with No Name, however, doesn't make Jésus his business, and he rides off toward San Miguel. Everything in this opening scene reflects what constituted the Spaghetti western. The sun baked, southwestern setting; the pugnacious Mexican gunmen, and the dysfunctional family with the screaming child yearning to be reunited with his mother, while his defenseless father is battered all attract our attention. Joe's refusal to intervene reflects the difference between the traditional values of Hollywood westerns and the dystopian values of the Spaghetti western. Eventually, Joe will intervene, but it seems like a last resort.

Society barely exists in "**Fistful**." Marisol, Julio, and Jésus represent society as much as the widows of San Miguel. Moreover, the reimagined Italian western hero isn't clad in fringed buckskins, like earlier western heroes such as Buffalo Bill and Wild Bill Hickok. At this point, we know precious little about any of these characters. Nevertheless, all will play an integral role in what happens later in this tightly-knit western. Expository dialogue is often used to keep spectators apprised about plot mechanics. No Hollywood western had ever unfolded with such a grim scene. Unlike "**Yojimbo**," "**A Fistful of Dollars**" introduces the dysfunctional family at the outset and later weaves it back into the plot.

The Man with No Name rides beneath a skeletal tree with a hangman's noose dangling in the breeze like the sword of Damocles. As he enters San Miguel, black-clad female mourners disperse at his approach. Furthermore, a horse carrying a dead man propped up in the saddle trots past him. A paper sign attached to the corpse's back reads: "Adios, Amigo."

This is roughly equivalent to the scene in "**Yojimbo**" when Sanjuro spots a dog with a severed hand in its mouth. No sooner has this ominous figure ridden past than the bell ringer, Juan De Dios (Raf Baldassarre), prances into the scene like a harlequin. This loquacious fellow serves the function of a Greek chorus. He will be seen only once more. He briefs Joe about San Miguel, its two-party family structure, and the prevalence of death. Later, the cantina proprietor Silvanito will repeat virtually everything the bell ringer has said.

A dilapidated, ramshackle, lawless town, San Miguel differs from most towns in a Hollywood western, except perhaps a ghost town. Seldom is a soul seen on its single street unless he is an armed smuggler from across the border. People, particularly women and children, are few and far between. The standard business enterprises in a traditional Hollywood western are conspicuously absent, too. San Miguel boasts no barbershops, no churches, no dressmakers, no general merchandise stores, and no doctors/dentists/lawyer's shingles swinging in the breeze. No stables with the inevitable blacksmith ringing his hammer on an anvil as he shapes a horseshoe and then submerges it into a water bucket can be heard. San Miguel might have been a town before the Baxters and the Rojos took it over for their nefarious endeavors. Superficially, the town is as divided a city as Berlin during the Cold War, but without its red-light district.

Meanwhile, two heavily armed families rule San Miguel. The Baxter family with their army of Caucasian gunslingers occupy a large, two-story wooden house at one end of the town, while the Rojo clan with their Mexican pistoleros live in an imposing whitewashed hacienda at the other end. When the stranger rides into San Miguel, three of the Baxter gunmen accost him. Playfully, they reprimand him for being "a bad boy" and then stampede his mule. They blast geysers of dirt from around the mule's hooves with their six-guns, as the animal bolts hysterically away from them into town. Joe grabs an overhead cross pole support for a lantern and swings momentarily from it as his mule runs out from under him. Silvanito (José Calvo) peers over his cantina's batwing doors at him, and they silently acknowledge each other's presence. Our hero joins Silvanito inside for liquor and a plate of food.

Silvanito observes while Joe has a bite to eat in his cantina, "We spend our time here between funerals and burials." "Yeah," the Man with No Name agrees, "I never saw a town as dead as this one." "We've had too many killings," Silvanito explains. "All the women are widows, and the two rival families sell guns and liquor to the worst scum on the frontier." Silvanito elaborates, "Here you can only gain respect by killing other men. So, nobody works anymore."

At this moment, the bark of a hammer against wood halts their conversation. The only business that thrives in San Miguel belongs to a white-bearded old timer, Piripero (Joseph Egger), who bangs together plank coffins with a hammer. Of course, this is another example of Leone's tongue-in-cheek gallows humor. "I want to warn you," Silvanito advises him, "that those murderers will make a corpse out of you." The cantina owner warns the stranger that the Rojos are more dangerous than the Baxters. Later, after they have ascended to the balcony of the cantina, Leone places Joe visually between either end of the street with its heavily armed encampments. Our hero shakes his head in amusement, "Crazy bellringer was right, there's money to be made in a place like this."

"**Yojimbo**" and the second remake "**Last Man Standing**" (1996) with Bruce Willis, had placed their respective heroes at a crossroads tossing sticks up in the air or spinning bottles to determine which road they will take. Joe does neither. Instead, it appears he came to San Miquel for nothing more than a plate of food and whiskey. After Silvanito explains the lay of the land, the Man with No Name calculates that a golden opportunity awaits him.

Succinctly, Leone and his writers have done an exemplary job of establishing the setting, introducing the chief characters, and explaining the disreputable business of San Miguel, while dramatically delaying the introduction of the main villain Ramón Rojo (Gian Maria Volontè) and his ambitious plans.

The first major scene in "**Fistful**" establishes Joe's exceptional sharpshooting skills and his head scratching sense of humor. Clearly, he doesn't qualify as a traditional Hollywood western hero.

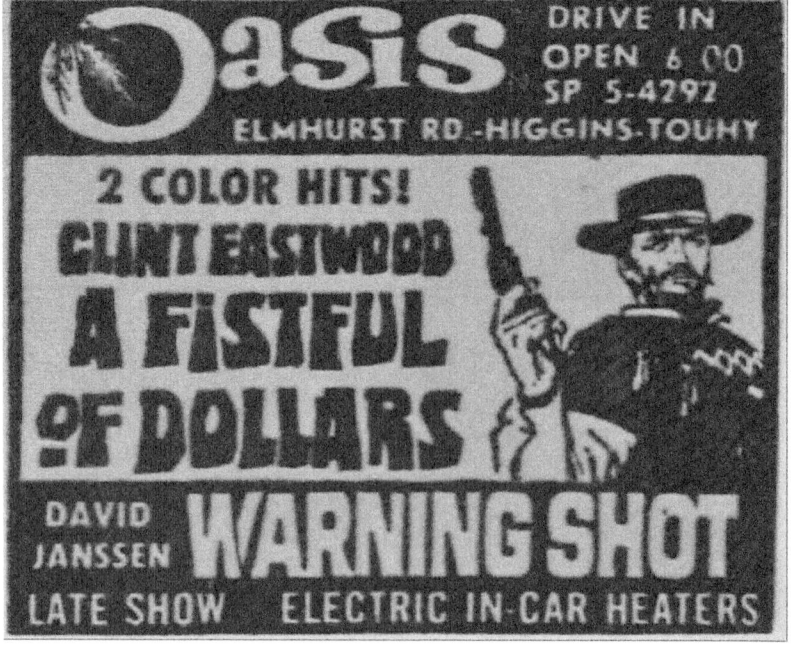

1. **JOE'S SHOWDOWN WITH THE BAXTER GUNMEN**

My favorite "**Fistful**" scene occurs within the first quarter hour when Joe taunts the four Baxter gunmen into a shootout. Whereas the traditional Hollywood western hero would let his adversaries do most of the talking, here the opposite occurs. Joe does most of the talking, and he insults the Baxters with his absurd tale about his mule's devastated sentiments over them shooting at its hooves to stampede it. As confrontations go, nothing about this initial face-off is straightforward. Our hero knows exactly what he is doing when he saunters down the street to goad them into a gundown. Indeed, as he approaches them, he alerts Piripero to prepare three coffins. Joe strings these gunmen along with his amusing yarn about his impressionable mule. "You see, that's what I want to talk to you about. He's feeling real bad." Joe particularizes: "He got all riled up when you men fired those shots at his feet." The gunmen regard Joe with deep suspicion, and one accuses him of making "some kind of joke." "See, I understand you men were just playing around," the Man with No Name says. "But the mule . . . He doesn't get it. Of course, if you were all to apologize." Gales of laughter burst from their incredulous faces. None of this hilarity matters to Joe. "You see my mule don't like people laughing. He gets the crazy idea you're laughing at him. Now, if you'll apologize, like I know you're going to, I might convince him you really didn't mean it."

Lenser Massimo Dallamano frames the scene from just behind Joe's right hip. We see our protagonist whip out his six-gun and knock down the gunmen like tenpins in a bowling alley. Once he has shot them, and they lay sprawled dead in the dust, Joe spins his revolver and seats it neatly in his holster. This added flourish along with the screwball story about a mule's bruised feelings suggests Joe had no doubts about his ability with a six-gun. Later, Don Miguel says as much to his brother Esteban about Joe when they discuss him before Ramón enters the action. "You cannot leave someone like that to do what he wants to around here. He's capable of doing anything." Don Miguel rejects Esteban's offer to shoot Joe in the back. "I want law and order in town. And with the cavalry arriving in town, and that Yankee was fast on the draw." Later, Don Miguel admonishes Ramón about Joe, "At shooting a pistol, nobody can touch him."

Page 66: Top Left: Chicago Tribune- May 16, 1969
Page 66: Top Right: Indianapolis Star- April 25, 1969
Page 66: Middle: Cincinnati Enquier- Jun 9, 1969
Page 66: Bottom: Chicago Tribune- April 8, 1967
Page 67: Dutch VHS

2.   THE RIO BRAVO MASSACRE

The Man with No Name nearly gets the seven-and-a-half-inch barrel of a Colt Single Action Army .45 caliber revolver shoved up his curious nose when he squints into the heavily guarded stagecoach after the Mexican cavalry arrives in San Miguel. The next morning the Mexican cavalry departs for the frontier. Joe and Silvanito follow them without attracting attention. Sprawling belly down on a slight rise overlooking the Rio Bravo River, they watch the Mexican cavalry reach their rendezvous point with the U.S. Cavalry. The Mexicans wait patiently as a dozen blue-clad cavalry riders escorting three covered wagons ford the Rio Bravo and pull up opposite them on the river bank. One of Ramón's most trustworthy gunmen, Rubio (Benito Stefanelli), rides at the head of the convoy. He gallops up to the Mexican captain as the soldiers remove a large, wooden strongbox from the stagecoach. "There's your gold as promised," the Hispanic captain points out. "I hope the guns you will be giving us will be equally as useful to our army." Rubio reins up near the Mexican officer. "Rest assured, Captain, we'll check them over together." At this point, wheeling his mount, Rubio gives a hand signal to the middle-most of the covered wagons.

Abruptly, Ramón open fires on the unsuspecting Mexican troops with a machine gun. He strafes the horsemen, toppling them from their saddles, picking off the wounded on foot, and killing as many as 38 of the khaki-clad troopers without giving them a chance to retaliate. Long before Sam Peckinpah staged his apocalyptic massacre in "**The Wild Bunch**" (1969) with every member of the bunch taking turns on a .30-06 water-cooled, Browning M1917 machine gun, Ramón has a field day wiping out every soldier in sight in a fusillade of gunfire without a qualm. He pauses now and then in his search for more targets and riddles those unfortunates with lead, too. Ennio Morricone's strident orchestral music captures the sudden fury as well as the enormity of the massacre. It is only after the fact we realize the U.S. Cavalry, which was supposed to rendezvous with the Mexicans, has been wiped out presumably by Ramón, too. Undoubtedly, like so many narrative ellipses in the story, Leone and his writers must have been forced to allow some action to occur off-screen because his low-budget didn't allow him to film them.

The single most problem with the Rio Bravo massacre is Ramón's method of accomplishing it. He couldn't have massacred the Mexican cavalry with such success without using a machine gun. Ramón's weapon of mass destruction is an early Franco-Belgian Mitrailleuse Machine Gun which saw use in the Franco-Prussian War of 1870-1871. After "**Fistful**" came out, the Gatling gun and similar Mitrailleuse machine guns became a staple of the genre. Leone may have inherited his ideas about weapons of mass destruction from Gordon Douglas' long forgotten Gregory Peck cavalry western "**Only the Valiant**" (1946) with its use of a Gatling gun to save the day. Similarly, Rudolph Maté's "**Siege at Red River**" (1954) concerned the cavalry's efforts to thwart the sales of Gatling guns to hostile Native Americans. Nearly every Spaghetti western after "**Fistful**" would feature either a Gatling gun or a machine gun like the Mitrailleuse. Later, Sergio Corbucci's "**Django**" (1966) featured a hero who dragged a coffin behind him with a machine gun in it. The titles are far too many to tabulate, but the most outrageous machine gun in a Spaghetti western would be Giuliano Carnimeo's "**Guns for Dollars**" (Testa t'ammazza, croce... sei morto - Mi chiamano Alleluja, 1971) where the hero Alleluja (George Hilton) converted a sewing machine into a machine gun! Altogether, by this point in "**Fistful**," the body count has surged exponentially far beyond the four Baxter gunmen that Joe had slain. The Rio Bravo Massacre has the added distinction of introducing Leone's chief villain Ramón (Gian Maria Volontè), and he emerges as a challenging adversary. Evidently, one Mexican trooper had played possum because he surprises Ramón and scrambles astride his horse to hightail it across the Rio Bravo in a desperate bid for freedom. Vaulting atop the seat of a wagon, Ramón snatches the Winchester that Rubio laterals to him. Crack shot that he is with a Winchester, Ramón fires one shot, and the fleeing rider pitches sideways off his horse with a bullet in his back. Afterward, Ramón reminds his henchmen to remove their blue uniforms and redress the corpses of the dead Americans piled in the other wagons. Ramón wants to make it appear that both cavalry units had engaged in a firefight and killed each other to the last man. As we learn more about Ramón, his notorious reputation looms above anybody else's thus far in "**Fistful**." Physically, Ramón is a wolfish looking dastard who does nothing by halves. The expression on Joe's face as he watches this massacre is that Ramón amounts to a sufficiently worthy opponent not only for his sheer audacity but also his relentless sadism. At this point, we haven't learned Ramón's preferred weapon of choice is a Winchester repeating rifle, and he handles it with the utter efficiency of a wizard with a wand of destruction. Rarely did traditional Hollywood westerns stage scenes like this as early as it occurred in "**Fistful**."

3. **THE CEMETERY SHOOTOUT**

The first time the Rojos and the Baxters exchange gunfire occurs during this scene. An appreciation of this pivotal encounter means tracing it back to its origins. Piripero (Joseph Egger) is the coffin maker in San Miguel. He isn't likely to go out of business what with the way gunmen die from lead poisoning. Stepping inside Silvanito's cantina, Piripero informs Joe he has loaded two coffins in a wagon for him. Joe invites Silvanito (José Calvo) to accompany him. Although Leone didn't film them visiting the site of the Rio Bravo massacre, they found two corpses and stashed them in the coffins. Silvanito is clearly alarmed by these shenanigans when they reach the graveyard. "I'm alive, and I want to remain with the living, understand? And when I'm dead, I want to remain with the dead. And I would be unhappy if somebody living forces me to remain with the living." Once Joe has the Mexican corpses slouched on either side of a tombstone, he follows a disgruntled Silvanito back to San Miguel.

Our manipulative hero fools both John Baxter and Ramón into believing that two soldiers not only managed to survive the massacre but they have also sought refuge in the graveyard. Hereafter, everything Joe does to instigate adversity between the Rojos and the Baxters will revolve around Marisol. Anyway, Joe declines the Rojo's offer to ride out to the graveyard with them. "When a man's got money in his pocket he begins to appreciate peace," he observes. While Joe may appreciate peace, he is clearly up to nothing but trouble.

After the Rojos thunder off to the cemetery, Joe boosts himself over the wall of the Rojos' hacienda. He catches a dutiful Chico patrolling the storehouse. The upper-half of the entrance consists of two ropes holding the door up. Playfully, Joe keeps Chico distracted with several random shots that keeps the big Mexican guessing about the locations of his unseen adversary. Eventually, Joe's bullets cut the ropes, and the upper-half of the door slams down, knocking Chico unconscious, and landing him in a pile of arms and legs.

Just as Joe enters the storehouse, Ramón and his gunmen as well as John Baxter and his gunmen confront each other at the cemetery. During the ensuing shootout, Ramón exhibits fearless disregard for his life as he charges the two corpses under withering gunfire and shoots both down. Earlier, during their rampaging ride off to the graveyard, John Baxter (Wolfgang Lukschy) explained to his son Antonio (Bruno Carotenuto) that if the two soldiers were witnesses to a massacre, the government would have grounds to arrest the Rojos, and San Miguel would have only one boss.

Meantime, as the Rojo and Baxter gunmen are blasting away at each other, Joe prowls around the storehouse. He taps the lids of innumerable kegs and barrels before he stumbles accidentally onto the location of the Mexican cavalry gold. By this time, Ramón and his brothers have captured Antonio Baxter, and they are riding back to San Miguel. Joe pauses from snooping about the premises when he sees a lantern. He confronts the lantern bearer and decks the individual with a knockout blow. Joe is completely surprised himself now because he has just knocked out Marisol. Later, he hands her over to Consuelo Baxter (Margarita Lozano) in return for another sheaf of dollars. Although he thought he had thwarted Baxter's plans to rescue the two Mexican cavalrymen and use their testimony to against him, Ramón's own plans to use Antonio as a bargaining chip has been similarly frustrated.

4. **JOE'S TORTURE**

Joe exhausted his luck when Ramón caught him sneaking back into his room in the Rojo's Hacienda after he had gunned down the five Rojo gunmen at the small house. He had given Julio, Marisol, and Jésus all his blood money and sent them off north to the border where they could live without fear from Ramón. From the torture chamber scene in the storehouse at the Rojo hacienda until his confrontation with Ramón in broad daylight on the streets of San Miguel, Joe has spent his time recovering from the whipping. During this violent, slam-bang, punching bag of a scene, Ramón howls insanely for the location of Marisol's whereabouts. During this grueling scene, Esteban cackles like a gleeful lunatic. Meanwhile, Rubio, Chico, and Ramón pound Joe's face and physique into pulp. They knock him up, down, and all around the storehouse. Occasionally, Joe throws a punch that connects, but he is more often on the receiving end. Finally, Esteban participates in the fun. He stubs out the glowing end of his cigar on the back of Joe's hand. Chico administers the final blow with his heel smashing into Joe's left hand. At first, you wonder why Chico ground up Joe's left hand since he shoots with his right hand. When Joe crumpled into a heap of arms and legs on the floor, his right hand with which he fires his revolver lies concealed beneath his chest. Like as not, Chico couldn't resist a last blow to Joe's conveniently exposed appendage. By this time, the make-up artists have done an impressive job of transforming Eastwood's face into a bruised, battered, blood-splattered mask of agony.

In some torture scenes, the villains take a break from their exercise in sadism. Usually, this provides the beleaguered hero with a golden opportunity to escape. First, Ramón halts the torture, because they can resume it later. Mind you, the Americano isn't going anywhere. Don Miguel has a better reason to cease the beatings. As bruised and battered as he is, Joe probably would not feel the pain of added blows inflicted on him. Now, that is a valid reason to pause the torture. After all, the hero must survive. Beaten as badly as he is, Joe still displays the unconquerable spirit of survival in his DNA that enables him to escape from the storehouse. Before he crawls away to safety, he sets up a booby-trap to pay back Chico. Remember Chico shooting the ground around little Jésus' feet as he ran crying to his father at the beginning? Joe has special reasons for wanting Chico dead, and he surprises everybody not only by his departure, but also in the way he has planned Chico's demise. A gigantic barrel of whiskey perched atop a ramp tumbles down with the force of an avalanche and smashes into Chico and another vaquero as they enter the facility. Meanwhile, Ramón and his pistoleros hear the crash of the barrel and rush to investigate. Scratching one of his matches, Joe sets the storehouse aflame. Ramón and his men are left scrambling to escape the inferno.

Now, Ramón is furious as he shouts to everybody to find the Americano. The repercussions of this scene escalate as Ramón attacks the Baxters while they are asleep. Nobody should be sleeping as peacefully as the Baxters are when Ramón launches a frontal assault on their premises. Presumably, Ramón must have thought Joe had taken refuge with the Baxters, so he attacks them. Ramón detonates multiple explosions in front of the Baxter's building. Afterward, he has his vaqueros back wagons up to the front of the building and roll out barrels of liquor on the grounds. The vaqueros smash these barrels with axes and saturate the façade. Ramón hurls a lantern, and flames engulf the residence. The Baxters pour out of their house in an exodus and plead for mercy. Some rush out shooting, too. Ramón greets them all with a barrage of gunfire, killing all of them.

Meantime, Joe has crawled into a coffin behind Silvanito's cantina, and Piripero drives him out of town. Before they depart from San Miguel, Joe watches as Ramón massacres the Baxters, bolstering his notoriety to greater heights of infamy! Ultimately, this scene illustrates Joe's instinct for survival as much as his cunning ability to fight back without a gun under the worst circumstances for him thus far! During the torture, he never begged for mercy. He took everything the Mexicans could give him, and they grew tired with their amusement.

5.   **THE FINALE IN SAN MIGUEL**

Earlier, Piripero drove Joe out of San Miguel in a coffin and hid him at an abandoned mine. As Joe recuperates from his terrible wounds, he practices with a six-gun and cuts an iron plate from a boiler. He plans to use this plate as a bulletproof vest. Leone foreshadowed an important element in this unusual duel earlier in the film, when Ramón touted the merits of his lever-action Winchester over Joe's Colt .45 revolver. "When you want to kill a man, you must shoot for his heart, and the Winchester is the best weapon." Joe didn't share Ramón's opinion. Nevertheless, Ramón adds, "When a man with a forty-five meets a man with a rifle, the man with the pistol will be a dead man. That's an old Mexican proverb, and it's true."

Arguably, the greatest use of foreshadowing in a movie takes place in "**Fistful**" when Joe is introduced wearing a poncho. Few traditional Hollywood western heroes had donned ponchos before Clint Eastwood. Robert Mitchum wore one very briefly at the outset of Robert Parrish's "**The Wonderful Country**" (1959), and Marlon Brando sported one in "**One-Eyed Jacks**" (1960). Mind you, he doesn't wear it in every scene. If you pay close attention, he had shed his poncho before the Mexican cavalry arrived in San Miguel. The next time we see Joe wearing his poncho is during the grand finale with Ramón. Remember, Ramón told Joe that he aims always for the heart. He demonstrated his accuracy during the Last Supper scene when he stitched the outline of a heart with bullet holes in the suit of armor. Joe could probably have gone throughout the remainder of "**Fistful**" without the poncho, but he has an indisputable reason for wearing it during the final showdown.

The poncho is an interesting cultural touch with Hispanic origins. Reportedly, costumer Carlo Simi created it for "**Fistful**."[24] The impression is that Joe wears the poncho like a coat when he is traveling, but once he holes up with Silvanito, he sheds it. Naturally, he would wear it to the finale with Ramón, so that the Winchester loving villain wouldn't see the metal plate. The surprise is Ramón's bullets cannot penetrate the plate. Joe is virtually bullet-proof. No matter how many times Ramón knocks Joe down, Joe gets back up. Finally, once an incredulous Ramón has emptied his Winchester, Joe wipes out the four pistoleros standing around Ramón. With his last bullet, Joe cuts the rope that Silvanito dangles from in front of the cantina.

Now, the final showdown between Ramón and Joe commences. The rules are one bullet per man. Joe has leveled the playing field in his favor.

A Colt Single Action .45 revolver is a quarter of the size of a Winchester repeater, but far easier to handle in closed quarters. Previously, Ramón enjoyed a margin of superiority over Joe because his Winchester could fire farther than Joe's six-shooter. Moreover, Ramón's Winchester held up to fifteen cartridges in a tubular magazine under the barrel. Of course, Joe dispatches Ramón with a single shot. As "**A Fistful of Dollars**" ends, Joe leaves San Miguel apparently penniless. Not only did he give everything that he had earned to Marisol and her family, but he wants Silvanito to return the stolen gold to the Mexican authorities.

The significance of the finale on the surface escaped me, until I appreciated Joe's audacity in orchestrating the showdown as he did. Principally, the finale qualifies as the best of all scenes owing to our hero's audacity. First, Joe deployed the two sticks of dynamite which Piripero had provided him with as if it were a marching band to herald his return from the dead. Comparatively, Clint Eastwood's character in Don Siegel's "**Two Mules for Sister Sara**" (1970) used his dynamite to kill his foes rather than simply get their attention as he does in "**Fistful**." Once he sauntered out of a cloud of dust, Joe goaded Ramón in much the same way he did the quartet of Baxter gunmen in the first scene. Naturally, Ramón shoots Joe five times in the heart, but Joe refuses to draw on him until Ramón's Winchester clicks on empty. No traditional Hollywood western hero would have conducted himself in this manner. Fortunately, an incredulous Ramón has filled his head full of hoopla about his proficiency with a Winchester, and he is mortified by Joe's survival. Indeed, Joe kept taunting Ramón. "The heart, Ramon. Don't forget the heart. Aim for the heart, or you'll never stop me." Joe taunted Ramón with Ramón's own words. Otherwise, the wily Hispanic would have realized his error and cut Joe down as easily as he had the fleeing trooper in the Rio Bravo. The spectacle of Joe exposing himself to potential death on the gamble that Ramón would keep shooting for the heart illustrates his bravery as well as his audacity. Few traditional Hollywood western heroes would have dared to gamble with their lives as flagrantly as Joe did and emerge triumphant in the end. Generally, the traditional Hollywood hero allows the villain time enough draw his six-gun before the hero empties his holster and disposes of the dastard.

CONCLUSION

What Sergio Leone and "**A Fistful of Dollars**" started would rise to another level entirely with "**For A Few Dollars More**" in 1965. Leone would part company with Jolly Film and attain greater autonomy with producer Alberto Grimaldi on "**For A Few Dollars More**" and "**The Good, the Bad, and the Ugly**." Ultimately, he would sever ties with Grimaldi and produce "**Once Upon A Time in the West**" with his own production company. Meantime, the meteoric rise of "**Fistful**" would retool the approach that the Italians had taken initially with their earlier westerns that carbon-copied the values of the traditional Hollywood western. After dying a premature death prior to "**A Fistful of Dollars**," the Spaghetti western would surge forward in into double- and triple-digit body counts and eclipse the competition. Eventually, Hollywood would join the ranks of European producers and shoot their westerns on the same dusty locations around Almeria, Spain. By 1966, the Spaghetti western had decimated the once popular peplum cycle of sword-and-sandal epics that had proliferated in the wake of Pietro Francisci's highly successful "**Hercules**" (Le fatiche di Ercole, (1958) with Steve Reeves. Many of the filmmakers who had made the peplum potboilers traded in their toga-clad heroes for heroes in ponchos sporting six-guns. Although Leone denied being the Father of the Spaghetti western, he gave birth to it with his first western "**A Fistful of Dollars**!"

-Van Roberts

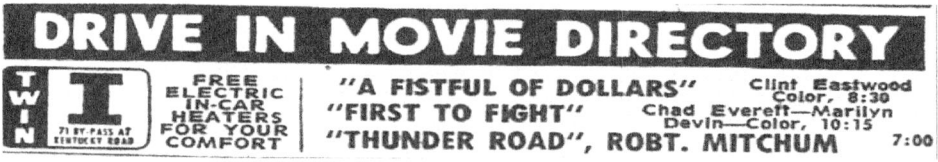

U.S. Newspaper ad: The Kansas City Star, April, 1967

**Turn to pages 208-209 to see Clint Eastwood's Contract from A Fistful of Dollars!

NOTES

1. Christopher Frayling, *Sergio Leone: Something to Do with Death* (New York: Faber and Faber, 2000), 118-119; Roberto Curti, *Tonino Valerii: The Films,* with a foreword by Christopher Frayling, and an afterward by Ernesto Gastaldi (Jefferson, North Carolina: McFarland & Company, Inc., Publishers, 2016), 25
2. Curti, *Tonino Valerii: The Films*, 87.
3. Trailer for **A Fistful of Dollars**, United Artists, 1967.
4. Ennio Morricone, "**A Fistful of Dollars**? It's my worst ever score," interview by Will Hodgkinson in The Guardian, July 14, 2006.
5. Robert C. Cumbow, *Once Upon A Time: The Films of Sergio Leone* (London: The Scarecrow Press Inc., 1987), 2.
6. Howard Hughes, *Once Upon A Time in the Italian West: The Filmgoers' Guide to Spaghetti Westerns* (New York & London: I.B. Tauris, 2004), 14.
7. Hughes, 14-15.
8. Terence Denman, *Fistfuls of Dollars in Almeria*: The Spanish Landscape that Shaped the Spaghetti Western, 1961-1977 (Independently published, 2019), 206.
9. Christopher Frayling, *Spaghetti Westerns*, p. 118-164.
10. Oreste De Fornari, *All About Sergio Leone* (Rome: Gremese International, 2019), 37.
11. Denham, 65.
12. Denham, 63-68.
13. Frayling, 120-121
14. Oreste De Fornari, 133.
15. **A Fistful of Dollars**, Credits, The Internet Movie Database; Frayling, 161.
16. Joseph McBride, *Hawks on Hawks* (Los Angeles: University of California Press, 1982), 29
17. David Lusted, *The Western* (New York: Pearson & Longman, 2003), 185-187
18. Frayling, 132.
19. Hughes, 11.
20. Hughes, 15.
21. Frayling, 254.
22. De Fornari, 133.
23. William Darby, *John Ford's Westerns*: A Thematic Analysis, with a Filmography (Jefferson, North Carolina: McFarland & Company, Inc., Publishers, 1996), 153.
24. Michael T. Marsden, "*Savior in the Saddle: The Sagebrush Testament,*" in Focus on the Western, ed. JackNachbar (New Jersey: Prentice-Hall, Inc, 1974), 98.

U.S. Newspaper ad, The Winina Daily News (Winona, Minnstota), Feb 12, 1967

https://www.artusfilms.com/

Goodbye Maestro!

Above: Left "*Here is the photo I took of Morricone on Thursday March 17, 1994 at the Red Lion Inn for his 1994 Career Achievement Award Tribute Dinner put on by The Society for the Preservation of Film Music.*" -Tom Betts. Above Right: Maurizio Baroni's brilliant book that encompasse all of Morriocone's scores. Highly recommended!
Bottom: Al Murloch (Knuckles), Once Upon a Time in the West. Paramount Pictures.

Remembering Ennio

The Maestro left us on July 6, 2020. He was 91. He had fallen some time before and had broken his leg. I never saw anything about it in the media. The next thing I know is I hear of his passing on the news on July 6th. Born in Rome on November 10, 1928. Over the years he wrote scores for over 500 films. He won 2 Oscars and was screwed out of at least 5 others. He also won 3 Grammy Awards, 4 Golden Globes, 6 Bafta, 10 David di Donatello, 11 Silver Ribbons, 2 European Film Awards, a Golden Lion for Lifetime Achievement and a Polar Music Prize. In 2017 he received the honor of Knight of the Grand Cross of the Order of Merit of the Italian Republic. He was an Academician of Santa Cecilia.

For me he was the heart and soul of the Spaghetti Western. I remember the first time I saw "**A Fistful of Dollars**" in 1966 and was prepared to laugh at what I saw on the screen. The film blew me away and like many changed my life. The haunting score ran through my head for weeks as I hunted in music stores for a copy of the score. After almost giving up I found a cover copy from Leroy Holmes and a better version released by Hugo Montenegro which also contained the other two scores of the Dollar Trilogy that had already been filmed and released in Europe but weren't released in the U.S. until 1967.

His scores for the Leone films were similar but different than the American western soundtracks I grew up with. They contained whistling but a different sound, whip cracks, bells and a chorus singing undecipherable lyrics. As each Leone film was released, I was rewarded with bigger and better scores. This led me to try and find other western scores he may have composed. I searched through Italian delis that offered Italian food and products including LPs for their customers. This led to finding record stores that offered monthly catalogs which they would mail to customers and we would order and wait two months before receiving scores for films I had never heard of let alone seen. I was never disappointed. He was a master of putting music to film when music was part of the film and helped the director establish feelings we were witnessing on the screen or inner feelings of characters that were not shown via dialogue on the screen.

He could do it all. Westerns, Horror, drama, love, adventure and war films. His music reached our ears, hearts and our souls. As his career advanced, he was at first pigeonholed as a pop composer but as time went on he was seen as a true music composer. Yes, several of his compositions were made into songs with lyrics and performed by leading singers of the day such as Mina, Andrea Bocelli, and Paul Anka. Then classical musicians like Yo Yo Ma and philharmonic orchestras picked up the torch. His track "*Ecstasy of Gold*" from "**The Good, the Bad and the Ugly**" became one of the most recognizable pieces of music in the world and heard on endless commercials.

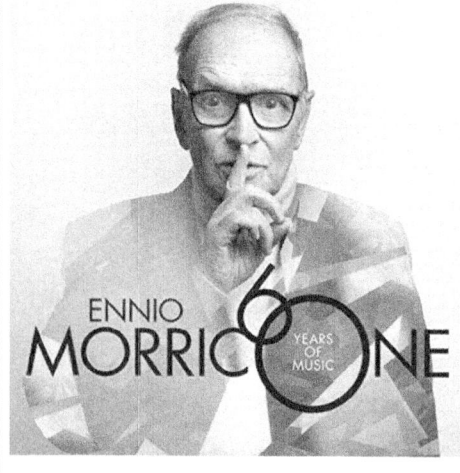

Ennio was a bigger than life figure and yet a very private person who bent to the pressure put on him by his millions of fans to perform in person at music venues throughout the world. His concerts were almost always sold out no matter where he performed, and he showcased all aspects of his musical repertoire and turned more of his admirers on to new pieces of music they may not have been aware of.

In the end we are sad that he has left us after all the years of pleasure he has given us, but he leaves behind a legacy of music that we can listen to for decades to come. We should be glad we were living when his compositions and scores were first released that brought us such delight.

RIP Ennio Morricone. Ennio Morricone the Oscar winner whose haunting, inventive scores expertly accentuated the simmering, dialogue-free tension of the spaghetti Westerns directed by Sergio Leone, died in Rome, Italy on July 6, 2020. He was 91.

 The Italian composer was born in Rome on November 10, 1928, scored more than 500 films, seven for his countryman Sergio Leone and fellow classmate in elementary school. Ennio, whose first instrument was the trumpet, won his Oscar for his work on Quentin Tarantino's **The Hateful Eight** (2015) and also was nominated and robbed for his original scores for Terrence Malick's **Days of Heaven** (1978), Roland Joffe's **The Mission** (1986), Brian De Palma's **The Untouchables** (1987), Barry Levinson's **Bugsy** (1991) and Giuseppe Tornatore's **Malena** (2000). Known as "The Maestro," he also received an honorary Oscar in 2007 (presented by Clint Eastwood) for his "magnificent and multifaceted contributions to the art of film music," and he collected 11 David di Donatello Awards, Italy's highest film honors. Morricone's ripe, pulsating sounds enriched Leone's low-budget Spaghetti westerns: **A Fistful of Dollars** (1964), **For a Few Dollars More** (1965), **The Good, the Bad and the Ugly** (1966), starring Clint Eastwood, and his masterpiece, **Once Upon a Time in the West** (1968) and **Duck, You Sucker** (1971). "The music is indispensable, because my films could practically be silent movies, the dialogue counts for relatively little, and so the music underlines actions and feelings more than the dialogue," Leone, who died in 1989, once said. "I've had him write the music before shooting, really as a part of the screenplay itself." The composer loved the sound of the electric guitar and the Jew's harp and employed whistles, church bells, whips, coyote howls, chirping birds, ticking clocks, gunshots and women's voices to add textures to scores not associated with the typical studio arrangement.

He leaves his wife Maria Travia whom he married in 1956 and four children Marco, Alessandra, Andrea and Giovanni

                                            -Tom Betts

Page 76:
Left: One of Morricone's most iconic scores was for the classic The Good, The Bad and The Ugly- United Artists.
Right: Ennio Morricone: 60 Years of Music from Ennio Morricone- 2016. Universal Music.

Page 77: Camden Release of A Fistful of Dollars and For A Few Dollars More. 1968 UK. Camden/RCA. Rerelease.

Any Gun Can Play
An Interview with Kevin Grant!

S.W. Your book *Any Gun Can Play* is by far the best book written on Italian westerns! Tell us how you got to the point of writing the book and some back history on how you became a film historian.

K.G. The idea for the book had been churning for a number of years, since I began writing about films as a hobby. I'd been a fan of spaghetti westerns for as long as I'd been a fan of Clint Eastwood – that is, since I was a boy, and first saw **A Fistful of Dollars** on television. Films other than the Dollars trilogy would occasionally air on British TV, so I became acquainted with different actors and characters – I remember seeing Lee Van Cleef as **Sabata** and Terence Hill as **Trinity** at an early age – and came to appreciate the quirks of the genre, the amazing landscapes, distinctive music and the incredible faces.

I gained a deeper understanding of the films' social and historical context from reading Christopher Frayling's Spaghetti Westerns and the equally indispensable Opera of Violence, by Tony Williams and Laurence Staig. (I suppose that's also where my interest began in film history as opposed to the related but distinct discipline of film criticism.) The video-trading scene was another vital development. Suddenly I had access to hundreds of movies I had been reading about and was able to form my own opinions. I could begin tracing the threads that bound them all together – recurring themes, directorial techniques, and so on. The book was my attempt to put everything I had learnt into perspective.

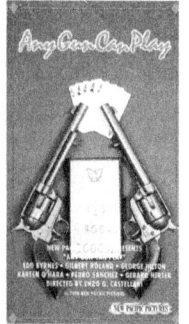

Left: Italian Western: The Opera of Violence- Laurence Staig and Tony Williams. Lorrimer Books- 1975.
Center: Spaghetti Westerns: Cowboys and Europeans from Karl May to Sergio Leone- Christopher Frayling. I.B, Tauris- 1981, 1998.
Right: VHS of Any Gun Can Play. New Pacific Pictures-1990

S.W. You made a notation on the back of *Any Gun Can Play*, which states, "The Euro-Western beyond Leone!" What're your thoughts on not only Leone but also how his vast shadow looms over the genre?

K.G. As with the majority of people, Leone was my starting point for appreciating these movies. I'd seen enough American westerns to notice immediately that the Dollars films were a radical departure in terms of tone and style and moral values. Leone was as shrewd as he was talented. He realised that you could harness all the traditional elements of the classic western – and the ancient myths that underpinned them – to the exuberance and irreverence of his own country's cultural heritage. Together with his collaborators, not least Ennio Morricone, he gave audiences something new yet oddly familiar. With each successive film he raised the bar for his competitors; none of them was quite able to reach it, in my opinion, but a few came close. His influence is apparent not just in the many copycat productions – those "bastard children" he spoke about – but also in films by other directors considered trendsetters in their own right – Sollima, Corbucci, certainly Valerii (a former assistant to Leone of course). Not so much in the case of Duccio Tessari, perhaps. So much had been written about Leone, however, even in English – again, Christopher Frayling set a kind of benchmark – that I didn't see the point of adding to it when there was more to say about spaghetti westerns in general and so many other gifted individuals whose work deserved appraisal.

S.W. Talk if you will about the genre birth and the noteworthy films that predated and were contemporaries of A Fistful of Dollars.

K.G. Most of the Italian-made westerns before **A Fistful of Dollars** were either comedy vehicles for popular stars like Walter Chiari and Ugo Tognazzi, or straightforward B-western imitations played straight. Watching films like **Stranger in Sacramento** or **The Last Gun** today, you struggle to imagine how the trend would have carried on. Before Leone, you might say, the 'Italian' western was stillborn. The best European westerns from the early 1960s were made elsewhere. The wholesome Winnetou series is most famous, of course, and made enough money to enable other filmmakers to find financial backing for westerns. I have always preferred the output of Spain's Joaquin Romero Marchent. His films were equally heartfelt, but they had a tough emotional core, and were more likely to end tragically than with the hero riding off in triumph. For my money, the best pre-Fistful European western is Marchent's **El Sabor de la venganza**, or **Gunfight at High Noon** (a meaningless title), which manages to be both gritty and sentimental and treats the subject of revenge seriously. Nice roles for Robert Hundar and Fernando Sancho, too.

S.W. I believe that one would be foolish when speaking of some of the influences of the Italian westerns to overlook the more violent 1950s Hollywood "B" westerns. Not that they were anywhere close in the tally of bodies, but some are downright harrowing and unsettling for the time frame- Speaking of films like Ambush at Tomahawk Gap, Rebel in Town, Kid Domino and others that pushed the violence.

K.G, We know from their own statements, and it is obvious from their films, that the leading directors and actors were well versed not only in classic Hollywood westerns but also second-tier productions like **The Halliday Brand**, **The Bravados** and **Day of the Outlaw**, to give a few fairly obvious examples. But I think these were more influential in terms of plot points and details – items of costume, character quirks – than violence and sadism. These qualities were already intrinsic to popular Italian genres – costume adventures and the peplum in particular – and carried over quite naturally into spaghetti westerns.

As for the American variety, the 1950s was both a golden age and a turning point. I think the genre reached a peak of maturity in that decade by questioning the basis of its own existence. It gave legendary actors like James Stewart, Henry Fonda, Gary Cooper and John Wayne some of the best and most challenging roles of their careers, and directors like Anthony Mann, Budd Boetticher and Robert Aldrich achieved parity with John Ford. You also had lesser-known filmmakers like Alfred Werker producing consistently interesting work.

This process continued in the early 1960s, when Sam Peckinpah galvanized the genre, but in other respects the Hollywood western appeared moribund. There were plenty of tired B-films starring ageing icons like Audie Murphy, but these offered nothing that TV westerns weren't showing regularly on the small screen. At the other extreme were big-budget widescreen epics, which only rarely advanced the genre in the same way that the Europeans would do with Sergio Leone's prompting (partly by stealing from the same films of course).

In the middle were a number of fine films about ageing gunmen and the end of the west, from Will Penny to The Wild Bunch and Monte Walsh. All these films seemed like epitaphs.

S.W. In my opinion, one of the essential things to occur the Italian westerns were the work of Giuliano Gemma in 1965. I think it was important for the genre to have a homegrown star, and his films helped further the genre. What're your thoughts on the pivotal year of 1965?
You're right, Gemma's advent was crucial. As well as possessing the physical attributes, he had the charisma not only to carry his own films, but to stand his ground alongside seasoned Americans like Lee Van Cleef and Eli Wallach. All his 1965 westerns were outstanding financial successes. The Duccio Tessari Ringo films have always been respected, even by critics who don't usually care for Italian westerns, and they prove Gemma's versatility as an actor with their very different moods. I enjoy **Adios Gringo** and **One Silver Dollar** as well, but I can't help feeling that without Gemma's vigour and charm, they'd have been forgettable. That's the difference he made.

Of course, the most significant film of 1965 appeared right at the end, when Leone proved with **For a Few Dollars More** that **Fistful** was not just a flash in the pan. Duccio Tessari gave him a run for his money that year though.

S.W. Django forever changed the Italian western landscape and is ultimately the reason that the genre exploded with more violence? What is Django's legacy, in your opinion?
Django was important for producing a home-grown character who not only struck a chord with Italian audiences – even more than Gemma's 'Ringo' persona – but became a distinctive brand overseas as well, something to signify 'Italian western'. There was no regard for intellectual property rights of course, so the name 'Django' gave a financial fillip to scores of entirely unrelated movies when they were released across Europe, especially in Germany and France – the centres of the 'Django cult'. Only a few of these resembled the Corbucci original – the distinctive costuming, for example, or the morbid humour. I suppose it gave a licence to other filmmakers to push the cartoonish aspect of Italian westerns even further.

Its explicit bloody violence did not become the new normal, however. We can point to **Django Kill**, but that was not conceived as a 'Django' film. Torture and sadism remained rife in the genre, but they had taken root well before Corbucci made **Django**. As for the splattery gunplay in **Django Unchained**, I'd say that owed more to Sam Peckinpah and John Woo than to Corbucci.

Left: Italian 4F Poster.
Above: For A Few Dollars More, Novel based on the movie of the same name. Written by Joe Millard, who wrote a number of movie tie-in books. Award Books, first printing, 1967. Published by agreement with The United Artists Corporation.

S.W. The Zapata westerns, a subgenre was, of course, more politically motivated and held more richly developed stories within. A subgenre that doesn't command a lot of respect as a whole and is overlooked in my eyes! What're your thoughts on the Zapata western subgenre?
K.G. I think the Zapata westerns flowed naturally from the political sympathies of many Italian filmmakers. At the same time, political subjects and rebel characters were very fashionable, so it was inevitable that the canny Italian popular film industry would seek to exploit them. The films greatly reduced the complexity of Third World conflicts, but it was refreshing – or seems so in retrospect – to see secondary or marginal characters promoted to the role of protagonist. Italian westerns are usually considered to be cynical – and many of them are – but the idealism of films like **A Bullet for the General** and **Companeros** appears to have been sincere. Other examples, like **Tepepa** and **A Fistful of Dynamite**, were less straightforward.

S.W.. The late 60s/early 70s in all reality was the beginning of the end of the genre. The Trinity films revived if for a bit, but the end was close. While there are some very good Italian comedy-westerns, most were awful examples. Do you believe the comedies harmed the overall reputation of the genre, and are non-Italian viewers missing something in the translation when it comes to the comedies?
I don't think comedies can be blamed entirely for the decline of the genre. Comedy westerns had always existed alongside the serious ones. Indeed, parodies were among the first westerns produced in Europe in the late 1950s-early 1960s. Nevertheless, when they came to be produced in such numbers after the Trinity films had made a killing, it must have portended the end of an era even to the people who were making them. Not even the specialists were taking the genre seriously any more – Leone, Petroni, Damiani... Corbucci always had a fondness for farce, so it was no great leap for him.

It's probably safe to say that the majority of Italian comedy westerns were intended primarily for domestic consumption, as they had been in the mid-1960s when Franco and Ciccio were at their peak. It's probably also the case that a lot of the gags and references would have made more sense to Italian audiences than they do in translation. Whether they would have seemed funnier is another matter.

S.W. What is your take on why the Italian genre died out?
K.G. Like other popular formulas before it, it outstayed its welcome. There had always been plenty of bad or mediocre productions, even in the mid and late 1960s, but these had been offset by a substantial number of superior films. By the early 70s this was no longer the case. Quality control was lacking, if not actually nonexistent, even before the Italians began sending themselves up.

Also, westerns everywhere had fallen out of fashion. Even those produced by Hollywood – and there were some great westerns, made in the 70s – tended to undermine the myths that had sustained the genre for so long. In both America and Italy, people preferred tough cops to gunslingers, and city streets replaced the open range as the setting for violent adventure.

S.W. You, along with Clark Hodgkiss, wrote an excellent book on westerns called *Renegade Westerns*! **Can you tell our readers a bit about it and some of the films you covered?**
K.G. *Renegade Westerns* covers what are broadly considered revisionist westerns – films that disputed the arguments associated with more traditional examples. 'Revisionist' is a very subjective term. We gave ourselves considerable latitude when selecting which titles to include, but they all had to go against the grain in some way. They had to ask more of the audience than simply to cheer on the hero – whether they presented that 'hero' in an unflattering light, as in many of the Anthony Mann westerns or **The Searchers**, for example, or looked critically at the settling of the frontier, as in **Soldier Blue** and **Little Big Man**. We also wanted to acknowledge films that gave women a more prominent and proactive role than viewers are accustomed to seeing in such a masculine genre – Barbara Stanwyck made a particularly strong impression in westerns like **The Furies** and **Cattle Queen of Montana**. And because we are both fans of film noir, we felt honour-bound to include films like **Pursued** and **Blood on the Moon** where the same visual and thematic qualities that defined noir were present in western period settings. It was all about illustrating the diversity of the genre and hopefully expanding the popular perception of what westerns are all about.

*Both *Renegade Westerns* and *Any Gun Can Play* are available from Amazon, the world over!

VAN ROBERTS' DAY OF ANGER!

INTRODUCTION

Tonino Valerii is one of the least appreciated Spaghetti western film directors in the genre. Recently, Italian critic Roberto Curti salvaged Valerii's maligned critical reputation with his insightful monograph *Tonino Valerii: His Films*. More importantly, Sergio Leone's biographer Sir Christopher Frayling penned a reappraisal of Valerii for Curti's book. Essentially, Frayling said Valerii has been overshadowed by his mentor Sergio Leone, and then Frayling gave Valerii full credit for directing the Sergio Leone produced western comedy "**My Name is Nobody**" (Il mio nome è Nessuno, 1973). Indisputably, Valerii was influenced by Leone, with whom he worked as an assistant director on both "**A Fistful of Dollars**" (Per un pugno di dollari, 1964) and "**For A Few Dollars More**" (Per qualche dollaro in più, 1965), as much as many other Spaghetti western directors who followed in the wake of Leone's groundbreaking horse opera "**A Fistful of Dollars**." Nevertheless, after he left Leone to become a director himself, Valerii established himself as a successful, competitive filmmaker in his own right, and his second Spaghetti western "**Day of Anger**" (I giorni dell'ira, 1967) bears out his virtuosity.1

Sadly, like his tarnished but rehabilitated reputation, Valerii and his films haven't garnered the recognition and respect they deserve from inside the genre as well as outside.2 For example, Valerii's "**Day of Anger**" epitomizes the elements and attitude that made Valerii not only an outstanding storytelling director, but also what differentiated his westerns from those of Leone and other esteemed genre practitioners. Nobody could rival Sergio Corbucci's output. He made more Spaghettis than Leone. Nevertheless, everything boiled down to quality versus quantity. Leone made fewer movies of greater quality, while Corbucci stretched his creativity thin with a larger number of films of lesser quality. Nevertheless, Corbucci made several entertaining westerns, including the blind man western "**Minnesota Clay**" (1964), with Cameron Mitchell; the machine gun wielding "**Django**" (1966), with Franco Nero; the Lost Cause western "**The Cruel Ones**" (I crudeli, 1967), with Joseph Cotton; the revenge-themed "**Navajo Joe**" (1968), with Burt Reynolds; the mute hero saga "**The Grand Silence**" (Il grande silenzio, 1968), with Jean-Louis Trintignant; and the high-body count Zapata western "**The Mercenary**" (Il mercenario, 1968), with Franco Nero. As entertaining as it is, "**Companeros**" (Vamos a matar, compañeros, 1970), with Franco Nero, doesn't make the cut, because it feels like an uninspired remake of "**The Mercenary**." Comparably, Sergio Sollima made

Left to Right- Top to Bottom:
1. USA VHS. Mintex Entertainment. 100 Mins.
2. Arrow Blu-Ray release. U.K.
3. Riz Ortolani "Day of Anger" Soundtrack LP RCA LSO-1165 1970
4. German DVD Release. Filmjuwelen. German/Italian Audio. German/English Subs. Also available on Blu-Ray.
5. Wild East Productions DVD release.
6. German DVD release. Studiocanal. German Audio. German and Italian subs.

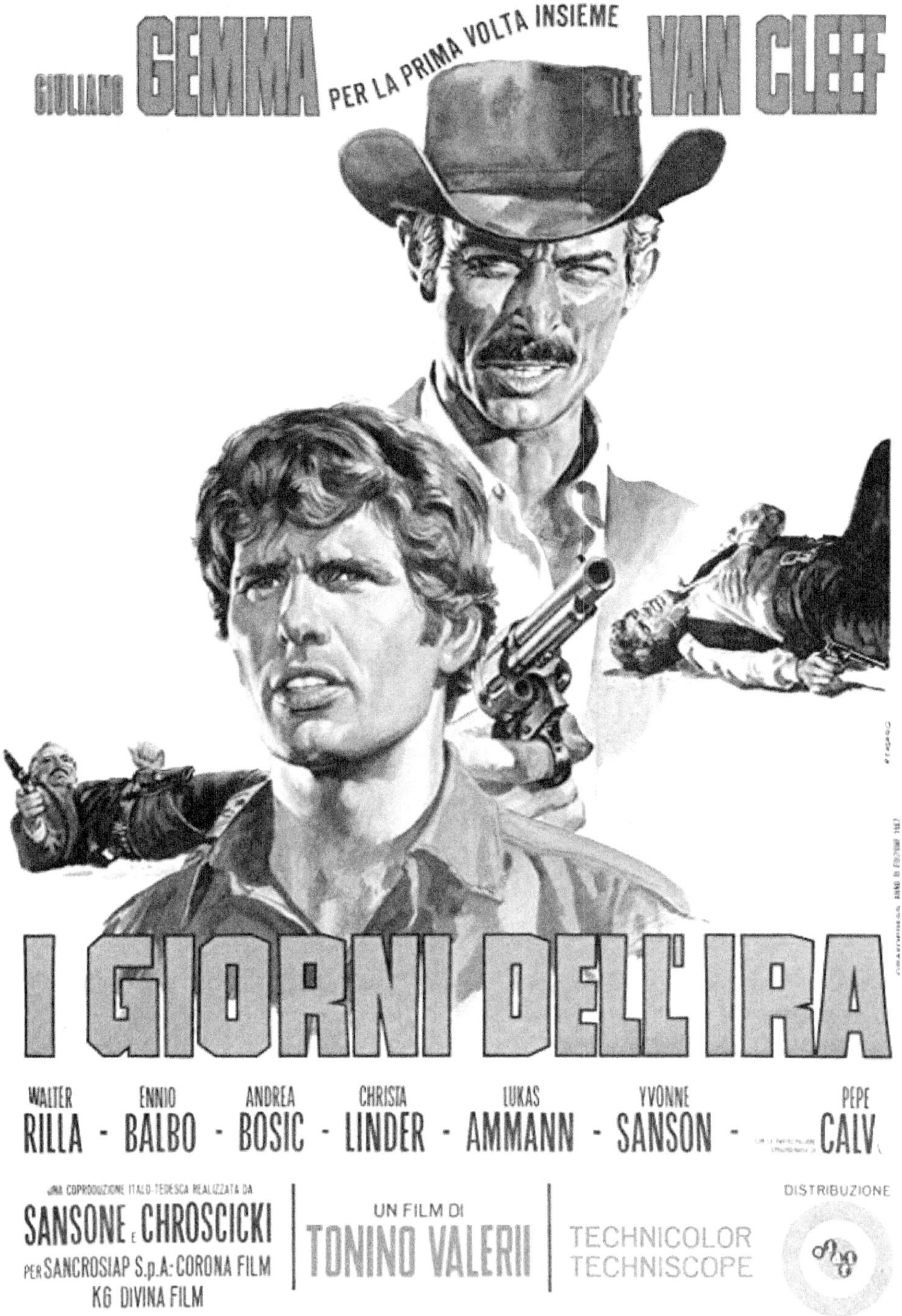
GIULIANO GEMMA
PER LA PRIMA VOLTA INSIEME
LEE VAN CLEEF
I GIORNI DELL'IRA
WALTER RILLA - ENNIO BALBO - ANDREA BOSIC - CHRISTA LINDER - LUKAS AMMANN - YVONNE SANSON - PEPE CALV
UNA COPRODUZIONE ITALO-TEDESCA REALIZZATA DA
SANSONE E CHROSCICKI
PER SANCROSIAP S.p.A.-CORONA FILM
KG DIVINA FILM
UN FILM DI
TONINO VALERII
TECHNICOLOR
TECHNISCOPE
DISTRIBUZIONE

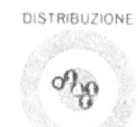

Page 84: Italain Poster
Page 85: Left: USA VHS release of Day of ANger under the title of "Days of Wrath (1987). Imperial Entertainment Corp. 6430 Sunset Blvd, Suite 1500, Hollywood Ca 90028
Right: Italian Title card

fewer Spaghetti westerns than both Leone and Corbucci. Sollima's three sturdy Spaghetti westerns were "**The Big Gundown**" (La resa dei conti, 1966), with Lee Van Cleef; "**Face to Face**" (Faccia a facia, 1967), starring "**Fistful of Dollars**" villain Gian Maria Volontè, and "**The Big Gundown**" sequel "**Run, Man, Run**" (Corri uomo corri, 1968), with Tomas Milian reprising his role from Sollima's first western.

Meantime, Valerii helmed five Spaghetti westerns, same as Leone but less than Corbucci. His initial Spaghetti western "**Taste of Killing**" (Per il gusto di uccidire, 1966), followed a shrewd but illiterate hero, Hank Fellows (Craig Hill), armed with a Winchester repeating rifle equipped with a telescopic sight. This cynical protagonist shadows stagecoaches from afar and uses his telescopic sight to spy on outlaws when they rob them. Afterward, he trails the thieves and recovers the loot as well as the bounty on them rather than intervene directly on the spot. Valerii's "**Day of Anger**" would serve as a warm-up for the lighter weight "**My Name is Nobody,**" and paired him with prolific Spaghetti western scribe Ernesto Gastaldi, who had written almost a dozen horse operas. Later, they collaborated again on "**A Reason to Live, A Reason to Die**" (Una ragione per vivere e una per morire, 1972), an American Civil War adventure bristling with treachery, betrayal, and violence, co-starring James Coburn, Telly Savalas, and Bud Spencer. Gastaldi brandished his pen for Valerii on his third western "**The Price of Power**" (Il prezzo del potere, 1969), a radical departure from any Spaghetti western ever made, considering it constitutes a 'what-if' re-enactment of the JFK assassination set in 1880s. "**Day of Anger**," however, remains Valerii's least contrived western. Basically, "**Day of Anger**" qualifies as a tragedy, but Valerii doesn't shirk his responsibility as a storyteller when he concludes it with an appropriate but sad ending. Reminiscent in different ways to Anthony Mann's traditional Hollywood oater "**The Tin Star**" (1957), co-starring Henry Fonda and Anthony Perkins, "**Day of Anger**" explores a similar tutorial plot about a master and protégé relationship. As Morgan Hickman, Fonda played an older, wiser, former sheriff who shows a callow youth, Ben Owens (Anthony Perkins), the ropes about how to survive as a conscientious lawman. When I first saw "**Day of Anger**" in 1967, I found the comparison between the two films inescapable. The primary difference was "**The Tin Star**" protagonists were sympathetic lawmen saving an irate citizenry from their own destructive urges. Conversely, "**Day of Anger**" concerns a twenty-year old who yearns to be a gunfighter and learns everything he must know like an apprentice from a seasoned gunfighter. The relationship between the "**Day of Anger**" protagonists contains greater depth and maturity than Mann's remarkable western. Curti has written definitively about "**Day of Anger**" in his superb book about Valerii's cinema. Since he knew Valerii, Curti is to Valerii what Sir Christopher Frayling was to Sergio Leone. No shallow, simple-minded, shoot'em up, "**Day of Anger**" emerges as a stunning western about a hero with an Oedipus complex. On-camera interviews with Valerii and Curti both affirm this psychological point abundantly, so this author has scoured the text of the film to a greater degree in search of other insights. Again, Curti enters the picture and provides road signs for criticism. Valerii never attracted the worldwide acclaim that flourished around Leone. Principally, Valerii was not as flamboyant a filmmaker as Leone. Instead, Valerii shares the characteristics of many traditional Hollywood filmmakers during the studio years in the early twentieth century.

A director with an unobtrusive style, he attended to the visual needs of his narrative, but he also was forged in the furnace of Italian exploitation cinema. Furthermore, Valerii appears to have gone out of his way to distinguish this western from the rest of the genre. Rather than situating "**Day of Anger**" on the arid, southwest border, most of it unfolds in the town of Clifton, Arizona. Like "**The Tin Star**," "**Day of Anger**" exposes the social, political, and moral dynamics within a small-town setting from the perspective of a contentious surrogate father & son relationship between the subversive gunfighter and the naïve youth who aspires to emulate him. The beauty of "**Day of Anger**" is Valerii doesn't pull any punches, so little comes across as being contrived. Indeed, every time I watch it, I wish the Lee Van Cleef character Frank Talby had not been such a dastard and the Giuliano Gemma character Scott Mary had not been quite so starry-eyed. In some ways, "**Day of Anger**" channels the traditional Hollywood western, because Valerii's message is clear at fadeout: if you live by the gun, you will just as surely die by the gun. In John Sturges' "**Gunfight at the O.K. Corral**" (1957), Wyatt Earp (Burt Lancaster) summarized the gunfighter's curse when the marshal lectures a wayward youth, Billy Clanton (Dennis Hopper), about the life trajectory of a gunfighter. "I learned one rule about gunslingers. There's always a man faster on the draw than you are, and the more you use a gun, the sooner you're gonna run into that man." Although it is a Spaghetti western, and most Spaghettis were an excuse for amoral characters to run rampant and rack up a double-digit body count set to vibrant music, "**Day of Anger**" preaches similar anti-gunfighting rhetoric that westerns like the Sturges' film and others hammered into the hearts and minds of youngsters coming of age during the post-World War II era in the aftermath of a national juvenile delinquency crisis.

After co-starring in two classic Leone Spaghettis, "**For A Few Dollars More**" and "**The Good, the Bad, and the Ugly**" (Il buono, il brutto, il cattivo, 1966), Lee Van Cleef ventured out on his own to star in several other memorable horse operas. In his Spaghetti westerns, the lupine New Jersey native played three basic western stereotypes. First, he portrayed an invincible man in black with gadgets, in "**For A Few Dollars More**," in Gianfranco Parolini's two Sabata sagebrushers, "**Sabata**" (Ehi amico... c'è Sabata. Hai chiuso! 1969) and "**Return of Sabata**" (È tornato Sabata... hai chiuso un'altra volta! 1971), and in Giancarlo Santi's "**The Grand Duel**" (Il grande duello, 1972). Second, he played an amoral gunfighter in "**The Good, the Bad, and the Ugly**," in Giulio Petroni's "**Death Rides a Horse**"(Da uomo a uomo, 1967), in Eugenio Martín's "**Bad Man's River**" (El hombre de Río Malo, 1968), in Giorgio Stegani's "**Beyond the Law**" (Al di là della legge, 1968), in Antonio Margheriti's "**Blood Money**" (El karate el Colt y el impostor, 1974), in Margheriti's "**Take A Hard Ride**" (1975), and in Margheriti's "**Kid Vengeance**" (1977). Third, he represented law and order in "**The Big Gundown**," and as a twin brother priest/gunfighter in Gianfranco Parolini's "**God's Gun**" (Diamante Lobo, 1976). Of his Spaghetti westerns, I prefer "**Death Rides a Horse**" (Da uomo a uomo, 1967) over "**Day of Anger**" for scenarist Luciano Vincenzoni's exciting heroes and villains as well as its upbeat Sergio Corbucci style ending. Although it concludes with a happier ending than "**Day of Anger**," Valerii's western supersedes it, based on the gravity of its morality enhanced ending. Ultimately, a complex master and protégé western, "**Day of Anger**" ranks as perhaps Valerii's best horse opera.

In his non-Spaghetti westerns, Van Cleef portrayed good guys in Gordon Douglas' ferry master shoot'em up "**Barquero**" (1968); in Alexander Singer's "**Captain Apache**," where he appeared as a Native American cavalry captain; a charming but villainous gunslinger in John Guillermin's "**El Condor**" (1970), and as a married lawman in George McCowan's "**The Magnificent Seven Ride**" (1972).

Lee Van Cleef made his cinematic debut as a hired gunman in Fred Zinnemann's classic western "**High Noon**" (1952) starring Gary Cooper. Van Cleef was typecast as ephemeral villains in as many as twenty-five traditional Hollywood westerns between "**High Noon**" and John Ford's "**The Man Who Shot Liberty Valance**" (1962). When he wasn't getting gunned down on the silver screen, he appeared as a guest star on virtually every prime-time western television series, among them "**Gunsmoke**," "**Bonanza**," "**Branded**," "**The Lone Ranger**," "**The Rifleman**," "**Cheyenne**," "**The Deputy**," "**Colt .45**," "**Laredo**," "**Lawman**," "**Tombstone Territory**," "**The Range Rider**," and "**The Gene Autry Show**." Indeed, based on the content of the role in "**Day of Anger**," Van Cleef was destined to play Frank Talby. Ironically, the advertising for both "**The Big Gundown**" and "**Day of Anger**" touted the hook-nosed American western heavy inaccurately as "*Mr. Ugly*" in "**The Big Gundown**" and referred to him as "*Ugly*" in "**Day of Anger.**" In "**The Good, the Bad, and the Ugly**," Van Cleef played "the Bad," while Eli Wallach was "the Ugly." It is amazing that the publicists for both movies as well as the companies who released the films made such egregious errors. Fans of Van Cleef's career would do well to peruse Mike Malloy's comprehensive reference guide, though we disagree on some points about the artistry of "**Day of Anger**." I don't share Mike Malloy's criticisms of "**Day of Anger**" about the so-called "predilection for pointless excesses, some of which are laughably campy" as well as "many unnecessary scenes of outrageous violence." 3 Leonard Maltin disparages "**Day of Anger**" as "below par, even for an Italian western . . ." 4 Western film historian Phil Hardy seems to miss the point and the style when he describes Valerii's film as "routine, but cheerful." 5 *The Film Buff's Bible of Motion Pictures*, edited by D. Richard Baer, categories "**Day of Anger**" as "Only fair, Not Worth Watching." 6 *New York Times* film critic Roger Greenspun felt the film was "strange and muddled [...] very long and mostly boring, depending for its plot upon notions of class and caste that seem foreign to the genre if not to real history." 7

According to Roberto Curti, Giuliano Gemma wasn't the first choice to play the protégé. 8 Initially, Valerii had sought baby-faced actor Lou Castel who had made three fascinating Spaghetti westerns during his 56-year film career, but was best known at the time for Marco Bellocchio's "**Fists in the Pocket**." Damiano Damiani's "**A Bullet for the General**" (Quién sabe? 1967), Carlo Lizzani's "**Requiescant**" (1968), and Cesare Canevari's **Matalo!** aka "**Kill Him!**"

(ADVANCE ANNOUNCEMENT)

ACTION-PACKED WESTERN TO OPEN

"Day of Anger," action-packed western starring Lee Van Cleef and Giuliano Gemma, released by National General Pictures in Technicolor and Techniscope, will open at the .... Theatre on ....

The drama about a gunfighter and his protege, who is taught the use of a gun and its consequences, was filmed in Spain and Italy. It was produced by Alfonso Sansone and Enrico Chroscicky and directed by Tonino Valerii.

"DAY OF ANGER" (2A)

Lee Van Cleef (left) and Giuliano Gemma are starred in the action-packed western "Day of Anger" released in Technicolor and Techniscope by National General Pictures.
(Still No. DOA Pos 5)

(¡Mátalo! 1970) were three noteworthy Spaghettis. Instead of the cherubic Castel, Valerii wound up casting the lanky, acrobatic Gemma. Gemma made sixteen Spaghetti westerns. These included Duccio Tessari's "**Ballad of Death Valley**" (Una pistola per Ringo, 1965), Giorgio Ferroni's "**Blood for a Silver Dollar**" (Un dollaro bucato, 1965), Tessari's "**The Return of Ringo**" (Il ritorno di Ringo, 1966), Giorgio Stegani's "**Adiós Gringo**" (1965), Michele Lupo's "**Man from Nowhere**" (Arizona Colt, 1966), Ferroni's "**For a Few Extra Dollars**" (Per pochi dollari ancora, 1966), Florestano Vancini's "**Long Days of Vengeance**" (I lunghi giorni della vendetta, 1967), Ferroni's "**Wanted**" (1967), "**Day of Anger**" (1967), Giulio Petroni's "**A Sky Full of Stars for a Roof**" (E per tetto un cielo di stelle, 1968), Tessari's "**Alive or Preferably Dead**" (Vivi o preferibilmente morti, 1969), Valerii's "**The Price of Power**" (1969), Lupo's "**Amigo, Stay Away**" (Amico, stammi lontano almeno un palmo, 1972), and Sergio Corbucci's "**Shoot First... Ask Questions Later**" (Il bianco il giallo il nero, 1975), with Eli Wallach; Lupo's "**California**" (1977), and finally Lucio Fulci's "**Silver Saddle**" (1978).

Not only will a synopsis of "**Day of Anger**" plumb the depths of this deeply psychological horse opera with its Freudian Oedipus complex, but it will also show how Valerii dramatized the thematic concerns primarily through its narrative elements. Valerii doesn't exaggerate any of the events with either baroque camera angles or elaborate set-ups which detract attention from the essential storyline. This approach gives Valerii's Spaghetti western a greater sense of realism. Riz Ortolani's orchestral music score, which punches up the action considerably, qualifies as the only apparent overindulgence. Furthermore, "**Day of Anger**" shuns conspicuous comic relief both humorous or ghoulish. However, moments occur when you wonder if Ernesto Gastaldi and Valerii weren't amusing themselves. For example, Scott barely conceals his sarcasm when he comments about the origins of the evil smelling contents of his sewage barrels. Says Scott, "It's all from the respectable citizens of Clifton." Later, Scott rides a mule inexplicably named Sartana, undoubtedly an in-joke on one of the most dangerous Spaghetti gunslingers in all Italian cinema. After it's colorful, flashy, head-swapping, rotoscoped title credits set to Ortolani's brassy orchestral score, "**Day of Anger**" opens quietly in Clifton with a close-up of the town sign. This frontier municipality boasts a veneer of affluence, with many shops and businesses lining each side of Main Street, with a fringe of forest on the outskirts. According to Spaghetti western historian Howard Hughes in "*Once Upon A Time in the Italian West*, Valerii lensed all the town scenes in Rome at Cinecitta Studios, so the town doesn't appear as ramshackle as most Spaghetti western towns lensed on location in Spain." 9 Few people are awake this early in the morning. A glimpse at the clock in a bordello indicates it is about six o'clock.

The first scene seems unusual for a western, especially a Spaghetti western. Nothing exciting about it clamors for our attention. It doesn't open with a gunfight. Instead, a tall, rangy, young man with unkempt hair, wearing ill-fitting garments, is shown hauling a crude, wooden cart by hand which contains two barrels. Fortunately, *Smell-O-Vision* didn't last long in Hollywood. Otherwise, we would have smelled the awful, reeking stench from those buckets that Scott (Giuliano Gemma) trundles around town without a care in the world. Scott looks and dresses like a lower working class refugee from Italian Neorealism films of the late 1940s and early 1950s. Various businessmen have set out wooden buckets brimming with either slop or sewage which Scott cheerfully empties into his barrels as he makes his rounds. When he tries to strike up a conversation with barbershop owner Sam Corbitt (Ferruccio Viotti), Corbitt is so sickened by the vile smell fuming from those barrels that he runs Scott off. Apart from a friendly but naïve prostitute, Gwen (Christa Linder) as well as the sympathetic whorehouse madame, Vivien Skills (Yvonne Sanson), everybody in Clifton looks down their collective nose at him as if he is the scum of the earth.

Scott has only one name--his first name. Basically, he was born out of wedlock. He neither knew his prostitute mother nor his lusty father. During his conversation with Vivien, we learn Scott grew up in the bordello. Dutifully, he handles the worst jobs nobody else would stoop to perform. Later, Scott encounters the town tramp, Blind Bill (José Calvo), sitting outside the Gala Saloon. Bill amuses himself tossing pebbles into empty liquor bottles. Saloon proprietor Abel Murray (Andrea Bosic) storms up in a red, hot rage with his shotgun. He chews Bill out for tampering with his bottles, strewn in a careless pile outside the premises, which he claims he will wash and recycle. When Bill flees in terror, Murray lets him have a barrel full of buckshot in the buttocks. Scott tries without success to placate the furious saloon owner. Murray warns Scott not to touch him. He scorns Scott as "an ugly son of a bitch."

Valerii presents an image of Clifton as a peaceful, civilized town. Predictably, Murray's early morning shotgun blast awakens several townspeople. "It's years since we heard shooting in Clifton," a nightshirt-clad husband despairs to his drowsy-eyed wife on their Main Street balcony, until they learn about the circumstances of the shooting. Two similar citizens chuckle about Murray blasting away at Blind Bill and then return to their rooms. The paunchy town sheriff, Nigel (Giorgio Gargiullo), wears a gun belt, but neglects to carry a six-gun. He cuts an absurd figure when Murray confronts him. The saloon proprietor explains he was cleaning out the barrel of his shotgun. Nodding to Nigel's empty holster, Murray advises the sheriff, "you should do the same every so often." You know a town is civilized when the lawman forgets to pack a pistol. Nigel grimaces at Murray's disapproval. "I'm the law here," Nigel contends. "In Clifton that's more than an old weapon." Clearly, a long time has passed since anybody has raised a ruckus in Clifton. The powers that be and the sheriff are in league with each other, and they all despise Scott for his accidental birth.

Nothing has changed for Scott during the twenty years he has lived in Clifton. Once he has finished his rounds, Scott returns to the stable and disposes of the sewage. He knots a length of rope around his hips, with a wooden gun stuck in a shabby holster. Repeatedly, Scott practices his fast draw, while an older, avuncular fellow, Murph Allan Short (Walter Rilla), regrets ever having provided Scott with a facsimile firearm. Coincidentally, Valerii found a variation on Scott's character in Allen H. Minor's "**Black Patch**" (1957), a black & white George Montgomery western, about an errand boy, Flytrap (Tom Pittman), who acquired a gun and defied those townspeople who had bullied him. 10 Later, as Scott is sweeping off the boardwalk in front of the bordello, he spots a stranger on a horse approaching him.

Composer Riz Ortolani strikes a couple of sinister chords as an older man, wearing a tied down six-gun, reins his horse up in front of Scott. He asks for the location of the stable. After Scott furnishes directions, the grateful but gimlet-eyed stranger, Frank Talby (Lee Van Cleef) inquires about the best place to eat, drink, and sleep. Scott recommends the Gala Saloon, and Talby promises him a dollar if he will stable his horse. In all of ten minutes time, Valerii has introduced the most woebegone specimen of humanity in Clifton. Little do we know Scott will emerge as the protagonist of "**Day of Anger.**" Everybody treats Scott like a leper. Talby's arrival in Clifton changes Scott's life. Talby asks for the youth's name. "Scott," replies the gawky twenty-year old. Talby frowns. "Just Scott?" Sheepishly, Scott concedes, "I never knew my father." Predictably, Talby questions Scott about his mother. "Everybody called her Mary," Scott remembers. "That can be your surname," Talby suggests. "Call yourself Scott Mary." Visibly embarrassed by such a proposal, Scott blurts out, "Everybody would laugh at me if I called myself Scott Mary." Talby bristles irritably. "So what? Who knows for sure whether they would laugh at it?" The gunfighter invites Scott to join him at the saloon where he will await him with his dollar. At this point, Talby doesn't realize Scott is a persona non grata in the eyes of most Clifton citizens.

Not only has Valerii established Clifton as a quiet, peaceful town populated by a snobbish elite, but also that Scott grovels before everybody in the town. After Talby has arrived, Scott experiences a sea change. Talby has given Scott a last name and an entirely new identity. Scott is no longer simply Scott. Furthermore, Talby treats the twenty-year old with greater respect than anybody else, apart from Murph Allan Short. At the stable, Scott brags about Talby's saddle and the dollar Talby has promised him. Earlier, Vivian had offered Scott a mere quarter for sweeping her boardwalk, but Scott remains too grateful for Vivian's kindness of allowing him to grow up at the bordello to take her quarter. When Murph asks about Scott's plans for his new-found wealth, Scott tells him he plans to save up some extra dollars and buy himself a Colt .45 revolver.

Murph grimaces at the prospect of Scott buying a gun. "The days of fast guns are over," he reminisces, "Once upon a time, a good pistol was worth more than money in the bank." Briefly, Murph tells Scott being quick on the draw isn't adequate, especially if your adversary has tricks with which you aren't acquainted. "In my day, we had to either learn the tricks or we gave work to the gravediggers." Clearly, Valerii and Gastaldi have planted an example of foreshadowing here which will haunt Scott until the end of "Day of Anger." Scott remains adamant about purchasing a pistol. "I'll buy myself a Colt." Resentment creeps into Scott's voice. "I want to see if anyone will have the courage to call me a 'bastard.'" Now, Murph regrets having ever taught Scott how to draw. He frowns when Scott reveals the stranger's name. "Talby?" Murph searches his memory, "I think I've heard that name before."

Heading to rendezvous with Talby at the saloon, Scott approaches Judge Cutcher's beautiful daughter, Eileen (Anna Orso), and she warns him her father doesn't want him around her. Cutcher (Lukas Ammann) himself personally warns Scott to lay off Eileen. "You're a good boy, Scott," Cutcher concedes. "But you're an illegitimate bastard. Your mother was one of Vivian Skill's girls, and your father who knows who your father was. You mustn't raise your eyes to look at my daughter. You must never talk to her or stop here again." Later, once he arrives at Murray's saloon to collect his dollar, Scott encounters more trouble. Initially, Murray wanted to evict him, but Talby insists Scott is his guest. He treats Scott to his first shot of whiskey. Another local citizen, Hart Perkins (Romano Puppo), whose wife has just given birth to twins, objects to Scott's presence. He makes the fatal mistake of pulling his gun on Talby. Talby kills him without a qualm. This lands the gunfighter in Judge Cutcher's court, but the judge exonerates him. Cutcher rules the shooting a clear case of self-defense. Hurriedly, Talby shoulders his way through the crowd of locals and leaves the courtroom. After everybody has cleared out of the courtroom, Murray and Nigel use Scott as a punching bag.

Abruptly, Talby rides out of Clifton. A desperate Scott pursues him on his mule Sartana. Finally, when he catches up with Talby, the rugged old gunfighter isn't as friendly as he was in Clifton. Nevertheless, Scott is determined to be a gunfighter, so Talby takes charge of his education, with the equivalent of the Ten Commandments. "I want to get to be like you," Scott announces. "I know how to draw, but I've never had a real pistol. If I'm taught right, I'm pretty bright. I'd be useful to you as a sort of partner."

Talby ponders Scott's proposition. "Alright, the first lesson is never beg another man." Talby asks for Scott's eight dollars, and the kid hands it over without question. Abruptly, Talby lashes out with the back of his hand, striking the youth in the face, and knocking him flat in the dust. "Lesson number two: never trust anybody." Swinging astride his horse, Talby rides away without looking back. This setback redoubles Scott's resolution to learn Talby's third lesson. Those first two lessons are about to occur before Scott's eyes as he pursues Talby into the hardscrabble hamlet of Bowie, Arizona, near the Mexican border. The notorious outlaw, Wild Jack (Al Mulock), has holed up in Bowie with his gang. He owes Talby the sum of $50-thousand dollars. A hard luck, ex-convict, Wild Jack already has a price on his head after having just gotten out of prison. He explains to Talby that he took on three silent partners when he decided to steal a gold shipment.

Page 90: George Montgomery as Black Patch; Walter Rilla- Murph; Leo Gordon as Hank Danner (Black Patch); Giuliano Gemma and Lee Van Cleef in Day of Anger; Al Murloch- Juan Wild (Day of Anger)
Page 91: Top to Bottom: Gemma; Tom Pittman as "Flytrap" (Black Patch); Gemma; Pittman; Black Patch- Warner Bros Archive DVD

As it turns out, those silent partners were none other than Clifton's most respectable citizens: Turner the banker (Ennio Balbo), Judge Cutcher, and Abel Murray. Turner alerted Wild Jack about the gold shipment. The judge prepared an alibi for him, and Murray drove the train. Talby reminds Wild Jack that he has been waiting ten years for Jack to pay his debt. The ex-convict pleads for Talby to give him a chance to collect his loot. "I'm not after revenge, Wild," Talby asserts. "Give me my fifty-thousand, and we'll be friends again." Wild says he doesn't have "one stinking dollar." He explains everything went fine, until the honest people of Clifton swindled him. "We were all set to pull the job in Abilene." Moreover, Wild was prepared to divide the loot with these honest men. Talby fidgets with his pipe as Wild pauses in his explanation. "And the clean hands tricked you," Talby interjects before Wild can continue. The outlaw grimaces. "They testified against me, and the money disappeared." Talby appreciates Wild's predicament. "And so, my $50,000 ended up in their pockets, too." Wild adds he cannot enter Clifton with a bounty on his head. Talby prompts Wild to reveal the names of those honest citizens.

Afterward, he suggests Wild cross the Mexican border and spend the rest of his life in exile. "Let's say I'm buying our revenge for $50,000 and those honest people in Clifton can owe their debt to Frank Talby instead." Wild doesn't argue with Talby. He knows Talby is far too fast on the draw for him. Wild orders drinks for everybody. Scott refuses to toast Wild's health, and the vicious outlaw beats him unconscious. Just as Wild is poised to gouge a hole in Scott's throat with the jagged end of a smashed tequila bottle, Talby intervenes. He attends to Scott and slaps him around with a series of stinging blows until Scott regains consciousness. "Fourth lesson," Talby states. "Punches are like bullets, if you don't make the first one's count, Scotty, you just might be finished."

Meantime, Wild sends three of his gang off to Bill Farrell's place. Farrell was one of Wild's other accomplices. Outside the cantina, Wild tries foolishly to kill Talby, but the old gunfighter outdraws him. He wounds Wild with his first shot. Scott makes the error of blocking Talby's line of fire. Wounded and sprawled face down on his chest, Wild Jack pleads with Talby to spare his life. Kneeling in front of Scott, Talby shoots between the arch of Scott's legs and kills Wild as the outlaw struggles futilely to return gunfire.

Talby delivers the fifth lesson: "When you wound a man, you better kill him. Sooner or later, he is going to kill you."

Page 92: Image from the USA pressbook
Page 93: Left: Spanish Poster;
page 93: Right: Ernesto Gastaldi scripts for Day of Anger and My Name is Nobody in Italian language. Available at www.facebook.com/gastaldiernesto.

Leaving Scott behind, Talby rides off for Bill Farrell's ranch. Arriving there too late, he finds Farrell dangling from the roof, his neck in a noose. Wild's three henchmen sneak up on the unsuspecting Talby. Relieving him of both gun and gun belt, these snickering ruffians drag him belly down across the inhospitable terrain, laughing as they spur their horses for greater speed. When they take a momentary break to rest their mounts, Scott surprises Talby and pitches him his six-gun. Before Wild Jack's three gunmen realize it, Talby has toppled them from their saddles, thumbing the hammer of his revolver in rapid succession as his bullets thud into them.

"The sixth lesson," Talby grins. "The right bullet at the right time, well aimed. Bravo, Scott, bravo! Looks like I owe you my life." Scott dismisses Talby's gratitude. "You owe me nothing, but take me along." Talby surprises Scott when he thrusts the muzzle of his gun into his chest. "Seventh lesson," Talby resumes, "When you untie a man, take his guns before that." Now, it is Scott's turn to trump Talby. "Eighth lesson," Scott smiles, "don't give a man any more bullets than he's got use for." Surprisingly, Talby's six-gun clicks on a spent cartridge. Finally, the protégé has impressed the master! Talby invites Scott to accompany him. "But don't get your hopes up too high," he advises him, "because it's a dirty life."

Talby and Scott return to Clifton. Talby ushers Scott into the general store and buys him a Colt .45 Single-Action Army revolver with a seven-and-a-half-inch barrel, along with a gun belt, holster, and three cases of .45 caliber ammunition. Actually, Talby sought more bullets, but the salesman lacked a sufficient inventory to accommodate him. This is another allusion to Clifton as a peaceful town, since nobody seems to have a reason to buy such large orders of bullets until Talby comes to town. Meanwhile, Talby teaches Scott the proper way to carry his gun. "Your belt's too high. Put the butt of your gun down by your wrist." Talby hands him a wad of cash for a new wardrobe and approaches Wild's 'clean hand' accomplices. Although he has no account at the Bank of Clifton, Talby enters the bank and converses with Turner about Wild Jack's account. He informs Turner about the deaths of Wild Jack and Bill Farrell. He also tells him about Farrell's confession with a list of his accomplices. Reluctantly, Turner forks over a thousand dollars. After Talby leaves, Turner hastens to see Judge Cutcher. Meantime, Talby visits Murray at the saloon. He blackmails him into signing away half of his interest in the Gala Saloon, making them partners. Talby inherits Wild Jack's half of the saloon. "These scales of justice will be leaning the way I tell them to and you just watch the way I tell them to." Murray is powerless to retaliate. Farrell's confession would put his head in a noose on the gallows. Talby doesn't rely on the speed and accuracy of his gun now. Since he is tangling with the honest white-collar citizen criminals who played by a different set of rules, Talby adopts those rules to dominate them as they dominated Wild Jack.

The next time we see Scott Mary, he has a new wardrobe. Meantime, word has reached the friends of the late Hart Perkins that Talby is back in Clifton. Sheriff Nigel warns Talby about their imminent arrival. Talby settles into a chair on the boardwalk to bide his time. Before he sends Scott across the street to catch Perkins's pals in a cross-fire, Talby advises him to open fire only after him. "A man on horseback has to divide his attention between his horse and his gun, so you cannot let them dismount." When Perkins' well-armed relatives—six of them--ride into Clifton, Nigel confronts them with a shotgun in his fists. The sheriff tries to avert a showdown. The leader of the bunch, Mackenzie Perkins (Mauro Mannatrizio), shoots first and nails Nigel in the thigh. Promptly, Talby empties his holster and blazes away at them. Scott hesitates, perhaps out of some shred of decency Murph Allan taught him, before he follows Talby's lead, shooting, wounding and killing their assailants. Surprisingly, Talby catches a bullet in his left shoulder. Scott wounds two of Perkins' friends and kills a third. "Four dead," Nigel announces gravely. "And two wounded. I want to know what the devil you want, Talby." Talby retorts, "I only shot after they knocked you down, Nigel." Later, as the town physician inspects the dead and the wounded, he tells an incredulous Cutcher, "You'll have to acquit him again, Judge."

After the Main Street gunfight with the Perkins clan, Scott rebukes Judge Cutcher and calls him a "bastard" twice. Scott's abuse of Cutcher shocks the town physician. He wants to know what Talby has done to Scott. "He's like some rabid wolf," the physician protests. Talby's reply is appropriately provocative. "He was born a wolf. You made him rabid, not me." Later, Abel Murray eagerly praises Scott for his swift shooting against Perkins' friends. "Good boy, Scott," the saloon man applauds him. "You're always been underestimated, and I'm the first to recognize it and ask you to excuse me." Scott ignores Abel's compliment. Nigel tries to bully Scott into relinquishing his gun and resuming his duties at Ron Miller's stable. Unfortunately, Nigel doesn't realize how irrevocable matters have become for Scott. Despite his shoulder wound, Talby is pleased with the outcome of the gunfight as well as his young apprentice's dexterity with firearms. "Scott," Talby announces triumphantly, "I think this town is ours."

Afterward, Talby learns about Scott's first surrogate father figure Murph Allan Short. Scott reacts with surprise when Talby recognizes the old sheriff. "Ran me out of town with a rifle in my back." Clearly, Talby grimaces at this humiliating incident. "It was a long time ago, but I won't forget it." Talby pauses, considers how much Scott has accomplished for him, and then ponders Murph's influence over him. "Maybe he was right. I should take your gun away and send you back to the stable." Scott frowns at this prospect. "Don't try it, Talby, it's too late." This is the first sign of hostility between them as Scott clashes with Talby. The old gunfighter relents. "Yeah, it's too late."

Vibrant Spanish Poster of Day of Anger.

Initially, when Talby rode into Clifton, he had been traveling to Bowie to collect fifty-thousand dollars from Wild Jack. After Judge Cutcher cleared him of killing Perkins in self-defense, Talby wanted nothing more than to shake the dust of Clifton. Indeed, he rushes off without a fond farewell to Scott Mary. Presumably, at this point, Talby as well as others think he will never return to Clifton. Nevertheless, fate prompted Talby to return, and the incident outside Bowie fortified the apprenticeship between Scott and Talby. Clearly, it was no mistake Talby rode into Clifton for a night's rest because it lay on his journey to Bowie. "**Day of Anger**" isn't an episodic, picaresque Spaghetti western, with carefree heroes rampaging all over the west. Comparably, it shares something in common with an empire building gangster movie. Typically, the aspiring mobster ascends to the heights of notoriety over a town before he crashes and burns from dissension within his ranks!

The first half of "**Day of Anger**" concludes with Talby gaining the upper hand. No longer must Scott kowtow to Clifton's haughty citizens. Indeed, things have come 180 degrees for the youth. He has achieved part of his dream. Now, nobody can impugn his illegitimate origins without inciting the wrath of his revolver! This moment of triumph doesn't last long, because Scott will turn against Talby after the veteran gunfighter makes the fatal mistake of murdering Murph Allan Short. Scott wants to be so much like his idol Talby that he follows the dictates of Sigmund Freud's psychoanalytic theory the Oedipus complex. Indeed, Scott has three fathers! First, there was his birth father who he never knew. Second, Murph and Talby both represent the different halves of the father figure that he cannot reconcile as one because they represent different ends on the spectrum. Ironically, when one kills the other, Scott must punish the survivor with death. Sex has no place, however, in this variation of the Oedipus complex. The values that Murph instilled in Scott are the same instincts that prompt Scott to take arms against Talby. Another way of looking at this discrepancy in his father figures is to compare Scott's predicament with a similar predicament that the traditional Hollywood western hero faces when he must choose between a good, moral woman, such as a schoolmarm and a bad, immoral woman, like a prostitute. Meantime, Clifton's leading citizens dream up a scheme to drive a wedge between Scott Mary and Talby.

At this point, it is useful to review what has occurred in "**Day of Anger**." Valerii and Gastaldi have done a splendid job of introducing characters as either heroes or villains, establishing the locale of Clifton as the arena of combat, and sowing the seeds of conflict foe the unrelenting class warfare waged by the villains against Scott as a humble sanitation worker. Ironically, Talby behaves more tolerantly to Scott's underprivileged, blue-collar status. He treats Scott with greater respect, and he provides a dimension to Scott's identity with a surname that bolsters the youth's self-confidence. Later, Scott will serve as Talby's partner until their predestined discord. Meantime, not only is Talby a formidable gunfighter, but he is the bigger fish that devours Clifton's smaller, white-collar, criminal fish. Instead of blasting his way to the top of the hierarchy with his forty-five, Talby resorts to the same methods Cutcher and company used to manipulate Wild Jack. Initially, Talby uses blackmail to keep Tanner, Cutcher, and Murray in line, before he destroys them with his gun.

The irony of this situation cannot be taken for granted! These elite role models of virtue, the cream of Clifton with their 'clean hands,' have been thriving off the ill-gotten gains they acquired after they double-crossed Wild Jack. They have abused law and order to ensure their own prosperity in Clifton, even as they have concealed their corruption. Gunshots were once a rarity in Clifton until Frank Talby appeared. Indeed, corruption in Clifton is just business as usual, until Talby returns. Now, since he knows they are bereft of virtue, Talby treats them much as they have treated poor Scott since his birth. In a sense, Talby emerges as a greater evil that eradicates a lesser evil. This Darwinian survival of the fittest is entirely appropriate for the Spaghetti western. Life is hard, brutal, and deadly. Talby himself warned Scott when the youth approached him that to live by the gun he would discover life is a dirty business.

Society in Spaghetti westerns differs from society in traditional Hollywood westerns. Spaghetti westerns rarely depict good neighbors pitching in to help one another, celebrating with Saturday night social dances, and gathering for Sunday morning worship services to warble hymns. Indeed, a church stands on main street, but no preacher is ever seen prowling the premises. Moreover, the local bordello lies within the city limits of Clifton rather than without as is usually the case in traditional Hollywood westerns. "**Day of Anger**" hypothesizes that society is susceptible to the evil that men do, and this corruption enables them to maintain their status quo power. Meantime, Talby qualifies as an anti-hero.

Typically, in the traditional Hollywood western, the hero rides into a corrupt town and liberates its citizens from the clutches of evil. Valerii and Gastaldi have subverted one of the most popular traditional Hollywood western plots about the town taming hero. "**Day of Anger**," however, is far more than just another sagebrush saga about a town tamer. Just as he sets Scott free from Clifton's social class bondage, Talby emerges as a greater force that alters the power structure. Now, Scott can enjoy his new status as an equal member of the town. Most Spaghetti westerns don't dwell this deeply on the dynamics of town politics like "**Day of Anger**." Talby and Scott as well as the Clifton syndicate circle each other warily throughout the remainder of the action. Initially, Talby had whittled them down with at least a pretense of law on his side, but he goes beyond the pale when he embarks on murder.

Meantime, Scott started out as a social pariah, the most unlikely candidate for a Spaghetti western protagonist. Talby delivered him from his pauper's destiny, and Scott achieves far more than he would have had he gone on filling the sewage barrels of his wheeled cart. Later, Scott's dream degenerates into a nightmare. Earlier, Scott is shown intervening on behalf of his friends and adversaries for their clemency. He tried to intercede for Blind Bill against Abel Murray as well as Wild Jack against Talby. As for Talby, the old gunfighter lives by the lessons with which he has indoctrinated Scott. In this respect, "**Day of Anger**" boils down to an anatomy of a gunfighter. Talby has survived as long as he has because he is a trickster. In Clint Eastwood's "**The Outlaw Josey Wales**," the eponymous hero assures his companions that a man must always have an edge over his adversaries. This same edge applies to Talby when a hired assassin, a buffalo hunter named Owen White (Benito Stefanelli), arrives in Clifton by stagecoach to challenge Talby to an atypical duel.

Before they set out to divide Talby and Scott, the city fathers try to eliminate Talby themselves. "Talby wants to become the owner of the whole town," Cutcher dreads. "And he'll succeed if we don't find a way to isolate him. Which means getting rid of Scott." The villains have imported White, who has traveled 500 miles, and offered him $10-thousand to kill Talby. Scott, Talby, and his architect are discussing Talby's plans for his new saloon when White approaches them on Main Street. "You've made yourself a lot of enemies, mister Talby," White observes as he notices Sam Corbitt's barber shop. Ominously, Corbitt himself is loading a rifle in plain sight of everybody. White glances from Corbitt to Talby. Taking White's subtle hint, Talby hurls himself face down into the street to dodge Corbitt's bullet. He kills the barber with three bullets. Later, Nigel warns Talby that White "is able to shoot ten buffalo while riding at full speed." Talby dismisses this statistic. "Nigel, the gun hasn't been invented that's going to kill me." Ultimately, what Talby doesn't know is going to be the death of him!

Naturally, Cutcher and company are furious with White for saving Talby's life. White argues he wasn't going to allow another man to thwart his chances of receiving the full amount of his contract to terminate Talby. At dawn on the following day, Talby and Scott rendezvous with White in the desert, and the buffalo hunter explains the rules of the duel. They will use muzzle loading rifles, dumping powder and shot down the barrel and then attaching a percussion cap to the nipple for the hammer to strike. They will perform this complicated procedure while riding hell-bent-for-leather astride their horses toward each other like knights in a medieval jousting tournament. Before he mounts his horse for the duel to commence, Talby slips the ball-shaped rifle bullet under his tongue. Not only is Talby able to load his rifle faster than White, because he spits the bullet down the barrel while White fumbles for his own ammo, but he discharges his weapon split-seconds before they ride past each other on their thundering horses. Earlier, Scott didn't understand why Talby accommodated White on the latter's own terms. "Ninth lesson," Talby explains. "There are times you have to accept a challenge or lose everything in life anyway. This is one of those times, but I wouldn't worry about it too much." Talby remains supremely confident about his odds of survival.

This galloping duel is picturesque, and Valerii stages it with verve. You'll have to look long and hard to find a comparable duel between equestrians as singular as this in any Spaghetti western. Afterward, Talby embarks on his own urban renewal project when he cancels his partnership with Murray. This marks Talby's change in strategy. Now, he will murder rather than blackmail his adversaries. Opening the taps on all the liquor kegs, he swamps the premises with the combustible liquid. Setting fire to the Gala Saloon is a clear case of arson, and Talby abandons Murray to die an agonizing death, wreathed in a blazing inferno.

Outside, Clifton's horse-drawn fire pumper careens to a halt in front of the Gala Saloon, and Nigel wields the water hose. Unfortunately, the saloon is fully engulfed. The entire town turns out to witness this conflagration. It isn't often either you see a fire brigade, another example of Clifton's prosperity, in a Spaghetti western. Alfio Caltabiano's **"They Still Call Me Amen"** (Oremus, Alleluia e Così Sia, 1973) is one of the few Spaghetti westerns to boast a fire brigade.

Talby names his new saloon and gambling hall after his trusty six-gun. You won't find a saloon like this in any Spaghetti western. The four stanchions supporting the façade's entrance have replicas of gigantic Colt .45 revolvers carved into them. Inside, Talby introduces a musical band with a singer like an emcee, and then invites his guests to try their luck out on his roulette wheels. Before this happens, an important scene transpires in the stable. When Scott revisits his old stomping grounds, he encounters Murph. The stableman warns Scott about Talby. "You watch out." He elaborates, "They've been saying you're faster than him. You may be faster and quicker with your eyes and hands, but in order to survive, you need something else—experience." Murph estimates Talby must be at least 45 years old, "a bad age for a gunfighter." Scott listens with narrowed eyes. "Every day you feel yourself getting slower. Your muscles still react, but your reflexes aren't as quick. Talby has done the same like a lot of others before him—he's taken a helper. Somebody young who shoots for him when things get too difficult." Murph pauses, "The day will come when you will throw too big a shadow on him. This is his last chance, his last city. Either he sets himself up here for life or he leaves his skin." The importance of a name as well as an identity crops up momentarily again in this scene. Curiously, Scott inquires of his oldest mentor, "Who are you now? Murph Allan Short or are simply plain Murph?"

Murph compares the different ways that Scott and Talby use firearms. He slides the heel of his hand along the top of the barrel, over the cylinder strap, so that his hand cocks the hammer of the revolver with each pass. Afterward, he demonstrates Talby's more efficient method of shooting. Repeatedly, Murph flicks the hammer with his thumb. He explains that Talby can discharge six shots in the same length of time Scott could fire three. If you look at the way Talby wielded his forty-five after Wild Jack's henchmen dragged him, you'll see him thumbing the hammer. "And he's more accurate," Murph adds. Again, Murph explains it's all about the firearm. Earlier, Murph had told Scott about Doc Holiday and how the notorious gambler modified his own revolver for greater speed and accuracy. Murph argues that Talby deliberately bought Scott a gun with a longer barrel, so Talby would have an advantage over him. Scott understands now why Talby removed two inches of his own gun barrel along with the muzzle sight to accelerate the speed of his draw.

Murph Allan Short is an important character. Never off-screen for long after the shootout with Perkins' friends, he serves as Scott's initial role model, though Murph wishes now he had never carved the wooden gun for Scott and showed him how to draw it so swiftly. Murph qualified as Scott's surrogate father figure before Talby came to Clifton. Clearly, Murph never took Scott as seriously as Talby did. However, Murph had been a lawman who knew the difference between good and evil, whereas Talby is just plain evil. Scott has heard enough of what Murph has warned him about, and he imagines erroneously that the former Abilene lawman wants to turn him against Talby. The last person Scott ever plans to turn against is Talby, though his mind changes after he kills two of Nigel's deputies hired to kill Talby.

"Day of Anger" doesn't let its female characters accumulate many screen minutes, but women teem on the periphery of the action. It is interesting to note in this civilized town the married women do not campaign against the prostitutes at Vivian Skills' bordello. Although she has a minor role, Gwen (Christa Linder) is the woman most sympathetic to Scott's cause and entirely without guile. She treated him with a modicum of respect early in the film because she knew him and didn't share society's contempt for his illegitimacy. Later, she warned Scott about Nigel's two gunslinging deputies--Cross and the Harmonica Kid—who were skulking around the premises. Later, she rushed to his side when the town physician treated the arm wound that he received at the mill when the emporium salesman ambushed him. Indeed, everybody in Clifton wonders if Scott's arm wound will make it impossible for him to use a gun. Fortunately, this doesn't turn out to be the case. Meanwhile, Scott has begun to question his own motives when he cuts down that pair of deputies that Nigel had hired. When Talby offers to celebrate the demise of the deputies, Scott refuses and plays the dead man's harmonica with remorse: "His songs were sad, but he knew how to play them."

The turning point in Talby's rule over Clifton occurs when Judge Cutcher hatches a devious plan to exploit Scott's infatuation with his beautiful daughter Eileen (Anna Orso) so they can turn Scott against Talby. Remember, thus far everybody Talby has killed, he has shot in self-defense until he ended his partnership with Murray. Now, Eileen lures Scott to a telegraph station outside Clifton where her father Judge Cutcher, Turner, Nigel, and Murph Allan Short await him. Before they ride off to the rendezvous, Eileen confides in Scott, "If you do what my pa says, he won't object anymore to our seeing each other." Significantly, Scott and Eileen kiss each other. This is the only time in "**Day of Anger**" that anybody indulges in a display of public affection.

During this brief meeting, all four men struggle to convince Scott that order must be restored in Clifton. "You have learned a few tricks, boy," Cutcher acknowledges Scott. "Listen, we want you to come over to our side, so we can bring some order back to Clifton. This is as much your town as ours." Scott refuses to let Cutcher deceive him. "I've known your order for more than twenty years." Scott defends Talby, describing his actions as motivated by justice. When he backs out of the meeting with his drawn revolver, Scott saunters out the door and the emporium salesman ambushes him from the concealment of a covered wagon, shooting Scott in his right arm. However, Scott manages to kill him.

Frank Talby surprises everybody with his presence. He kills Turner in cold blood while Eileen shields her father with her body. Finally, Nigel has the goods on Talby. "This time it's got nothing to do with self-defense, Talby!" He prepares to arrest Talby, and Talby submissively reverses his gun, offering the revolver butt first to Nigel as the wary lawman approaches. Suddenly, without warning, Talby flips the gun around and cuts down Nigel. Cutcher takes advantage of the situation to coddle up to Talby. "What's done inside the law is safer than what is done outside the law." The judge bows to Talby's terms and agrees he owes him the $50-thousand that Wild Jack owed Talby. "A reasonable price, but our alliance will yield twice that every month."

When Scott learns Murph has replaced Nigel as town sheriff, he cautions Talby, "In Clifton, I owe nothing to nobody, but to Murph, I'm very indebted. Of course, I'm indebted to you, too. I wouldn't want to be between two fires." Talby doesn't think Scott can take him in a gunfight.

He believes Scott would hesitate long enough for him to kill the youth. Scott warns Talby in no uncertain

EFFECTIVE IMMEDIATELY
THESE NEW MPAA RATINGS
ARE TO REPLACE THE "M" RATING
IN ALL "DAY OF ANGER"
ADVERTISING.

Top: Day of Anger was originally released in the U.S. with an "M" rating in late 1969. The "M" rating was disolved in 1970 and was changed to "GP" rating.
Middle: In the USA, Lee Van Cleef was Top-Billed and in Italy and Spain Giuliano Germma. Title credits adjusted for each.
Bottom: German Film Program

Top and Bottom: U.S. Newspaper ad, 1970, Kansas City Missouri
Middle: U.S. Newspaper ad, 1970, Philadelphia Pennsylvania; High Point, North Carolina

terms about Murph, "You do anything against Murph, it's also against me." Murph makes it harder on Talby and Scott than Nigel after he wins passage of a city-wide ordinance banning firearms in public. Informing his adversary about this new edict, Murph demands that Talby surrender his weapon. One of Talby's henchmen slips up behind Scott, holds him at gunpoint, and confiscates his six-gun so Scott cannot shoot Talby. Just as he fooled Nigel, Talby pulls a similar trick on Murph. Unbuckling his gun belt with his holstered revolver, Talby hands it toward Murph with every apparent intention of relinquishing it. At the last second, Talby fires his revolver while it is still in its holster, and Murph keels over dead from a bullet in the chest.

Escaping from Talby's henchmen, Scott rushes to the stable where Murph had stashed Doc Holiday's venerable six-shooter. Talby's gunmen search for the youth, and Scott eliminates them in individual showdowns. Significantly, one of the first enemies that Scott dispatches is Cutcher, as the evil judge tries to bushwhack him from an upstairs window. Scott drops Cutcher as effortlessly as Talby shot Corbitt. One of the coolest encounters occurs when a Talby gunman gets the drop on Scott. Holding him at gunpoint from behind, the Talby gunman orders the youth to discard his gun. Scott appears to dispose of it. What he really does, however, is flip the weapon in the air, adroitly snatching it as it falls, whirls, and plugs the unsuspecting gunman!

Finally, Talby and Scott meet for their long-awaited showdown! Shrewdly, Talby has positioned himself so the sun glints in Scott's eyes, another example of an edge Talby gains over his adversary. Scott isn't impressed. "I don't believe your tricks will be enough," he retorts. "If I was alone," Scott explains, "maybe you could have done it. But not against me and Murph. Now, I've got a pistol equal to yours. Sight missing, calibrated perfectly." Of course, Scott is bragging about Doc Holiday's pistol. Metaphorically, this revolver roughly amounts to the equivalent of King Arthur's legendary sword Excalibur.
Talby prepares for what he believes will be inevitable. "Your last lesson, Scotty. When you start killing, you cannot stop it." Unlike Sergio Leone, Valerii doesn't let the two antagonists stare at each other for an eternity before one decides to draw. Surprise of surprises, Scott beats Talby on the draw, and the veteran gunfighter crumples on his stomach in the street. As Scott approaches his master, Talby violates his own first rule. He pleads for his horse so he can leave Clifton. Actually, not only does Talby sound convincing, but he also behaves unusually contrite. "You know," Scott mentions, "I'd be stupid to help you. I've learned your lessons like a good boy." Indeed, during his earlier gunfights with Talby's gunslingers, Scott had recited a lesson to each killing. "When a man has been wounded, you've got to end it. Or it may be that later he might kill you." Scott finishes Talby off with a bullet in the head.

Hurling his gun away in disgust, he smashes a window with it. He walks arm in arm with Blind Bill as "**Day of Anger**" concludes, after one hour and fifty-three minutes, without a single second squandered! Tiresome as this synopsis may seem, it illustrates beyond a doubt that Tonino Valerii and Ernesto Gastaldi created a genuine Spaghetti western classic with "**Day of Anger**." Literate, complexly-plotted, imaginatively-helmed, with an ideal cast, "**Day of Anger**" lives up to its wrathful title. Valerii and Gastaldi chronicled virtually every known western gunfighter secret. None of the scenes wallow in exposition. Every character has a reason that rationalizes their behavior, and the dialogue is rarely garrulous. While he confines his gunplay within the letter of the law, Talby remains immune from prosecution, but his empire crumbles after he crosses the line and slaughters Tanner, Nigel, and Murph, all in cold blood. Ultimately, Scott rebels against him after Talby murders Murph. Altogether, a morality tale about greed, corruption, class warfare, and authority, "**Day of Anger**" winds down on a less than heroic note. Scott doesn't toast his triumph with Blind Bill after he guns down Talby. Staggering away with each other, Scott and Blind Bill are presumably bound for a more rewarding future. Most Spaghetti westerns conclude on a triumphant note for the hero, but this isn't the case with "**Day of Anger**." The lingering question is did Scott shirk his responsibility at fadeout? When he renounced the way of the gun, did he renounce its use or its abuse? Could he have taken over as town sheriff once Cutcher, Tanner, Murray, and Nigel were dead and charted a new path for Clifton?

"**Day of Anger**" ends with cynicism similar to the town sheriff's action in "**High Noon**" when he pitched his star in the dust. The ultimate tragedy here is Scott's belief from the beginning that he could compensate for his illegitimate birth by using a gun to reprimand his enemies. None of Scott's three fathers have done him any favors. Scott's first father abandoned him without a qualm. Murph set Scott on the path to becoming a gunfighter, and Talby taught him how to survive in a morally corrupt world. Ultimately, from the beginning, Scott's thinking was inherently flawed, but the repercussions toppled a crooked cabal of prominent citizens who would have remained in power had he not chosen his ill-fated path.

End Notes

1. Roberto Curti, *Tonino Valerii: His Films,* with a foreword by Sir Christopher Frayling and an afterword by Enresto Gastaldi (North Carolina, McFarland & Company, Inc., Publishers, 2016). Curti's book is an invaluable reference guide and biography of Valerii that no genuine Spaghetti western scholar should be without.
2. Leonard Maltin, *Leonard Maltin's 2009 Movie Guide* (New York, Signet Books, 2009), 322.
3. Mike Malloy, *Lee Van Cleef: A Biographical, Film and Television Reference* (North Carolina, McFarland & Company, Inc., Publishers, 1998), 62. Despite our divergent opinions about "Day of Anger," any die-hard Lee Van Cleef aficionado will do well to peruse Malloy's informative text.
4. Leonard Maltin, *Leonard Maltin's 2009 Movie Guide* (New York, Signet Books, 2009), 322.
5. Phil Hardy, *The Western: The Film Encyclopedia* (New York, William Morrow and Company, Inc, 1983), 301.
6. D. Richard Baer, ed., *The Film Buff's Bible of Motion Pictures, 1915-1972* (Hollywood: Hollywood Film Archive, 1972), 32.
7. Roger Greenspun, review of Day of Anger, directed by Tonino Valerii. *New York Times,* (December 5, 1970).
8. Roberto Curti, Tonino Valerii, 39-40.
9. Howard Hughes, *Once Upon A Time in the Italian West* (London & New York: I.B. Tauris, 2004),186. Hughes' book is another work of scholarship that the conscientious Spaghetti western aficionado should have at their disposal, too.
10. Although I own a copy of this western and have seen it repeatedly, my editor Mike Hauss had to point out to me the resemblance between the two characters. Thanks, Mike!

Japanese Poster of Day of Anger

Wild East Productions: The Spaghetti Western Collection - Volume 64

In the 64th installment of their superlative "Spaghetti Western Collection", Wild East brings us a double-bill with the common theme of featuring the obscure Steven Tedd in the lead roles.

In **Thou Shalt Not Kill** (Quinto: non ammazzare, Italy, Spain, 1969) a loosely-assembled group of bank robbers take over an isolated stagecoach stop to hideout following a heist. Their bags of stolen money, however, have disappeared in the chaos following the robbery and the gang members begin to accuse one another of absconding with the money (Morphing the film into a whodunit, of sorts) as alliances and loyalties among the bandits take some surprising twists and turns. Among the civilians being held hostage at the locale are a few prostitutes, the saloon owner and a naïve young traveler, Bill, as played by Tedd. Bill, it turns out, is timid to the point of shaking like a Don Knotts character at the first sign of trouble. "I'm no fighter, I'm against guns," he explains. The bandits have some time to kill, waiting on a couple more of their squad to arrive, and one of them, "Sucre," takes sympathy on Bill and gives him some personal lessons to "toughen him up,"

Though he's introduced as a secondary character, "Sucre" (German Cobos) emerges as, arguably, the star of the film. His progression from "third cowboy on the right" to the co-protagonist makes for an unexpected plot turn in the well-crafted screenplay. Sucre totes a guitar throughout the film and even croons a couple of verses of the theme song while relaxing in bed. Actress Sarah Ross also makes an impression as Eliana, who uses her sex appeal to manipulate a number of her male cohorts. With her sweeping red hair and alluring eyes, she bears more than a passing resemblance to a 60's-era Ann Margret.

The overall production values are solid; Piero Umiliani's score complements the proceedings nicely and "Quintana", as vocalized by Peter Tevis, is a pleasant theme song. The cinematography by Giuseppe La Torre is good, and makeup artist Duilio Giustini provides a couple of bloody effects to complement the action.

Director Leon Klimovsky began making movies in his native Argentina before relocating to Spain in the 1950's, ultimately directing 75 features over his 30-year career (1948-1978). He's probably best-remembered for his horror films, most-notably a series of cult-favorites with actor/writer Jacinto Molina (i.e. Paul Naschy, "The Spanish Lon Chaney") including the self-explanatory **The Werewolf Versus the Vampire Woman** (La noche de Walpurgis, Spain West Germany, 1971)

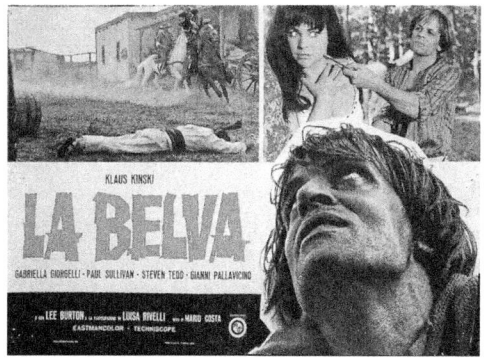

Page 102: Wild East Productions Volume #64. Spaghetti Western Collections.
Page 103:
Top: Quinto aka Thou Shall Not Kill- Italian Poster.
Bottom: The Beast- Italian fotobusta.

and **Dr. Jekyll Versus The Werewolf** (Doctor Jekyll y el Hombre Lobo, Spain, 1972), and also the George Romero-esque **The People Who Own the Dark** (Ultimo deseo, Spain, 1976). Klimovsky also directed eleven other westerns, including a couple from early in the cycle, **Torrejon City** (Spain, 1962) and **Fura de la ley** (Spain, 1964).

The second feature, **The Beast** (La Belva, Italy, 1970) tells the story of a peasant, Ricardo (Tedd), who longs to provide for his hard-working girlfriend, "Juanita" (Gabriella Giorgelli) and decides that that taking part in a kidnapping/extortion scheme can be their ticket to the good life. Klaus Kinski plays "Crazy" Johnny Laster, one of the crooks that Ricardo must align himself with. "If he couldn't be trusted, I wouldn't have brought him here," says a co-conspirator (Paolo Casella), referring to Laster, in a statement that will have the audience scratching their heads; Whether he's getting caught cheating at poker , killing hostages required to be kept alive or clumsily manhandling (and repulsing) every woman he comes into contact with, Laster appears to be a character with the unique ability to screw up everything he touches. Assuming that he's in fact the titular character, one might wonder why the film wasn't instead titled "The Bungler."

Ostensibly, the audience is expected to sympathize with Ricardo, although he appears to enjoy taking part in a felony-level crime which includes the aforementioned kidnapping and the threatening (at gunpoint) of law-abiding citizens. He's not a "hero," by any stretch, but he's not really an "anti-hero" either. He's simply another among the film's poorly-defined characters in a disjointed screenplay rife with awkward dialogue where characters have to explain the confusing plot (The term "basal exposition" comes to mind). Jarring shifts in tone also hamper the movie, including a painfully awkward attempt at pathos in the final act.

Despite its shortcomings, **The Beast** does have a couple of redeeming qualities; Stelvio Cipriani's score is quite good, although mostly cues recycled from **The Stranger Returns** (Un uomo, un cavallo, una pistola, Italy, West Germany, United States, 1967). Also, Kinski chews up the scenery (as usual) in a role patterned after his alleged real-life persona; Namely that of a man who can't control his primal urges and emotions. Accordingly, fans of Kinski and his trademark histrionics will not be disappointed.

The film was the final directing (and writing) effort from Mario Costa, whose lengthy career (1946-1970) included 33 feature films of various genres. He directed only one other western was **Buffalo Bill, Hero of the West** (Buffalo Bill, l'eroe del far west, Italy, France, West Germany, 1964), an entertaining film patterned after "big" Hollywood westerns with large-scale "Cowboys vs. Indians" battle scenes and a prototypical hero played by former-Tarzan actor Gordon Scott.

Appearing very Elvis-like with his black hair and sideburns, Steven Tedd makes for an offbeat leading man. He appeared in 12 movies over a brief career (1968-1973). His other westerns included the Klimovsky-directed **Reverend's Colt** (Reverendo Colt, Spain, 1970) in a primarily "love-interest" bit-part, the mean-spirited **Requiem for a Bounty Hunter/Death Played the Flute** (Lo ammazzò come un cane... ma lui rideva ancoraunter, Italy, 1972) as a flute-toting gunman, "Whistler," clearly patterned after Charles Bronson's "Harmonica," and **You are a Traitor and I'll Kill You!** (Una cuerda al amanecer, Spain, Italy, 1972) wherein he co-starred with Piere Brice and Fernando Sancho. His first film appearance was in the nudie **Guess Who's Coming for Breakfast** (Die Nichten der Frau Oberst, West Germany, Switzerland, Italy, 1968) as a young Italian lover - A role with no dialogue but a good deal of bare-naked action. Perhaps he was then typecast, because the balance of his non-western films would all be "adult-themed" comedies and dramas, including Lesbo (Italy, 1969) – directed by Edoardo Mulargia, **Revelations of a Psychiatrist on the World of Sexual Perversion** (Rivelazioni di uno psichiatra sul mondo perverso del sesso, Italy, 1973) and the psycho-sexual potboiler La casa delle mele mature (Italy, 1971). His final film was **The Lonely Woman** (No encontré rosas para mi madre, Spain, France, Italy, 1973) starring Gina Lollobrigida. An unconfirmed report indicates that Steven Tedd passed away circa 2000.

As typical of Wild East DVDs, a great deal of care and effort is evidenced in the final product. The extras include an assemblage of international VHS covers, posters, lobby cards and press-kits. The overall picture and sound quality of both features is exceptional, as well, especially in consideration of the obscure nature of the films and the relative scarcity of available prints.

-Steve Mason

** All photos except for the Star-Cine Aventures panels, courtesy of Eric Mache

Random panels from Star-Cine Aventures. This October 1972 issue features Thou Shall Not Kill. Star-Cine was a french magazine. The magazine would use blown up portions of a film to tell its story.

Italian Posters for Thou Shall Not Kill and The Beast

Notes

"Steven Tedd" was born as Giuseppe Cardillo. Apparently, he was sometimes also credited as "Pippo Cardillo."

Cobos appeared in over 120 films, including the westerns **Massacre at Fort Grant** (Fuerte perdido, Spain, 1964) and **Reverend's Colt** (Reverendo Colt, Spain, Italy, 1970).

The screenplay is credited to Manuel Martínez Remís and Dino de Rugieriis. Remis also scripted Il magnifico Texano (Italy, Spain, 1967) and Reverend's Colt.

Tedd's character in The Beast is dubbed by the same actor that voiced-over for Giuliano Gemma in most of his westerns.

Cheating at poker in the actual historic American West was an offense punishable by serious (often fatal) consequences (legal or otherwise), though in the context of the film the indiscretion is simply brushed-off. In a second implausible situation (within the same day nonetheless), Laster is thwarted from attempting to rape a woman by a tough-looking man wielding a gun (presumably her husband) and allowed to simply walk away unharmed.

Costa directed Buffalo Bill under the pseudonym "John W. Fordson" in an obvious nod to John Ford. The film, imitative of many of Ford's westerns in style, is clearly a further tribute to the legendary director in and of itself.

I've been informed that Tedd also worked as a photo-novel model.

There is some question as to whether Klimovsky actually directed **Reverend's Colt**. Richard Harrison, in an interview with Tom Betts and William Connolly, stated that Marino Girolami was the actual director. A note in the Internet Movie Database attributes the Klimovsky/Girolami switch to "funding reasons."

The plot of **Death Played the Flute** is also lifted from another film, **Death Rides a Horse** (Da uomo a uomo, Italy, 1967)

The lurid proceedings of **Guess Who's Coming for Breakfast** are presented under the guise of being based on a Guy de Maupassant story.

Thomas Weisser, in his 1992 reference book "*Spaghetti Westerns – the Good the Bad and the Violent*" refers to Thou Shalt Not Kill ("Quinta") as being a "lost" film.

Italian Lobby Cards - Thou Shall Not Kill

mondo-macabro.com

THE WILD SIDE OF WORLD CINEMA

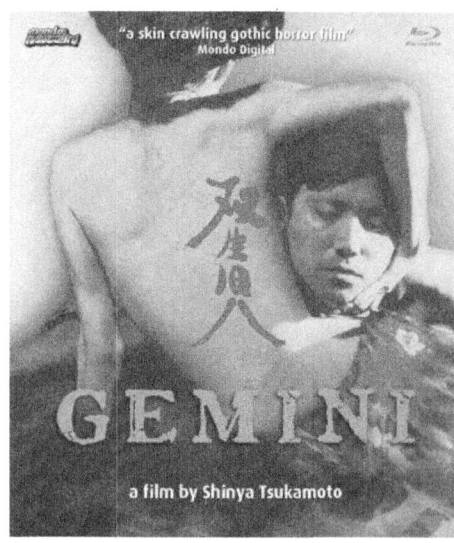

GLENN SAXSON
Interview

INTERVIEWED BY RENE HOGGUER

Recently a Dutch morning paper ran an article about the Dutch actor Roel Bos. This name won't ring a bell with any of you, but the article went on to state that he used the name Glenn Saxson in Italian films. We're all familiar, of course, with his DJANGO SHOOTS FIRST (DJANGO SPARA PER PRIMO).

I didn't hesitate to phone his agency to ask for an interview with this fellow Dutchman who could tell me much about working in Italian Westerns. I was allowed to interview him for 30 minutes.

The interview took place in the Hotel Bell Air in the Hauque in October 1991. My wife Barbara and I arrived a little earlier than Glenn, so we decorated the table with three issues of **Westerns... All'Italiana!** and the video jacket for DJANGO SHOOTS FIRST. Glenn greeted us and took a seat.

G = Glenn Saxson
B = Barbara
R = Rene

G: Yeah, I saw DJANGO SHOOTS FIRST in a video store here in Holland. I didn't really have the time to watch my movies in the cinema when they were released because at the time I was already on another location to shoot another movie. I'd go to Africa or somewhere else, and when I'd come back the movie wouldn't be in circulation anymore.

R: When were you born?

G: March 5, 1942, in Scheveningen, Holland. (He picks up a copy of WAI!)

R: Even though the Italian Western genre has been dead for years there are still many fans worldwide who've come together through this magazine.

G: (He looks at WAI! #30 with George

Glenn Saxson meets WAI correspondent Rene Hogguer.

Hilton on the cover) I know George well. He is South American, from Argentina. He has lived in Italy for a very long time. (Still browsing) Peter Lee Lawrence came from Austria and died, unfortunately, a couple of years ago. He had a brain tumor.

R: Did you know Klaus Kinski too?

G: Yes, Klaus is crazy.

R: How old were you when you went to Italy?

G: I went in 1964, so I was 22 years old.

R: What made you go there?

G: I had just finished acting school and met a girl who later became my wife. I had read an article about

---

With the legendary Spaghetti Western expert Tom Betts' approval, we will try and bring to each issue an interview that originally ran in Tom's long runiing 'zine Westerns All'Italiana!. In this issue, as you can see above, we are including an Interview with the Dutch actor Glenn Saxson that appeared in issue #38 from 1998,, conducted by Rene Hogguer. In fact it was Rene's idea to run this interview here in the pages of the Spaghetti Western Digest and much thanks is owned to Rene and of course Tom!. Plus Two bonus Retro-reviews from Eric Mache.

Retro Interview: Glenn Saxson

her in the newspaper. She was a Dutch girl who had a role in a Lebanese movie. She came to Holland to do a TV commercial that I also had a part in. During that period I didn't earn much. I could get a contract for a month and with that paycheck I could just pay my rent, with nothing left over for food. She advised me to drop stage plays and go into movies. I said, "OK, let's go to Beirut." She said, "No, the big center at the moment is Rome..." So with a few things we had and very little money (about $600 U.S.) we went to Rome.

R: Glenn Saxson became your acting name.

G: Yes. It was given to me by the producer of my first movie. He had no comprehension of Dutch names. My full name is Roel Eckard Bos and that didn't sound American enough. At that time it all had to sound American. Giuliano Gemma later took back his real name and didn't go on being Montgomery Wood. Actually it was ridiculous since the audience could see very well that the Italian Westerns were technically much better than the American ones.

R: Did the producer have a specific

reason for giving you that name?

G: No, he suggested Sean Jackson, but I didn't like that. Later we agreed on Glenn Saxson. And now 15 years later everybody in Italy still calls me Glenn Saxson.

R: What was the first Western you made in Italy?

G: VAYA CON DIOS GRINGO (GOOD LUCK GRINGO). That was a movie shot on a very low budget. It was my first important role. Before that I had a small role in a Lex Barker film (24 HOURS TO KILL). The funny thing about VAYA CON DIOS GRINGO was because it was made with so little money, they had to use all unknown actors. In the screen test I had said my mother came from Texas. That wasn't true, both my parents came from Holland. I had said it so there wouldn't be any doubt about my riding abilities. In truth, I had never ridden a horse before. I knew that shooting would start in only a few days with two other actors, and they couldn't ride horses either. So I tried to learn in 1½ days and, of course, it didn't work out. On the day shooting started I had muscular pains everywhere. The director saw very quickly that there were three lumps on horseback! Then came the great improvisation gift of the Italians and he suddenly came up with the idea that we wouldn't ride horses at all. In the movie we sit in an open stolen stagecoach pulled by four horses.

R: That was a good solution.

G: Perfect! Another strange problem the movie had was that one actor, I believe his name was Lino Desmond, could not act for anything. He was so bad... the director ordered him to count to ten each time so that his lips moved for dubbing later. The problem with Lino was that he started counting at all the wrong times. The producer saw that we were doing retake after retake and he became so mad that he kicked Lino off the set. But there were still 10 or 12 shots to be done with Lino... so the funny thing was that the producer put on Lino's clothes and he played the scenes. Of course, you

Retro Interview: Glenn Saxson

only see "Lino" in those shots from the back. Nobody would have noticed it, except for his mother.

B: Now you can ride a horse?

G: Yes, and I was lucky I never fell off my horse in the movies. Years later there was a series of Westerns on TV and next to my house was a stable. The owner worked with socially difficult youth and asked me if I was willing to ride a horse for them. He said that they knew me and he would supply me with boots and a hat. So that afternoon there were at least 20 boys who came to see my riding abilities and wanted my autograph. As destiny would have it, my horse stepped on a hornets nest and threw me off! The boys couldn't believe their eyes - the hero never falls off his horse. So most of them never asked for my autograph that day.

R: Your second Western was DJANGO SHOOTS FIRST.

G: DJANGO SHOOTS FIRST was the most exhausting movie I ever made.

R: There was a lot of action in it.

G: I worked every day and when I had a free day we did night shots. All in all it took 8 weeks. It was a very heavy schedule.

R: The Django you played did not have the real Django character.

G: No, this was one of the first times comedy was used in the Italian Western. Until then the films were hard. Women also played a key part in this film.

The cast and artwork for DJANGO SHOOTS FIRST grace the Dutch video cover for DON'T WAIT DJANGO, SHOOT!

Westerns All'Italiana

Retro Interview: Glenn Saxson

R: So comedy was the movie's main point of view?

G: Yes. I also remember that little tuft of blond hair came out from under my hat. The movie was a big success in Italy. It became Campione dell Casso when it was released just as **VAYA CON DIOS GRINGO** did.

R: **DJANGO SHOOTS FIRST** was directed by Albert de Martino. How was it to work with him?

G: Albert cared more for action and less for the actors. He found the fights in the saloon of more importance than the dialogue. So that was a disadvantage for him. On the other hand he was able to guide the movie in a competent way from beginning to end. But he isn't my favorite director.

R: You starred with Fernando Sancho in **DJANGO SHOOTS FIRST**...

G: He made an awful lot of Westerns.

R: Did you know he died recently?

G: No, I did not. He was a very kind person. He took me to the bullfights for the first time. I didn't like it much.

R: How was it to work with him?

G: Nice, because he was an experienced Western actor, and I had only made one to that point. Yes, he was a very nice guy with whom you could laugh a lot.

R: How many Westerns did you do?

G: Five, and then I got sick of them. After **DJANGO SHOOTS FIRST** I made **IL MAGNIFICO TEXICANO**, then **CAROGNA SI NASCE**, and then the last one was **IL LUNGO GIORNO DELLA MASSACRO** with Peter Martell.

R: In **LYNCHING (CAROGNA SI NASCE)** you played with Gordon Mitchell.

G: I think Gordon and I were some of the few who stayed in Rome. All the other guys went back. I haven't seen Gordon in years, but he's a very nice guy. The opposite of the hard "mask" he wears.

R: He has a <u>very</u> hard face!

G: Yes, but a great heart.
Do you know Peter Martell?

R: Yes, sure.

Glenn Saxson in CAROGNE SI NASCE.

Retro Interview: Glenn Saxson

G: Well, here's a funny story about him. Peter missed his BIG moment in his career due to a crazy succession of circumstances which led to another man becoming a star. It was all because of a little accident Peter had. It was around '65 or '66, and all the actors were busy making Westerns. Peter was supposed to do a Western which I believe was titled THE CAT, THE WOLF, AND THE DOG.

Well, funny enough, although for him it was a disaster, the evening before the shooting started he got into an argument with his girlfriend and got so mad that he tried to kick her with his foot (typical western style), but he missed her, kicked his iron bed, and broke his leg. The movie was completely organized and ready to start. The producer called every Western actor to see if anyone else was available but nobody was. He became desperate and said, "I don't care who we get as long as he has blond hair, blue eyes and must be able to ride a horse. That's the minimum." Somebody said he knew an actor like that who had only done figurative roles and some bit parts. That was Mario Girotti.

R: Terence Hill.

G: That movie was not called THE CAT, THE WOLF, AND THE DOG but GOD FORGIVES... I DON'T! It was a big box-office success and it was the first big success for Terence Hill.

R: Together with Bud Spencer.

G: It was one of the first times the Italians brought a lot of comedy into the Western. DJANGO SHOOTS FIRST also had a little. Well, we all know what Terence Hill did after that, and Peter Martell failed ignominously. He is now blind in one eye, lives very sadly, and tried to commit suicide once.

B: In THE MAGNIFICENT TEXAN you played a masked hero.

G: Yes, it was kind of a Zorro idea.

R: Did anyone in particular influence you in the Western?

G: No, but before I started I had seen a movie by Sergio Leone. I admired the way he made his movies. He was the first one with those magnificent close-ups and who visualized so many details. In this way he brought more action into the Western. If you compare his Westerns with the American ones, the American ones are quite boring. His contribution was enormous and undoubtedly many American directors adopted his style. And, of course, the music played an important role.

R: How many movies did you make in all?

G: About 16. I just finished the TV series PIAZZE DI SPANJA in Italy. Now I am working in Holland in the TV series DE DAGERAAD and TAKE-OFF.

R: Looking back on your career were you satisfied with all the roles you did?

G: In the beginning I did everything. Every role meant money and I couldn't be choosy. Later I could adjust scripts, but it was hard to avoid being type-cast. I always had

Retro Interview: Glenn Saxson

to play the hero. Now I can finally get roles that have more character. I was so sick of the type-casting that I decided to produce. That was in the period from '74 to '83. Many of my films were shown in festivals all over the world. I made movies with little manpower - movies on a low budget, but with profound stories. They received fantastic criticism and I was very proud, since as a producer the films are a little like your own babies.

R: Did you win any prizes?

G: In Cannes **SA PROVITA** won the "Prix Cretia". The movie tells the story of a parasite who lives on dead bodies. Another, a very controversial movie in Italy modeled after **LA DOLCE VITA** by Fellini, was called **A VIRGIN NAMED MARIAN**. With that movie I learned how great the influence of the Vatican can be. Even in the House of Parliament questions were asked about this movie, but to our advantage. They wanted to know why the Vatican was trying to ban this movie. It is a

magnificent movie, but due to Vatican resistance the movie came into circulation months later under a different title. The movie got incredibly good reviews.

R: The Western has died in the cinema for a long time now.

G: They still try to resurrect it - **DJANGO STRIKES AGAIN** and now **DANCES WITH WOLVES**. It's a cycle. Who knows, maybe the epic movies will come back again. The Westerns, however, will never come back in the way they were made at the high point in Italy.

R: Glenn, I thank you kindly for the interview.

G: It was nice to talk with a Western fan, and I'd be happy to receive some **Westerns... All'Italiana**'s!

The interview lasted over an hour. It went very smoothly since we could both speak our native Dutch language. Video sleeves were autographed and pictures were taken. Thank you Glenn.

Westerns All'Italiana

Retro Interview: Glenn Saxson

Westerns All' Italiana

GLENN SAXSON
Filmography

1966 - "GOOD LUCK GRINGO" (English Title)
"VAYAS CON DIOS GRINGO" (Italian Title)
"DIEU EST AVEC TOI, GRINGO (French Title)
Production: CIO Film and International Production SAP
Director: Edward G. Muller (Eduardo Mulargia)
Screenplay: Glenn Vincent Davis, Edward G. Muller
Photography: Renato Doria
Music: Felice DiStefano
Cast: Glenn Saxson, Lucretia Love, Pedro Sanchez, Aldo Berti, Livio Lorenzon.

1966 - "DJANGO SHOOTS FIRST" (English Title)
"DJANGO SPARA PER PRIMO" (Italian Title)
"DJANGO TIRE LE PREMIER" (French Title)
"DJANGO NUR DER COLT WAR SEIN FREUND" (German Title)
Production: Fida Cinematografia (Rome)
Director: Alberto De Martino
Screenplay: Continenza , Capriccioli, Carpi, Flamini, Simonelli, De Martino.
Cameraman: Riccardo Pallottino
Music: Bruno Nicolai
Cast: Glenn Saxson, Fernando Sancho, Evelyn Stewart, Nando Gazzolo, Erika Blanc, Lee Burton.

1967 - "THE MAGNIFICENT TEXAN" (English Title)
"IL MAGNIFICO TEXANO" (Italian Title)
" TEXAN LE MAGNIFIQUE" (French Title)
"DIEZ HORCAS PARA UN PISTOLERO" (Spanish Title)
Production: Selenia Cinematografica (Rome), R.M. Films (Spain)
Director: Lewis King (Luigi Capuana)
Screenplay: Robert Keaton, Lewis King
Photography: Pablo Ripoll
Music: Francesco DeMasi
Cast: Glenn Saxson, John Barracuda, Barbara Loy, George Greenwood, Louis Induni.

1968 - "LYNCHING" (English Title)
"CAROGNE SI NASCE" (Italian Title)
"WER EIN HUNDSFOTT IST, KOMMT ALS SOLCHER ZUR WELT" (German)
Production: Sipal Cinematografica
Director: Al Bradley (Alfonso Brescia)
Screenplay: Lado, Finocchi
Music: Coriolano Gori
Cast: Glenn Saxson, Gordon Mitchell, Maria Vittoria Bardanzellu, Phillipe Hersent, Renato Baldini, Giovanni Pazzafini.

(continued)

1968 - "THE LONG DAY OF THE MASSACRE" (English Title)
"IL LUNGO GIORNO DEL MASSACRO" (Italian Title)
"MASSACRE POUR UN SHERIF" (French Title)
"DAS GESETZ DER ERBARMUNGSLOSEN" (German Title)
Production: Boston Cinematografica
Director: Albert Cardiff (Alberto Cardone)
Screenplay: Alberto Cardone
Music: Michele Lacarenza
Cast: Peter Martell, Glenn Saxson, Manuel Serrano, Liz Barrett.

GLENN SAXSON REVIEWS

VAYAS CON DIOS GRINGO

VAYA CON DIOS GRINGO (1966- Italy)
Director: Edward G. Muller.

Director Muller makes the most of an obviously low budget in this unpretentious actioner. Gringo (Glenn Saxson) is out to avenge his brother's murder by the Criss Brothers. The murder is shown in a great pre-credit sequence that mixes terrific music by Felice Di Stefano with dramatic violence.

Gringo and his side kick Mexico (Pedro Sanchez) escape from a Wichita jail in a stagecoach along with a murderous band that includes Dean Stratford and Aldo Berti. The episodic, free-wheeling plot follows the band as they kill, steal railroad funds and kidnap a Mexican girl, Carmen. They double-cross each other until only Gringo, Mexico and Carmen are left. They return to Wichita and Gringo faces the Criss Brothers for the climactic showdown.

Stratford and Berti are excellent as the totally unprincipled bandits. Saxson, to his benefit, is a bit scruffier than usual. VAYA CON DIOS GRINGO is a notch above average; a fast-paced, straight forward western that is worth checking out.

Thanks to Rene Hogguer for providing a letter-boxed English language t.v. version under the title, GOOD LUCK GRINGO.

- Eric Maché

WAI Rating: 3 Pistols

Westerns All' Italiana

GLENN SAXSON REVIEWS

IL LUNGO GIORNO DEL MASSACRO

IL LUNGO GIORNO DEL MASSACRO (1968- Italy)
D: Albert Cardiff.

Director Cardiff is responsible for several fine examples of the Italian Western genre such as $7 TO KILL and BLOOD AT SUNDOWN and he does not let audiences down with this one. Joe Williams (Peter Martell) is an ex-sheriff unjustly accused of murder. He tracks down the real killer, a Mexican bandit called "La Muerte." The new sheriff (Glenn Saxson) is also hot on the trail. There is a great massacre sequence as Saxson's men surround the Mexican bandits. Acknowledging Joe's innocence, the sheriff lets him escape.

This well-photographed film is ultra widescreen and needs more severe letterboxing than is offered on the German cassette. Although the plot is fairly routine, the solid score by Lacarenza, the great-looking women and plentiful action make for an enjoyable film. The film's originality allows for Martell to be captured by the Mexicans with bolos. Peter Martell, who subsequently acted in some dismal comedic westerns (PATIENCE HAS A LIMIT... WE DON'T, HIS NAME WAS POT), acts too serious and comes off zombie-like. Saxson's performance is superior despite his clean-cut Glen Campbell image.

In his controversial book, author Tom Weisser claims this film to be "lost!" The excellent quality PAL German cassette, DAS GESETZ DER ERBARMUNGSLOSEN has been available on the American Video label for many years. The only thing "lost" is the enticing nude scene promised on the video sleeve cover that does not appear in the film!

— Eric Maché

WAI Rating: $2\frac{1}{2}$ Pistols

Tom Betts has a look at 1966, the most pivotal year of the spaghetti westerns. The year of heightened social unrest throughout the world, the Spaghetti westerns are hot! And Django!

1966, The Spaghetti Western becomes estab lished! Or when Django became Unchained!

If we look back at 1964 and **A Fistful of Dollars** as the beginning of what most of us consider the Spaghetti Western, then 1965 was the year of trial and error when the Italian, Spanish and German directors, and writers were trying out formulas and ingredients that would result in box office hits. Many of these filmmakers grew up watching American westerns but had never attempted to make one because it was not a native genre to their particular countries. With Sergio Leone's international success, it opened up the door for them to try out stories and characters based on the American hero and the new anti-hero. In 1966 we saw the rise of directors such as the Spanish Marchent brothers, Roberto Bianchi, Alberto Cardone, Michaele Lupo, Harald Reinl, Duccio Tessari, Ignacio Iquino, Sergio Bergonzelli, Giorgio Ferroni, Giorgio Simonelli, Mateo Cano, Joaquín Luis Romero Marchent, Alberto De Martino and several others.

That same year we started to see a developed theme of a strong western hero usually out for revenge or standing up to evil land barons and town bosses defending settlers or downtrodden widows. He usually had a unique wardrobe and used gimmicks in the way of weapons and tricks to outsmart his opponents, whatever the odds. Sometimes he had an accomplice but never a sidekick as in the old B westerns of the U.S. Whatever he did, he was usually thinking of himself first and in self-preservation and maybe making some money. Bounty hunters became respected heroes along with gunfighters. He liked women, but they had their time and place.

New heroes now emerged, such as Django, Ringo, "The Stranger," and other characters that would find themselves resurrected in future films even though the actors would change the character remained the same, at least in name.

Some of the genre's biggest and most remembered films were released in 1966 such as **Django** (Italy, Spain, 1966), **The Good, the Bad and the Ugly** (Il buono, il brutto, il cattivo, Italy, Spain, W. Germany), **7 Guns for the MacGregors** (7 pistole per i MacGregor, Italy, Spain), **Ringo and His Golden Pistol** (Johnny Oro, Italy), **Johnny Yuma** (Italy), **Massacre Time** (Le colt cantarono la morte e fu... tempo di massacre, Italy), **Texas, Adios** (Texas, Addio, Italy, Spain), **Navajo Joe** (Italy, Spain), **The Ugly Ones** (El precio de un hombre: **The Bounty Killer,** Spain, Italy), **A Bullet for the General** (Quién sabe?, Italy), **My Name is Pecos** (2 once di piombo, Italy), **Sugar Colt** (Italy, Spain), **Yankee** (Italy, Spain), **Taste of Killing** (Per il gusto di uccidere, Spain, Italy), **Arizona Colt** (Italy, France), **Fort Yuma Gold** (Per pochi dollari ancora, Italy, France, Spain), **El Rojo** (Italy, Spain), **Django Shoots First** (Django spara per primo, Italy), **A Gunman Called Nebraska** (Ringo del Nebraska, Italy, Spain), **$1,000 on the Black** (1000 dollari sul nero, Italy, W. Germany) and **The Hills Run Red** (Un fiume di dollari, Italy).

Western stars were born or solidified themselves as heroes in 1966, such as Franco Nero, Giuliano Gemma using his real name, Gianni Garko, Hunt Powers, George Eastman, Richard Harrison, Craig Hill, Glenn Saxson, Tomas Milian and Robert Woods. These names would go on for several years to come, to become several became icons of the genre.

We also saw several actresses establish themselves as leading ladies of the genre. Evelyn Stewart, Chelo Alonso, Loredana Nusciak, Rada Rassimov, Agata Flori, Giulia Rubini, Rosalba Neri, Elisa Montés, Nieves Navarro and Nicoletta Machiavelli.

The supporting actors were becoming regulars of the genre and would be as recognizable as the stars, and often in smaller budgeted films, they became bigger names than the lead actors. Actors like Frank Brana, Fernando Sancho, Luigi Pistilli, Livio Lornezon, and Benito Stefanelli became fan favorites still remembered fondly today. 1966 was the year the Spaghetti western became a reliable member of the International film industry. So much so, that big-name Hollywood actors were now approachable. And some were even asking to be in the new genre. Names like Burt Reynolds, Henry Silva, Guy Madison, Mark Damon became active in the genre. Simultaneously, others like Yul Brynner, Jack Palance Gilbert Roland, and Woody Strode became approachable and would travel across the Atlantic to become stars and keep their careers going in the years to come. Although their careers may have been on the downside in the U.S., they were stars in Europe, and they were treated as such, and their names still sold tickets.

The genre may still have been looked down upon by critics. Yet, it was not seen as such by Hollywood actors and studios that were eager to cash in on the so-called fad and make co-productions with the Italians, Spanish and Germans and take advantage of the inexpensive costs to film in Europe for their films.

1966 was the year the genre matured and became an actual genre to be reckoned with in the world film industry. The Spaghetti western was here to stay, at least for the foreseeable future.

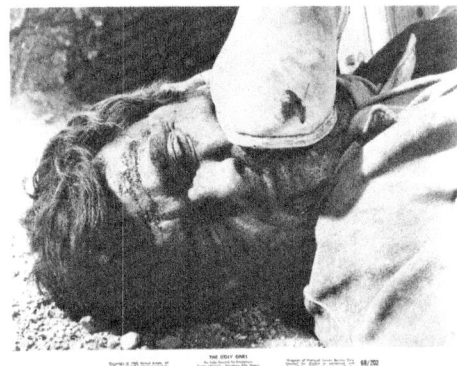

Top: Richard Wyler co-star of The Ugly Ones with boot to his face
Bottom: Henry Silva, Nicolettaa Machiavelli and Nando Gazzolo.

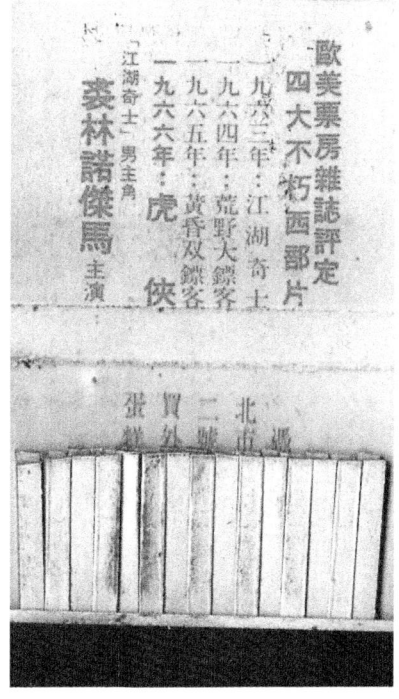

Left, Top: Lucio Fulci's Massacre Time "in English with Dutch subtitles."
Left, Bottom: GBU
Above: Japanese Fort Yuma Gold Matches

121

Coming Soon.....

From Wild East Productions!

Euro-Westerns 1919-1961.

ANTHONY THORNE HAS A LOOK AT THE EURO-WESTERNS FROM 1919-1961

BULL ARIZONA, DER WÜSTENADLER 1919
BULL ARIZONA. 2. DAS VERMÄCHTNIS DER PRÄRIE 1920
LEDERSTRUMPF, 1. TEIL: DER WILDTÖTER UND CHINGACHGO-OK 1920
LEDERSTRUMPF, 2. TEIL: DER LETZTE DER MOHIKANER 1920
ORO VIL 1941
FANCIULLO DEL WEST, Il 1942
SOGNO DI ZORRO, Il 1952
EL COYOTE 1955
LA JUSTICIA DEL COYOTE 1956
FERNAND COWBOY 1956
SÉRÉNADE AU TEXAS 1958
STRADA DEI GIGANTI, La 1960
DINAMITE JACK 1961
GOÛT DE LA VIOLENCE, Le 1961

Scene from BULL ARIZONA, DER WÜSTENADLER (1919)

BULL ARIZONA, DER WÜSTENADLER
Germany 1919 [Chateau Kunstfilm-Werke] 52 min.
AT: Bull Arizona – the Desert Eagle (Eng.)
Dir: Philipp Jutzi Prod: Adolf Basler St and Sc: Hermann Basler
starring Hermann Basler, Sonya Bernini, Sepha Bernay, Robert Moser, Mary Basler, Horst Krahè

Bank robber Bull Arizona (Hermann Basler) falls in love with Mary Davis (Esther Farlan). They travel west on a wagon train, and suffer in the desert heat, before Arizona protects the group from an Indian attack.

This silent era German production is among the first documented European westerns. Contemporary musician Michael Klubertanz posted a short fragment of the film on YouTube in 2009. We see horses galloping, gunfights, and an argument between cowboys at a card table. Indians in native headdress peer over an outcrop of rocks, and the hero travels with a friend on a stagecoach. Another rider chases them, and holds up the pair at gunpoint. Arizona fires his gun, and a huge cloud of smoke fills the screen. Arizona leads his horse through a forest, and it stops to eat foliage. When Arizona walks his horse to a mountain edge, he looks out over the landscape. A storm of scratches and damage takes over the image, signaling the end of the reel. The title 'ENDE' comes up briefly, and music plays over a black screen. The rest of the film is left to our imagination.

Co-director Jutzi had a background in painting and cinema advertising. He worked as a cameraman and director at Internationale Film-Industrie in Heidelberg, where the company produced slapstick and Wild West films, then became involved in left-wing filmmaking after contacting the Berlin communist group Internationale Arbeiterhilfe (IAH – International Workers Relief) in the early 1920's, to help document political activities. Jutzi then joined Prometheus Film-Verleih as an employee, where he prepared the German version of Eisenstein's **BRONENOSETS PATYOMKIN** (1925), and worked as a cinematographer. Jutzi's documentary **UM'S TÄGLICHE BROT** (1929), and the silent drama **MUTTER KRAUSENS FAHRT INS GLÜCK** (1929), both depictions of poverty, were banned by the Nazis in 1933. He joined the NSDAP (Nationalsozialistische Deutsche Arbeiterpartei – Nazi Party) in March that year, and directed more features in Austria. In 1939, he helped film the trial of the security personnel captured during the SS Heimwehr Danzig attack on the Polish Post Office. The prisoners, found guilty, were later executed by firing squad. After years of declining health, Jutzi died in 1946.

BULL ARIZONA, DER WÜSTENADLER was filmed on the Baden Road, Dossenheim, in Ludwigshafen, and at the Glashaus am Neckar studio in Schlierbach, Austria. Followed by **BULL ARIZONA. 2. DAS VERMÄCHTNIS DER PRÄRIE** (1920). Black and white.

1920

BULL ARIZONA. 2. DAS VERMÄCHTNIS DER PRÄRIE
Germany 1920 [Chateau Kunstfilm-Werke] 65 min.
AT: Bull Arizona – the Legacy of the Prairie (Eng.)
Dir: Philipp Jutzi Prod: Hermann Basler St and Sc: Hermann Basler Ph: Hermann Basler
starring Hermann Basler, Esther Farlan, Leo Westphal, Mizzi Ship (as 'Mi Ship'), Curt Schreck

This is Philipp Jutzi's sequel to **BULL ARIZONA, DER WÜSTENADLER** (1919). A fragment of the first film is viewable online, but no copies of the second episode are currently available. Hermann Basler's Chateau Kunstfilm-Werke later suffered financial losses after the Weimar government passed the May 1920 'Lichtspielgesetz' (Cinema Act). The new law restricted the screening of violent movies, including westerns, for younger audiences. The company went bankrupt in 1924. Black and white.

LEDERSTRUMPF, 1. TEIL: DER WILDTÖTER UND CHINGACHGOOK.(1920)
Left: Alpha Video   Right: Grapevine Video

LEDERSTRUMPF, 1. TEIL: DER WILDTÖTER UND CHINGACHGOOK
Germany 1920 [Luna Film (Berlin)] Twelve reels, (cut to five for US release)
AT: The Deerslayer and Chingachgook (Eng.); The Deerslayer (USA)
Dir: Arthur Wellin Prod: Arthur Wellin St: based on the novel 'Leatherstocking Tales' by James Fenimore Cooper Sc: Robert Heymann Ph: Ernest Plhak
starring Emil Mamelok, Béla Lugosi, Herta Héden, Gottfried Krause, Edward Eyseneck, Margot Sokolowska, Kurt Rottenburg, Erna Rehberger, Willy Schröder, Egon Söhnlein, Heddy Sven, Frau Wenkhaus, Charles Barley, Kurt Rehberger

In New York State, 1740, an orphan boy (Emil Mamelok) is adopted by Delaware Indians and given the name Deerslayer. His boyhood friend Chingachgook (Bela Lugosi) is the son of an Indian chief. On reaching adulthood, Deerslayer must protect his friends, and his beloved Herta (Judith Hutter) from enemy soldiers and a neighboring tribe.

This silent era western was released in two parts in Germany, then cut for the US market by Cameo Distributing Co, and released as **THE DEERSLAYER**. The remaining footage is unexceptional compared to other, more renowned silent films from the period, and gives no insight into how the original version played. The dialogue is performed like a stage play, and the camera remains static, except for moments where the actors travel on a river. A battle has soldiers firing muskets, and a wounded Indian gives a speech conveyed via title cards that ends with "Ugh, now I die!". Lugosi, wearing body paint, gives a credible and committed performance as the Indian Chingachgook, but his scenes often feature more title cards than footage. The murky cinematography has occasional moments of interest, such as an evocative shot of a canoe passing across a lake. At the end, the Deerslayer and Chingachgook, having survived their adventures, share a handshake. It's possible that more interesting scenes were dumped when the film was cut. The original German version was followed by **LEDERSTRUMPF, 2. TEIL: DER LETZTE DER MOHIKANER** (1920). The story was revisited in Harald Reinl's **DER LETZE MOHIKANER** (1965), and Richard Groschopp's **CHINGACHGOOK – DIE GROSSE SCHLANGE** (1967). Black and white.

LEDERSTRUMPF, 2. TEIL: DER LETZTE DER MOHIKANER
Germany 1920 [Luna Film (Berlin)]
AT: The Last of the Mohicans (Eng.); The Deerslayer (USA)
Dir: Arthur Wellin Prod: Arthur Wellin St: based on the novel 'Leatherstocking Tales' by James Fenimore Cooper Sc: Robert Heymann Ph: Ernest Plhak
starring Emil Mamelok, Béla Lugosi, Herta Héden, Gottfried Krause, Edward Eyseneck, Margot Sokolowska, Kurt Rottenburg, Erna Rehberger, Willy Schröder, Egon Söhnlein, Heddy Sven, Frau Wenkhaus, Charles Barley, Kurt Rehberger

This is the second episode of Luna Film's Chingachgook adaptation, following the same year's **LEDERSTRUMPF, 1. TEIL: DER WILDTÖTER UND CHINGACHGOOK** (1920). Like that film, it remains lost, and the cut version is the only way to see some of what was intended. Lugosi later left Germany for the US, a decade away from his acclaimed run of 1930's horror films. Wellin directed more silent films, and acted at the Volksbühne Berlin theatre. In October 1941, Wellin was transported with other Jewish citizens from Prague to the Ghetto Litzmannstadt residential district. The area served as a stopover point before the Nazi extermination camps. There is no record of his fate after that.

Above: Oro Vil (1941). Photo courtesy of Javier Ramos.
Page 127: **FANCIULLO DEL WEST, IL (1942)**

ORO VIL

Spain 1941 [C.E.A (Madrid)] 72 min.
AT: Dirty Gold (Eng)
Dir: Eduardo García Maroto Prod: Eduardo García Maroto St: Antonio Martin Sc: Eduardo García Maroto Ph: Andrés Pérez Cubero Mus: Daniel Montorio
starring Pablo Álvarez Rubio, Florencia Bécquer (Erna Bécquer), Rufino Inglés, Ricardo Merino, Conrado San Martin, Mary Santamaría (Maria Santamaría), Manuel de Hita, Pilar Delgado, Erasmo Pascual, Emilio Santiago

Alberto, a doctor working outside of Spain, is abandoned by his fiancée before their wedding. He consoles himself by travelling to America and chasing riches during the gold rush. A parody of the genre, **ORO VIL** was one of the earliest European westerns, filmed on the southern slopes of the Guadarrama mountain range north of Madrid. In his autobiography, Aventuras y desventuras del cine español, published in 1988, director Eduardo García Maroto described it as

"...a film without excessive violence, filmed with great ingenuity. The action took place in the Pedriza, a place that would be repeatedly exploited later by Italian and American producers. The budget was very limited - an almost pitiful hundred and fifty thousand pesetas..."

Director Maroto started his career as a correspondent for '*Cine Revist*a', a local cinema journal. At the age of 20, he was enlisted to fight with the Segundo Regimiento de Zapadores Minadores in Morocco during the military dictatorship of Miguel Primo de Rivera. He returned from military service to work as an editor for Madrid Film in 1924, and trained in Paris at the end of the silent era alongside René Clair, before returning to Spain to direct several other features and documentaries. Maroto also wrote articles for the long-running magazine Hermano Lobo, under the pseudonym 'Marisa Barba'. Late in his career, Maroto would work as the production manager for Kubrick's **SPARTACUS** (1960), Schaffner's **PATTON** (1970), and other big-budget American epics from the period. His autobiography was later used as the basis for a documentary, **Memorias de un peliculero**, in 2004. **ORO VIL** was his only western. Black and white.

FANCIULLO DEL WEST, IL
Italy 1942 [Scalera Films] 85 min. 12.24.1942
AT: Macario au Far West (Fr); Boy of the Golden West (USA); The Kid of the West
Dir: Giorgio Ferroni Prod: Liborio Capitani St: Leo Bomba, Silvano Castellani, Vincenzo Talarico Sc: Gian Paolo Callegari, Giorgio Ferroni, Vittorio Metz, Vincenzo Rovi Ph: Sergio Pesce Mus: Amedeo Escobar Ed: Vittorio Solito
starring Erminio Macario, Elli Parvo, Giovanni Grasso, Nino Pavese, Adriana Sivieri, Egisto Olivieri, Carlo Rizzo, Tino Scotti, Nada Fiorelli, Marisa Valli, Aldo Pini, Piero Pastore, Erminio Spalla, Giovanni Onorato, Vinicio Sofia, Renata Capanna, Gian Paolo Rosmino, Giulio Battiferri, Ciro Beradi, Luisa Agosti, Oreste Onorato, Pasquale Fasciano, Giorgio Ferroni, Renato Navarrini

Frontier doctor Mac Carey (Macario) attempts to end the rivalry between the Carey and the Donovan families, and hopes to marry the Donovan's beautiful daughter, Margherita (Sivieri). While trying to gain her affection, Mac seeks temporary solace in the arms of beautiful Spanish singer Lolita de Fuego (Parvo), but Margherita remains the object of his desire. To win the hand of his beloved, Mac will need to defeat the group of bandits that continually threaten the town.

This WW2 era Cinecitta production from director Giorgio Ferroni – promoted during its initial release as a comedic retelling of *ROMEO AND JULIET* - was among the very first spaghetti westerns. (Carl Koch's **LA SIGNORA DELL'OVEST**, listed below, preceded **IL FANCIULLO DEL WEST** in cinemas by a few months. Both films were produced at a time when American films were prohibited for distribution within Italy). The title of Ferroni's film derives from Puccini's 1910 opera *"La Fanciulla del West"* [trans. "Girl of the Golden West"], which Koch's feature references more directly.

The light-hearted Trinity films with Terence Hill would achieve enormous success in the 1970s – and encouraged a spate of less successful imitators - but as an initial precursor, **IL FANCIULLO DEL WEST** probably has more in common with the locally popular comedies of Franco and Ciccio than the films Hill did with, or without his co-star Bud Spencer. Short, nerdy, and with an exaggerated and theatrical manner developed from a career in Italian music halls, the un-heroic but amiable Macario – sporting pale make-up, painted lips and brows, and wearing a natty suit – resembles Pee Wee Herman in both performance and appearance. Accordingly, the comedy in **IL FANCIULLO DEL WEST** is agreeable, deadpan, and often dumb. A stagecoach is stopped during the opening scenes so a cowboy conductor can validate each passenger's fare. He uses his pistol to blast a hole in the tickets before passing them back to the travellers. Elsewhere, the story detours to visit the 'Village of Abandoned Women", a ramshackle collection of decrepit huts inhabited by a gang of hooked-nosed Italian men in drag, some of whom are the approximate height of Richard Kiel. Macario wanders wide-eyed through various scenes and blows his nose into a handkerchief when the passage of events becomes stressful. Helpful Indians cast a love spell for Macario by dancing around a fire to the sound of jungle drums, and the 'Abandoned Women' stagger out of their homes like possessed zombies to locate the sound. Sexy Elli Parvo (who plays hot saloon dancer Lolita de Fuego) has a spirited song and dance number late in the film, but it's unfortunately too brief to be memorable. (Pretty actresses abound in the crowded saloon scenes, but none are given much screen time). The film's occasional gunfights are perfunctory and depicted mainly for purposes of slapstick. (Macario raids a chicken nest near the climax to pelt anonymous baddies with eggs). An admirably stupid finale sees Macario captured and tied to a Rube Goldberg contraption within a decrepit hut. A winched rope is tied to a burning candle, the end of which supports a hanging bottle of wine. The wine bottle dangles above a snoozing Indian, who cradles a sleeping chicken under his arm. The chicken is tied to another winched rope that leads to a box with a cannonball placed within, and the cannonball is poised above some scales. The scales attach to another rope, which leads by winches to the hammer of a loaded pistol that is pointed at a bucket of dynamite. The hogtied Macario sits atop the explosive bucket and awaits his doom, staring glumly at the sleeping Indian. When Margherita enters the hut, Macario is able to struggle free, and a climactic gunfight ensues, with the townsfolk ultimately victorious. The townsfolk celebrate their triumph and Macario embraces his love, but the happy ending is interrupted when the town villain, yelling for vengeance, emerges with a shotgun from the doorway of the shack. The mustached baddie raises his weapon to fire. At this point, the candle burns through the rope, which drops the bottle, waking both the chicken and the Indian, sending the cannonball rolling, landing on the scale which shoots the pistol, detonating the bucket of dynamite and blowing the gunman off the face of the earth.

Clever opening titles feature credits and wild-west imagery roughly sketched across the planks of a wooden wall. The dark, scratchy print under review (taken from Italian TV) shows the ravages of time, but still maintains visual interest. The sets, period detail and bustling crowd scenes featured in **IL FANCIULLO DEL WEST** are occasionally more lavish and convincing than those seen in westerns from the 60's and 70's, a possible result of the film being produced a few decades closer to the historical reality depicted onscreen. Macario continued to act in numerous films well into the (and his) 70's, among them the Mario Amendola cheesecake burlesque compilation **TOTO SEXY** (1963). The gorgeous Parvo would act in dozens more films until her retirement in 1960. Ferroni would direct peplum **[LA GUERRA DI TROIA** (1961) with Steve Reeves, and **IL COLOSSO DI ROMA** (1964) with Gordon Scott], horror films [the stylish **IL MULINO DELLE DONNE DI PIETRA / MILL OF THE STONE WOMEN** (1963), a career highlight] and westerns [including several with iconic spaghetti hero Giuliano Gemma – **UN DOLLARO BUCATO** (1965), **PER POCHI DOLLARI ANCORA** (1966), and **WANTED** (1967)] for a few more decades. Black and white.

BANDOLERO STANCO, IL
Italy 1952 87 min. 22.12.1952
Dir: Fernando Cerchio Prod: Ezio Gagliardo, Emo Bistolfi St: Emo Bistolfi Sc: Mario Guerra, Carlo Romano, Renato Rascel, Emo Bistolfi, O.G. Caramazza, Alessandro Continenza, V. Veltroni, J. Comin Ph: Tino Santoni Mus: Angelo Francesco Lavagnino Ed: Maria Rosada
Starring Renato Rascel, Lauretta Masiero, Franco Jamonte, Lia Di Leo, Tino Buazzelli, Silvio Bagolini, Gigi Bonos, Mimmo Craig, Peppino Ferrara, Rodolfo Salinas, Bianca Maria Mascolo, Arnaldo Arnaldi, Rio De Sonay, Gabriella Graziotto, Ettore Bevilacqua, Carlo Cori, Amerigo Santarelli, Lino Banfi
DVD: Millenium Storm (Italy, 2008), PAL 4:3 Ital. Mono, 86 min.

Left: Millenium Storm DVD. Italian language with no subs.

Parodic comedy western with actor / singer Renato Rascel as Pepito, an impoverished peasant looking for gold, finding it, and attempting to win the heart of his beloved. Unbeknownst to Pepito, Sheriff Fred (Franco Jamonte) plans to rob him of his girl and his money. Stelvio Massi, cinematographer on several later westerns (and director of satisfying trash like the 70's 'Marc the Narc' cop trilogy - **MARK IL POLIZIOTTO** (1975), **MARK IL POLIZIOTTO SPARA PER PRIMO** (1976) and **MARK COLPISCE ANCORA** (1976) - with Franco Gasparri) was a camera assistant

---

SOGNO DI ZORRO, IL
Italy 1951 [I.C.S. (Rom)] 93 min. 26.3.52
AT: Zorro der Held (Ger); Le hertier de Zorro (Fr); De Erfgenaan van Zorro (Nl); El sueno de Zorro (Spa); El ultimo Zorro (alt. Spa); Zorro's Dream (UK); The Dream of Zorro (USA)
Dir: Mario Soldati Prod: Niccolo Theodoli St: Mario Amendola, Ruggero Maccari, Marcello Marchesi Sc: Mario Amendola, Alessandro Continenza, Ruggero Maccari, Marcello Marchesi, Vittorio Metz Ph: Mario Montuori (black & white) Mus: Mario Nascimbene
starring Walter Chiari, Vittorio Gassman, Carlo Ninchi, Delia Scala, Umberto Aquilino, Sandro Bianchi, Juan DeLanda, Gisella Monaldi, Piero Capanna, Michele Philippe, Anna Arena, Giorgio Costantini, Augusto Di Giovanni, Giovanni Dolfini, Claudio Ermelli, Giacomo Furia, Sophia Loren (as 'Sofia Scicolone'), Michele Malaspina, Guido Morisi, Lugi Pavese, Riccardo Rioli, Gualtiero Tumiati, Antonietta Zocchi

Above: **IL SOGNO DI ZORRO** from 1951, not to be confused with the Franco Franchi film of the same name from 1975, bottom photo

Don Raimundo Esteban (Chiari), the grandson of Zorro, and an innocent plotted against by foes bearing faces of friendship, becomes timid and fearful after a fall from his horse. A later blow to the head transforms him into a master swordsman and seducer of beautiful women. Don Raimundo will need to keep his wits about him if he is to defeat his rival Don Antonio (Gassman) and win the hand of his beloved Estrella (Scalia).

This antiquated but effective comedy (with minimal western elements – there are characters on horseback and a chase featuring a horse-drawn carriage, but no cowboys or gunfights) provides a few genuine laughs and chuckles amidst other gags that have lost some of their appeal with the passage of time. Chiari, playing a character who vacillates between able-bodied swordsmanship and grotesque, Jerry Lewis-style mugging, provides numerous examples of each, and is responsible for both the film's funniest and most painful moments. Sporting an ill-fitting hat and a variety of infantile expressions at the film's beginning, Chiari convincingly inhabits the role of a gormless dope, skipping gleefully down the street picking petals from flowers, humming obnoxious tunes, and poking his tongue out at friends and family when they offer advice. (Soldati wrings much humour from the wry, tolerant expressions of the elder townsfolk, all of whom appear to have developed a patient manner in dealing with the town retard). Mercifully, Chiari's persona grows in appeal when a comical blow to his head – one of many throughout the movie - transforms his personality, allowing him to evolve from an obnoxious simpleton to a swaggering, loud-mouthed, sex-crazed lout. Circa this eccentric development, the film's restrained tone is energised when Sofia Loren (billed as Sofia Scicolone) walks onscreen in a skirt and tight-fitting top, carefully lit to emphasize her voluptuous curves and pointing her oversized, perfectly shaped bust at the camera. Chiari, busy flirting with some attractive female admirers in the dining room of his lodgings, interrupts the story he was telling and leaps over three different tables to ravish and passionately kiss Loren, who desperately tries to fend off his advances. Chiari ignores her pleas and the crowds at the surrounding bar all have a good chuckle, just before the scene fades to black as a symbolic prelude to Chiari presumably carting the squealing Loren off to the boudoir to consummate his raging lust. In 1950's Italy, gags like this were presumably not too far off the mark in depicting the off-screen behavior of much of the audience.

Some later, tamer jokes hit the spot with precision. Don Esteban wishes to woo his beloved Estrella - (Delia Scalia, the film's pouting, attractive female lead) - so he stands beneath a balcony with a guitar and sings a song of romance. Behind a tree a short distance away stands a short, mustached guitar-playing bandit, hired to play and sing whilst Chiari badly mimes the vocals. Chiari's deadpan, perfectly stupid performance misses the song's conclusion and mimics the bandit's climactic 'Ole!' several beats too late. Elsewhere, Chiari's opponents rig a bedroom with every imaginable booby trap, including mallets falling from the ceiling and a chair that catapults the sitter into another room to be beaten by thugs. Chiari strides around, setting off the traps for his opponents rather than himself, and remains blandly oblivious when his conversational partners are thrown to their doom. (When he receives a mallet to the head late in the film, the powers of transformation inherent in the blow regress him to being a juvenile dunce in the middle of a clinch with the gorgeous Scalia. After fortuitously reclining into a booby-trapped chair that thwacks him on the skull yet again, Chiari regains his cojones in time for the final fight). Soldati's direction, with a frequently mobile camera and some elegant framing, is better than expected for the period and the genre. The cleverly staged scene where Chiari tries out multiple dance partners at a town ball, in particular, is a tour de force of choreography, performance and scoring.

IL SOGNO DI ZORRO is not a traditional spaghetti western, but it offers evidence that some of the genre's textural pleasures were present early on. The black-and-white photography brings a sense of lyricism to opening shots of landscape and clouds, and the pictorial qualities of the movie are quite fine, with lots of rural detail, rustic buildings glimpsed in the distance, and shots of farmland populated by characters in period dress. The opening credits (backed by evocative orchestral and mariachi music) roll over an evocative shot of an open road, the frame equally divided between land, cloud and sky. The elaborate art direction throughout the movie is also quite witty. The villa of the elderly Zorro (a relative of Don Raimundo, shown prior to the introduction of Chari's character at the beginning of the film) is decorated with elaborate letter 'Z's on the walls and doorways, and a musical performance within a country church (in which Chiari plays the triangle) features a grinning, decorated skull sitting near the conductor. **IL SOGNO DI ZORRO** shows its age more through some occasionally staid editorial rhythms than any visible pictorial or technical deficiencies – the elder Zorro lassos a bottle of wine from across the room rather than getting out of his chair, and the shots comprising the gag are lingered on in a sluggish manner. The film's vintage is also revealed during a brief 'comic' scene involving a cockfighting match where animal welfare clearly wasn't a priority. The final swordfight between Chiari and Gassman, where they battle for Scalia's affections, features dozens of stupid and amusing visual gags performed with precision, moving from a carriage chase, to a courtyard fight, through a baker's kitchen, across a rooftop, and into a barnyard stable. The confrontation in the kitchen allows Chiari and his opponent to slice the local peasant's meals for them with each thrust and parry. Elsewhere, Chiari and Gassman fall into a tub of flour and transform their costumes to pure white, regaining their appearance only after dropping into a giant vat of wine that renders the pair of them briefly, amicably drunk before they regain their sobriety and continue the fight.

Novelist, playwright and actor Soldati started his directorial career just prior to World War 2, and worked in various genres for almost 50 years (including, apparently, uncredited second A.D work on **BEN-HUR** (1959)), but this is his only semi-western. Co-scriptwriter Mario Amendola would have greater involvement with the genre, directing **IL TERRORE DELL'OKLAHOMA** (1959) and **...DAI NEMICI MI GUARDO IO!** (1968), while scripting many others. Chiari appeared in the comedy western **GLI EROI DEL WEST** in 1965, and would eventually star in films as diverse as Orson Welles' **CHIMES AT MIDNIGHT** (1965), Michael Powell's **THEY'RE A WEIRD MOB** (1966), and Terence Young's **THE VALACHI PAPERS** (1972). Gassman later appeared in Sergio Corbucci's **CHE C'ENTRIAMO NOI CON LA RIVOLUZIONE?**, and worked prolifically until his death in 2000. The print reviewed was a MediaSet TV copy. A later, unrelated **IL SOGNO DI ZORRO** appeared in 1975. Black and white.

COYOTE, EL
Mex/Spa 1955 84 min. 5.5.1955
AT: Der Coyote (Ger); Il Coyote (It); The Coyote (USA)
Dir: Joaquin Luis Romero Marchent, Fernando Soler Prod: Ismael Palacio Bolufer, Salvador Elizondo, Eduardo Manzanos St: Pedro Masó, Pedro Chamorro, Jesus Franco (from the book by Jose Mallorqui)
Sc: Pedro Chamorro, Antonio Abad Ojuel, Jesus Franco, Joaquin Romero Marchent, Jose Mallorqui
Ph: Ricardo Torres [black and white] Mus: Odón Alonso, Jesus Franco Ed: Antonio Gimeno

starring Abel Salazar, Gloria Marín, Manuel Monroy, Santiago Rivero, Rafael Bardem, Jose Calvo, Lys Rogi, Xan das Bolas, Carlos Otero, Antonio García Quijada, Mario Moreno, Julio Goróstegui, Rufino Ingles, Jose Maria Prada, Victor Proncet, Mari Sol Luna, Alfredo Muniz, Angela Tamayo, Pedro Ignacio de Paul, Pepita Bravo, Antonio Moreno, Jeronimo Montoro, Jose G. Rey, Pepa Ruiz, Ignacio de Cordoba, Fernando Delgado, Joaquin Burgos, Luis Dominguez Luna, Antonio Fornis, Hector Mayo, Miguel Pastor Mata, Jose Riesgo, Emilio Rodriguez, Manuel San Ramon, Ángel Álvarez

Poster for El Coyote (1955)

In 1848, the United States of America invades the former Mexican colony of California. Captain Potts (Santiago Rivero), a commander in the US Cavalry, seeks peace, while landowner Don de Echague (Rafael Bardem) orders his son Cesar (Abel Salazar) home from his studies in Europe to aid the Mexican rebellion. Cesar befriends Captain Potts as a ruse, and keeps his involvement in the rebellion secret from his fiancé Leonor (Gloria Marín). When Cesar's two patriot friends, Valdez and Artiga, are captured, Cesar disguises himself as a masked avenger, the Coyote, to fight the invaders. When Potts is relieved of his duty on criminal charges, he vows to kill the Coyote before his departure from California.

The first western from Joaquin Marchent, **EL COYOTE** is a low-budget production compared to what followed, but it convincingly evokes the old west, and provides entertainment even for non-Spanish speaking viewers watching an un-subtitled print. Salazar is a likeable hero, exchanging dandyish civilian clothes for his darker El Coyote costume when preparing to fight the enemy. Marchent evokes the turbulent politics of the period with evocative visual details. We see scenes of warfare, cannons firing, and Cavalry soldiers passing on horseback. A low angle shot of a soldier playing the bugle captures a flock of birds in the sky behind him, and townsfolk hanging from nooses are shown in silhouette. The symbol of the coyote – a fun motif to inspire a heroic western character – appears throughout. During the opening titles, as folk guitar plays, a painted backdrop depicts a rocky outcrop and a coyote howling at the sky. When de Echague is distraught at witnessing another hanging, a silhouetted coyote in the distance is heard. The coyote is heard a final time when the hero grabs his gun, preparing for retribution. De Echague rides into town, leaving a calling card threatening vengeance, and his note has a coyote sketched at the bottom. A stylish climactic gunfight utilizes stark lighting, with the shadows of de Echague and Captain Potts looming high on background walls as the pair stalk each other at night.

This was the first of two Coyote films based on novels by Spanish journalist Jose Mallorqui (1913 – 1972). Mallorqui was inspired by Robert Mamoulian's **THE MARK OF ZORRO** (1940), and wanted to create a similar character. The Coyote first appeared in the *Novelas del Oeste* western collection between 1943 and 1949, and grew in popularity to have adventures through fumetti, a musical parody, spin-off novels written by other authors, and over 100 additional novels from Mallorqui himself. A film of the Coyote's adventures was proposed in the late 1940's, and Antonio Abad Ojuel wrote a script based on the character. The script went through the offices of several producers, and was offered to various directors, including Leon Klimovsky. The project became a co-production with Mexico, and Fernando Soler was hired to film it. Early in the shoot, Soler, romantically attached to actress Gloria Marín, found that she was having an affair with her leading man, Abel Salazar. Tension between the trio led to Soler quitting the production. Joaquin Marchent was then hired to direct, and the sequel **LA JUSTICIA DEL COYOTE** was shot simultaneously, using the same cast and crew. A young Jesus Franco assisted Marchent, working as an assistant director, co-authoring the script, and writing some of the music. (For Franco fans, a scene of a cute dancer swaying her hips onstage hints at the depictions of nightclub cheesecake Franco inserted into his own work from **GRITOS EN LA NOCHE (**1961) onwards.) The scratchy full-screen print of **EL COYOTE** shows signs of age and damage, conveying the impression of a rarity rescued from oblivion. (A sharper transfer and subtitles would make the film more engaging).

This was Marchent's third movie, and first western. After some comedies, he returned to the western genre with **LA SOMBRA DEL ZORRO** and **LA VENGANZA DEL ZORRO** (both 1962), and continued to direct westerns through the 60's and early 70's. Franco, Marchent's assistant, was 5 years away from making his own directorial debut with the eclectic teen comedy **TENEMOS 18 ANOS** (1959), and the later **GRITOS EN LA NOCHE** (1961). Franco would direct more than 200 horror, exploitation and erotic movies over the next four decades, but only one western – **EL LLANERO** (1963). In the second issue of Positivo, Marchent noted:

"It was quite complicated because the films were shot simultaneously, and the producer didn't like the scripts so we were doing re-writes every morning before shooting. Jesus Franco was my assistant director and co-script writer. Since we were making two films, we had to alternate the sets and characters, but more than once we realized that we had used characters who were supposed to have died in previous sequences! It was an awful mess, but we wrapped each film in 29 days. That is how I started in Westerns."

Salazar later starred in Mexican horror films, including Fernando Mendez's **EL ATAUD DEL VAMPIRE / THE VAMPIRE'S COFFIN** (1958), Rafael Baledon's **EL HOMBRE Y EL MONSTRUO / THE MAN AND THE MONSTER** (1959), and Chano Urueta's immortal **EL BARON DEL TERROR / THE BRAINIAC** (1962). He married Gloria Marín in 1958. The atmospheric photography in **EL COYOTE** is by Ricardo Torres, and the film was shot in the municipality of Titulcia, in Madrid. After Marchent's two films, the character of the Coyote returned in Mario Caiano's **IL SEGNO DEL COYOTE** (1963), scripted by Mallorqui, and Mario Camus' **EL COYOTE** (LA PELICULA) (1998). Black and white

 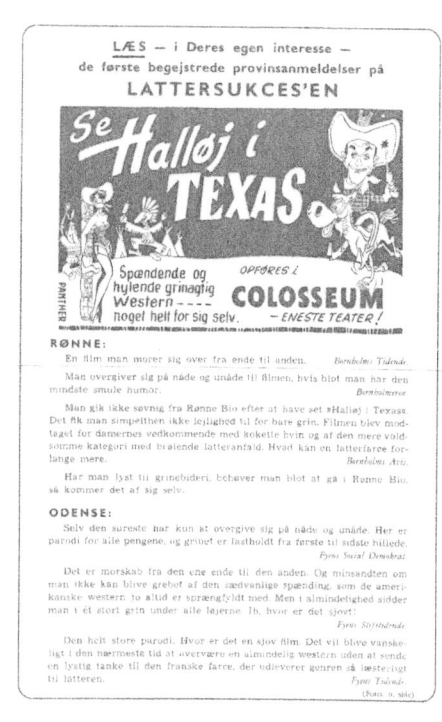

Left: Poster of LA JUSTICIA DEL COYOTE (1955)
Right: Danish Press Release- FERNAND COWBOY (1956)

FERNAND COW-BOY
France 1956 85 min. [Cinéphonic, SGGC, Pathé Cinéma] 7.9.1956
AT: El conquistador de Texas (Spa); Fernand Cowboy (Eng)
Dir: Guy Lefranc Prod: Francoise Chavane St: Yvan Audouard, Jean Redon Sc: Yvan Audouard, Jean Redon Ph: Maurice Barry [black and white] Mus: Louis Guglielmi (as 'Louiguy') Ed: Monique Kirsanoff Art Dir: Georges Lévy
starring Fernand Raynaud, Noël Roquevert, Nadine Tallier, Jean-Marie Amato, Amédée, Raoul Billerey, Jean-Roger Caussimon, Pierre Darçay, Hubert Deschamps, Françoise Favier, Maurice Gardett, Jim Gérald, Jess Hahn, Albert Michel, Bernard Noël, André Weber, Maurice Magalon, Pierre Dudan, Dora Doll, Antonin, Michel de Bonnay, Lucien Guervil, Guy Henry, Marcel Bernier, Joé Davray, Georges Demas, Paul Faivre, Jean Franval, Henri Guégan, Jean Lara, Sylvain Levignac, Jean Minisini, Félix Miquet, Albert Médina, Jacques Préboist, Marc Taylor
DVD: TF1 Vidéo (France, 2007), PAL

Fernand Mignot (Fernand Raynaud), a villager from deepest France, inherits his uncle's saloon and travels to Carson City in Texas. On his arrival, Mignot meets Any (Nadine Tallier), a beautiful dancer. As Mignot falls in love, hotel manager Jim Harlan (Jess Hahn) and his wife Mae Marlane (Dora Doll) frame Mignot for the murder of old Richardson (Jim Gérald), a friendly customer of the saloon. As the townsfolk prepare to hang Mignot, local bandit William Black (Pierre Dudan) kidnaps him, forcing Mignot to help Black's gang search for stolen money. When Orissa (Françoise Favier), a young Indian witness, tells her story to the townsfolk, the sheriff and his companions vow to rescue Mignot from his captors.

This mildly funny comedy western has a few well-staged gunfights and brawls, and sexy female co-stars. The nervous, cheerful Raynaud, a mannered performer with a repertoire of shrugs and grimaces, falls afoul of rowdy physical gags perpetrated by others, and repeatedly screws things up himself. A funeral near a train station at the start of the movie shows Mignot stuck in the rain, clapping and putting his hat on when he thinks the eulogy has finished, and removing his hat to get drenched when the speech starts up again. During his journey to Carson City, Mignot is squashed between two sleeping guys on the coach, and when he tries to uncork a bottle for Any in the saloon, he sprays wine over everyone, including his date. During a later gunfight, a cowboy shoots Mignot's hat off as he looks out of a window. When Mignot is eventually framed for murder, a cellmate helps him escape jail through a hole in the wall. Mignot sneaks around to the front of tbe prison, steals the keys, and accidentally wakes the guard, who shrugs and chucks Mignot in his cell before going back to sleep. Mignot then climbs out the hole again, runs around to the front, back into the jail, tiptoes past the guard, and re-opens the cell to free his buddy. The noise of the keys wakes the guard, so Mignot jumps back into the cell to hide his escape attempt. The guard walks back to the cell, takes the keys, locks the door and leaves Mignot where he started.

Much of **FERNAND COWBOY**'s appeal is in its actresses, and its action. Dora Doll is a hoot as Mae Marlane, wife of the hotel manager. She wears a low-cut, tight-fitting dress that shows lots of cleavage, and tries to seduce Mignot. Elsewhere, Nadine Tallier dances in a corset, revealing her great legs and hips, and reclines over guys sitting in the saloon. Mignot watches in admiration, and spends half a minute trying different finger combinations in his mouth in an attempt to whistle. When Black kidnaps Any, she's tied up, then stripped down to lingerie for the pleasure of Black's men. A card game in the saloon erupts into a fight where the stunt guys destroy much of the set, and a pianist shoves a falling body out of the way so he can keep playing. A later shootout features dozens of combatants, and a gunslinger falls from the top of some stairs on to a piano with a loud bang. When the townsfolk discover the truth of Anderson's killing, and learn that Mignot has been kidnapped, they lead an assault on Black's cabin, while Mignot hides under a pile of corpses. The celebrating townsfolk dance to a violin and fiddle, and Mignot hooks up with Orissa, the young Indian girl, while Any leaves with another cowboy. Mignot finishes the film smoking an Indian peace pipe with his betrothed.

FERNAND COWBOY has good costumes, attractive camerawork, and locations full of stagecoaches and extras. Regardless, Pascal Merigeau's 2012 biography of Jean Renoir alludes to Lefranc not being fond of the production. During his association with Renoir, when he worked on **LE CAPORAL ÉPINGLÉ** (1962), Lefranc had "…just turned forty, and since the last Jouvet film he had made only some forgettable works, ordinary comedies with Fernand Raynaud or others, which allowed him to wait for this big film of which he'd been dreaming, not to mention that he himself had had the experience of being an "elusive" prisoner of war. Claude Sautet, who was his assistant, presented him as a "very cultivated boy [who] felt demeaned having to direct **La Bande a papa** [Daddy's Gang] or **Fernand cow-boy**."

This was Raynaud's only western. He appeared in two more films for Lefranc, **SALUT BERTHE!** (1968) and **L'AUVERGNAT ET L'AUTOBUS** (1969), before dying in a 1973 car crash. Doll remained a prolific performer for decades, and appeared in more than a hundred films during her career. She starred in Edward Dmytryk's **THE YOUNG LIONS** (1958), appeared in movies by Renoir, Claude Chabrol, Henri-Georges Clouzot and others, and was made a Knight of France's National Order of Merit in 2000. Tallier (born Nadine Lhopitalier), starred in the 1958 British comedy **GIRLS AT SEA** and other movies before retiring from acting in 1964. In 1962, she married Edmond Adolphe de Rothschild, a Swiss member of the Rothschild banking and winemaking family. She later wrote a book on etiquette, Le Bonheur de Séduire l'Art de Réussir, republished in English as Savoir-vivre in the 21st century. Louis Guglielmi's upbeat saloon theme, featuring zany bonks and whistles on the soundtrack, is first heard during the opening

credits, which show Raynaud's head on top of a totem pole. **FERNAND COWBOY** skipped theatres in Germany, premiering on television there a half-century later in 2004. Black and white.
[Jean Renior: A Biography by Pascal Merigeau]

JUSTICIA DEL COYOTE, LA
1956 84 min. 8.3.1956
AT: Justice du Coyote (Fr); Die Rache des Coyoten (Ger); Oxifomahos tou Sacramento (Gr); Giustizia del Coyote, La (It); Coyote (English title); Judgement of the Coyote (alt. English title)
Dir: Joaquin Luis Romero Marchent Prod: Eduardo Manzanos Brochero, Gonzalo Elvira St: Pedro Maso, Pedro Chamorro, Jesus Franco (from the book by Jose Mallorqui) Sc: Joaquin Romero Marchent, Jesus Franco, Antonio Abad Ojuel, Jose Mallorqui, Pedro Maso, Antonio Chamorro Ph: Ricardo Torres [black and white] Mus: Odon Alonso Ed:
starring Abel Salazar, Gloria Marin, Manuel Monroy, Santiago Rivera, Rafael Bardem, Miguel Pastor Mata, Julio Gorostegui, Antonio Garcia Quijada, Angel Alvarez, Jose Riesgo, Emilio Rodriguez, Mario Moreno, Jose G. Rey, Luis Dominguez Luna, Antonio Fornis, Manuel San Ramon, Alfonso Ruiz, Pepita Bran, Jose Riesgo, Joaquin Burges, Antonio Moreno, Hector Mayo, Mary Sol Luna

Colonel Clarke (Miguel Pastor Mata), a representative of the US Government, attempts to confiscate land from the settlers of Los Angeles. When the peasants meet to discuss their predicament, a dagger appears at their door, with a note reading "Have confidence in me. I will save you." The message bears the sketch of a coyote. Cesar de Echagüe (Abel Salazar), known as El Coyote, has returned to defend his countrymen. Cesar's father, Don de Echagüe (Rafael Bardem), shares a meal with his friend Acevedo, who refuses to sell his property. When Acevedo is murdered by Clarke's henchmen, Acevedo's daughter Leonor (Gloria Marín) tries to avenge his death, but is unable to shoot the men responsible. Leonor is arrested for attempted murder, and Clarke attempts to win her gratitude by influencing the jury. After El Coyote intevenes and convinces the court of Leonor's innocence, Clark orders the death of a juror, Yanguas the blacksmith. When Yanguas is murdered along with his family, El Coyote vows to avenge his death by killing Clarke and his men.

Joaquin Marchent's shorter follow up to **EL COYOTE** (1955) was shot alongside it, is talkier and has just a few action scenes. It benefits from a brisk narrative, good photography (by Rafael Pacheco, who worked frequently with Marchent afterwards), and a grimly effective killing midway. The most gripping scenes in the film hinge on the threat of violence, or depict it through gunplay. The opening of the film, with a young woman wordlessly threatened by bandits, is effective and – despite chaste imagery - mildly erotic, perhaps due to the involvement of assistant director Jess Franco, an unrepentant voyeur who later made sex films. Bandits tend a fire in a field, and a conversation between them erupts into a fist fight, which spooks a tethered horse. The men notice a dark-haired woman in the distance, and watch as she heads towards the river's edge behind some trees. She undresses to bathe. The camera shows a swaying tree branch in close up, and items of clothing are hung on it as the woman strips off. She swims naked in the river, unaware of the men, and a bandit rides his horse through shallow water towards her, watched by the others. As he approaches, El Coyote appears in the distance on horseback, and fires a warning shot. The bandit takes shelter behind a tree, and the men exchange gunfire. The woman, still naked, hides in the grass, her hair wet, with the river flowing behind her as the men fight. We watch her breathless reactions as each man shoots, until El Coyote chases the bandits away. The woman dresses, and El Coyote pulls her onto the back of his horse, with the two seen in silhouette as they depart. The scene is tense, with minimal dialogue.

Clarke's murder of Yanguas is carried out by the same bandits. The killers confront Yanguas at night near his homestead, and shoot bullets near his feet. He stands unmoved, and they shoot him dead. The killing is witnessed by Yanguas' wife and child, who flee into the house. The leader of the bandits walks inside, and we hear gunfire and screaming. When the killers leave, they torch the building with their cheroots. El Coyote arrives later, and vows revenge over the dying body of Yanguas. He confronts the bandits at a saloon, and tells them to prepare to duel at midnight. The bandits, tired and afraid, loiter over their drinks and watch a ticking clock, before heading out into the street to face their enemy. At midnight, El Coyote avenges the death of his friend.

The finale features a mistaken-identity ruse with two men wearing El Coyote's outfit, and a lengthy swordfight between Clarke and de Echagüe. Both actors display impressive fighting skills. When Cesar finishes his career as El Coyote, he throws his disguise down to his father while embracing Leonor on a balcony. As the lovers kiss, Don de Echagüe stares at the mask, which we see in close-up as the movie fades out. Rafael Pacheco's photography uses beautiful studio lighting and deserves a sharper print. Other moments suggest Franco's involvement. A scene where Salazar approaches a mirror to remove his mask is filmed at a distorted angle, and a dinner sequence viewed through a candelabra looks like the work of the director who later shot love-scenes through fish-tanks for eccentric visual thrills. The film is dialogue-heavy, and a chase scene on horseback outstays its welcome. The period setting is convincing, and a sequence of the bandits resting in a field is richly evocative of country life. **The COYOTE** films are atmospheric, better-than-average westerns with a sense of the gothic, but Marchent's later work would be received more warmly. Emilio García Riera, in his history of Mexican cinema, was unimpressed. **LA JUSTICIA DEL COYOTE** is much shorter than its predecessor, he noted, "but not less boring."

Marchent's next westerns were **LA SOMBRA DEL ZORRO** and **LA VENGANZA DEL ZORRO** (both 1962), then **EL SABOR DE LA VENGANZA** (1963). Black and white.

I, 7.1953-1954. University of Guadalajara, Government of Jalisco, National Council for Culture and the Arts and Mexican Institute of Cinematography. Mexico, 1993. Pages 319 and 320.

(Emilio García Riera: Historia documental del cine mexicano)

SÉRÉNADE AU TEXAS (1958)
Studiocanal release, French Language, No Subs.

SÉRÉNADE AU TEXAS
France 1958 98 min. [Jason Films] 17.12.1958
AT: Texas Mädel (At); Texasmädel (Ger); Texas (It); Serenata de Texas (Spa); Serenade of Texas (Eng)
Dir: Richard Pottier Prod: Suzanne Goosens St and Sc: Jean Ferry, Richard Pottier Ph: Lucien Joulin Mus: Francis Lopez (song "Serenade au Texas" sung by Luis Mariano) Ed: Lilyane Fattori, Maurice Serein Art Dir: Rino Mondellini starring Luis Mariano, Bourvil, Germaine Damar, René Blancard, Robert Rocca, Jean Pâqui, Paul Mercey, Gil Delamare, André Philip, Albert Michel, Jean-François Martial, Henri Arius, Micheline Gary, Liliane Bel, Arlette Poirier, Yves Deniaud, Les Bluebell Girls, Sonja Ziemann, Miguel Gamy, Jacqueline Georges, Nicole Jonesco, Lucien Raimbourg, Sylvain
DVD: Studiocanal (France, 2012), PAL, Mono 2.0
1959

Shy music seller Jacques Gardel (Luis Mariano) learns from his notary Jérôme Quilleboeuf (André Bourvil) that he has inherited an oil field in the town of Big Bend, Texas. En route to Big Bend, Jacques is recognised by a travelling comedian, Roderick (Yves Deniaud) and his actress daughters Sylvia (Sonja Ziemann) and Rose (Germaine Damar). Jacques and Jérôme join the troupe of players as singers, and strike up romances with the girls. When the travellers arrive at Big Bend, they encounter a masked gang, the Black Riders, who are driving ranchers from the town to steal their land. Jacques attempts to rid the town of the bandits, but the gang's leader, city banker Dawson (Jean Pâqui), is determined to kill Jacques and steal the girls for himself.

This French western musical mixes comedy with a light-hearted plot, has lots of songs, and is notable for the sexy appeal of Ziemann and Damar, who have great dancer's bodies and who each play their perky singing cowgirl roles in tight-fitting pants. Bandits attack the group as they travel to the town, and a gunfight is played for laughs, with the women stopping the bandits and the men hiding. The battle is won when sticks of dynamite are thrown onto a campfire and explode like fireworks. When the group arrives in Big Bend, the travellers prepare a show. Jerome sings the upbeat title track, and friends of Roderick perform for the townsfolk. A guy in a top hat croons a sad song while winding the handle of a large music box, as onlookers watch in silence. When he finishes, the crowd boos, so he turns the handle again and keeps singing. The crowd eventually throws pies and fruit at him to shut him up.

The decorative qualities of **SERENADE AU TEXAS** are notable. The film was shot in Eastmancolor, has a vibrant colour scheme, and features evocative sets by Rino Mondellini, who worked on Louis Malle's **ASCENSEUR POUR L'ÉCHAFAUD** (1958) the same year. A dimly lit auditorium in front of a stage during rehearsal is beautifully designed. Crossbeams cast shadows through the room, and extravagant costumes and scenery line the walls. When the girls later perform in the Theatre Roderick, the crowd is lit by hanging lamps that light the walls with colour, and a dancer in pink performs in front of a backdrop painted blue. The colourful design continues during a night-time gunfight outside, where members of the Black Riders fire their weapons across a red-lit courtyard, and are silhouetted by bursting clouds of backlit smoke. When Dawson is killed at the end of the film, midway through an attempted rape of Sylvia, the fourth wall is broken and the actors join with other performers on a large stage. A closing dance number takes place in a brightly lit metropolis, with incongruous neon signs advertising a casino, gin and tonic, Vogue magazine and the Sony Corporation. Mariano, a Spanish-born tenor, is a cheerful presence and performs the upbeat title tune more than once. Arlette Poirier, who appears briefly as Dawson's girlfriend Dolorès, is a good sport. During a saloon argument, she accepts two hard slaps in the face from Pâqui when he urges her to shut up. Zieman and Damar are extremely fetching onscreen, and display their spectacular figures while practicing a dance routine in the mountains, but French performer Claire Guibert dubs Ziemann throughout the movie. Ziemann later appeared in Cy Endfield's **DE SADE** (1969). Damar was the subject of a documentary, **GERMAINE DAMAR – DER TANZENDE STERN** [Germaine Damar – the Dancing Star], and sang at its Luxembourg premiere in 2011. The second reel of the film has different colour to the first, suggesting that the DVD was compiled from different prints. The theme of female cabaret performers moonlighting as gunslingers returned in later westerns. Brigitte Bardot and Jeanne Moreau appeared in Louis Malle's **VIVA MARIA!** (1965) while Lola Falana and Rita Pavone starred as lone heroes in Siro Marcellini's **LOLA COLT** (1967) and Ferdinando Baldi's **LITTLE RITA NEL WEST** (1967).

STRADA DEI GIGANTI, La
Italy 1960 90 min. 8.4.1960
AT: Alarm im Tunnel (At); Lannistumattomat (Fin); Les conquérants de la vallée sauvage (Fr); Die Furchtlosen von Parma (Ger); Kataskopos ypo 2 simaias (Gr); O Caminho dos Gigantes (Por); Ruta de titanes (Spa); Road of the Giants (USA); Valley of the Doomed (alt. USA / TV title)
Dir: Guido Malatesta Prod: Roberto Capitani, Luigi Mondello St and Sc: Guido Malatesta, Arpad De Riso Ph: Enzo Serafin Mus: Guido Robuschi, Gian Stellari, Roberto Nicolai Ed: Gino Talamo
starring Don Megowan, Chelo Alonso, Hildegaard Knef, Ivo Garrani, Dario Michaelis, Jole Fierro, Paul Muller, Nerio Bernardi, Mario Passante, Daniele Vargas, Fedele Gentile, Mara Fie, Amedeo Trilli, Carlo Pisacane, Renato Tontini, Gianfranco Pinelli, Benito Stefanelli, Alfio Caltabiano, Nello Pazzafini, Mimmo Poli, Spartaco Natale, Ivy Holzer, Renato Malavasi, Franco Cobianchi, Ida Masetti, Mario Margnelli
S: LP Philips P 08514 L (Italy, 1960)

Left: Poster for **STRADA DEI GIGANTI, La (1960)**
Right: Can't let the opportunity pass with the mention of Don Megowan's name to plug the way ahead of its tilme, sexualized, violent 1959 westen A Lust to Kill

Nominal western set in 1860 on the border between Parma and Austria. Grand duchess Maria Luisa (Hildegaard Knef) commissions beefy American engineer Clint Farrell (Don Megowan) to supervise the building of a new railway amid mountainous terrain. The Austrian government, opposing the plan, sends sultry Countess Stella Von Kruger (Chelo Alonso) to sabotage the construction, seduce Farrell, and disrupt his work. After Countess Von Kruger opens a nearby dancehall saloon, a love triangle develops as both women fall for the American. The Austrians continue their attempts at sabotage with increasing violence, until war breaks out between the two States.

This entertaining hybrid of romance, historical western and 19th century period drama benefits from impressive widescreen scenery and a succession of violent, well-staged action scenes. It temporarily suffers from a talky, visually incongruous opening focused on court intrigue when engineer Farrell arrives amid stagecoaches and extras in period finery to enter the Royal chambers and visit the grand duchess, before his departure to the mountain worksite. (The spectacular castle interior seen throughout the film's opening was filmed at the Royal Palace of Caserta, and the film makes elaborate use throughout this sequence of the Palace's giant, ornate stairwell. A lavish ballroom scene allows for some sweeping camera moves on the ballroom floor with numerous extras moving in the background, providing extravagant visuals similar to those seen in Umberto Lenzi's historical pictures from this period). After Farrell finally departs to the frontier town, (heralded by shots of explosive demolition work in the hills outside the village, as engineers prepare groundwork for the construction of a bridge), the exterior sequences filmed amid the mountains of Tuscany are spectacular and give **LA STRADA DEI GIGANTI** the rich visual texture of a western for the remainder of its running time.

As the story unfolds, the engineer faces unexpected setbacks with his work, some caused by saboteurs who attempt to disrupt construction of the railway, or to kill Farrell and his workers. A dynamite explosion in the town mine leads to the collapse of an underground tunnel, and the bare-chested Farrell is forced to run and hold up some toppling wooden support structures as his co-workers attempt to shore up the walls. In a later scene, the same saboteurs set a train engine in reverse and send it backwards across a bridge, with the drivers trapped on board and the engine gaining speed at a dangerous rate. In an expertly directed sequence, the engineer takes chase on horseback, and his pursuit is shown through beautifully framed shots of horse and rider silhouetted in front of the mountainside as they race after the engine. Farrell reaches the out-of-control train within a ravine, and jumps on as it travels past, bringing the machine under control just before it reaches another carriage stationed on the tracks ahead.

Farrell's efforts to complete his project are eventually rewarded by the romantic attentions of Countess Von Kruger, who falls for the big lug pretty quickly. **LA STRADA DEI GIGANTI** benefits from the casting and spectacular physical presence of Cuban bombshell Chelo Alonso, who plays the Countess as a feisty woman of means with a taste for erotic dancing. Alonso had gained widespread attention the previous year performing a sexy dance in Guido Brignone's peplum **NEL SEGNO DI ROMA** (1959), and her hot, desirable body is on full display when she performs a seductive dancehall show for the men in the saloon. Alonso's provocative, come-hither routine, lingered on by the director, is a showstopper and a highlight of the movie. As drunken louts paw the women in the crowd, and Farrell and his men toss back beers, a tuneful acoustic guitar heralds Alonso's entrance at the top of the stairs. Dressed in fur, a translucent bodystocking and a jewel-encrusted bikini, Alonso lounges around seductively, giving the crowd and appreciative viewer a good look at her scantily clad body. (As the music swells, Alonso sings a mournful ballad of womanly longing to the crowd. Her vocals are dubbed by Mara Del Rio, whose high-pitched voice sounds like Kate Bush). A satisfying widescreen shot captures Alonso reclining against a bannister, as the town band play their instruments behind her. Besotted drunks hoist the Countess up onto the bar, and she vamps and wiggles her way across it, with the camera panning down to hip level to show her from the waist down before she slinks back down to the floor. Alonso lies invitingly across a table at the end of her song, and draws cheers from the crowd. Farrell (presumably distracted from the performance by topics such as underground rock density and the fuel-to-distance ratio of trains carrying different loads) watches from the sidelines and walks off, leaving the Countess unhappy with the engineer's cold fish response. Deciding that further enticements are required, the Countess takes a bubble bath in her room and strategically shows Farrell her bare back and a hint of her glistening, freshly washed bottom when a maid opens the door to bring more water. (Alonso is sitting in the bath as Megowan talks behind the door, but when the maid enters she's out of the water, looking behind herself and then dropping back into the water with a splash). The engineer gets the message and romance develops between the two, allowing Alonso to transform from a sultry femme fatale to a more sympathetic lead as she falls for Megowan's rugged charms.

The saboteurs continue their attempts to destroy Farrell's handiwork. During a costumed waltz in the saloon one night, a building outside is set on fire. The chaos in the town that follows is well staged by director Malatesta, and a larger number of extras than usual for the period portray the panicked townsfolk. The criminals return for another explosive attempt at sealing the dig, and this second attack causes flooding and large-scale water and stunt scenes as men flee the torrents pouring into the mine. Farrell urges his co-workers to run but is caught, along with several others, in a sealed-off cavern as the disaster unfolds. The eventual set of the collapsed mine is impressive – a maze of collapsed timber in the darkened tunnel, filling the widescreen frame, lies atop a path of muddy, running water, and the rescuers must climb through the wreckage to reach their trapped friends. When the Countess and Farrell embrace after the engineer is freed from the cavern, music swells with an orchestral surge that silences Alonso, even though her lips are moving while she talks onscreen. The dialogue track comes back afterwards and allows her a final "Ahh!" of pleasure as she embraces her lover while the screen fades to black.

LA STRADA DEI GIGANTI features crowd-pleasing action that ranges from the dramatic to the comedic. A long barroom fight near the end is surprisingly violent, features a huge crowd of extras, and gives the stuntmen a workout with flips, a knife fight and breaking furniture amid a few amusing gags. The funniest is a dwarf who rises from a wicker basket to bash a bad guy on the head with a hammer, and who then rises again to scratch a line on a chalk board to keep tally of his victims. (Being a 1960 production, the stunt men getting thumped in this scene probably helped train their later protégés who would eventually get hammered by Bud Spencer in the 1970's). A final shootout in the hills around the railroad features a confrontation with enemy soldiers, and a cannon brought into the fray to blow up the scenery as both sides shoot it out. The climactic stunt during the battle is remarkable. Countess Von Kruger locates the bad guys and alerts Farrell of their escape. Farrell starts the train, rides it across the bridge at high speed, then jumps at the last minute. The driverless engine leaves the tracks, plunges off the bridge and lands amid the men in a destructive explosion. The train derailment is staged for real, and multiple cameras capture it plunging off the ravine and tumbling down the mountain embankment in a huge cloud of steam and smoke. The good guys must have had a train to spare as another engine is shown transporting cheering soldiers and miners from the worksite at the end of the movie, as Farrell and the Countess embrace and wave to the departing men.

The attractive pictorial qualities of this classically shot studio production compensate for its predictable narrative. A widescreen image of a train heading into town across the main bridge lingers on plumes of white steam billowing in front of the landscape. In the frontier village, crowds of workers and townspeople construct buildings amid a town square surrounded by impressive set design. Shots of Megowan talking to other characters carry visual impact by being framed in front of the picturesque mountainside at different times of the day. The indoor sets are nicely textured with a lot of wood panelling, but have a cleaner look than the gritty visual qualities inherent in later westerns. (Megowan's checkered shirt in the outdoor sequences is reminiscent of Eric Idle in costume about to sing his Lumberjack song). The score (credited to Guido Robuschi, Gian Stellari and Roberto Nicolai) is elegant, and emphasizes traditional orchestral work from the period, but only occasionally sounds like a western. (Alonso's show tune is given a melancholy reprise on guitar when the Countess declares her feelings for Farrell, and the melody later returns as an affecting background theme on harmonica). The location footage shot by Enzo Serafin in the Apuan Alps in northern Tuscany loses much of its appeal in the print currently available, and deserves a more flattering transfer.

Malatesta would direct peplum and adventure films for another decade. Although this was his only western, he contributed as a writer to two others, Mario Caiano's **UNA BARA PER LO SCERIFFO** (1965), and Monter and Polselli's **EL SHERIFF NO DISPARA** (1965). Megowan maintained a prolific career in film and TV for the next twenty years, appearing in shows such as **The Rifleman**, **Bonanza**, and **Gunsmoke**, and films such as **BLAZING SADDLES** (1974) and **TRUCK TURNER** (1974). Alonso starred in a handful of peplum and adventure movies after this, then concluded her film career with a trio of important westerns – Sergio Leone's **IL BUONO, IL BRUTTO, IL CATTIVO** (1966), Sergio Sollima's **CORRI UOMO CORRI** (1968), and Giulio Petroni's **LA NOTTE DEI SERPENTI** (1969). Alfio Caltabiano, Nello Pazzafini and Benito Stefanelli, who only have small roles here, would appear in numerous westerns later. Future spaghetti director Guido Zurli (**THOMPSON 1880** (1966), **COWBOY KID** (1973)) was an assistant director.

DINAMITE JACK

France / Italy 1961 [Bertrand Federation International (Paris), Radici (Italy)] 103 min. 3.11.1961
AT: Dynamittii Jack (Fin); Dynamite Jack, le terreur de Arizona (Fr); Le demon de l'Arizona (alt. Fr); Jack, o dynamitis (Gr); Dinamite Jack (It); Il terrore del Texas (alt. It); Dynamite Jack (USA)
Dir: Jean Bastia Prod: Jacques-Paul Bertrand St: Jacques Ary, Jean Bastia Sc: Jacques Ary, Jean Bastia, Jacques Emmanuel, Jean Manse Ph: Roger Hubert (Eastmancolor) Mus: Pascal Bastia, Jean-Pierre Landreau
starring Fernandel, Eleonora Vargas, Adrienne Corri, Lucien Rainbourg, Claude d'Yd, Marcelle Fery, Jess Hahn, Josette Jordan, Georges Lycan, Todd Martin, Alfonso Mathis, Viviane Mery, Jo Warfield, Margaret Rossel, Perry Smith, Colin Drake, Carl J. Studer, Fortunato Arena, Donald O'Brien (as 'Donal O'Brien'), Arthur Endreze, Maurice Derumaux, Billy Callaway, Jean Caltat, José Yamuza Dugo, El Coyote, Maurice Magalon, Jack Ary, Nadine Bellaigue, Evelyne Dassas, Alfonso Mathis, Arlette Redon, Daniel Ivernel
DVD: Inconnu (France, 2010), PAL, 103 min.
Arizona, 1880. French immigrant Antoine Esperandieu (Fernandel) journeys to Widow's Canyon during the Gold Rush in the hope of becoming as rich as his friend Jules Lavisse. Upon Esperandieu's arrival, the town's elderly sheriff informs Antoine that his friend is buried in the local cemetery, as Lavisse was a victim of Dynamite Jack, the town outlaw. Jack is the spitting image of Esperandieu, and the sheriff hires Antoine as a tax collector, hoping his resemblance to the bandit will persuade local settlers to repay their debts. When Jack and his gang stage another attack on the town, Esperandieu confronts his double, and each man finds that survival requires them to embrace their opponent's identity.

Veteran French comic Fernandel plays a dual role in this colourful, slightly overlong comedy that combines easygoing gags and dramatic gunplay. After an opening depicting a stagecoach travelling across desert terrain, Esperandieu pokes his head out of the coach window to complain in sarcastic fashion to the driver. The horse-faced Fernandel is immediately funny as Esperandieu, who suffers droll misfortunes throughout the film but maintains an eye for the ladies. When the driver kicks Esperandieu out, Esperandieu makes his way to Widow's Canyon on foot, taking a nap in the hills at dusk with a cactus silhouetted against the sky. Waking the next morning, Esperandieu is spooked by a cow skeleton lying on the desert sand, and makes haste down-road. The elderly town sheriff, Scotty (Lucien Raimbourg) greets him, gives Esperandieu a hit of booze and points him towards Lavisse's grave. Discussing the women attending Lavisse's funeral with the sheriff, Esperandieu learns that his deceased friend was a Mormon, and the women were all Lavisse's wives. Esperandieu contemplates his late friend's sexual exhaustion with admiration: "Jules, old boy. Several women... that was fatal." After seeking lodgings in town, Esperandieu greets the attractive saloon manager, Dolores (Eleonora Vargas), and then notices the cleavage under the low-cut top of another pretty woman cleaning the saloon. Esperandieu retires to unpack, and the cleaning woman ascends the stairs to tidy his room. When she walks inside, Esperandieu yells "Ahah!" with pleasure, and the sound of a struggle ensues before the woman runs out to avoid his lechery. The cleaning woman is the owner's wife, and Dolores marches Esperandieu out of his room at gunpoint. Esperandieu bargains his way out of trouble, and Dolores departs with cautionary advice: "Stay away from married women."

Now settled in, Esperandieu heads out on horseback the next day to look for gold, and returns with a bad case of sunstroke. The sheriff gives him a job as the local tax collector, warning Esperandieu to beware his debtors as "taxpayers are bloodthirsty animals". Esperandieu returns from this second mission with a ripped shirt and tattered clothes, and staggers into the bar for a drink. Dynamite Jack, his double, is inside, and has his back turned at the counter.

Fernandel's portrayal of Esperandieu as a romantic dupe contrasts with his performance as Jack, who menaces the town with threats of violence and creates tension whenever he appears. Weary-eyed, and radiating hostility, Jack is an expert shot who is comfortable killing with a gun or a knife. Esperandieu enters into a card game with Jack for money when the rest of the townsfolk choose to keep their distance. The game plays as a succession of desperate gags as Esperandieu first wants to win, then to lose once he realises the identity of his opponent. The confrontation ends when townsfolk and widows draw guns on the captured Jack. A light is shot and in the dark all sides shoot it out as a knocked calliope piano in the saloon starts to play. Jack and Esperandieu escape, then encounter each other in a barn. The recently bereaved widow Daisy (Adrienne Corri) approaches with a gun outside, and Jack departs on horseback. With Esperandieu desperate to survive, and Jack determined to escape, the scene mixes humour and suspense throughout.

As the townsfolk gather in determination to kill Jack and his band of outlaws, various mistaken-identity gags fill the rest of the story. Esperandieu dresses as a sheriff to help with his tax collecting, but the spooked townsfolk think he is Jack, and pay their debts before running for safety. A lynch mob forms to confront Jack, but grabs Esperandieu and prepares him for hanging. Dolores rescues Esperandieu at gunpoint, then confesses her feelings for the bandit Jack, who was once her lover. Esperandieu flees for the country, and Jack's men think he is the bandit. The real Jack gets knocked out, and Esperandieu returns to town as a hero boasting tales of defeating the outlaw. The town organises a medal for the conquering hero, and the real Jack shows up to claim it. The double-crosses and confrontations culminate in a final duel where both Jacks stalk each other through town, and clever shot choreography uses a variety of tricks and editing techniques to show both protagonists at the same time. (When Jack shoots a mirror during the final scene, it gently echoes Peckinpah's later **PAT GARRETT**). The final mistaken identity gag is a clever one. Sheriff Scotty comes to the rescue during the climactic duel and saves Esperandieu's life with a well-timed shot. Since the sheriff was hidden from view when he fired his rifle, the townsfolk think Esperandieu was the triggerman and crowd around to listen as he begins another of his boastful tales.

DINAMITE JACK flavours its story with sex gags. The attractive Dolores (played enticingly by Vargas, who shows good cleavage throughout) strips off to change when she and Esperandieu are in hiding, revealing a hot body and sexy undergarments that leave Esperandieu dumbfounded with lust. When a stranger enters the attic, Esperandieu takes the persona of Jack, kisses her passionately, and the two sink beneath the frame. At the end of the film, Dolores, realising her onetime lover's true identity, marches Esperandieu away at gunpoint and demands he marry her in the saloon. En route, Esperandieu stares longingly at another cute chick in town and asks the sheriff what he should do to become a Mormon. "Antoine, you old pervert!" says the sheriff with an appreciative grin. Roger Hubert's stylish colour cinematography often glides through scenes to make a narrative point. A shot early in the film tracks past multiple gravestones bearing names of various deceased who were "killed by Dynamite Jack", while Jack himself is introduced at the end of a duel, with the camera tracking backwards to reveal the victim. Attractive exterior scenes linger on well-framed shots of characters on horseback galloping past mountains, and a spectacular town in front of the Spanish hills. Pascal Bastia's score features a whistled tune backed by guitar, and a harmonica theme that sounds particularly French and carries allusions of the old west.

Spanish actress Eleonora Varga later starred in the Paul Naschy horror **LA ORGIA DE LOS MUERTOS / THE HANGING WOMAN** (1973), while British actress Corri was still some years away from her role as Mrs Alexander in **A CLOCKWORK ORANGE** (1971). Raimbourg would appear in TV and films (including Jean Brismée's surreal **LA PLUS LONGUE NUIT DU DIABLE / THE DEVIL'S NIGHTMARE** (1971)) for two more decades. Donald O'Brien (better known as Donal O'Brien in some quarters) has only a small role here but appeared in numerous spaghetti titles later (including **CORRI UOMO CORRI** (1967), **KEOMA** (1976), **MANNAJA** (1977) and the **ZANNA BIANCA** sequels), before starring in a formidable run of pure European trash, (Massaccesi's **EMANUELLE AND THE LAST CANNIBALS** (1977), Gianfranco Parolini's rotten **YETI-GIANT OF THE 20TH CENTURY** (1977), Marino Girolami's Z-grade Sybil Danning actioner **PANTHER SQUAD** (1984), and Michele Soavi's stylish **THE SECT** (1991), to name a few). The Spanish village seen in **DINAMITE JACK** later became a key location for Leone's **PER UN PUGNO DI DOLLARI** (1964). The storyline of **DINAMITE JACK** bears similarities to Fernandel's earlier **L'ENNEMI PUBLIC NO 1** (1953), another mistaken identity satire.

GOÛT DE LA VIOLENCE, Le
France / Italy / West Germany 1961 [Franco London Films, Societe Nouvelle des Etablissements Gaumont (Paris), Continental Produzione (Rom), Universum Film A.G. (München)] 89 min. 11.8.1961
AT: Haut fur Haut (Ger); Febbre di rivolta (It); El sabor de la violencia (Spa); The Taste of Violence (USA)
Dir: Robert Hossein Prod: Alain Podre, Ralph Baum St: Clade Desailly, Robert Hossein, Louis Martin, Jules Roy Sc: Claude Desailly, Robert Hossein, Louis Martin, Dany Jacquet, Hans Neubert, Jules Roy Ph: Jacques Robin (black & white, Dyaliscope) Mus: Andre Hossein; Song: "Poderoso senor" sung by Severiano Alvarez Ed: Boris Lewin Dec: Jean Mandaroux
starring Robert Hossein, Giovanna Ralli, Mario Adorf, Madeleine Robinson, Dany Jacquet, Hans H. Neubert
DVD: Gaumont (France, 2012), PAL 2.35:1 French Mono, 82 min.

Perez (Robert Hossain), a revolutionary leader in early 20th century Latin America, leads his men in holding up a military train and kidnapping Maria (Giovanna Ralli), the daughter of a local dictator, hoping her ransom will secure the exchange of 50 of their jailed compatriots. As Perez and two fellow rebels, Chico (Hans H. Neubert) and Chamaco (Mario Adorf) transport the young woman back to their base, unexpected emotions build between Maria and the three men, each of whom develops ambitions in conflict with the others. With some of the group fated not to complete their journey, the final destination at the Capital will hold tragic revelations for the rebel Captain.

LE GOÛT DE LA VIOLENCE, written and directed by lead actor Hossain, features multiple twists and double-crosses among its quartet of lead characters as they journey through the Oriente province, and its storyline of political conflict within Central America marks it as one of the earlier examples of the revolutionary (or 'Zapata') western that would later include such films as Damiano Damiani's **QUIÉN SABE?** (1967) and Sergio Corbucci's **VAMOS A MATAR, COMPAÑEROS** (1970). Hossain threads the story with hostile enemy encounters, melancholy interludes among the downtrodden peasant inhabitants, and stark depictions of the aftermath of war. As the grim tale progresses, expertly choreographed scenes of violence inflict casualties on the group, until the remaining protagonists, and the audience, are led to a downbeat conclusion. This was Hossain's sixth film as director (following an eclectic series of noir and crime films, with **TOI… LE VENIN** (1958) the most highly regarded) and **LE GOÛT DE LA VIOLENCE** displays an accomplished command of drama, narrative drive and stark cinematic atmosphere. Hossain, in collaboration with cinematographer Jacques Robin, makes the journey of the four protagonists an impressively textured visual experience, capturing the arid beauty of the railroads and mountain landscape at dawn, dusk and night, then populating those locations with impressive period set design. (Some westerns manage a lot of the same, but on the cheap. **LE GOÛT DE LA VIOLENCE**'s budget seems to have been high enough to utilise quality design and craftsmanship, and to fill the sets with sufficient extras to give a sense of verisimilitude and authentic period atmosphere. At the beginning of the film, a military train travels with dozens of armed guards sitting in the open air. At film's end, a monastery overrun by ranks of marching soldiers has its walls lined with endless rows of hanged men). Hossain also makes frequent use of depth within the frame. At one point, Perez traverses a mountain range, and the widescreen framing reveals a village in the valley below. The next shot shows Perez and his men entering the village with the same mountain range behind them. Inside the village, the Captain meets a compatriot, Paco, and the two men talk inside Paco's house. They hold their conversation near an open window, and we see through the window to the rest of the village outside, with villagers walking the streets. Perez eventually mentions a monastery, and behind the villagers we see the monastery under discussion through the window in the far distance, atop the mountain overlooking the village. Each scene casually emphasizes the relevant geography visible in the background, easing the film into the subsequent locale and accompanying chapter of the story with a satisfying sense of narrative economy.

In keeping with **LE GOÛT DE LA VIOLENCE**'s recurrent imagery of women as unwilling captives or victims, an undercurrent of sexual danger runs throughout the movie, continually threatening to explode into overt violence. When Perez approaches a lone woman in the village, and interrupts her while she washes clothing, the woman registers surprise before silently adjusting her dress to cover a bare shoulder, providing a glimmer of tension and suggesting just how cautious women must be in this locale. The perils of transporting an attractive woman through a hostile land are eventually made apparent when the strikingly beautiful Maria brings unwanted attention to the group. In a chilling sequence, male villagers assemble on the mountain road at dusk as Captain Perez and his fellow travellers attempt to leave the village. Armed with machetes, they greatly outnumber the plainly dressed Perez and his companions. Perez talks his way through the crowd, and the villagers follow Perez and his group across an open field a short distance behind them, harbouring obvious intentions for the general's daughter. The sound of wind blowing across the field plays on the soundtrack, and Perez stops at the edge of a tall cornfield. After conferring with his men, Perez and his group head into the maze of crops, and the villagers follow them into the thicket of corn stalks and leaves. Moving quickly, the Captain's men split up and light torches to start spot fires throughout the field, as Perez and Maria hurry across the plain. The villagers advance, and eventually confront a tall wall of flame blocking their path. It shields Perez and his companions as they leave, and the villagers are forced to turn back. When Perez and his men escape to the safety of a coastal waterway, they are confronted by a hundred soldiers on horseback. Perez has to show his willingness to kill the general's daughter to get them to retreat, and as the fugitives row away from the shoreline, we see

their pointof-view of the soldiers gathered with their horses on the receding shore. Chamaco makes an observation about their predicament: "It's not a woman we have with us, it's dynamite."
The ongoing rivalry between members of the group is depicted through confrontations that only temporarily allow any one person to have the upper hand – a mirror of the struggle the revolutionaries in the country have against their military oppressors. In an early sequence, Chamaco goes into the underbrush to kill Perez, and the audience is encouraged to expect one of two outcomes – the first where Perez has killed Chamaco, and the second where Chamaco has killed Perez. Gunshots are fired, and Maria and Chico wait for a victor to emerge. The outcome is unexpected – enemy soldiers had surprised the duo, and both men have helped save the life of the other. A later scene shows Perez and Chamaco sleeping lightly, neither one now trusting the other. Chamaco reaches for his weapon, and cocks the rifle. Perez does the same. A weapon is eventually lowered, then the other. Neither man says a word, and the scene fades to black. In a final confrontation on a beach, Maria gains temporary control over the group and must choose who she might kill among equally threatening opponents. When she wounds one of the group, and the dying man prepares to take revenge, Perez must choose where his ultimate loyalties lie.

There is romance in the film (no surprise considering the appeal of hot bombshell brunette Ralli) but it is fragile, and temporary. In **LE GOÛT DE LA VIOLENCE**, where Perez and his rebels are outnumbered and outgunned, victory merely delays the return of defeat, and of death. The film opens with dozens of armed soldiers travelling on a train through desolate countryside, and then shows the capture and mass execution of those soldiers by rebel bandits. At the end of the movie, the balance of power is reversed, and soldiers gather on horseback among the corpses of their recent rebel victims. Following the murder of a companion, Perez's advice to Maria sums up the film's portrayal of a land bereft of hope: "If you know a prayer, say it. I don't know any."

French actor Robert Hossain made a strong mark on the genre with only two westerns. He followed up this fine film with the outstanding, equally impressive **CIMITERO SENZA CROCI / CEMETARY WITHOUT CROSSES** (1968), where he again wrote, directed and starred. Mario Adorf would have a more prolific career in the genre and appears in several fine westerns - Harald Reinl's **WINNETOU I** (1963), Paul Martin's **DIE GOLDSUCHER VON ARKANSAS** (1964), Rolf Olsen's **DER LETZTE RITT NACH SANTA CRUZ**, Jaime Balcazar's **TIERRA DE FUEGO** (1965), Giulio Petroni's **...E PER TETTO UN CIELO DI STELE** (1968) and Corbucci's **GLI SPECIALISTI** (1969). (Admirers of Adorf's excellent performance in this movie should also check him out in Fernando Di Leo's tough urban Eurocrime noir flick **MILANO CALIBRO 9** (1972), where he's even better). Giovanni Ralli later appeared in Corbucci's outstanding **IL MERCENARIO** (1968) and **CANNON FOR CORDOBA** (1970). Eurocult fans should note that she also stars in Massimo Dallamano's trashy **LA POLIZIA CHIEDE AIUTO** (1974 – aka **WHAT HAVE THEY DONE TO YOUR DAUGHTERS?**). The sparse, acoustic folk music score by Andre Hossein (the director's father) is lovely, and offers its most lyrical and engaging tune late in the film when Maria and Perez are shown falling for each other during a wordless sequence on an empty mountain plain. (Director Hossein shoots this scene with an abundance of smooth tracking shots that repeatedly and elegantly track into the face of each actor from wide-shot to close-up, like something out of a P.T. Anderson film). Elsewhere, the score makes accomplished use of a female vocalist during a scene in the monastery where the women of the town gather to mourn the death of the men. Reviewed via a widescreen and subtitled TV copy. Gaumont released a remastered DVD of the film in France in 2012. Filmed in former Yugoslavia, in black and white.

MAGNIFICI TRE, I
Italy 1961 [Cineproduzioni (Rom)] 105 min. 10.11.1961
AT: The Magnificent Three (Eng. title)
Dir: Giorgio Simonelli Prod: Emo Bistolfi St and Sc: Bruno Corbucci, Giovanni Grimaldi, Mario Guerra, Giulio Scarnicci, Renzo Tarabusi, Vittorio Vighi Ph: Franco Villa [Eastmancolor, Widescreen] Mus: Gianni Ferrio; song "Un Uomo Vivo" sung by Gino Paoli Ed: Dolores Tamburini
starring Walter Chiari, Ugo Tognazzi, Raimondo Vianello, Dominique Boschero, Aroldo Tieri, Anna Ranalli, Margaret Rose Keil, Luigi Visconti (as 'Fanfulla'), Tom Felleghi, Lucia Modugno, Ciccio Barbi, Nietta Zocchi, Franco Jamonte, Nando Angelini, Giuliano Mancini, Eugenio Galadini, Tullio Altamura, Revides Alex, Aldo Pini, Bruno Tocci

Comedy set in Latin America in 1866, with three dopes mistaken for skilled gunslingers. Parody of John Sturges **THE MAGNIFICENT SEVEN** (1960), and one of many western comedies made by Chiari and Tognazzi in the early 1960's. Simonelli's next western was **DUE MAFIOSI NEL FAR WEST**, with Franco and Ciccio.

Above: Italian Fotobusta of I Magnifici Tre (1961)

Left: Robert Hossein in a scene from A Taste of Violence (1961)

En Cine Del Oeste
En La Comunidad De Madrid
by Javier Ramos and Angel Caldito Castellano

Available on Amazon

THE NOIR AND THE WEST: HOW SPAGHETTI WESTERN AND NOIR CHARACTERS SHARE A SHAPED PERSONALITY

BY TONY NASH

World War II changed everything, and the Vietnam War changed everything all over again and spun it around on its head. In both circumstances, people worldwide came to an unspoken realization that what they believed before was no longer relevant in the wake of the various devastation. This shattered idealism and hopelessness were accurately depicted by the Noir films of the late 1940s, early 1950s, and the Italian Spaghetti Westerns of the 1960s, early 1970s.

Noirs and Spaghetti Westerns may sound like two complete opposites when it comes to having similarities to its characters, but they do share some things in common. Characters changed by life-altering events, the world in a constant state of uncertainty and change, and society's structure always teetering between being good, bad, and downright ugly. Split half and half, what both genres don't share in terms of their overall design, they make up for in giving their unique interpretation of them.

In both cases, objectivity in terms of relationships between people was completely lost. Where people once kept a kind of distance before they felt it was safe to give someone their trust was no longer possible. Any desire or feeling to attempt trust was now gone, and everyone was out for themselves. Within the terms of Film-Noir via the Post War Period, genre expert Eddie Muller stated the genre began as:
"The American public had lost its innocence and it wanted more adult stories about the way people actually behaved" (1), as people became more aware that nothing was black and white in terms of human beings, and that everyone was capable of deceitfulness, greed, and duplicity.

In terms of the Spaghetti Westerns, the Vietnam War had gone full tilt by 1963-64, and filmmaker and SW regular Ferdinando Baldi best stated, in regards to the genre's origins, that "the good guy who wins in the name of the law and restores the law was no longer valid. So, a new, ambiguous character was born, a character that played both sides, a person who didn't want to have anything to do with anyone." (2) *. This ambiguousness primarily spoke towards Europe's dissatisfied youth who felt their parents' old ways no longer worked in an era where even grade school kids were more intellectually aware of things going on in the world. Still, the idea does indeed harken back to the Post War period of America. Ideals that were once highly valued no longer made sense, and realizations that you were on your own for the majority of life made people less inclined to give their trust and friendship to anyone.

"The right now is essential, I wanna know what's going on right now. I live for the moment; I don't know when the bomb is gonna fall….. There's only now, and making money. And taking care of myself," (3) said writer Stuart Kaminsky in an interview he did in discussing the two film versions of Ernest Hemmingway's The Killers (1946 & 1964).

Mr. Kaminsky's comment is mostly related to the turbulent 1960s and The Cold War- but applies to both Post War Noir and the Spaghetti Westerns in relation to the mindset of the varied characters that made up the genres. When people become disillusioned after great tragedies like war, their demeanors change as well. Caring for oneself and only oneself at the expense of others, whether intentionally or collateral damage, is true of both Noir and SW characters. For many people in Noirs and SWs, money is the only thing that matters; how much can be gotten and how quickly before the targets realize they've been scammed. Sometimes bigger situations occur that make money seem less important, but a profit would still get made for the (anti) hero. By only living in the here and now, and having no concern for what tomorrow, and even the future, will hold, makes both Noir and SW characters less inclined to feel a connection of anyone outside of themselves. A kind of beginning as dirt, and ending as dirt if viewers were to look for philosophical meaning. Whereas in Noir, where the final outcome can be ambiguous, even if the intention is straightforward for the hero and justice, the SW outcome is either absolutely final or a continuation of what viewers saw at the beginning of some films in the genre. In the days of the Old West, the rules regarding law and order were often made up of what the people of the varied little communities believed they should be. While there were certainly sheriffs, marshals, judges, etc. even in the slowly prospering areas, more often than not, these figures held very little power in terms of actually exercising it. Whether they were cowards, beset by strict instructions from the main politicians of the state or Washington D.C., or simply plain crooked, individuals not only felt let down by their fellow man but now the laws that are supposed to protect them are either willingly incapable or don't care to uphold their authority. This combination of life's uncertainty, from both man and Nature, a sad realization of human frailty, and the hatred of violent inhumane treatment, played a large role in SW characters.

Soldiers in combat played the most significant role in shaping both the Noirs and the SW's characters. What people were reading about in regards to war was nothing compared to those who witnessed things first hand. What those men saw and experienced in the trenches and jungles of both periods had profound effects on their return to civilian life. Not only did their ideas and views of life change, but their connection to people and the world as a whole changed as well. Faith was not only lost in other people, but faith in themselves was gone as well. These men no longer felt they belonged in the world, that they died spiritually on the battlefield, and that only their bodily shell and brain functions returned, merely going through the motions."I fight only for myself now," (4) claimed SW character Nathaniel Cassidy (played by Donal O'Brien from **Corri Uomo Corri** (Run Man Run, 1968) and sadly he was very right. Characters of both the Noirs and SW's are always on the move, never remaining very long in one place, and only giving of themselves the basics- to the people these characters make the briefest connections with. While the majority of Post War Noir protagonists were disillusioned war veterans whose humanity returns all too late as their decisions often lead to their demise, this isn't always the case for SW characters. Many of them did most likely see action during the Civil War, the Mexican-American War of 1848, or even aided in Texas' war for independence in 1836. But for the majority of these characters, the harshness of the still untamed Western Frontier landscape, the raids by hostile Native American tribes and brutal Mexican Bandidos, the uncertainty of who around them could be trusted, and the all-around unforgiving power of nature is what led to their current feelings.

Not only were these SW characters affected by the varied wars of the burgeoning United States, but their losses and failures as they were making their way in the frontier made even broader impacts for them. These men didn't just feel disconnected from such experiences; some even felt the need for revenge on the world for the raw deal they believed they got. This revenge is usually fueled by the feeling of being far too slighted by both society and life by breaking a few rules regarding conduct in handling the deception of those they've set their sights on in whatever scheme they're thinking of. Even forging uneasy alliances with those who're simply greedy and ruthless became commonplace within the genre, sometimes followed by a foreboding of betrayal to come. The SW characters often border on being no better than the characters they eventually will come into conflict with and take down, sometimes more so because audiences realize that they weren't bad once upon a

Top: Arrow Video: The Sartana Collection
Middle: Still from Sabata
Bottom: Koch Media release of Run, Man, Run

Top: Explosive Media: The Big Gundown
Middle: Wild East twofer: Garringo & Two Crosses at Danger Pass
Bottom: German Film Program: The Stranger Returns

time. What keeps the characters of both the SW and Noirs likable is that someone or something will come into play within the various films that remind them of what they once stood for. This spark of revelation is usually never permanent as the character will often go back to his previous shifty ways once the task at hand is done. Still, it does give such characters a little of their humanity back, and even a little more philosophically enlightened.

What few people outside of both the SW genre and the film world, in general, know about these characters is that their origin came in the form of a Japanese Samurai film. In 1961, Akira Kurosawa redefined his country's brand of action cinema with **Yojinbo** (Yojimbo/The Bodyguard), starring Toshiro Mifune. Despite being world-weary, cynical, and out for himself, the Mifune character displays some empathy and compassion for the woman held hostage by one of the bad guys and her suffering husband and young son. While no explanation is given explicitly for his brief humanity- maybe the woman reminds him of someone from his past (perhaps his mother?) is a definite possibility.

Clint Eastwood's genre-defining role as the Man with No Name in Leone's Dollars Trilogy (**Per un Pugni di Dollari** (A Fistful of Dollars, 1964), **Per Qualche Dollaro in Pui** (For a Few Dollars More, 1965), and **Il Bouno, il Brutto, il Cattivo** (The Good, the Bad, and the Ugly, 1966) is, of course, the model for the SW Anti-Hero who has no qualms about double-dealing and double-crossing people for his own personal gain, but also depicts a little of the disillusioned man in his moments where he shows genuine care and sympathy for certain characters throughout the films. Other characters of this type were played by: Giuliano Gemma in **Una Pistola per Ringo** (A Pistol for Ringo, 1965), Tony Anthony in **Un Dollaro Tra I Denti** (A Dollar Between the Teeth/A Stranger in Town, 1966), Craig Hill in **Per Gusto di Uccidere** (A Taste of Killing, 1966), and Peter Lee Lawrence in **Garringo** (1969). The majority of these characters are of the deliberate loner types. Whether the victims of consistent lousy luck, war experiences, etc., the characters in question have rebuked society in whatever way they choose and make marks out of anyone who crosses their paths. Usually, their revenge against the targets (marks) is based on them getting double-crossed- Echoes of the past equally play a part, but usually, the former has the strongest point. In the case of Peter Lee Lawrence's Johnny in Garringo, scars of a traumatic past and total hatred of any kind of authority have been the cause of his traits. That he has friends and has a good relationship with his adoptive family shows a man of split personality, not dubious or methodical tendencies. Lawrence's Johnny is very much akin to the kinds of lost souls returning from Vietnam in the late 1960s who saw the heaviest and most devastating forms of violence and combat that left them as nearly complete shells of their former selves, living unusual double lives.

Three Spaghetti characters associated the closest to the Noir characters playing the likes of Humphrey Bogart, John Garfield, Robert Mitchum, Robert Ryan, and, to a somewhat lesser extent, Sterling Hayden, - Django (the original **Django** (1966) played by Franco Nero), Jonathan "Colorado" Corbett (Lee Van Cleef in Sergio Sollima's **La Resa di Conti** aka The Big Gundown, also 1966), and Manuel (Robert Hossein in his grossly underrated **Une Corde, un Colt...** [Cimitero senza Croci, The Rope and the Colt, Cemetery Without Crosses, 1968-69]). While these three characters are certainly ambiguous in what they'll do to reach their goals, they do not entirely lack humanity, and indeed have a set of standards of moral conduct, ethics, and honor.

For Django, the war, racism, and hardship took far too much than he thought he would have to give up and left him with dark, unrelenting painful scars, trauma, and depression. One of the few true examples of man left hollowed by war within the genre, Django's very much like a ghost- existing, but not really alive.

"I left love behind many years ago. It's buried under a cross in the Tombstone cemetery," (5) * he says as he prepares to depart in a less than honorable fashion prior to the climax of the film
 That he wants to forget somehow all that's happened to him and move on to live a life with some sort of contentment makes him not only a tragic figure but one that audiences can care about and empathize with. The love of the mixed-race woman Maria gives him that second chance he's long desired. However, he first tries to fight the reciprocating feelings they share and gives him not only the courage to face his past and conquer it but to avenge the murder of the first woman he loved and give her spirit, and himself, peace.

"You can't run away forever. ……. I realized it when I was holding your hand so tightly, while the coffin was sinking into the quicksand. If I don't succeed, at least I will have tried to…redeem my life." (6) * He tells a wounded Maria as he decides the time has come to make a final stand against the odious Confederate villain Jackson and his band of racist cutthroats.

In an interesting case of irony, this makes Django one of the few SW protagonists/Anti-Heroes to have a full circle in their previous life view! After the war ended in that he could find a reason to go on living, he was able to love again, and could reciprocate that love, and have some form of normalcy in a crazy world.

Corbett from **Le Resa di Conti** (The Big Gundown, 1966) is a man who's seen quite a bit in his life: war, murderers, thieves, etc. All these experiences numbed him to a degree- in his treatment of suspects whether as a lawman or bounty hunter.

"I stopped playing with guns when I was a boy of 12. When I draw a gun now, it's only to kill," (7) * he explains to Mr. Brokston (Walter Barnes) and his friend/bodyguard Baron von Schulenberg (Gerard Herter), indicating his days of being a boastful show off are over.

Even though he's wary of many people, he still maintains a degree of ethics, a code of conduct, and, most importantly, honor. He naturally believes his quarry Cuchillo Sanchez (SW familiar face Tomas Milian) is guilty of murder and pedophilia, the latter an act even the most hardened and vicious to life are appalled by and intends to bring the man in to stand trial, only planning to kill him if he has no other option. When he gets to know the man and the circumstances surrounding key people involved in the case, Corbett's humanity comes back to life, and realizes he's turned away from not only the truth but life itself in his self-pity. Corbett isn't really an Anti-Hero like many of the SW stars, though he does display many of the classic tropes of the style, but too much time dealing with the guilty has led down a rocky terrain that he has to come to grips with and remember the values he holds dear.

"... something seemed wrong. And when you involved yourself personally in this thing… I knew it was wrong. You thought I'd shoot first and think later, is that it? You were wrong." (8) *
Corbett defiantly tells Brokston when he realizes the cover-up against Cuchillo in the rape-murder case.

Corbett is also unique in that he never enters the specific realm that some of his predecessors, contemporaries, and successors do. He hasn't completely separated himself from society and rejected it. While a loner to an extent in that he seems always to be going from place to place, this has more to do with being restless and the law enforcement jobs he's held that require extended periods of being alone.

Manuel (from **Une Corde, Un Colt**… (Cimitero senza Croci/The Rope and the Colt/Cemetery Without Crosses [1969]) is quite different from his predecessors here mentioned, and in the genre in general: He's been on the wrong side of the law his whole life, a rarity in the SW genre, and to an extent the Noir genre as well, though some Noir characters are revealed as good men having gone bad. For Manuel, being a gun for hire and killer of men had been a choice, and one he had indeed come to regret, though not completely. Manuel also differs in that his experiences have taught him that revenge, grudges, and hatred toward society as a whole is useless as it robs people of the lives they could be leading and the fulfillment they could still have if they didn't hold on to their anger and hostilities.

"Revenge is a bad seed. It bears bitter fruit. For everyone." (9) * he tells Maria Caine (played by Michele Mercier) when she comes to seek his help. Only the love he has for Maria is what purely drives him to help her in her quest to avenge her late husband. While it's debatable on many levels as to whether Manuel in some fashion had no issues in returning to his old ways, it's clear he does try to talk the woman he loves out of her scheme and that it's still possible for both of them to be happy and do it together as they had once planned.

Maria can be applied to the canon of SW Anti-Heroes as one of the few Anti-Heroines! The dogged life she and her husband were forced to live made her bitter to most of those around, especially the Rogers clan, who hated anyone who tried to be as prosperous as them. While wanting to get some revenge and peace for her husband was noble in her devotion, it left Maria with a hole that she can't fill, and has permanently marked her as a doomed woman, even though the Rogers were in the wrong in the first place.

"I'm so tired, Manuel. I did my duty. That's all I wanted. I'm all alone." (10) * Maria tells Manuel when they come to an important decision in their plan.

"I know a place in the South. We can go there together, if you want." (11) * he responds to her, knowing that things can never be the same for them as before.

In his own way, Manuel had come full circle even before viewers get to see him for the first time in the film, but then it's realized he has another crossroad to venture to and make one last decision when it becomes clear what he wants with Maria will not go how he planned.

Two characters that also follow this pattern, albeit in a far lighter tone, are Sartana and Sabata. These characters live on society's fringes, but more so in that, they can operate their various schemes with little or no interference from people they would otherwise get close to. Unlike their predecessors and contemporaries, Sartana and Sabata aren't plagued by demons like the horrors of war, the loss of many loved ones, and the slew of hardships and bad experiences that would otherwise make them bitter and resentful. They're still untrusting of most of the people around them! But this has more to do with being able to read faces and tell people from their movements, etc., traits usually honed by gamblers, so instead of being resentful of society, they treat it like players in a card game, keeping an eye on everyone. Both men are also a bit more honest than their contemporaries and predecessors. Neither Sartana nor Sabata will take more than what's deemed a fair amount in exchange for their services; they only steal from the bad guys and share the spoils equally with their accomplices. Sartana even goes a step further in that he won't take money off of a dead man, though whether this is moral or religious is left for the viewer to ponder. To say they're above stealing, in general, would be a complete misnomer as they do work scams. Still, the targets are usually very unscrupulous types who not only can afford to lose money but also don't want their squeaky-clean images busted and their true intentions made known. They also try to avoid complications with law enforcement officials, so while they're not pillars of the community, they also don't intend to obstruct justice.
"I'm on the right side…..not the side against the law," (12) Sabata tells his untrustworthy buddy Banjo, who planned to double-cross him from the original **Ehi Amico… C'e Sabata, hai Chiuso!** (Sabata, 1969) film.

The above antidote can be applied to Sartana as well, though he never uses a phrase like it. What he does say in the third film of the series, **C'e Sartana… Vendi la Pistola e Comprati la Bara!** (Sartana's Here, Trade Your Pistols for a Coffin!/I Am Sartana, Trade Your Guns for a Coffin/A Fistful of Lead, 1970)

"You must never pay a man to kill," (13) * he says to a youngster asking him to save his mother from the clutches of a bandito, showing he values the innocence of youth and wants the kid to believe in the positives of life and people.

Still maintaining many of the classic tropes of the SW icons, Sartana and Sabata are a breath of fresh air in that they lack the hostility, hatred, and distance of the usual Anti-Hero and can be more openly rooted for as they have a higher value for code, ethics, and decency.

The only other items separating these characters besides genre are locations, storytelling, and era. For Noirs, the isolation and separation from society were the concrete jungles of places like Los Angeles and New York. The labyrinths of buildings, streets, and alleyways made disappearing and hiding all the more suitable for those who not only wanted to evade the law and justice, but for those who couldn't stand the world they were living in anymore. That everything seemed close together, and on top of each other added to that dizzying effect of the unease people were feeling in post-WWII. The Western frontier for the Westerns was a seemingly never-ending stretch of barren desert, with only the occasional small burgeoning community. This dry and sandy wilderness could be unforgiving for those unprepared or naïve to enter into it, hence why outlaws and loners looking to get lost were the only ones who could survive such hostile environment/terrain. The frontier could be scarier as, at times, there was nothing for miles around, and if severe injury or loss of vital supplies happened, often it was days or even weeks to the nearest little hamlet to get aid. The landscapes these characters inhabit- serve more as extensions of the characters themselves, giving a little extra depth to the type of lives they live and the thought process going through their minds that drive them into the various schemes, adventures, and dangers they engage in and face, though sometimes the land can also act as a metaphor for the times these same characters inhabited.

In many Noir films, including **The Maltese Falcon** (1941), **The Big Sleep** (1945), **Double Indemnity** (1944), **The Postman Always Rings Twice** (1946), and **Mildred Pierce** (1945), the plot's center on murder, greed, deception, and unrequited love. The fourth item tends to rarely play a role in the SWs, instead replaced by lost love through murder or unforeseen tragic circumstances beyond human control. Death happens quite a bit in the SW genre, but usually, the heroes or Anti-Heroes know the identity of the killer and are out for revenge, and rarely do the characters engage in investigations into such affairs as is done in Noirs.

Of course, three exceptions to this would be Sergio Corbucci's **Gli Specialisti** (The Specialists/The Specialist, 1969), Giuliano Carnimeo's **Una Nuvola di Polvere…un Grido di Morte…Arriva Sartana** (A Cloud of Dust..a Cry of Death…Sartana is Coming/Light the Fuse… Sartana is Coming, 1970), and Enzo Gicca Palli's **Il Venditore di Morte** (The Price of Death, 1971). In Gli Specialisi, the main character Hud comes back to his old home town to find out who framed his brother for taking part in a bank robbery and then had him killed. In the fifth and final film of the official Sartana series, the mysterious gunman tries to figure out what really happened in a deal for counterfeit money and illegal weaponry that went wrong- and who masterminded the agreement and the double-crosses. **Venditore di Morte** has a gunslinging detective trying to clear the name of a man believed to be framed for a crime he didn't commit, only to discover something more sinister. All three play up the mystery theme very well, particularly Venditore as it has the most Noirish and early Gialli (Italian Mystery Thrillers) aspects to it that, while basic, work well for the material at hand. Of course, deception and greed play significant roles in both genres; the SW characters tending to go further than their Noir counterparts due to the lack of stable law and order.

A lingering question for anyone unfamiliar with both genres is why anyone would find such characters exciting and root for them. As mentioned earlier in the article, Eddie Muller stated that people were more interested in seeing on-screen characters as very much like those they saw on the streets, read about in the paper, etc. Heroes played by the likes of John Wayne, Roy Rogers, Clayton Moore, William Boyd, and even Gene Autry, seemed a little too clean-cut for audiences in the wake of one conflict, and later in a much more controversial conflict. The characters these men played worked well for the wide-eyed youngsters- full of dreams, goals, and ideas in making things better, but as with maturity and age, sometimes what was idolized in childhood made less sense when knowledge flowed. These characters were almost unrealistic to the point of being almost immortal, whose qualities were unattainable to the common man! This seemingly unattainable status made the flawed characters, even to the point of being corrupted types in Noirs and SWs, more appealing because the common man could relate to on some level to them!

Despite coming from two completely different eras, Noir and SW characters have fairly similar traits that make them akin to each other. Living in worlds they no longer understand, everything they once believed in- in shambles, the horrors of war, loss, and misfortune hardening them to the point of being stone-cold to everything! The loss of human emotions, the varied men of Noir, and SWs now live in an invisible barrier that separates from society and allows them to act on their own rules within the same society they now hate and avoid. Some on both sides aren't completely without redeemability and show they can still display forms of humanity. Even the changes they experienced have forever marked them so that they can never be who they were before, but it doesn't mean they can't regain a decent quality of life. Unfortunately, some can't make the change in that far too much damage has been done, while others simply stick with their loner lifestyle by choice. These characters reflect the generations who went to see them on the big screens: the Post WWII audiences who came to the sobering revelation that life wasn't as simple as they first thought, and darkness existed within everyone and the Counter Culture of the 1960s that were wary of all the lying, scheming, and the duality of the current governments of the world, and that the values their parents had, didn't work anymore. Audiences in the last twenty years or so can equally relate to these characters as the past generations' feelings have as much and/or more relevance today. The near-unlimited resources to people and their backgrounds gives people all the more reason to be wary and untrusting of others around them. Even today, characters from both genres are necessary as they offer a glimmer of hope and control in otherwise consistent chaotic times.

Two highly recommended books on Film Noirs.

Left: The Noir Western by David Meuel: Mcfarland and Compnay. 2015

Right: The Dark side of the screen: Film Noir by Foster Hirsch: Da Capo Press. 2008

(*) Asterisk indicates a quote is the English subtitle translation of the original Italian audio track

Sources
1. From the documentary Shadows of Suspense (2006), included on the Eureka! Masters of Cinema Blu Ray of Double Indemnity (1944). Eureka! Entertainment 2012
2. From the documentary The Spaghetti West (2005) presented by IFC Films. IFC Films 2005
3. Stuart Kaminsky on the Killers, included in the Criterion Collection Double DVD of The Killers (1946)/ The Killers (1964). The Criterion Collection 2004
4. From the Blue Underground DVD of **Corri Uomo Corri** (Run Man Run) (1968). Blue Underground 2006
5. From the Arrow Video Steelbook release of **Django** (1966). Arrow Video 2018
6. From the Arrow Video Steelbook release of **Django** (1966) Arrow Video 2018
7. From the Grindhouse Releasing Blu Ray of **Le Resa di Conti** (The Big Gundown) (1966). Grindhouse Releasing 2013
8. From the Grindhouse Releasing Blu Ray of **La Resa di Conti** (The Big Gundown) (1966). Grindhouse Releasing 2013
9. From the Arrow Video Release of **Une Corde, Un Colt…** (Cimitero senza Croci/The Rope and the Colt/ Cemetery Without Crosses) (1969). Arrow Video 2015
10. From the Arrow Video Release of **Une Corde, Un Colt…** (Cimitero senza Croci/The Rope and the Colt/Cemetery Without Crosses) (1969). Arrow Video 2015
11. From the Arrow Video Release of **Une Corde, Un Colt…** (Cimitero senza Croci/The Rope and the Colt/Cemetery Without Crosses) (1969). Arrow Video 2015
12. From Ehi Amico… **C'e Sabata, hai Chiuso!** (Sabata) (1969)
13. From the Arrow Video release of **C'e Sartana… Vendi la Pistola e Comprati la Bara!** (I Am Sartana, Trade Your Pistol for a Coffin!/ Sartana's Here, Trade Your Guns for a Coffin/Fistful of Lead) (1970), via The Complete Sartana Boxset. Arrow Video 2017

Coming in Issue #3 of The Spaghetti Western Digest! An interview with the Legendary Fred "The Hammer" Williamson!

**Photo Courtesy of Eric Mache

COVER REVIEW:
KILLER KID

-DENNIS CAPICIK

KILLER KID (Italy, 1967)

Director Leopoldo Savona had previously made **El Rojo** (Italy/Spain, 1966), his first—and probably least-appealing—foray into the world of spaghetti westerns. Starring American ex-pat Richard Harrison as the confusingly-titled lead (a.k.a. "Red"), this Leone-inspired revenge western was a generally uneventful affair. But with **Killer Kid**, which was also prepped as yet another action quickie, this time starring the ubiquitous Anthony Steffen, Savona fashioned a far more interesting, politically-inclined low-budgeter, which was clearly influenced by the first-and-finest "spaghetti zapata", Damiano Damiani's **A Bullet for the General** (Quien Sabe?, Italy, 1966). [Caution: The following paragraph of synopsis contains spoilers!]

While in prison awaiting his transfer to Fort Knox, the infamous "Killer Kid" (Anthony Steffen) is allowed to mysteriously escape to try and prevent the sale of a shipment of stolen army rifles, which has the potential to compromise the United States government and become a (quote) "embarrassing situation diplomatically." After witnessing an unscrupulous double-cross during what was supposed to be a routine sale of munitions ("You double-crossin' polecat! You're gonna pay for this in gold, or you can keep that revolution of yours goin' with matchsticks!"), the Kid reluctantly sides with the duplicitous Vilar (Fernando Sancho) and infiltrates this band of revolutionaries, led by the elderly and far-more-composed El Santo (Nelson Rubien). At the start of this shaky alliance, the Kid attempts to prevent said shipment of rifles from ever finding their way into the revolutionaries' hands. Along the way, federale Lieutenant Ramírez ("Ken Wood"/Giovanni Cianfriglia) also learns of the shipment—that was (quote) "plucked from the U.S. Army's well-guarded arsenal"—and the real truth about the Killer Kid, who may or may not actually be an undercover army operative named Captain Morrison. However, after witnessing the brutal slaughter of innocent Mexican villagers at the hands of the Ramírez gang ("Those who aid the revolutionaries are enemies of the State!"), the Kid—who is indeed really Capt. Morrison—embraces the revolutionary cause and stays on to fight for its cause…

Translated Spanish ad-catchline: **"The Mexican People Defend Their Freedom In Acts Of True Heroism!"**

Above: German Film Program
Bottom: Italian Fotobusta- Killer Kid
Page 160: German vhs release of Killer Kid under the title Chamaco

As with most politically-motivated Italo-westerns of the time, **Killer Kid**'s topical Mexican Revolution backdrop is most definitely used as a metaphor for any number of contemporaneous issues troubling the world during the Vietnam-era, social unrest-filled late 'Sixties. This was especially evident in many of the more prominent and upscale westerns to come out of Italy at that time, such as the aforementioned **A Bullet for the General**, along with Sergio Sollima's **The Big Gundown** (La resa di conti, Italy/Spain, 1966) and its follow-up **Run, Man, Run** (Corri uomo corri, Italy, 1968); Sergio Corbucci's playfully-political triumvirate consisting of **The Mercenary** (Il Mercenario, Italy/Spain, 1968), **Companeros!** (Vamos a matar, compañeros, Italy/West Germany/Spain, 1970) and **What Am I Doing in the Middle of the Revolution?** (Che c'entriamo noi con la rivoluzione?, Italy/Spain, 1972); and, of course, Sergio Leone's **Duck, You Sucker!** (Giù la testa, Italy, 1971), to name but a few. In his essential and pioneering book, *Spaghetti Westerns – Cowboys and Europeans from Karl May to Sergio Leone* (Routledge & Kegan Paul, 1981), author (the future Sir) Christopher Frayling points out that directors Sergio Sollima, Damiano Damiani and actor Gian Maria Volontè had (quote):

"…all stressed, in interviews, that the Westerns in this sub-genre were intended to be read as parables about the relations between the Third World (represented by 'Mexico') and the capitalist countries of the West (represented by the 'outsider'): the unstable relationship between bandit/rebel and 'Gringo' was apparently meant to illustrate 'the difficulty of sustaining a dialogue between the Third World and the industrial world', the 'outsider' was meant to 'recall the anti-colonial struggles of the peoples of Latin America, of Vietnam, and of minorities within the United States."

In the hands of such leftist directors and writers as Franco Solinas (a prolific and very politically-minded writer who penned a number of the above-mentioned films), many of these westerns attempted to convey their sociopolitical views through what was ostensibly escapist entertainment meant for the masses; a perfect platform for many of these outspoken individuals within the film industry who made an effort to expose not only the anxieties of Italy at the time, but the rest of the world as well.

As it moves swiftly from one action scene to another, Savona's present modest little film never overtly pushes its underlying political agenda, but several of its characteristics were emblematic of other, better-known films in the cycle: which include the shadowy American interloper (i.e., Steffen) who surrenders to the Mexican patriots' cause, and the contemptuous insurgent (i.e., the always-entertaining Fernando Sancho); both of whom gradually and grudgingly develop bonds of kinship despite their differing philosophies. But, as with most westerns steeped in ideological themes, each character eventually evolves to having a new, more ethical—albeit solemn—worldview. However, part of the Kid's changing viewpoint also stems from the film's more traditional love/hate relationship with El Santo's niece, Mercedes ("Liz Barrett"/Luisa Baratto) when he emphatically declares:

"I wanna talk straight! When you folks welcomed me without question, I was hoping I'd found a new life. The men and women I've been watching die with courage, I thought were peasants without ideals or an ounce of dignity. I've changed my mind about that!"

First seen languishing in an Army stockade, Steffen as "Kid" plays his usual, hard-edged enigmatic self, whose character is further obscured at the outset by some lazy scripting, much of which revolves around the convoluted subplot involving stolen weapons. Given that this was the initial reason why Steffen's character is allowed to sneakily escape, the commanding officer of the garrison then confusingly states, "We finally got our hands on the most dangerous gunman in the West, and we let him slip through our fingers, gentleman! He made fools of the pack of us!" Whereas, later in the narrative, in what amounts to an almost incidental, throwaway bit of dialogue, this same C.O. praises Kid's methods of impersonation ("He is an excellent officer, but is completely devoid of scruples when it comes to a fight!"). Elsewhere, when Vilar questions the Kid's true identity, Kid/Morrison demonstrates his prowess with a six-shooter by blasting (quote) "a hole in a silver dollar… while it's moving!" further stressing our hero's ambiguity, a point which is never resolved by the film's end.

After meeting the charismatic El Santo, who quietly governs using his intellect and sheer force of will, Steffen's character remains in a constant mental/moral struggle with his loyalty to the U.S. Army. It's only after he witnesses Ramírez's brutal slaughter of innocent Mexican villagers that Kid/Morrison's personal convictions begin to outweigh and eclipse his obligations to his capitalist employers. This sentiment was reiterated in any number of political spaghetti westerns, as well as in higher-profile, more mainstream Hollywood movies like Richard Brooks' **The Professionals** (USA, 1966). In spite of his unscrupulous reputation, Morrison strives to impart some basic rules of wartime conduct when he witnesses the revolutionaries blindly killing enemy captives ("What makes you think you can't kill without manners?!"), yet this imperialistic/paternalistic stereotype (also echoed in Brooks' film), which implies that the Mexicans are incapable of governing themselves, is thrown on its head, when, after witnessing further carnage in the film's climactic battle, Morrison orders the execution of a number of 'POWs', an action which not only echoes his ex-commander's earlier estimation of him, but also the lingering consequences of war itself.

In what amounts to one of his more tastefully-reserved performances, Steffen still participates in a number of his trademark action scenes, which, despite the film's underlying would-be 'intellectual' stance, remain the primary driving force of the film (this is essentially an actioner over a heavy political statement, after all). Sancho, on the other hand, delivers yet another colorfully outrageous performance as the blustery Vilar, whose antagonism towards Kid/Morrison ("PIG! I spit on you! Filthy gringo!") also drives much of film, but in an uncharacteristic—and highly welcome—turnaround, he becomes adversely affected when the war hits a little too close to home. Here seen in one of his more substantial supporting roles as the ruthlessly-unwavering Ramírez, actor-stuntman "Ken Wood"/Giovanni Cianfriglia likewise adds some extra spurts of energy as the sole representative of the brutally dictatorial Mexican government.

Shot entirely in Italy and utilizing many of the similar abandoned quarry locations that later popped up in just about every poverty-row "Miles Deem"/Demofilo Fidani oater, DP Sandro Mancori makes the most out of his meager locations and succeeds in giving the proceedings a much grander scale than its modest budget could probably have afforded without him. While Savona's career became increasingly spotty over the course of the 'Seventies, he did direct three additional westerns, one of which, **A Man Called Apocalypse Joe** (Un uomo chiamato Apocalisse Joe, Italy/Spain, 1970), also starred Anthony Steffen as yet another ruthless gunman, this time masquerading as a wannabe Shakespearean actor (!?). Among the more appealing ingredients of **Killer Kid** is Berto Pisano's rousing score, which brings extra oomph to the numerous action scenes, while his impressive flamenco guitar title theme conveys all the necessary melancholy that Savona's little action picture ultimately delivers.

Although several of Anthony Steffen's westerns became available to North American audiences on Beta/VHS cassette throughout the home video boom of the 'Eighties, **KK** remained absent to most English-speaking viewers during this time, while some steadfast spaghetti western aficionados succeeded in tracking-down copies from such faraway places as South Korea and Venezuela. As of this writing, the only official English-friendly DVD currently on the market (but now OOP) remains Koch Media's 2008 German release, which retained the film's crucial 2.35:1 scope aspect ratio and offered a choice of either

German or Italian language audio options with optional removable German or English subtitles. **KK** was later released on disc in France by Artus Films, but alas, that version wasn't English-friendly.

Although sophisticated enough, **Killer Kid** never attains the astute political insights of a Damiani or Sollima film, but despite being nothing more than a routine programmer, Savona manages to shrewdly imbue a number of interesting themes and perspectives into his action-oriented narrative. For that reason alone (but for other reasons besides), it remains one of Steffen's and Savona's best efforts.

Top to Bottom:
Fidani's Production copmay
English Title card
Hunt Powers as Django
Dennic Colt listed as playing both Sanchez brothers

THE BALLAD OF DJANGO (Giù le mani… carogna!, Italy, 1971)

Continuing his economical mock-"Django" series, it seems that Demofilo Fidani, a prolific director of notoriously-cheapjack westerns, had also begun to run out of ideas by the time the 'Seventies rolled around, as evidenced by this lowly, piecemeal effort (a.k.a. **Down with Your Hands… You Scum!**).

Using much 'repurposed' footage from a number of his earlier—much more engaging—westerns, this story of aging bounty hunter Django ("Hunt Powers"/Jack Betts) commences amidst the hoariest of western clichés—a barroom brawl. Django, the (quote) "most famous bounty killer of the West" meets up with a young Bill Hickok ("Jerry Ross"/Gerardo Rossi), a fervent admirer of Django's skill with a pistol, who enthusiastically urges the senior shootist to recount a couple of stories for his entertainment and edification. The first involves the notorious Sánchez Twins (both played by "Dennis Colt" aka Benito Pacifico), one of whom was (quote) "hard and cruel," while the other was all (quote) "fire and hate! An animal who killed for the fun of it!" In the second story, he tells of the infamous outlaw Dean O'Neil ("Dean Stratford"/Dino Strano), who gunned folks down just for laughs, but in this case, Django's undertaking was also a (quote) "question of honor… and revenge!" As Django prepares to leave the bar for (quote) "one last job", "Wild" Bill asks to tag along in his pursuit of Buck Bradley (Gordon Mitchell), but Django, ever the loner, assures him that this game is not for him…

As with most of Fidani's, uh, 'thrifty' westerns, **The Ballad of Django** places most of its emphasis on lengthy, seemingly-endless action scenes, with seldom a minute spared to focus on its clunky, halfhearted plotline. Judging by its recycled footage and meager sets (many of which got reused over and over [and over!] again at the Elios Studios backlot), **TBoD** was shot using a tighter-than-usual budget even for "Deem"/Fidani (and that's sure saying something!), but despite its exceedingly humble origins, Fidani and his trusted stock players still manage to muster-up the odd burst of energy here and there. Using his usual pseudonym of Hunt Powers, Jack Betts is actually quite good as the seen-it-all bounty hunter (nicely dubbed on English prints by veteran voice actor Tony La Penna) with his graying hair, weathered all-black attire and distinctive limp (a condition which, of course, allows him to sneakily hide a trusty 4-barreled mini-derringer in the handle of his walking cane).

Gordon Mitchell, the **TBoD**'s other 'name' star, appears in the film's last twenty minutes for an extended shootout, which has a succession of stuntman shooting each other in an abandoned quarry (a frequently-used low-rent location that appeared in most of Fidani's westerns) as they energetically run, dive and tumble from rocks on cue. Other scenery-chomping performances include veteran stuntman/actor Benito Pacifico as the villainous Sánchez Twins, whose backstory involves little more than a string of robberies and indiscriminate murders, which culminates with an amusing Leone-esque stand-off. Z-grade leading man Dino Strano—better-known to some as "Dean Stratford"—is also on board as the trigger-happy Dean O'Neil, who is suitably over-the-top, cackling incessantly and cold-bloodedly murdering whoever crosses his path.

- Dennis Capicik

Italain Fotobustas The Ballad of Django

By spaghetti western cowboy
Denver, Italian style, abuilding south of Rome

By Nino Lo Bello

CAVE, Italy — Plunked amid some rolling hills here about 25 miles south of Rome is a Wild West cowboy town that was built by an American actor with his own two hands.

"I've built it from my mind's eye plan the way I think Denver, Colorado, must have looked in the days of the Gold Rush," explains he-man Gordon Mitchell, himself of Denver, Colorado. Mitchell, who has been living in Italy for the past decade, makes seven or eight so-called "spaghetti Westerns" a year.

"Denver, Colorado Jr." is eventually destined, when the right time comes, to be used as a free home for war waifs and for families whose luck has run out because of the ravages of war.

Meanwhile, though Mitchell continues to labor on his one-man whistle-stop on an average of about 15 hours a week (often picking up his tools at 3 in the morning when he can put in a few uninterrupted hours), he rents out his cowboy town to film companies that shoot Westerns.

"All the money I get from renting the location and most of my own salary from films goes into the buying of wood, nails, cement, equipment and what-have-you for this mad-mad project of mine. The first year I put up four wooden buildings. Last year I managed to get up another 12 structures, and this year I hope to have five more finished," he says.

So far Gordon Mitchell has done everything by himself — with nary a stitch of help. Eventually he will need some professional construction workers to help him install a plumbing system, but in the meantime whatever water may be needed by the movie crews on the set is brought in by truck.

"When the time comes, I plan to do the electricity and the wiring myself. And I think I can do the job because I've been reading up on the subject."

Mitchell, 48, whose real name is Charles Pendleton, has a legion of fans here, thanks to some 70 films he's made in Italy since coming to Rome in 1961. He started out as a bare-chested Hercules, went over to making war movies and is now doing six-shooter, good-guy parts for Italy's fettuccine flicks.

His experiences during the Korean War, in which he rose from Air Force sergeant to major, were to bring him here to Cave (pronounced Cah'-vay) to build a town in the image of pioneer Denver, where he was born. A Catholic priest one day in 1953 took Mitchell to a children's hospital in Sholow, Korea, a town that the Americans had just captured. Visiting the wards, Mitchell saw hundreds of innocent kids whose bodies and limbs had been shattered by bombs and guns.

By his own admission, Mitchell says he did not believe in any religion at that time, nor even in God. But what he saw in those wards made a deep, lasting impact on him. He knew that when he got out of the service, he wanted to do charitable work in the name of God — but with no specific religious denomination in mind.

Forced to give up these intentions for a while, Mitchell applied himself to a career and became an established B-movie film star, a line of work that enabled him to put away regular sums in the bank. Thus when the opportunity came, he bought seven acres of land a few kilometers outside of Cave.

Even before the ink was dry on the contract, Mitchell plunged in and began to build the cowboy town — chopping down his own trees, lugging his own logs, sawing the boards to size and nailing the planks with his trusty hammer — sometimes even with the butt of his trusty six-shooter, if he happened to be in costume already for some early camera chores.

But of the some 20 structures that he has put up, Mitchell is most proud of a church building he has built on large white stones he lugged in.

"Christ said, 'I will build my church on rocks,' and that is where I wanted to build the church. It's called Church of the Flowers of the Far, Far West. I've also written a song — both the music and the words — about the Church of the Flowers."

ACTOR GORDON MITCHELL AT WORK

AND A CHILD SHALL LEAD—Procession of jumbos shuffle along in single file, following the footsteps of Shane Smart, 4, who simply holds onto a stick which the lead elephant grips in its trunk. Shane's father is an animal trainer for Billy Smart's Circus in Windsor, England, and little Shane has learned some of the cues that start the elephant troupe performing tricks, like taking a walk around the block. Complains Shane's dad, "He can do tricks with elephants, but he hasn't learned the alphabet yet."

The Boston Globe (Boston Massachusetts), Jan 16, 1972

Sergio Martino Interview

Translation by Eugenio Ercolani
Conducted via email by Michael Hauss

S.W. Noting that your grandfather was the great director Gennaro Righelli, was it presumed that you too would enter the filmmaking world?
S.M. If you read my book, I talk in detail about my relationship with cinema and my beginnings in the industry. My grandfather would take me often to the cinema and on his sets. On one occasion I remember meeting Anna Magnani and Vittorio De Sica. He would push me to invent stories and when he called my mother to ask how I was, he would say "how is my little director?"

S.W. Were your parents involved in the film industry?
S.M. My mother, as a young girl, appeared in a silent movie directed by her father. I have beautiful photos of these sets, they were pioneering times. My father was a bank manager instead, but he had a passion for Super8 cameras. When I was sixteen I wrote a kind of Dr. Jekyll and Mr. Hyde story and we had fun shooting it together, I was the protagonist. My brother had a cameo. My mother and grandmother had supporting roles and the maids smaller ones. I still have a copy somewhere…

S.W. Were you a fan of the western genre growing up?
S.M. Like many filmmakers of my generation, we grew up with the great American westerns. Epic and perhaps over time a little repetitive but still very important to us. I remember the most important: **Stagecoach**, High Noon, **Gunfight at the O.K Corral**. Sergio Leone found a new approach with his stylized stories, which were profoundly different to the American ones.

S.W. You worked together with your brother Luciano on numerous films. What was the working relationship with him like? He was a producer on your two Italian westerns Arizona Colt Returns and A Man Called Blade.
My brother had a lot of faith in me, after all I grew up on his sets in which I had different tasks and roles. My first test as a director were my two early films, pseudo-documentaries. That investigated the youth of the sixties, and he produced both of those.

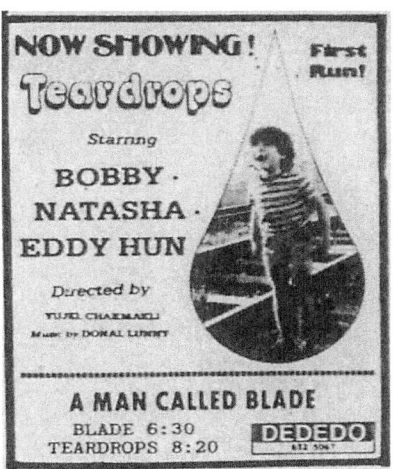

S.W. You contributed to the script for the very underrated $100,000 For A Killing, along with Luciano, what was that like and were you involved with the film after the script writing duties?
S.M. Certainly Italian cinema had, and still has, an artisan's approach and especially at that time roles were often exchanged. At the time I worked mostly in the production side of things, but at the same time I sometimes collaborated on the scripts and directing.

S.W. Tell us about Arizona Colt Returns, which is your first feature film directed after the two documentaries Wages Of Sins and Naked and Violent?

S.M. Obviously it was a more demanding experience, also because I had real professional actors to direct. Filmed largely in Madrid with a Spanish crew and few Italians. I perhaps had some initial anxiety but then I managed to take hold of the situation and after the first few days it was easy sailing. Many years have passed since that film and I have a nostalgic memory of it. Those were good times for Italian cinema...

S.W. You had a wonderful cast on Arizona Colt Returns, what do you remember as far as actors are concerned?
Antonio De Teffè, a.k.a. Anthony Steffen, remained a friend of mine even though I never worked with him after that. The atmosphere on set was cheerful and pleasant and the crew was highly professional. On that film, I just remembered, I had an actor I later used for one of my giallo films, a Herculean man who was called Barboo (**The Case of the Scorpion's Tail**).

S.W. Anthony Steffen was the star of the film, what was he like to work with?
S.M. Maybe the first few days he had a little mistrust but then he understood that I wasn't a naive newcomer that didn't know where to place the camera and he started listening and trusting me. He moved to Brazil when the western genre began its decline. I met up with him many years later when I went to Brazil to shoot some films and he would also give me a call when he would pop by Rome.

What are your thoughts on the film?
S.M. I can't really answer because I haven't seen it in many years. All I can say is that I have very fond memories of the making.

S.W. After Arizona Colt Returns in 1970, you did not return to the western genre until 1978 with A Man Called Blade.

S.M. **A Man Called Blade**, I think, was the last western shot in Italy, it was an attempt to reinvigorate the genre. I think it is a good film, reviewing the initial sequence I find that it is still effective nowadays. The story also contained an environmental message: in those days, this issue was not given much importance, whereas today it has become an urgency for all humankind. The music by the De Angelis brothers also gives great value to the film.

S.W. You directed some of the most iconic Italian films, how does it feel to know you left such a profound mark on the film industry?
S.M. I believe I did every single genre out there, which have been reevaluated by such directors as Quentin Tarantino and Guillermo del Toro. In Italy for many years, genre cinema was considered rubbish. Only the new generations consider it valid, despite thanks to directors of my generation Italy was the second biggest film industry in the Western world and the first in Europe.

S.W. Tells us about the use of the fog machines and the mud in the film A Man Called Blade.
S.M. The fog was an expedient to hide the old and crumbling western village of the Elios Studios, which was falling apart. The Italian art of adapting brought us to come up with this idea. It was a little tiring to make it credible on windy days, because of course it is all artificial smoke.

S.W. Maurizio Merli was an excellent choice to play the Mannaja character, how did you aquire his services?
S.M. Maurizio was the star of the moment thanks to a long string of successful police thrillers and action flicks. He was thrilled to try his hand in the western genre and devoted himself with great vigor to the difficulties of some particularly dynamic scenes, such as the mud fight in the cold winter weather. Unfortunately our collaboration and friendship ended with that film. He was the one who suggested that the character use an ax instead of a gun or rifle. I wrote the film with Ernesto Gastaldi, I don't recall if Scavolini's pen was also involved in that script. I also remember with pleasure the idea of alternating the girls' dance with the images of the train being attacked. An effective and suggestive sequence with quick and precise intercutting.
** **Scavolini did indeed work on the film…**
S.M. Sauro has been a collaborator of mine in many films. He had nice ideas especially when it came to dialogues or finding narrative solutions that had a romantic note to them. I believe that in many of my films from that period, I was able to mix Gastaldi's style which is more dramatic with Scavolini's, more literary one.

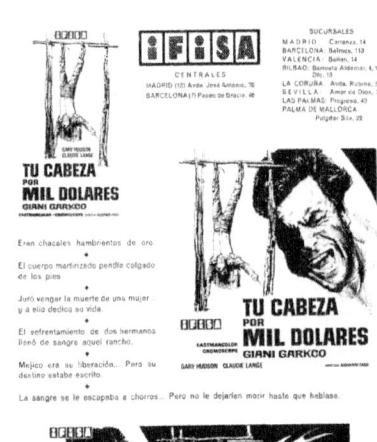

Page 167: Top to Bottom: Italian Poster Mannaja aka A Man Called Blade; Guam newspaper ad from June 28, 1982 A Man Called Blade on a Double bill
Above: Still from Arizona Colt Returns
Bottom: A Page from the Spanish Pressbook for Per 100,000 dollari ti ammazzo

The Western Films of Alberto De Martino!

— Michael Hauss

"De Martino has never been a trendsetter, he has never been a director who wanted or was capable of revolutionizing a genre, of giving birth to a new current but he has always distinguished himself in each one he got close to and right from the start of directorial career, dedicated himself to the most popular genres."

Eugenio Ercolani- Darkening the Italian Screen

(17) Foreign Film Festival $100,000 for Ringo." Richard Harrison, Fernando Sanco.

(1)

2:00 Big 3 Theater 3
"$100,000 for Ringo" Knowledge of hidden treasure filters throughout town. Richard Harrison, Fernando Sancha. (1965)

(2)

(11) CINE EN CASA
"El Sheriff Terrible," 1962 western comedy with Walter Chiari. Spanish-language movie. (2 hrs.)

(3)

Ft. Worth, Italian Style

Italian movie houses are doing great business with a movie titled "Heroes of Fort Worth," but you'd have a hard time recognizing the city —or Texas, for that matter.

(4)

10:50 (5) Western Jamboree
(10) Movie "Django Shoots First," Evelyn Stewart

(5)

11:30 "Heroes of Fort Worth" (Italian-Spanish; 1956 Western) Edmund Purdom, Priscilla Steele. Ch. 5

(6)

Cuban-naturalized Italian actor Tomas Milian will play a new Biblical-named western character, "Providence," in new film. The character will be a Chaplinesque type. Milian is only member of family who has not become an American citizen.

(7)

1. .Philadelphia, Pennsylvania, April, 12, 1968
2. Hartford, Connectticut, Dec, 9, 1967
3. Tucson, Arizona, Jan, 31, 1975
4. Fort Worth, Texas, Jan, 22, 1965
5.. Victoria, Texas, November, 15, 1969
6. Ithaca, Ny, March, 5, 1969
7. San Francisco, Calf, July 9, 1972

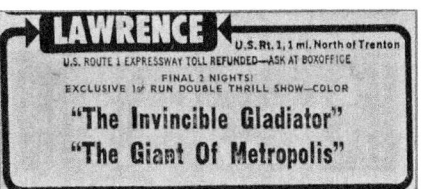

Top: Italian Poster: Terrible Sheriff
Middle: Italian Fotobusta: Terrible Sherriff
Bottom: Drive-in ad USA, Bristol, Pennsylvania, 1965

The first thing one notices about the film career of Alberto De Martino is how fluidly he moved from one genre to another. That ease of movement is how he avoided being labeled as a particular "genre" director. Because of De Martino's ability to adjust and adapt, he moved into more extensive and better-financed productions. His aptitude in working with foreign actors and getting desirable results is another key to his success. The list of American actors (Kirk Douglas, Dorothy Malone, Telly Savalas, John Cassavetes, Martin Balsam) De Martino worked with is quite extensive, and he became known as a director who could produce films that could be exported outside of Italy. Thus, he was labeled an "American director." [1] Alberto De Martino's father was the makeup artist Romolo De Martino, and Alberto grew up on film sets. After a brief on-screen career as a child actor, he eventually become an assistant director in 1952. He would perform that duty until 1961 when he directed his first film, the peplum **The Invincible Gladiator.** (Il gladiatore invincibile, Italy, Spain, 1961). [2] De Martino mostly worked on melodramas as an assistant director but transitioned over to other genres, most notably for the film **The Minotaur, the Wild Beast of Crete** (Teseo contro il minotauro, Italy, 1960), which was the film that signified he was ready to handle directorial chores. Concerning **The Invisible Gladiator**, it is the European film debut of the American actor Richard Harrison, who was brought over to Italy from the U.S. by the producer Italio Zingarelli to test for the part of Reezius. Harrison would go on to a lengthy film career in Europe and Asia. Harrison and De Martino would work together a few more times but most notably in 1965 in arguably each man's best western, **One Hundred Thousand Dollars for Ringo** (100.000 dollari per Ringo, Italy, Spain, 1965).

The Invincible Gladiator was a financial success and De Martino's services were in demand as a director. When the original director left during the pre-production of the western **Terrible Sheriff** (Due contro tutti, Italy, Spain, 1962), the producer Emo Bistolfi called De Martino to take over the directorial duties..[3] While the **Terrible Sheriff** is not a great film by any stretch of the imagination, it is not as terrible as some suggest. But a word of warning, it does contain a few points of highly offensive racial content. As hard as those moments are to overcome, if one is so inclined to, they are rewarded with a nicely structured film with solid direction from De Martino and two excellent leads in Walter Chiari and Raimondo Vianello as the half-wit scheming brothers Bull and Jonathon Bullivan.

171

The brothers go to the town of Golden City to defraud the citizens of their savings- but stay around to defend the town. But the boys are no heroes; in fact, they are chickens and speaking of chicken's, when the boys steal and eat a chicken who was given a secret tonic by its owner, the boys become superhuman in their fighting skills. Those skills come in handy to help save the town from a gang of desperados. Chiari and Vianello, two seasoned actors, work well together and have enough of a handle on performing comedy to not overact or become caricatures. Terrible Sheriff was not the first time Chiari and Vianello had appeared in a comedy-western together as they had done so in the 1961 film **The Magnificent Three** (I magnifici tre, Italy, 1961), and the familiarity with each other in a western setting pays dividends. The director of **The Magnificent Three**, Giorgio Simonelli, would go on to form a long working relationship with the Italian comedian team of Franco and Ciccio, even directing the duo in three western parodies, **Two Gangsters in the Wild West** (Due mafiosi nel Far West, Italy, Spain, 1964), **Two Sergeants of General Custer** (I due sergenti del generale Custer, Italy, Spain, 1965) and **Two Sons on Ringo** (I due figli di Ringo, Italy, Spain, 1966). [4]

Terrible Sheriff proved to be a success, and Chiari and Vianello would appear together in two more westerns, both from 1964, directed by Steno, **Heroes of the West** (Gli eroi del West, Italy, Spain, 1964), and **Twins from Texas** (I gemelli del Texas, Italy, Spain, 1964). Chiari also appeared in the westerns, **The Dream of Zorro** in (Il sogno di Zorro, Italy, 1952, and a comedy-western that predated **Terrible Sheriff** in **Dollar of Fear** (Un dollaro di fifa, Italy, 1960). Vianello would team up a few years later with Lando Buzzanca for two comedy-westerns, **For a Few Dollars Less** (Per qualche dollaro in meno, Italy, 1966) and **Ringo and Gringo Against All** (Ringo e Gringo contro tutti, Italy, Spain, 1966)), with the former being directed by Mario Mattoli and the later by Bruno Corbucci. **Terrible Sheriff** is of importance because it was the film that the first permanent western town was built for in Spain called Golden City- Hoyo de Manzanares, Spain.

De Martino seemed to acquaint himself very well with the western genre, and with veteran actors in the leads and a solid supporting cast, the film is flawed but decent enough watch. **The Terrible Sheriff**'s pacing is slow as are the lead characters' Hollywood cowboy styled mannerisms, but the ending with the ingestion of the toxic chicken sends the film into overdrive and ends the movie on a high note. The writing of the film was done by Vittorio Vighi (Story, screenplay), Mario Guerra (Story, screenplay), Ruggero Maccari (Screenplay), Jose Mallorqui (Screenplay), Giulio Scarnicci (Screenplay), and Ettore Scola (Screenplay). That many hands involved in the writing of the film, makes the film uneven. Some of the gags work well as do some of the comedic lines, including making a note of how the boys never reload their guns, because they are in a western and a road sign along the boys' journey that says "Rome," to which Bull replies that "All roads lead to Rome." Romolo De Martino was one of the makeup artists on the Terrible Sheriff a duty he had performed the previous year on his son's directorial debut, **The Invisible Gladiator.** Romolo De Martino would perform makeup duties on a total of eight of his son's films, **The Invisible Gladiator, Terrible Sheriff, Perseus Against the Monster** (Perseo l'invincibile, Italy, Spain, 1963), **The Secret Seven** (Gli invincibili sette, Italy, Spain, 1963), **The Revolt of the Seven** (La rivolta dei sette, Italy, 1964), **Special Mission Lady Chaplin** (Missione speciale Lady Chaplin, Italy, France, Spain, 1966), **Django Shoot First** (Django spara per primo, Italy, 1966) and **Operation Kid Brother** (OK Connery, Italy, 1967). Alberto De Martino would follow up **Terrible Sheriff** with another peplum with Richard Harrison, **Persues Against the Monsters** in 1963 [5]. Also, in 1963 De Martino would helm the flawed Gothic horror film **The Blancheville Monster** (Horror, Italy, Spain, 1963) and The Secret Seven, which starred the American ex-pat Tony Russel and spawned a loose sequel The Revolt of the Seven in 1964. One last peplum was in store for De Martino in 1964, the Dan Vadis' starring **Hercules vs. the Giant Warriors** (Il trionfo di Ercole, Italy, Frabce, 1964). De Martino would make two westerns in 1965, one an unmitigated disaster and the other a minor classic that performed very well at the box office and allowed De Martino to move onto bigger-budgeted pictures. De Martino's first western of 1965 would be the unmitigated disaster I spoke of above- **Assault on Fort Texan** (Gli eroi di Fort Worth, Italy, Spain, 1965) is a lousy film that tries too hard to be an American western and fails on all levels. Over the opening credits rides the 7th Cavalry, and as this insanely chaotic sequence unfolds, you see riders falling off their horses. The whole film would go on to be as frenzied as the opening credits and jumps about too much leaving character details to the imagination and plot threads unfulfilled. It must be noted that the action scenes in **Persues Against the Monsters** were excellently handled including the cavalry tracking shots, and one would assume hopefully that De Martino could transfer that knowledge to the western setting in **Assault on Fort Texan** (He didn't).

Hercules Marathon playing in Charlotte North Carolina, December 18, 1970. Included in this Marathon is Albeerto De Martino's Perseus Against Monster, appearing here under its U.S. Title Medusa Against the Son of Hercules.

After the disjointed opening, on-screen text unfolds, "July 1863. The Civil War continues in Virginia, but Mississippi is in the Union's hands and Louisiana, Arkansas, and Texas have all been separated from the rest of the confederation territory. There is a group of Confederate troops that, so far, have not been located by the enemy, and they are now attempting to flee to Mexico."

The film then suddenly takes a violent turn when two confederate soldiers in civilian duds hold up a stagecoach. They are trying to pass information to a Confederate spy, a young woman named Nelly (Evelyn Stewart) riding the stage. But one of the passengers riding the stage realizes one of the men is a confederate soldier, and when the smoke clears, four men lay dead. In the hills above, Fort Worth is a confederate battalion whose goal is to march into Mexico and ask Emperor Maximilian to help the rebel side out in the states' war. But Union troops have two strongholds in Fort Worth and Wichita Pass, and the only way to Mexico is along those Union encampments. The South, though, has devised a plan to save their battalion by enlisting the aid of a local tribe of Apaches and have them pull off a series of orchestrated attacks against Fort Worth and the outlying town. Colonel George Bonnet (Eduardo Fajardo) is sent to organize Wild Horse, and his Apaches braves for their attacks against first the 5th Cavalry who are stationed in Fort Worth and then the 7th Cavalry once they advance towards Fort Worth from Wichita Pass. The first attack by the Apaches on Fort Worth is a brutal affair as each member of the town is killed. The scenes of the towns massacre play out in a brisk and violent style as the bodies pile up in the streets including women and children. After the 5th rides out from the fort to assist the town, another band of Apaches rides up behind the soldiers. The braves who had assaulted the town assemble to attack the soldiers from the front, thus trapping the 5th calvary between them and eliminating them.

From scenes of carnage, we are then introduced to a man in a jail cell, drawing pictures of women on the wall with charcoal. Archibald Timothy Patterson, aka "Sugar" (Edmund Purdom), is in jail for insubordination and has been busted down ranks from Captain to Sergeant. In that introduction of the "Sugar" character, we find out he is an artist and thus not one to comply with strict military rules; he is a senator's son, loves wine, women, and poker. So, after the unevenness of the opening scenes, we finally meet a character who the film can build its plot around, or so one would think. "Sugar" is only four hours away from being discharged from the military and, after being released from jail, beats a path straight to the local saloon where he quickly becomes entangled in fisticuffs! He is forced by Major Shane to ride along with the 7th Cavalry to Fort Worth after the news of the attack has reached Wichita Pass. Along the ride, "Sugar's" time is up in the military, and he decides to leave his fellow soldiers and head back to Wichita Pass. As he rides off, he is shadowed by a couple of Indians, whose horses he notices have saddles on them; therefore, they are not part of Wild Horse's tribe. "Sugar" in fear and respect for his compadres returns to his outfit and rides with them to Fort Worth. The 7th Cavalry believe that an attack is imminent, and that night Major Shane and "Sugar" sneak into Wild Horses village. There "Sugar" finds and quickly becomes engaged to an Indian maiden named Amanda (Monica Randall), who will chase after the character throughout the film. Major Shane notices at Wild Horses village that no scalps were hanging, and all he surveyed was older rifles; therefore, he assumes the attackers came from far away and already left the area. But the 7th Cavalry is being duped by Wild Horse (and Colonel Bonnett behind the scenes) who rides to the fort and sacrifices a few braves who he says were part of an outside tribe who were drumming up trouble but were actually a couple of his braves. We find this out when Amanda rides to the fort looking for "Sugar" and finds her brother dead. Amanda is told by a couple of soldiers on burial detail to look for "Sugar" at the saloon's doors in Wichita Pass, as he will show up there eventually. "Sugar" is delivering a message to the General in Wichita Pass when he is caught by the Apaches and is held long enough for Bonnett to read the message he is carrying. The Apaches allow "Sugar" to escape, but little do they know the message is written in code.

Amanda finds "Sugar" in town and tells him that a "white man ordered Wild Horse to kill settlers. A white man named Colonel, who orders all of you to be killed." Nelly, who is working at the saloon, hears this information, and when a wagon train pulls out for Fort Worth, full of mostly women, she joins the wagon train with Amanda alongside her. Once the wagon train arrives in Fort Worth, Major Shane and Nelly fall in love, she after all is a conflicted Southern spy, and after a kiss from Major Shane, she changes her alliances over to the union and more specifically Major Shane. When the first attack happens this time, the Indians, who expect a town full of women, come across men dressed as women, and a battle rather than a massacre ensues. The 7th Calvary leaves the fort, which is the signal for Bonnett and his charges to ride up behind them! And once the 7th is on the outskirts of town, the two forces will sandwich them in between, like they did the 5th Calvary. But Once in town, Bonnett finds that the tables have been turned and his men are massacred.

Alberto De Martino on **Assault on Fort Texan**, "That's a film I'm not very fond of. Probably the problem was that I was still anchored to an old way of perceiving westerns, with a style that tried to mimic the classic American style." [6]. The problem with Assault on Fort Texan is it lacks style and character depth and a basic understanding of western film construction. It starts out in a frenzy and jumps about too much and tries to be too tricky with its plot and all hell breaks loose as it just a runaway disaster. The only character we feel any connection with is "Sugar", but he begins an aimless young man, and he is never allowed to redeem himself. Although "Sugar" does plan a future at the end with Amanda, it feels rushed and empty. Because De Martino allowed the "Sugar" character to remain vain, self-indulging, and almost buffoonish, he left the picture without a true protagonist. There was hope, though when "Sugar" is introduced when you see a bit of the Richard Harrison Lee "Ringo" Barton characters mischievousness in him- you hold out hope for a character to emerge out of the chaos. But "Sugar" is constructed as a foolish lad who is after wine, women, and poker and remains a fool until the end and is vapid in the viewer's eyes. The secondary character Major Shane is devoid of emotion, and his character is essentially a good soldier who complies with the military rules. How he seduces the beautiful Nelly in a matter of minutes with his uptight mannerisms is another problem with the film. Nelly is a throwaway character, and one would think that at the end when she finds out her father is dead that it would result in an emotional payoff, but it is not well handled and devoid of emotion. De Martino also never really chooses sides in the film and, in a typical American style, exploits the Indians and makes the Wild Horse character to be greedy and violent even though he was only trying to reclaim his ancestral lands for the Apache nation. And when Wild Horse is led by the White man Bonnett it seems to say that the Chief was not intelligent enough to pull off the attacks. Although not above killing women and children (remember war is hell), Colonel Bonnett is never presented as anything other than a military man who is trying to help the South enlist the aid of Emperor Maximilian. Eduardo Fajardo, as Colonel Bonnett, keeps his characterization in check and does not create enough animosity with his portrayal. Fajardo would, of course, go on to understand the need for creating antagonists of more substance to help sell the protagonists of these films. Fajardo is best known for his portrayal of countless oily, slick antagonists in a host of western, including his most spectacularly sinister turn as Major Jackson in **Django**. Other notable western Fajardo appeared in include but are not limited to: **Gentleman Killer**

Two De Martino's non-western films
Left: Region 2, DVD of The Blancheville Monster
Right: Italian Poster: The Spy with Ten Faces

(Gentleman Jo... uccidi, Italy, Spain, 1967), **A Stranger in Paso Bravo** (Uno straniero a Paso Bravo, Italy, Spain, 1968), **The Mercenary** (Il mercenario, Italy, Spain, USA, 1968), **Death Knows no Time** (Pagó cara su muerte, Italy, Spain, 1969), **Shango** (Shango, la pistola infallibile, Italy, 1970) **Companeros** (Vamos a matar, compañeros, Italy, Spain, W. Germany, 1970) and **Sonny and Jed** (La banda J. & S. - Cronaca criminale del Far West, Italy, W. Germany, Spain, 1972).

The British actor Edmund Purdom handles the part of "Sugar" well enough, and if the character had been able to transition from the spoiled son of a senator to a hero, the film would have benefited greatly. But the decision was made to keep "Sugar" as a mischievous soul, who may be finally moving into adulthood, but then again... maybe not at the end. Purdom, a solid actor, first made a name for himself on stage in England , which eventually leads to some roles in a few British productions and ultimately to the USA, where he appeared in a slew of Big-Budgeted films, including **Titanic** (USA, 1953), **Julius Caesar** (USA, 1953), **The Student Prince** (USA, 1954), **The Egyptian** (USA, 1954) and **The Prodigal** (USA, 1955). Purdom would go to Italy in 1957 to appear in Riccardo Freda's crime film Agguato a Tangeri (Italy, Spain). As the years rolled by, Purdom would travel around quite a bit, appearing in many European countries' films. His first foray into the wild west would be as Rex Kelly in the Austria/ W. Germany produced **The Last Ride to Santa Cruz** (Der letzte Ritt nach Santa Cruz, 1964). While in the big scheme of things (**The Last Ride to Santa Cruz** is not very good and Purdom is highly ineffectual), it is not without merit. First off, the great Mario Adolf appears as the bandit Pedro Ortiz and is clad in all black and is channeling Burt Lancaster's turn as Joe Erin in Robert Aldrich's influential western **Vera Cruz** (USA, 1954). Adorf borders on histrionics at times, a trait that many Italian western antagonists would carry forward through the genre's life.

The cast of **The Last Ride to Santa Cruz** includes Klaus Kinski, Marianne Koch, and Sieghardt Rupp, and all three would appear later in 1964 in Sergio Leone's seminal **A Fistful of Dollars** (Per un pugno di dollari, Italy, Spain, W. Germany, 1964). Edmund Purdom's other westerns include **Texas Jim** (Los cuatreros, Spain, 1965), **Piluk. The Timid One** (Giurò... e li uccise ad uno ad uno... Piluk il timido, Italy. 1968), and **Chrysanthemums for a Bunch of Swine** (Crisantemi per un branco di carogne, Italy, 1968). Paul Piaget as Major Shane is not given a lot to do as the by-the-book-military officer who falls for the confederate spy Nelly. Piaget appeared in five westerns and two Zorro films. The highlight of the former stunt man's on-screen career is in the underrated **Seven from Texas** (Antes llega la muerte, Italy, Spain, 1964). Piaget appears as the lead in the film, a cowboy trying to win back his love and fight off various characters who are out for revenge or money- not to mention the Indians who attack a party he is traveling with. Piaget's other westerns are **The Shadow of Zorro** (La venganza del Zorro, Spain, 1962), **Zorro the Avenger** (L'ombra di Zorro, Italy, France, Spain, 1962), **Implacable Three** (Tres hombres buenos, Italy, Spain, 1963), **Four Bullets for Joe** (Cuatro balazos, Italy, Spain, 1964) **Black Angel of the Mississippi** (Bienvenido, padre Murray, Italy, Spain, 1964), **Texas Jim**, and **Assault on Fort Texan**.

Monica Randall essays the role of Amanda and Randall accrued 121 acting credits, most notably in the western genre in **One Hundred Thousand Dollars For Ringo**, where she worked once again for the director Alberto De Martino and as part of the international cast of **Red Sun** (Soleil rouge, Italy, France, Spain, 1971). The beautiful Evelyn Stewart is along for the ride as Nelly and Stewart appeared in numerous genres, including extensively in the westerns; her western credits, but not limited to: **Blood for a Silver Dollar** (Un dollaro bucato, Italy, France, 1965), **Adios Gringo** (Italy, France, Spain, 1965), **Blood at Sundown** (Perché uccidi ancora, Italy, Spain, 1965), **Gatling Gun** (Quel caldo maledetto giorno di fuoco, Italy, Spain, 1968), and in Alberto De Martino's 1966 oater **Django Shoots First.** The music is composed by Manuel Parada and is a typical Hollywood sounding score which fits perfectly with the overt aping of the Hollywood western genre on display here. A fatal flaw the film makes is its relatively limited visual scope; the west's vastness is lost on De Martino and his cinematographer Elloy Mella. The landscape cinematography, which in a picture trying to emulate the American west, needs to encompass the wide-open spaces, which Assault on Fort Texan does not. The riding and battle scenes need to adhere to the parameters of the shot. Sadly, the cinematography and direction are both sub-par on this film! Scenes are either cluttered or ineffectual because of the lack of style and discipline in the scenic constructions. Mella had worked with De Martino on both **The Secret 7** and **Perseus Against Monsters** and was the cinematographer on one other western, the 1965 Alfonso Brescia oater **My Gun is The Law** (La Colt è la mia legge, Italy, Spain, 1965). Cineproduzione Emo Bistolfi produced **Assault on Forth Texan** out of Rome along with Auturo Marcos and Edueuro Manzanos of Fenix Cooperativa Cinematografica, Madrid, Spain.

"Fully launched in production, in 1964, together with his friend Arturo Marcos Tejedor, he (Manzanos) created a new production company under the name of Cooperativa Fénix Films, taking advantage of the existing Fénix Films that Arturo Marcos had set up, together with his family in 1961. With this company, it would finance, among other productions, **Heroes of the West**, **Brandy**, **La tumba del Pistolero**, **Kid Rodelo**, **Uno straniero a Paso Bravo** or (and) **Django the Honorable Killer**." [7]

Eduardo Manzanos is one of the most important figures in Italian/Spanish westerns. Manzanos is responsible for constructing the first permanent western town built in Spain; a western village referred to as "Golden City, " erected in 1962 for the film the **Terrible Sheriff** in Hoyo de Manzanares, Spain. Eduardo Manzanos

Top to Bottom: Assault on Fort Texan: Eduardo Fajardo and Rafael Albaicin; Edmund Purdom and Paul Piaget; Edmund Purdom and Monica Randall; Monica Randall and Evelyn Stewart; Paul Piaget and Evelyn Stewart

**One wonders that with Edmund Purdom playing a womanizer in Assault On Fort Texan whether the producers were trying to capitilze on his notorious Hollywood years, raked with scandal?

Top to Bottom: One Hundred Thousand Dollars for Ringo:
Richard Harrison; Fernando Sancho; Richard Harrison and Rafael Albaicin; Richard Harrison and Fernando Sancho; Monica Randall

**Assault on Fort Texan original title was The Charge of the Seventh Cavalry but was changed to Heors of Fort Worth aka Assault on Fort Texan

had a hand in writing twenty-three westerns and produced or co-producing sixteen oaters- all films lensed in Golden City, which Manzanos leased from the local government from 1962 until 1973.

The misstep De Martino made on **Assault on Fort Texan** would not be repeated on his next western, the vastly underrated **One Hundred Thousand Dollars for Ringo**, which reunites the director and star Richard Harrison for the last time. From the minute the film begins, you are engulfed in the beautifully scenic construction, and its riveting Elmer Bernstein **Magnificent Seven** (USA, 1960) inspired score, including a wonderful vocal song opening called "*Ringo came to fight*," sung by Bobby Solo. The cinematography is breathtaking and fills its scope up with the magnificent Spanish landscape, all befitting this first-class adventure western. Federico Larraya is the cinematographer, and he had the year before worked as an assistant camera operator on Sergio Leone's seminal western **A Fistful of Dollars**. Larraya would also preform the cinematography duties on De Martino's 1966 film **Special Mission Lady Chaplin**.

It takes almost eleven minutes before the protagonist of the piece Lee 'Ringo' Barton is introduced and twelve for Fernando Sancho's dubious character Chuck. The minutes leading up to the introductions of the piece's stars are a bit of character building as we are introduced to the villain of the piece Tom Cherry (Gerald Tichy), and his two brothers. First off, Cherry pays some Indians off to kill the wife of a noted quick-draw expert Ward Cluster, who went away to fight in the civil war and never returned. The woman upon horseback rides at full speed as a group of braves race after her. In a saddlebag is a young male child. The woman stops and slaps her horse to send the boy off to safety while she holds off the Indians. As the Indians attack her, Tom Cherry steps forward and, with his Winchester, shoots all the Indians down. As he walks closer to the woman, Cherry bends down and picks up a Spear and heaves it into the woman's chest, and she dies. Tom Cherry goes to town and tells the townsfolk that the Indians have attacked and killed the woman. The townsmen band together and head out for a massacre of Gray Bear and his tribe. During the mayhem, Grey Bear, some braves, children, and women manage to escape, taking the child of Ward Cluster after the horse he was upon rode into the encampment. Tom Cherry is, of course, interested in the land, and by the time Lee Burton rides into town a few years later, Cherry controls the whole area and his driven most of the homesteaders off their lands.

Tom Cherry is molded after Ramon Rojo from **A Fistful of Dollars**- There's arms dealing with the Mexican military, a kept woman, who still loves her ex, and the three Cherry brothers, with Tom being the most forceful and violent of the three. When Lee Barton stops at an inn on his journey to Rainbow Valley, he is questioned by a couple of Cherry's thugs his reasoning for going there. After disturbing Burton's meal, one of the thugs receives a fork to the hand. Chuck (Fernando Sancho) is there and aids Barton with dispatching the three goons. Chuck takes the one man left alive and says he is the sheriff from Tucson and is taking him to jail. But Barton calls Chuck's bluff about being a lawman, and when Chuck pulls out a wanted poster, Barton figures him out to be a bounty hunter. After Barton saves Chuck's life from his bounties gun, the saloon's bartender notes that only one man is that quick with a gun, and that man had gone to war and not returned. The news spreads quickly that the quick-draw expert is Ward Cluster, even though it's not Cluster but Lee Barton. Once in Rainbow Valley, Barton is baffled as to why he is being called Ward Cluster, even by the sheriff! After defusing a tense situation in town involving Luke Cherry (Guido Lollobrigida), the sheriff takes Lee to the old Cluster homestead. There, lives an elderly caretaker named Jose (Paco Sanz), who has been keeping the house in order, awaiting the return of Ward Cluster. After Jose welcomes Ward (Barton) back, he gives him the lowdown on Tom Cherry and how he drove off all the homesteaders. Jose after hearing Barton speak and reading his face with his hands, realizes he's not Ward. But, as Jose is about to declare the man an impostor, an Indian woman India (Monica Randall), and a young boy named Sean walk into the cabin. The boy runs up to and hugs Barton, calling him "Father!" A few of Cherry's men led by Luke arrive and open fire and then start the cabin on fire! Jose grabs a rifle to defend the home, running out to confront the goons and is felled in a hail of bullets. Barton tells India and Sean to wait for him out back while he gets some horses. Barton pushes an old stand up piano out into the courtyard, all the while firing off shots and offing the bad guys until he gets to where the horses are tied up, and he takes off and v-lines to India and Sean and they quickly ride off with Luke Cherry and two other goons in pursuit. Luke and his men stop when they realize that their query is heading into the Apache village.

At the Indian village, Chief Gray Bear (Rafael Albaicin) tells Barton that he is "not his friend Ward Cluster!" To which Barton replies, "everyone who thought I was Ward Cluster, wanted me dead." As this goes on, a wagon train loaded with rifles from Tom Cherry makes its way across the desert to its rendezvous with the Mexican military unit. Back in

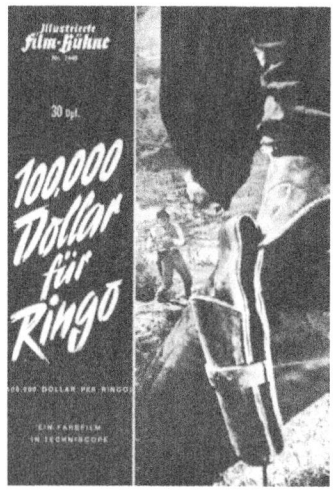

Top: Gerard Tichy: One Hundred Thousand Dollars for Ringo
Middle: German dvd of One Hundred Thousand Dollars for Ringo. Region 2, English and German language.
Bottom: German Program: One Hundred Thousand Dollars for Ringo

Rainbow valley, we are introduced to two lovers who are being torn apart by both Tom Cherry and alcohol. Deborah (Eleonora Bianchi) and Guy (Massimo Serato) are still in love despite Guy's drinking problem and Tom Cherry's interference in their life. Tom only allows Guy to live to please Deborah while pressuring her to succumb to his authoritative advances. Deborah still loves Guy and wants to find a new life someplace with him, and even after he assures her that he will quit drinking once they leave Rainbow Valley, she is still leery and deathly afraid of Cherry. When Cherry catches Deborah and Guy kissing, he becomes enraged and draws his gun to kill Guy, but Barton prevents him by holding a pistol to his head.

The commotion causes Luke Cherry and his goons along with the sheriff to enter the tense situation, Barton tells the sheriff (Luis Induni) that he's Ward Cluster and is taking Tom Cherry to the next town to stand trial for his crimes. The sheriff is more than happy to get rid of Cherry, but just after tying Cherry's hands together, he receives a bullet in the back and a skirmish breaks out between Cherry's men and Barton, Chuck (who has made his way to Rainbow Valley) and Guy. Eventually, Barton gets the situation under control and forces Tom Cherry's men to stand down, and he takes Tom Cherry along with him, followed by Chuck, Guy, and Deborah. The group has banded together gives one a momentary image of **Rio Bravo** (USA, 1959) with the mixing of the town drunk, beautiful woman, dubious characters, evil town boss, and long-held grudges. But the banding does not last long, as eventually Guy and Deborah ride off to start a new life together.

Lee Barton meets the Mexican military awaiting the shipment of guns and hands Tom Cherry over to them for $5,000. Therefore, Barton is nothing more than a bounty hunter, even though he scoffed at Chuck being one himself. After turning over Cherry, Barton gives Chuck the $500 he promised him to help, and they decide to separate. The only problem is that both men know that $200,000 is hidden somewhere in the abandoned church, and neither is planning on leaving without it. Barton heads to the surrounding hills and is accosted by Sean, who had been shadowing him. Sean tells Barton, "You traitor! You aren't my father! My father wouldn't turn someone in for money." This scene is pivotal because it shows Barton first looking towards where Sean has run off to and then towards the bell tower where the money is hidden. It places Barton right in the middle, with a monetary gain on one side and the love the child has placed upon him on the other. Richard Harrison, who was an adequate actor, really sells this scene- in this film, Harrison turns in his most satisfactory performance in a western, in my opinion.

Barton is looking to play both ends against each other ala Clint Eastwood in A Fistful of Dollars, informing Luke Cherry, after removing $1,000 for information from his prone body, that Tom is being held by the Mexican's. Barton's logic is to have the two parties eliminate each other, and with himself, right in the middle, he will walk right in and remove the cash. But things don't work out for Barton as the Mexicans are eliminated, and Cherry and his men quickly set out to find the money! With the Mexicans out of the way, Barton tries to persuade Gray Bear and his Apache warriors to attack Cherry and his men while they have the chance, thus getting revenge for the film's opening massacre. Gray Bear tells Barton that they have no money to pay him after Sean has told the tribe what had transpired between Barton and the Mexican general. Even after defeating Gray Bear's best warrior in hand to hand combat, Barton leaves the area alone, with only India's support, who has a growing affection for him. Barton is caught by Tom Cherry and his men, given a beating that is only interrupted by Luke returning with Guy and Deborah. With Barton tied to a post, Tom first shoots down Guy in anger and whips Deborah wildly until she collapses next to Guy's dead body, and as she lays there- is shot dead by the enraged Cherry. Chuck, who had been watching from the surrounding mounds, rushes in and saves Barton, but not before placing a knife to his neck and demanding to know where the money is hidden. Barton tells Chuck that the money is hidden in the bell tower, as Chuck begrudgingly cuts Barton loose, he says, "I'm too sentimental to be rich." Things are not looking good for Chuck and Barton as Cherry and his men have the duo pinned down, and both are running out of ammo. But what can only be described as a non-typical Hollywood ending, the Indians of Gray Bear rush in to save the day, defeating Cherry's gang. Tom Cherry and Lee Barton must have their final duel, and it does not disappoint as it has the men square off, with Barton standing on an elevated rock area looking down on Cherry, who is outdrawn and shot dead. While all the fighting is raging about, Chuck has climbed the bell tower and retrieved the loot! But Barton gets there before Chuck has descended the ladder and moves it so Chuck can't get down. As Chuck greedily rants that the cash is all his, it spells out from the chest, raining down on Sean and Barton. The two men split the money, and Lee Barton tells Gray Cloud that Sean is coming with him to start a new life on the ranch that Barton plans to buy with the money.

I have found that there are a lot of detractors of this film. I would imagine what detracts people from this film is because it is not a typical Italian Western with a slow, laconic anti-hero, as it's more of an adventure film. De Martino said that the film was his take on Shane's childhood based on George Sherman's seminal western Shane. The film was also not a take or a riff on Duccio Tessari's **A Pistol for Ringo** (Una pistola per Ringo, Italy, Spain, 1965), but the insertion of Ringo in the title was placed there obviously to capitalize on that film's success. De Martino noted that "Ringo was not referring to Tessari's Ringo films but John Wayne in **Stagecoach**." [8] Although De Martino references both of Tessari's Ringo films in the above quote, **The Return of Ringo** (Il ritorno di Ringo, Italy, Spain, 1965) was not released until December 8, 1965, in Italy, almost a month after **One Hundred Thousand Dollars for Ringo**. Therefore, **A Pistol for Ringo**, which premiered In Italy on May 12, 1965, was the film that De Martino lifted the Ringo moniker from. The film's original title was **Tre per il Texas** (Three for Texas), which would make more sense than a movie with "Ringo" in its title, that has no characters named Ringo in it. The European filmmakers and distributors never worried too much about using a name to sell a film- just think- Django, Trinity, Sartana, Ringo, or Sabata. And the name Ringo was a hot commodity after **A Pistol for Ringo**; therefore we got, **Ringo, Face of Revenge** (Los cuatro salvajes, Italy, Spain, 1966), **Ringo and Gringo Against All**, **Ringo and His Golden Pistol** (Johnny Oro, Italy, 1966), **Ringo, Its Massacre Time** (Giunse Ringo e... fu tempo di massacre, Italy, 1970), **Ringo, The Lone Rider** (Dos hombres van a morir, Italy, Spain, 1968) **Woman for Ringo** (Dos pistolas gemelas, Italy, Spain, 1966) and **Two R-R-Ringos From Texas** (Due rrringos nel Texas, Italy, 1967) to name but a few.

One Hundred Thousand Dollars for Ringo was a success, doing exceedingly well at the Italian box office. This film was the one that allowed De Martino to graduate to bigger budgeted films and was the one that made his mark within Italian popular cinema. The film is a big rousing spectacle that needs to be followed closely to figure out all the intricate working parts. One of De Martino's strengths was placing emotion in his films, which set him apart from other Italian western directors- most only wanted to copy the Leone film's 'Man with No Name' films to some extent. The Lee Barton character, while having some similarities to Giuliano Gemma's Ringo character in **A Pistol For Ringo**- was less of a glib, parody of Hollywood western heroes, and more of a conflicted hero, still Hollywood but with an edge.

Italian 45 rpm for One Hundred Dollars for Ringo, including "Ringo Dove VAI?" Sung by Bobby Solo

Middle & Bottom: Photos: Lee Barton (Richard Harrison) looking towards the fleeing Shane and then back at the bell tower where the money from the Mexican military is hidden.

While the lines are blurred between good and bad sometimes in the film, we understand with the heavy sentimentality how this thing will play out. And when Lee Barton tells the Apache's that Sean is coming with him, we know that he has been won over by love and not one of those dubious loner characters that littered the genre. We even get the sidebar of the doomed love between Guy and Deborah that helps build the emotional response one feels at the end after Barton has killed Tom Cherry! And when Barton decides to split the money with the suddenly greedy Chuck, we feel a sense of relief that things played out the way they did and the Italian west at least momentarily, although populated with plenty of bad people, has a few Hollywood styled heroes still riding the range. Therefore, the viewer, can wallow in the buffet of emotions that De Martino so exquisitely laid out for us in this spectacular adventure western.

The cast is outstanding, including the genre regular Richard Harrison as Lee Barton. After a few small acting jobs in film and television in the United States, Harrison headed to Italy to try his luck there and became a regular Italian cinema participant. After first trying his hand at peplums, Harrison began to work in the burgeoning western genre, appearing in some of the earlier films, including **Gunfight at Red Sands** (Duello nel Texas, Italy, Spain, 1963) and **Gunfight at High Noon** (El sabor de la venganza, Italy, Spain, 1964). Harrison would appear in seventeen Italian westerns with his most notables being, **El Rojo** (Italy, Spain, 1966), **Vengeance** (Joko invoca Dio... e muori, Italy, W. Germany, 1968), **One After Another** (Uno dopo l'altro, Italy, Spain, 1968), **Between God the Devil and the Winchester** (Anche nel west c'era una volta Dio, Italy, Spain, 1968) and **Shot Joe and Shoot Again** (Spara Joe... e così sia!, Italy, Spain, 1971). Fernando Sancho appeared in over fifty Italian westerns, including some of the earliest examples the genre has to offer including, **Zorro the Avenger**, **Gunfight at High Noon**, **Implacable Three**, **The Sign of Coyote** (Il segno del coyote, Italy, Spain, 1963), **Minnesota Clay** (Italy, France, Spain, 1964), **A Pistol for Ringo**, and **The Return of Ringo**. Sancho began his Italian western career appearing in somewhat sympathetic roles- But Sancho is, of course, best remembered as the over the top villain in many oaters. Sergio Corbucci's **Minnesota Clay** would help stereotype Sancho to a point as the uncouth, unclean Mexican bandit/general/leader type. Born January 16, 1916, in Zaragoza, Aragon, Spain, Fernando Sancho amassed an impressive 242 credits before dying on July 31, 1990, in Madrid, Spain, after undergoing an operation to remove a malignant tumor. Gerard Tichy (Gerhard Johannes Alexander Tichy Wondzinski), who is perfectly understated as Tom Cherry, was born in Germany in 1920 and fought in the second world war and migrated to Spain after the war and became a regular participant in Spanish and eventually Italian cinema. Tichy worked on many notable productions, including the international productions: Nicholas Ray's **King of Kings** (USA, 1961), Anthony Mann's **El Cid** (Italy, USA, 1961), and 1965's **Dr. Zhivago** (Italy, USA, 1965). Before appearing in **One Hundred Thousand Dollars for Ringo**, Tichy worked with De Martino on **Gladiators 7** (De Martino contributed to the story and screenplay, but did not direct [Italy, Spain, 1962]), **The Blancheville Monster,** and **The Secret Seven**. Tichy lent his considerable acting talents to a number of Italian westerns: **Gunmen of Rio Grande** (Desafío en Río Bravo, Italy, France, Spain, 1964), **Man from Canyon City** (L'uomo che viene da Canyon City, Italy, Spain, 1965), **Place Called Glory City** (Die Hölle von Manitoba, W. Germany, Spain, 1965), **4 Dollars of Revenge** (Cuatro dólares de venganza, Italy, Spain, 1966), **The Texican** (Italy, Spain, 1966), **Face to Face** (Faccia a facia, Italy, Spain, 1967), **Sartana Does not Forgive** (Sonora, Italy, Spain, 1968), and **Companeros** (Vamos a matar, compañeros, Italy, Spain, W. Germany, 1970). Monica Randall plays another Indian infatuated with the white hero, just as she had done in De Martino's earlier western **Assault on Fort Texan**. Other notables in the cast include Massimo Serato as Guy, Loris Loddi as Sean, and genre regulars Luis Induni and Paco Sanz in small parts.

Guido Zurli wrote the original story, but almost all of it was discarded, and a team of Alfonso Balcazar, Alberto De Martino, Vincenzo Mannio, and Giovanni Simonelli contributed to both the story and screenplay. The film was shot in Alcolea de Cinca/Rio Cincca (Huesca), Candasnos (Huesca), Fraga (Huesca), Esplugas City, and Elios Studios. The action that took place in town was filmed at the fabled 'Esplugas City' (Esplugues de Llobregat) western town, which, according to Enzo Castellari, was "Built on a mosquito-infested hill." [9] Espligas City was in use from 1964 until it was burnt to the ground in 1972 after General Franco's minister of information and tourism Alfredo Sanchez Bella ordered it to be demolished, remarking that it gave Spain "A Bad image."

Esplugas City was the second permanent western town constructed in Spain after Golden City in Hoyo de Manzanares. Sixty westerns performed some filming in Esplugas City including, **Five Thousand Dollars on One Ace** (Pistoleros de Arizona, Iyaly, Spain, W. Germany, 1965), **A Pistol for Ringo**, **One Hundred Thousand Dollars for Ringo**, **Oklahoma John** (Italy, Spain, W. Germany, 1965), **The Texican**, **The**

Return of Ringo, **Dynamite Jim** (Dinamite Jim, Italy, Spain, 1966), **Yankee** (Italy, Spain, 1966), **Five Giants From Texas** (I 5 della vendetta, Italy, Spain, 1966) and **Thompson 1880** (Italy, Spain, 1966).

The Balcazar brothers (Alfonso and Jamie Jesus), who had constructed the western town Esplugas city, wanted to turn the area into a western amusement park after the genre was dying off in the early 1970s, even getting permits from the local government, but the proposal was never moved forward. To have the town demolished would have proved costly, so the Balcazar's decided to film one more western there called, **Now They Call Him Sacramento** (I bandoleros della dodicesima ora, Italy, Spain, 1972) and then burn the town down in the finale.

As much as De Martino wants to distant his film from Tessari's **A Pistol for Ringo,** the inclusion of "Ringo" in the title did not invoke John Ford's **Stagecoach** in theatergoers minds! It was used to lure those masses who had visited the theater to watch Giuliano Gemma as Ringo. And the fact that Richard Harrison's character is never referred to as 'Ringo" should also alert one to the name's attempted box office draw. De Martino's next western, which we will look at here momentarily, **Django Shoots First,** was an obvious nod to not only Sergio Corbucci's Django (Italy, Spain, 1966) but the steady stream of like titled releases (Especially in Germany). In **Django Shoots First**, Glenn Saxson's character is addressed by his proper name Glenn Gavin, but he is also known by his deadly moniker "Django." Edmondo Amati (1920-2020) [10] and his son Mauizio Amati (1944-) served as producers on the film for their production company Fida Cinematografica out of Rome along with Francisco Balcazar for Balcazar Producciones Cinematograficas, Barcelona, Spain. Edmondo Amati was a producer of the highest order; even the notoriously gruff Fulci spoke highly of Edmondo, referring to Italian producers in general, "In Italy, the producer is generally a small speculator or, in the best cases like Amati, like Donati- the general organizer of the product." [11] Edmondo Amati's first success was the Franco and Ciccio 1964 film **I due Mafiosi** (Italy, Spain, 1964), directed by Giorgio Simonelli. With the western genre becoming a hot commodity, Amati produced, and Simonelli directed Franco and Ciccio in the oaters, **Two Gangsters in the Wild West**, and T**wo Sergeants of General Custer**. Amati, the founder of the production/distribution company Fida Cinematografics, would produce seventy films (sources vary on amount 55-70+) in various genres, including quite a few notables in the Italian western genre. Just a few of Amati's westerns:

Whats in a name?
Top: A Pistol For Ringo on the bottom of a double-bill with Picture Mommy Dead. New Jersey, November 22, 1966
Bottom: Ad Slick- Magnum Entertainment, Sagebrush Productions. 1985. Django and The Last Gun

Five Dollars on One Ace, **One Hundred Thousand Dollars for Ringo**, Django Shoots First, Fort Yuma Gold (Per pochi d ollari ancora, Italy, France, Spain, 1966), **Any Gun Can Play** (Vado... l'ammazzo e torno, Italy, 1967), **Gatling Gun**, **Kill Them All and Come Back Alone** (Ammazzali tutti e torna solo, Italy, Spain, 1968), **The Three Musketeers of the West** (Tutti per uno botte per tutti, Italy, Spain, W. Germany, 1973) and in an uncredited turn on Lucio Fulci's **The Four of the Apocalypse** (I quattro dell'Apocalisse, Italy, 1975) . Amati would produce a total of nine (1965-1977) De Martino films:

- One Hundred Thousand Dollars for Ringo,
- **Special Lady Chaplin,**
- **Django Shoots First,**
- **Dirty Heroes,**
- **Carnal Circuit,**
- **Counselor at Law,**
- **The Antichrist,**
- **Strange Shadows in an Empty Room (uncredited)**
- **The Chosen.**

The first thing you notice about **Django Shoots First** is how professionally the film is made, loaded with excellently staged punch-ups and shootouts. The film is a visual treat, sparked by the combined artistry of De Martino and his cinematographer Riccardo Pallottini. Speaking of Pallottini, he had an illustrious career as a cinematography, including working on several highly respected Italian westerns, **The Brute and the Beast** (Le colt cantarono la morte e fu... tempo di massacro, Italy, 1966), **Halleluja for Django** (La più grande rapina del west, Italy, 1967), **Vengeance, And God Said to Cain** (E Dio disse a Caino..., Italy, W. Germany, 1970), **Blindman** (Italy, USA, 1971), and **Take a Hard Ride** (Italy, Spain, USA, 1975). Pallottini worked in all the popular genres and became "Antonio Margheriti's regular d.o.p. starting with **Danza Macabra** (aka Castle of Blood, 1964) and worked with Margheriti, on 18 films, before his untimely death in 1982." [12] One noticeable thing is the higher budgets that De Martino was allotted for this film and his two 1966 spy films, **The Spy with Ten Faces** and **Special Mission Lady Chaplin**. And in the Euro-Spy genre, praised is to be lavished on **Special Mission Lady Chaplin** as not only one of the finest but also one of the most entertaining entries in the genre. So, after the phenomenal financial success of **One Hundred Thousand Dollars for Ringo** (1, 236.276.000 Lira-Italy), De Martino was, of course, allotted larger budgets. Still, **Django Shoots First** failed to even return in Italy half of **One Hundred Thousand Dollars for Ringo** box office, only posting box office receipts totaling 588.813.000 Lira. **Here We Go Again, Eh Providence?** (Ci risiamo, vero Provvidenza?, Italy, France, Spain, 1973) was De Martino's last western was his second highest-grossing western film at 1, 068.676 Lira after **One Hundred Thousand Dollars for Ringo**.

Below is a list of Alberto De Martino's five western in terms of Italian box office receipts. This list does not take into consideration the international box office of the films, only the Italian. The list was compiled by the Spaghetti scholar Austin Fisher and list the box office of four hundred and twenty-one films from 1961-1975 from the source *Catalogo generale dei film Italiani dai 1956 al 1975* (Associazione generale Italiana dello spettacolo, 3rd Edition, 1975). [13]

1. **One Hundred Thousand Dollars for Ringo, Italian Box Office- 1, 236.276 Lira. 34th All Time.**
2. **Here We Go Again, Eh Providence? Italian Box Office- 1, 068.676 Lira. 47th All Time.**
3. **Terrible Sheriff, Italian Box Office- 624.795 Lira. 88th All Time.**
4. **Django Shoots First, Italian Box Office- 588.813 Lira. 95th All Time.**
5. **Assault on Fort Texan, Italian Box Office- 216.933 Lira. 315th All Time.**

To break things down just a bit more, De Martino's average box office per film is 744.827 Lira, and his five films total box office is 3, 724.133. De Martino worked within the formative years of the genre, and after **Django Shoots First** in 1966, would not return until 1973 with Here We Go Again, Eh Providence? Thus,it must be noted that De Martino did not participate in the peak years of the film in 1967 and 1968 or even in 1971 or 1972 when the genre had a brief revival because of the **Trinity** films. It must also be noted that **Here We Go Again, Eh Providence?** was a sequel to Guido Petroni's **Life is Tough, Eh Providence?** (La vita, a volte, è molto dura, vero Provvidenza?, Italy, France, W. Germany, 1972) and is a comedy-western that did amazingly well at the shrinking 1973 Italian western Italian box office, with 1, 560.391 Lira, to

Dutch Vhs: Django Shoots First

place it 26th all-time on the list. While **Here We Go Again, Eh Providence?** may have fallen slightly beneath the total achieved by Petroni's film, it still performed surprisingly well at the box office, in a dire environment for Italian westerns. The price of a ticket had risen over time, so the numbers are not adjusted for inflation (along with escalating production costs) and may skewer the real non- adjusted inflation wise place. By the time De Martino directed **Here We Go Again, Eh Providence?** in 1973, the genre was at a place of no return. The genre peaked in 1967-1968 with seventy films each year of those years, to only twenty-eight in 1969, thirty-three in 1970, back up to forty-two in 1971, thirty-six in 1972, eighteen in 1973, and down to a few per year until its total demise in 1978.

What makes the serviceable but ultimately unsuccessful box office of **Django Shoots First** as compared to **One Hundred Thousand Dollars for Ringo** hard to swallow is that Glenn Saxson was not the first choice for the lead. De Martino wanted Giuliano Gemma for the part, but when the producer Amati organized a meeting between the director and Gemma, Alberto said, "yes, but this is a De Martino film, not a Giuliano Gemma film." Gemma left the production, and De Martino, who believed that a film didn't need a star if the director was talented, lost considerable box office revenue by not using the lead's very popular Gemma. [13a] Both Gemma's 1966 westerns did exceptionally well at the box office, doubling **Django Shoots First** take, Michele Lupo's **Arizona Colt** (Italy, France, 1966) at 1, 249, 041, and Giorgio Ferroni's **Fort Yuma Gold** 1, 309, 699. De Martino's thoughts that a star was not needed if a good director was at the helm was, in this case, off the mark and as strong as **Django Shoots First** is in all aspects, the film would have with Gemma in the lead fared much better at the box office than it did. The use of the word Django in the title was to capitalize on the success and notoriety of Sergio Corbucci's violent comic book western **Django**. And even though **Django** and **Django Shoots First** is similar in various ways, it's the tone of the two films that are miles apart, as is the angst of Franco Nero's Django as compared to Glenn Saxson's laid back and relaxed Glenn Garvin aka Django. To tell the viewer where he stands, De Martino has Django kill a bounty hunter named 'Ringo' (Jose Manuel Martin) who had killed Django's father and was taking his body to Silver Creek to collect a $5000 reward. De Martino seems to be trying to put his Ringo creation to rest and usher in his new Django creation. But one is quick to notice that besides the vast difference in the bodily shapes of Richard Harrison (muscular but concealed as not to appear too developed for westerns) and Glenn Saxson (Long and lean in the old Hollywood mode), that both men are somewhat similar in their facial constructions, hair color, and the use of a spaghetti western-style bead or long stubble.

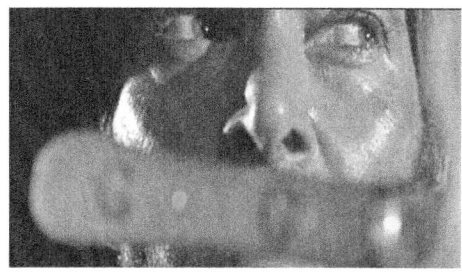

Top: Italian Title card: Django Shoots First
Middle Photos: Luke Cherry (Guido Lolobridgida) and the pivotal knife scene in Django Shoots First
Bottom: Wanted Poster for Django's Dad (John Bartha). John Bartha a fine actor never appeared in the film, only on the poster.

As Django prepares to bury his father, the thoughts of that $5000 start to gnaw on his mind, and in the end figures, its more beneficial if he collects the reward because his father, Thomas Garvin (John Bartha), wasn't much of a father anyways. Django even quipping about how his old man had left to get cigarettes and never returned. So, Django takes his father's body to Silver Creek to collect the reward money but is met there with suspicion by the sheriff (Marcello Tusco) and the bank owner Ken Kluster (Nando Gazzolo). The men wonder what happened to the bounty killer Ringo and whether Django killed his father for the reward? Both men are adamant about Django clearing out asap. Gordon (Fernando Sancho) is hanging around the bank, smelling in the sweet aroma of dollars, and sees what transpires between the men and follows Django out. Django is accosted outside of the bank by a couple of Kluster's henchmen, and a well-staged fight scene plays out until Gordon alerts Django to a shooter on a roof, whom Django shoots down. After the dust clears, Gordon tells Django that half the whole town belongs to him, and that's why Kluster wants him out of town. Thomas Garvin arrived in town and teamed up with Kluster and they bought the saloon together, and then one day Garvin was accused of smuggling guns and went to prison, and Kluster went scot-free. Kluster, just like his counterpart Tom Cherry in **One Hundred Thousand Dollars for Ringo**, is the ruthless town boss who is driving homesteaders off their lands and buying up their property. During a saloon punch up we are introduced to a character named 'Doc' who, at least in attire, is similarly dressed to Corbucci's Django character, a mystery man who stays at the saloon. Most of the action in **Django Shoots First** revolves around the town's saloon, just as in **Django**- and Django in both films falls for a female who works at the saloon. At the saloon in Rainbow Valley works Lucy (Erika Blanc) and her younger brother, who makes one think that his inclusion in the film attempts to tie the movie in the viewer's mind with **One Hundred Thousand Dollars for Ringo** and the boy named Sean.

Django is a legendary pistolero and Lucy's brother asks Gordon, "Say Gordon is it true whenever someone's as good with a pistol as Django- all the best gunslingers- come to challenge him? The answer is irrelevant to a point as we know that the best pistolero will always be challenged (from countless proceeding Westerns), by some young gun trying to make a name for himself. In **One Hundred Thousand Dollars for Ringo**, there is an exchange about the fastest man ever with a gun, a plot device used in countless Italian westerns.

One of the last Italian westerns **Keoma** (Italy, 1976) has similar moments expounding on the fastest gun, when Keoma's brothers talk about a shot only their father and Keoma could pull off and when Keoma and his father William (William Berger) are shooting targets, and William asks if Keoma (Franco Nero) has met anybody faster with a gun, to which Keoma responds he hasn't. Django moves in on Kluster, telling him he wants half of everything and will be around to collect it. Kluster has a wife named Jessica (Evelyn Stewart), who is as seemingly cruel and greedy as her husband- Who we will find out eventually has ties to the mysterious 'Doc.' While out scouting around, Django is trapped by three of Kluster's henchmen in the surrounding hills, and during the shootout, Django is shot (a surface wound) in the leg. Django kills off two of the men (Riccardo Pazzuti and Fortunato Arena) but narrowly escapes Kluster's right-hand man Ward (Guido Lollobrigida). Ward has retrieved Django's knife from one of the men's bodies and, in a pivotal scene, dejectedly stabs a post with it. The camera is tight on the blade and Lollobrigida's face as he looks off after the escaping Django; the scene which had started slightly out of focus on the knife, refocuses in on the knife and the initials G.G. on the blade as a light seems to go off in Ward's head to what potential this knife holds.

Well, it doesn't take Ward and Kluster long to figure out how to put that knife to good use. Kluster plants Django's knife in the bank tellers back, and then Ward takes off with the safe contents. The sheriff, backed by Kluster and his men, goes to the saloon to take Django in for questioning and a gun battle briefly erupts until Django flees on horseback followed by the posse. The tracks lead to Kluster's villa- the sheriff boldly enters the home but is revoked by Jessica Kluster, who demands him to leave her home at once. Django, though, was hiding in a bubble bath the whole time! It seems Jessica wants her and Django to snatch the cash that Ward is holding at the old abandoned mine and ride off together. The use of a knife or gun to wrongly implicate a person is a commonly used device, but one of prevalence to **Django Shoots First** occurs in the Gemma vehicle **Adios Gringo**. In that film, Brent Landers (Giuliano Gemma) is framed after his knife is used to kill a deputy and the evil town boss rallies the town against him. It must also be noted that Evelyn Stewart appeared in **Adios Gringo** as Lucy but appeared as Jessica in this film, but Erica Blanc is thusly named Lucy in **Django Shoots First**. Django wants to clear his name, realizing that sheriffs and bounty killers will pursue him for the rest of his life if he does not. Once Kluster returns home, Jessica gives him a sedative, and she takes Django into town to meet up with his two cohorts.

Jessica pushes into the saloon with Django; first off she is rude to Lucy, the barmaid who is in love with Django, and the two women have a brief fight; Doc then reveals that he not only knows Jessica, he is her husband (and has come to town to kill her). Once Jessica sees Doc, she is taken aback and flees from the saloon. Django, Gordon, and Doc head out to get to the old mine before Jessica does. The three Amigos trap Ward, Jessica, and the rest of the gang in a pass and wipe out most of the group, except Ward and Jessica, who ride off. 'Doc' shoots Jessica's horse out from under her, and Ward races off chased by Django. Quickly overtaking Ward,, Django and Ward fight among the cliffs, until Ward is killed after being tossed over a ledge. Jessica is taken into town, and when Django tells the sheriff and Kluster, they caught her heading off to Mexico with Ward and the money from the robbery- Kluster quickly turns on Jessica and tells the sheriff it was all her doing, and she is promptly locked up.

A trap is set for Kluster, and he follows 'Doc' to the sheriff's office where after knocking out, the deputy 'Doc' releases Jessica. As Kluster follows behind, a black cat runs across his path. Jessica tells 'Doc,' "you must love me still- you pretend to despise me, but you married me, and I'm still yours!" The pair kiss, and once they separate, Jessica has 'Doc's' gun in her hand, and after emptying the safe where the robbery money was placed, she tells 'Doc,' "You're such a fool darling! Sentiment is always a mistake!" After telling 'Doc' she "hates" him, she repeatedly pulls the trigger, but the gun is not loaded. As she fumbles with the door to escape from 'Doc,' he tells her Kluster is outside waiting to kill her. She does not believe 'Doc,' but upon stepping out the door, she is the recipient of a knife in her chest. Kluster's face, as he watches Jessica die, seems to be flush with relief in the killing of the woman he thought loved him. The two-timing woman killed for her betrayal is a relatively common Italian western plot device, included in such films as **Requiem for Gringo** (Réquiem para el gringo, Italy, Spain, 1968), **Blood Calls to Blood** (Sangue chiama sangue , Italy, 1968), and **Shotgun** (La vendetta è il mio perdono, Italy, 1968), to name a few.

Left: Studiocanal DVD release   Right: Dorado DVD release

Kluster then follows 'Doc' (who has left with the cash) to the cemetery where he finds the saddlebags laying on the ground, loaded with the robbery money; as he tries to exit with the money, he sees the open grave of Thomas Garvin. Django appears and tells Kluster he will make him pay for his father's death, and when Kluster goes with the old knife trick one more time, he is shot dead, falling into the open grave of Django's father. The men then hide the money in the basement, but Lucy has seen them hide it. The finale has Django, 'Doc,' and Gordon riding off until Django stops to give 'Doc' his share and realizes that there is no money in the saddlebags. In the bag is Lucy's picture, inscribed to Django, "I will always wait for you- Your Lucy." 'Doc' who is heading to Durango to start over tells Django to- go back and settle down with Lucy! The ending has a young hombre (Played by a young, uncredited George Eastman- minus his customary beard) entering the bank, which Django now runs, with Gordon as his teller. The young man tells the men he is Ken Kluster's son Jesse and he owns half of everything- Here we go again, eh Django? Django Shoots First is a thoroughly entertaining film. Besides all the punch ups and gun battles, at heart, it's a light-hearted affair. Glenn Saxson, in the lead, has a smooth, unassuming acting style that works perfectly here. The whole cast, for that matter, is outstanding. Even though the two females in the piece aren't fleshed out (which is nothing unusual for an Italian western), it doesn't hurt the results. And I must say that its refreshing to see the hero of the piece return to the woman he loves. The returning for love is an emotional lift for the viewer, just as Lee Barton and Sean setting off together at the end of **One Hundred Thousand Dollars for Ringo** was. The action scene in the film was adroitly handled by De Martino's A.D. Enzo Castellari. One thing De Martino knew how to deliver on was the emotion mentioned above, but also how to properly build and then dispose of the antagonist(s) at the correct time, allowing for the killing of the three villains of the piece a chance to play out spectacularly. The disposing of Ward being thrown from a cliff by Django, Jessica's deception being rewarded with a knife planted in her chest, and Kluster being shot down into Django's father's empty grave allowed for multiple emotional payoffs for the viewer. The only seed of doubt that runs across the mind at the conclusion is Django's uncaring attitude for his father, who was not much of a father to Django- and why he felt the need to avenge his death. So, ultimately one is left with that thought in one's mind, and just like Lee Barton, Django must decide whether love or money is more important and returns to claim the money but also Lucy. While Lee Barton and Django must decide at the end what is more important love or money, it must be noted that both received both money and love, even though their decision to accept love was not motivated by the money!

This is Glenn Saxson's (1942-) second credited acting gig, after two uncredited turns in **24 Hours to Kill** (U.K., 1965) and **Sandra** (Vaghe stelle dell'Orsa... , Italy, France, 1965). His first starring role was in the 1966 western **Go with God Gringo** (Vaya con dios gringo, Italy, Spain, 1966), where he showed a bit of that natural ease in front of the camera. Saxson's five Westerns' performances are all uniformly good, less Clint Eastwood type stoic detached anti-heroes and more classic, laconic Hollywood cowboys. Saxson followed his then-girlfriend from the Netherlands to Italy, which at the time was the movie-making capital of Europe, and after some modeling and commercials, he moved to feature films.

To understand the very subtle acting talents of Saxson, look at the memorable first scene of the film Django Shoots First; that scene, according to Glenn Saxson, was done in one take, "We shot the quite extensive scene in Almeria. Because of time, problem we had to shoot the scene in one take, with two cameras. And I succeeded to do it, which was very satisfactory, and the crew and director were very grateful" (*Spaghetti Westerns! Volume Two: interview with Glenn Saxson*). Saxson is probably best remembered for his turns in the films **Kriminal** (Italy, Spain, 1966) and **Il marchio di Kriminal**, Italy, Spain, 1968); his westerns credits: **Go with God Gringo**, **Django Shoots First, Magnificent Texan** (Il magnifico Texano , Italy, Spain, 1967), **Cry of Death** (Carogne si nasce , Italy, 1968), **The Long Day of Massacre** (Il lungo giorno del massacro, Italy, 1968). Erika Blanc (1942-) appears here as Lucy, the barmaid at the saloon, who falls in love with Django; in her first western **Colorado Charlie** (Italy, 1965), Blanc appeared as a saloon singer who receives her first on-screen kiss from the bulbous nosed Livio Lorenzon. A few of Blanc's other westerns are **Hallelujah for Django** (La più grande rapina del west, Italy, 1967), **Shoot, Gringo… Shoot** (Spara, Gringo, spara , Italy, France, 1968), **Shotgun**, **Stagecoach of the Condemned** (La diligencia de los condenados , Italy, Spain, 1970), and **Sartana's Here… Trade your Pistols for a Coffin** (C'è Sartana... vendi la pistola e comprati la bara!, Italy, 1970).

Nando Gazzolo is perfectly oily and menacing as Ken Kluster. Gazzolo worked in theater, feature films, and television and was also one of Italy's most famous voice actors. Gazzolo came from a theatrical family; his father Lauro was also an actor and accomplished voice actor- His mother, Aida Ottaviani, was an announcer on the radio- and his brother Virginio, an actor. Nando Gazzolo's western credits include **The Hills Run Red** (Un fiume di dollari, Italy, 1966) and uncredited as the Italian narrator of the Broderick Crawford Italian oater **Mutiny at Fort Sharpe** (Italy, Spain, 1966). Out of Nando's many voice dubbing credits, the one that jumps out at this writer is his dubbing Henry Fonda's Frank character from **Once Upon a Time in the West** (C'era una volta il West, Italy, USA, 1968) for the Italian language release. Gazzolo had previously worked with De Martino on **The Revolt of the Seven** and **The Spy with Ten Faces**. In Django Shoots First, Fernando Sancho plays an honest character who only wants to smell the scent of dollars and help out his new-found friend Django. Sancho's character Chuck in **One Hundred Thousand Dollars for Ringo** is very similar to his character Gordon in Django Shoots First; both help the hero of the piece out and are mystery men, but Gordon while motivated

Glenn Saxson

IN COLOR
232.
Django Shoots First

with
Glenn Saxon, Evelyn Stewart,
Alberto Lupo.

Dirtiest, bloodiest, deadliest,
Spaghetti Western ever!

See program notes on the back of this card.

Top: Videoyesteryear VHS insert: U.S. Django Shoots First

Bottom: GDM- GDM 4149 C.D. Italy. Django Shoots First

Top to Bottom:
Nando Gazzolo as Ken Kluster; Fernando Sancho, Albert Lupo, Glenn Saxson, Erica Blanc; Nando Gazzolo and Guido Lolobridgida; Evelyn Stewart and Albert Lupo

**Albert Lupo was effective as "Doc," and sadly this is his only Italan western credit!

by greed, is still a decent man, while Chuck seems to be only inspired by the intoxicating scent of dollars! Regardless of the role, he played upon the screen, any film Fernando Sancho appeared in was better because of his participation. As Jessica Kluster, Evelyn Stewart is riveting and as ruthless as any man but is a bit limited by the thinness of the construction of her character.

Aiding De Martino in the writing department was a collection of some notable writers including Sandro Continenza, Massililiano Copriccioli, Tito Capri, Vincenzo Mannino, and Giovanni Simonelli. Sandro Continenza was one of the most prolific Italian screenwriters, accruing one hundred and fifty-six credits. After writing for satirical and comedy magazines, Continenza began writing gags for the great Italian comedian Toto's films. His first two uncredited writing credits were for the Toto films, **The Two Orphans** (I due orfanelli, Italy, 1947) and **Fifa and Arena** (Fifa e arena, Italy, 1948). Continenza would have a hand in writing seven Toto films, and most of his early work was in comedies. To show how varied Continenza's writing credits are, here is a small sample of his notable accomplishments: Mario Bava's **Hercules in the World** (Ercole al centro della Terra , Italy, W. Germany, 1961), **Heroes of the West** (1964), Sugar Colt (Italy, Spain, 1966), **Let Sleeping Corpses Lie** (No profanar el sueño de los muertos Italy, Spain, 1974), and **The Inglorious Bastards** (Quel maledetto treno blindato , Italy, 1978). Continenza contributed to the screenplay and story along with De Martino on **Gladiator 7** (1962), **The Secret Seven**, **The Revolt of the Seven** (1964), **Django Shoots First**, and **Special Mission Lady Chaplin** (1966).

Tito Capri had a hand in writing one hundred feature films and television episodes. Capri is best known for his long association with Enzo Castellari, whom he wrote many scripts with, including but not limited to: **Any Gun Can Play**, **Payment in Blood** (7 winchester per un massacre, Italy, 1967), **Johnny Hamlet** (Quella sporca storia nel west, Italy, 1968), **Warriors of the Wasteland** (I nuovi barbari, Italy, USA, 1983), and **Escape from the Bronx** (Fuga dal Bronx, Italy, 1983). In 1966, Capri was involved in the writing of **Django Shoots First**, which Castellari, as noted above, was A.D. on. Capri was also involved in the writing of Castellari's directorial debut on the Leon Klimovsky credited (Castellari directed it after taking over for Klimovsky. Klimovsky did start out directing the film, but the scenes he directed were discarded) **A Few Dollars for Django** (Pochi dollari per Django, Italy, Spain, 1966).

Vincenzo Mannino was a high school friend of Alberto De Martino and tried his hand at screenwriting after graduating from law school. Mannino's first three writing credits were for Alberto De Martino on **The Revolt of the Seven, One Hundred Thousand Dollars for Ringo**, and **Django Shoots First.** Mannino had a hand in the writing of forty-nine films, including twelve for De Martino: **The Revolt of the Seven, One Hundred Thousand Dollars for Ringo, Django Shoots First, Dirty Heroes** (Dalle Ardenne all'inferno, Italy, France, W. Germany, 1968), **Carnal Circuit** (Femmine insaziabili, Italy, W. Germany, 1969), **The Man with Icy Eyes** (L'uomo dagli occhi di ghiaccio, Italy, 1970), **The Killer is on the Phone** (L'assassino... è al telefono, Italy, Belgium, 1972), **Counselor at Crime** (Il consigliori, Italy, Spain, 1973), The Antichrist (L'anticristo, Italy, 1974), **Strange Shadows in an Empty Room** (Una Magnum Special per Tony Saitta, Italy, Canada, 1976), **Formula for a Murder** (7, Hyden Park: la casa maledetta, Italy, 1985), and **Miami Golem** (Italy, USA, 1985). Out of his seventy-seven writing credits, Giovanni Simonelli worked with De Martino twice, both in 1966 on **Special Lady Chaplin** and **Django Shoots First.** Some of Simonelli's notable western writing credits include: **Gunmen of Rio Grande, Johnny Yuma** (Italy, 1966), **Any Gun Can Play, I'll Sell My Skin Dearly** (Vendo cara la pelle, Italy, 1968), and **Sartana Does not Forgive**. Massimiliano Capriccioli only was involved in the writing of four feature films: **Fort Yuma Gold, Django Shoots First, Wanted** (Italy, 1967), and **It's Your Move** (Uno scacco tutto matto, Italy, Spain, 1968). Capriccoli, who was active between 1952 and 1968, also worked as a set decorator/designer, art director, and production designer. He was a production designer on the very underrated **Sheriff with the Gold** (Uno sceriffo tutto d'oro, Italy, 1966), art director on **Wanted**, and set designer on **A Minute to Pray, a Second to Die** (Un minuto per pregare, un istante per morire, Italy, USA, 1968). **Django Shoots First** was filmed at Almeria; Ramblas Buho, Alfaro- Tabernas, Las Salinillas, Gergal, and Elios studios in Rome. This film was produced by Edmondo and Maurizio Amati for their Italian production company Fida Cinematografica.

Although **Django Shoots First** was not the success financially that **One Hundred Thousand Dollars for Ringo** was, it still performed well enough. Therefore, it would seem another western would be in the cards for De Martino as the genre was still operating in high gear. But being that De Martino was fluid in terms of his moving with the current genre "hot" trends, he moved next into war films with 1968's **Dirty Heroes**. From 1969 until 1972, De Martino worked on the newest "filones" -poliziottesco films, **Bandits in Rome** (Roma come Chicago (Banditi a Roma, Italy, 1968), **Crime Boss** (I familiari delle vittime non saranno avvertiti , Italy, 1972) and **Counselor at Crime** and the thrillers/giallo- **Carnal Circuit** (1969), **The Man with Icy Eyes** (1971) and **The Killer Is On the Phone** (1972). De Martino returned to the Euro-spy genre briefly in 1967 his first film after **Django Shoots First**, directing Neal Connery (Sean Connery's brother) in the amusingly bad **Operation Kid Brother.** De Martino was brought into direct Operation Kid Brother and was not involved in the film's writing, which is an exception instead of a rule as De Martino was commonly involved in the writing of the movies he directed. Out of De Martino's twenty-eight directing credits, he was involved (credited) in the writing of nineteen.

In late 1970 the film **They Call me Trinity** (Lo chiamavano Trinità..., Italy, 1970), directed by Enzo Barboni, was released in Italy and became a box office sensation! A follow up was quickly ordered, and **Trinity is Still My Name** (Continuavano a chiamarlo Trinità, Italy, 1971) became the highest-grossing Italian western ever in Italy. These two films revived the genre temporarily, but what followed was, for the most part, inferior Trinity inspired clones. That's not to say that there were not some excellent comedy-westerns post-Trinity, because there was. Still, for every **Guns for Dollars** (Testa t'ammazzo, croce... sei morto - Mi chiamano Alleluja, Italy, 1971), **Man of the East** (E poi lo chiamarono il magnifico, Italy, 1972), or **Jesse and Lester** (Jesse & Lester - Due fratelli in un posto chiamato Trinità, Italy, 1972), you get absolute rubbish like **An Animal Called Man** (Un animale chiamato uomo, Italy, 1972), **Trinity Plus the Clown and a Guitar** (Der Kleine Schwarze mit dem roten Hut, Austria, W. Germany and Italy, 1975), and host of others.

Some people falsely concur that the Italian western genre's demise was because of the comedy westerns, some even singling out the Trinity films as the main culprits. The truth is the genre was dying out after the peak years of 1967-1968, where over 70 films were made each year. And as the films fought for marquee space, the films' returns began to shrink, as did the budgets, and it showed as the films headed into the 1970s. [14] One can see the life the **Trinity** films pumped back into the genre at least momentarily. So, if one looks at the twenty-eight westerns of 1969 (After 70+ the two successive years), one realizes that the writing was on the wall! And with more films being lensed back in Italy to save on travel expenses to Spain and the escalating cost to operate there, the films, for the most part, became cheaper and dirtier and visually less accomplished. With fewer returns on their investments, more and more producers began to incur monetary problems and the films became less accomplished and more poverty-stricken looking. Just look at films like **Eh Amigo! A Toast to Your Death** (Ehi amigo... sei morto!, Italy, 1970), **Death Played the Flute** (Lo ammazzò come un cane... ma lui rideva ancora, Italy, 1972), or **Fasthand is Still My Name** (Mi chiamavano 'Requiescat'... ma avevano sbagliato, Italy, 1973) to see the diminishing quality of the product and how the western sets had fallen into disrepair.

Alberto De Martino had always been part of whatever genre was relevant or in fashion at the time, so when Giulio Petroni declined to direct the sequel to his successful Tom Milian Spaghetti-western-comedy vehicle Life is Tough, Eh Providence?, De Martino was offered the job and accepted. But first, we must have a quick look at the original film **Life is Tough, Eh Providence?** Giulio Petroni, when asked about his relationship with Franco Castellano and Giuseppe Moccia (as Pipolo), who wrote an early treatment of the script (**Life Is Tough, Eh Providence?**), "There wasn't any. Not ever. I can tell you that I was perplexed by the stupidity and vulgarity of their ideas when I first read their script. It was a hotch-potch of gags that were by no means funny, just … disgusting. A disgrace, a complete disgrace. We changed nearly everything on the set. Most situations and gags were invented and refined on the set, one by one, by me and the actors" [15]. I had the privilege of acquiring a copy of both Providence scripts from a second-hand dealer I assumed had purchased them from the estate of the late Gregg Palmer.

The script for Life Is **Tough, Eh Providence?** has Dean Craig credited as the screenwriter. Dean Craig was a pseudonym of Piero Regnoli, who was involved in writing one hundred and twenty films and directed nine. Regnoli was involved in the writing of seven westerns, including **The Hills Run Red** (1966), **Navajo Joe** (Italy, Spain, 1966), **Death Walks in Laredo** (3 pistole contro Cesare, Italy, Algeria, 1967), Law of Violence (La legge della violenza [Tutti o nessuno], Italy, Spain, 1969), **And They Smelled the Strange Exciting, Dangerous Scent of Dollars** (Sentivano uno strano, eccitante, pericoloso puzzo di dollari, Italy, 1973) and **White Fang** (Zanna Bianca, Italy, Spain, France, 1973). As noted above, Franco Castellano and Giuseppe Moccia (as Pipolo) wrote an early treatment of the script, which was deemed unusable. Eugenio Ercolani had this to say about how Regnoli got involved in the project, "Ok, this is how it went down: Castellano and Pipolo wrote the first treatment, the one Giulio Petroni was handed when he was offered the gig. Petroni (who, mind you, was not happy about having to do the film) accepted on condition that he could change some aspects of it. He called in, in accordance with the producers, Piero Regnoli. Then other little scenes and small gags were invented on set naturally." The rest of the writing on **Life is Tough, Eh Providence?** was performed by Petroni, Antonio Marino, and the dialogue collaborators Gunter Ebert (German) and Antoinette Pellevant (France).

And we might as well get this out there right now, Gregg Palmer was brought over to play a sidekick to Tomas Milian's character Providence. Palmer hated the filming experiences in Spain and Italy so much that although he had signed a five-picture deal- after the second Providence film, he broke the contract and headed back to the states. Tomas Milian, a notorious "ball-buster," was thoroughly disliked by Gregg Palmer, which should come as no surprise knowing a bit of Milian's problematic behavior (fueled at times by alcohol and drugs) with some of his male costars, including Maurizio Merli, Franco Nero, Orson Welles, and Richard Wyler to name but a few.

Giulio Petroni was not interested in making another western as he had respect for the genre and felt the current comedy-westerns were soiling the genre's reputation, noting, "Apart from my personal wishes, it was clear that the genre had run its course, and I didn't want to get involved in all this vulgarities that had started to dominate it"[16]. But when Tomas Milian, who was looking for a film to complete with the Trinity films, suggested Petroni's name to the producers Arrigo Colombo and Giorgio Papi, they offered the movie to Petroni. Giulio Petroni, who had just created his production company Azalea (Via Chimens, 3 – Rome) needed the capital and accepted. Papi And Colombo are best known for being the producers of the seminal Italian western **A Fistful of Dollars** for their Jolly films in 1964. It must also be noted that Mario Bava worked on the special effects on the film for a few days in an uncredited capacity. (Check out Bava's work on the billiards scene). Not to go too much into the **Life is Tough, Eh Providence?** as it will be discussed in a future issue, and after all, this is a look at the films of Alberto De Martino, but here

SOMETIMES LIFE'S TOUGH

AIN'T IT PROVIDENCE

April 3rd

No. 3

OCEANIA
PRODUZIONI INTERNAZIONALI
CINEMATOGRAFICHE s.r.l.
Via Romagnosi, 3 - ROMA

~~312726~~
351-235

~~45~~
38

23 - 48 - 95

8 - 37 - 1

George 27/6/7
758/515
mkb

"SOMETIMES LIFE'S TOUGH, AIN'T IT,
PROVIDENCE?"

Screenplay by:
    Dean Craig

25 FEB. 1972

goes a quick break down of the film. **Life Is Tough, Eh Providence?** aka **Sometimes Life's Tough Ain't it Providence?** premiered October 26, 1972, in Italy and did excellent box office, landing it in the top thirty grossing Italian western films (inflation not calculated in) of all-Time. Providence is introduced in the movie waking from a slumber; he is dressed in stylish but dirty duds, in need of mending, and a bowler hat to top it all off. The Charlie Chaplin "Little Tramp" character is just forming here, as can be seen in the manner of Providence's attire, Milian's mannerisms and the slapstick comedy elements. Now Milian would go full "Little Tramp" mode in the sequel, including sporting a "Toothbrush" mustache made famous by Charlie Chaplin. Providence is riding aboard a reconditioned Wells Fargo stagecoach, drawn by a team of horses, who seemingly always know where Providence is heading. We hear a voice from the back of the customized coach, and it's revealed to be a large, lumbering, bearded fellow who is tied to the stage and ambling behind it. That hulking character is named "The Hurricane Kid" and is played by the American actor Gregg Palmer and it's no coincidence that Milian, who was looking for a vehicle similar to the Trinity films- that Gregg Palmer was chosen because he resembled Bud Spencer. Eugenio Ercolani related a story concerning Palmer and his resemblance to Bud Spencer, "Giulio (Petroni) recalled that once Palmer got offended on set. They were setting up a scene, and cinematographer Alessandro D'Eva called Palmer jokingly 'Bud,' referring of course to Carlo Pedersoli. Palmer went back to his trailer and Giulio had to smooth things out. According to his recollection Palmer overreacted and refused for the following days to talk to D'Eva, who was mortified."

One thing one notices when comparing the script dated February 25, 1972, to the finished product (Viewed a dubbed English version) is that when Giulio Petroni said that much was improvised on the set, he was truthful in that statement. Another thing of note is that the script of **Life Is Tough, Eh Providence?** runs 128 pages, whereas **Here We Go Again, Eh Providence?** is a good one hundred pages more at a whopping 231 (The producers ran out of money and had to scrap some scenes, thankfully). **Life if Tough, Eh Providence?** borrows from **The Good, The Bad, and The Ugly** (Il buono, il brutto, il cattivo, Italy, Spain, W. Germany, 1966) in the use of turning in a wanted man (Tuco/Hurricane Kid) in for the bounty money and then helping free him and doing the whole thing over and over again in various towns. While Milian is not Terence Hill's equal in looks or of Eastwood's physical stature, it must be noted that no matter personality Milian's flaws, he was a wonderfully inventive actor.

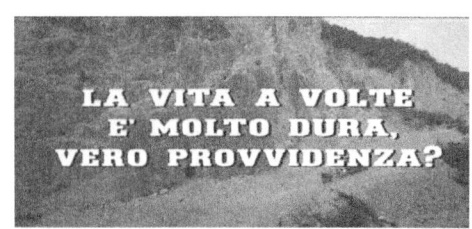

Top to Bottom: Italian Title card- Life is Tough, Eh Providence?; Tomas Milian as Providence; Tomas Milian; Providence's reconditioned Wells Fargo stage with Milian and Palmer on horseback; Gregg Palmer and Tomas Milian

Life is Tough, Eh Providence? Top to Bottom: Maurice Poli; Gabriella Giorgelli; Ken Wood (Giovanni Cianfriglia) and Tomas Milian in the billiards scene (Effects by Mario Bava); Swedish actress Janet Agren (talents wasted in her only Italio western); Paul Muller, Gregg Palmer and Milian

As the early 70s rolled around, Milian began to hide or disfigure himself in his made-up character roles. Besides being labeled as noted a "ball-buster" by some directors, another thing of note about Milian that seems to surface when he's discussed is his seemingly endless supply of ideas, his problems with staying within the script, and his overflowing creative juices. Giulio Petroni had this to say about Tomas Milian, "A great actor, by fits and starts, difficult to control. He was a volcano of ideas and had a tendency to overdo things. When we made Provvidenza he kept coming up with the craziest of ideas, and I literally had to slow him down" [17]. **Life is Tough, Eh Providence?** begins to shift gears once Providence heads to Owensboro, Kentucky, to claim the $10,000 reward on The Hurricane Kids head. The Hurricane Kid character, who had been a grating buffoonish caricature to this point, begins to show some development and becomes a fairly fleshed out character by the end, a character who garners more sympathy than the Providence character. Providence is a highly intelligent character, an expert criminologist, inventor, and a crack shot. On the way to Owensboro, Providence is momentarily tricked by The Hurricane Kid and is knocked out by a Bud Spencer fist bop to the head. The Hurricane Kid takes Providence to the sheriff in Owensboro, who is named Pendleton (Dieter Eppler). The Hurricane Kid tells the sheriff that Providence is The Hurricane Kid. After coming too, Providence disputes the claim, and the sheriff, unsure of who's who locks both of them up. The military is called in- .Providence is as noted above a renowned expert on criminals; he and The Hurricane Kid are part of Quiz show, given by the military commander Colonel Mike "Good Morning" on criminology. [18] It doesn't take the commander long to figure out who the real Providence is. Later that night, The Hurricane Kid receives a crowbar in his cell and escapes. The whole affair at sheriff Pendleton's office is relevant because it is eventually revealed that Pendleton has been making counterfeit money and exchanging it for real cash, including Providence's stash. From this point onwards, it a series of punch-ups and assorted people trying to get their hands-on Providence's loot. A Trinity-Esque scene revolves around a church's razing and the bad guy coming to collect the $4,000 owed to him. There is even an odd scene involving Providence doing yoga. During one of Providence and The Hurricane Kid's assorted punch-ups, The Hurricane Kid tells Providence as he tackles him, "Your washed-up Joe Namath." Joe Namath was a superstar quarterback of the New York Jets and was internationally known. Namath even appeared in an Italian western, **The Last Rebel**. The less said about **The Last Rebel** (USA, 1972) the better. But by 1972, Namath's on-field National Football League career was on the downside, the result of countless injuries and age.

While I have to say I enjoyed the film, it's very uneven, and it's almost like you have the beginning which builds the story, the end which resolves the story, and the middle consists of a bunch of unending meandering skits. The whole of the film is just surface entertainment and not a bit of depth or emotional attachment. The Providence character is limited in his construct; eccentric and intelligent, he is so anal retentive that he frustrates the viewer. Speaking for myself, I felt no connection or affinity for the character. There are many punch-ups, and while gun-play is displayed, its more comedic or to showcase Providence's prowess with a gun. There are a few funny gags, including one where the bulky Hurricane Kid jumps upon a horse from a balcony causing the horse to sink into the ground and when he tries to jump on Providence and lands on the ground, making a deep hole where his body landed. The billiards scene is inventive (Mario Bava did the special effects) and is essentially the Trinity poker scene but on a pool table.

Providence customized stagecoach is equipped with all kinds of gadgets shown to decent effect near the finale when it spews a smokescreen, ejects jets of water, and even a pie launcher. It is a lighthearted, lightheaded, uncomplicated film and leaves your mind as soon as the end credits are over. **While Life is Tough, Eh Providence?** is mostly inoffensive and keeps moving at a good pace- It's easy to see why the great Giulio Petroni decided to step away from westerns after this film. Petroni had directed the western masterpieces **Death Rides a Horse** (Da uomo a uomo, Italy, 1967) and **Tepepa** (Italy, Spain, 1969) and the second tier westerns **A Sky Full of Stars for a Roof** (E per tetto un cielo di stelle, Italy, 1968) and **Night of the Serpent** (La notte dei serpenti, Italy, 1969) and could see where the genre was heading and after directing **Life is Tough, Eh Providence?** did not want to mar the genre anymore- The westerns had given him much in terms of directorial clout and fame. While **Life is Tough, Eh Providence?** might be uneven and unremarkable; the score by Ennio Morricone is a joyous piece of infectious ear candy that fits the on-screen action to perfection. While littered with some terrific names, the supporting cast is used sparingly as the Providence character takes center stage and, to a lesser extent, The Hurricane Kid character. With the supporting players being forced to the peripherals, it doesn't allow them to be built to any depth and are just flimsy characterizations. Just looking at the cast list beyond the stars, its replete with some fine actors, but most are given so little screen time that they are deemed useless. The wonderful actress Gabriella Giorgelli (Here redheaded instead of her normal raven locks) is a throwaway character who is only in the film for the last fifteen minutes or so- as is the always excellent Paul Muller. Janet Argen, who is third billed, is used for a bit and then discarded. Maurice Poli gets about five minutes of screen time! Dieter Eppler gets a bit more screen time as sheriff Pendleton, but we get no foreshadowing that he is running a counterfeit ring- as if that idea was fleshed-out as they went along (which it probably was). France, W. Germany, and Italy co-Production. Production companies: Oceania Produzioni Internazionali Cinematografiche (Italy), Terra Filmkunst (W. Germany), Theatre La Rex (France), and Unidis (Italy). As noted above: Arrigo Colombo and Giorgio Papi were the producers on **Life is Tough, Eh Providence**, and were affiliated with Unidis, a production/distribution arm of Jolly Films.

Alberto De Martino had just finished up directing Tomas Milian in the rather dull crime film **Counselor at Crime** when he accepted the directorial chores on **Here We Go Again, Eh Providence?**. After blowing up Providence's customized stagecoach in the first film, a new vehicle was in order. What we get in the second film is a steam-powered car that looks like a space-age locomotive pulling a small passenger car. The vehicle is driven by Providence's Asian servant Ci- Hao, who caters to all the bosses wishes. After finding out that The Hurricane Kid was being sentenced that day in Galveston, Providence decides to head there to do the old release, recapture and collect the bounty thing like in the first film. But before they get to their destination, a stop is made at a saloon for water for the steamer. Providence is challenged to a shooting match inside the saloon (Used three times in the film), the prize- $100 (the cost of a barrel of water). Providence defeats the blonde cowboy named Shotgun (Rick Boyd). The scene features Shotgun shooting out a burning candle, and then Providence shoots the lone candle into the air and shoots it into four pieces. He then shoots and relights the candles, finally using his derringer (like a squirt gun) to extinguish the candles with a water stream. Providence recues The Hurricane Kid from life in prison, having his sentence communicated to death by hanging! As the Kid falls through the trapdoor, Providence shoots the rope in two (GBU again), and the duo take off.

Inside Providence's vehicle, The Hurricane Kid is locked behind bars when suddenly news comes across the ticker tape… "President Grant died… Rutherford has taken his place… The new president has proclaimed a general amnesty." With that, the jail cell door unlocks, and The Hurricane Kid is a free man. Providence is in a deep depression, and The Hurricane Kid tells him they should go and celebrate! The two wind up in a brightly lit saloon where a full-blown musical number is in process. A punch-up quickly occurs with The Hurricane Kid taking on four men as a solemn Providence sits and avoids the brawl, just tapping his fingers, obviously still saddened by the amnesty. The viewer quickly notices how bright and airy **Here We Go Again, Eh Providence?** is compared to the more rustic and earth-toned look of the first film. Most of the scenes are brightly lit, and the film looks like a million bucks, and one would imagine that the film had to have a larger budget than the first film. The film also uses some painted backdrops, which adds to the film's rather whimsical look and feel. Being that the first film was wildly successful, Milian was allowed to indulge more, including musical numbers showcasing his Providence character. After the saloon, Providence decides to go on vacation at the seaside, there, he rescues a beautiful girl named Pamela (Carol Andre) from drowning, who he instantly falls in love with- and if we can't guess that Providence is in love- Venus descends and shoots him in the heart with an arrow. Pamela is taken by Providence (or "Provvy" as Pamela calls him) to dine at a fancy restaurant; there, Milian (Providence) is allowed to indulge in a bit of sing and dance accompanied by two shapely black waitresses (Antonella and Nadia Cocconcelli) as Pamela looks on happily. During the dinner, the disguised Hurricane Kid attempts to rob the restaurant patrons. Providence foils the Kid's plans by revealing his true identity and insists he return the victims' their possessions. The Hurricane Kid, who is fed up, decides to shoot Providence, but "Provvy" has placed a metal tray in his shirt, and the first bullet bounces off! The second shot follows the first bullet's trajectory, but instead of harmlessly passing by The Hurricane Kid, it strikes his backside. The action then switches to Pamela's family's mansion in Wisconsin and the flamboyant Providence being introduced to the family. Once there, Providence finds out his beloved Pamela is set to marry the dashing Captain Bart (Manuel Gallardo) because her father Count de Ortega (Luciano Catenacci), owes the Captain $500,000. After a duel with swords between Providence and Captain Bart, which ends with Providence signing a bloody "P" into Bart's forehead and Zorro exclaiming, "Not bad Providence, you remembered Zorro's lessons- Providence promises to return with the money within the week in exchange for the hand of Pamela in marriage.

Providence goes to "*Hospice. Jesse James Foundation for Retired Bandits*," to enlist the help of The Hurricane Kid. As Providence makes his way through the home, The Hurricane Kid spies Providence and hides out, but Providence fishes him out with a bottle of whiskey. One humorous passage occurs in the Bandits retirement home, when one of the nuns tells an elderly bandit, "Trinity, how many times must I tell you! You must wash your hands before a meal." Of course, that exchange references Trinity's moniker as "The right hand of the devil" and his rather prodigious appetite. This line was changed from the script which read, "You don't get any, Santanna. First, wash your hands." To come up with the $500,000, Providence enlists the help of The Hurricane Kid in a series of crimes that turn into misadventures. First the boys cheat the saloon (featured in the first musical number), but The Hurricane Kid is too stupid to realize that it was Providence's magnet on the roulette wheel and not his luck that won him $500,000 in cash- so he quickly loses it at craps. Next up, they decide to rob the bank in Tucson! Problem is that there is no bank there- So, they build a bank out of what looks like giant Lego blocks and take the town's deposits, but when they attempt to make off with the loot, the Captain and his men thwart their attempt and then leave them stranded in the desert. While in the desert, they are captured by a tribe of Indians who plan on killing them until Providence does a rain dance, which brings the first rain to the area in seven weeks, and the duo are released. The chief has told Providence about a train that passes by there and is transporting $500,000 in gold. Providence comes up with a brilliant plan to make off with the gold from the train, which is again thwarted by Captain Bart. The two are brought before a military firing squad. After asking Captain Bart for a minute, Providence all of a sudden begins acting like a pigeon, his cooing brings a whole swarm of real pigeons who proceed to shit in the faces of the military personal allowing Providence and The Hurricane Kid to escape with the gold. Back in the steam car Providence uses the unique gadgets like in the first film, against the soldiers giving chase. This chaotic scene plays out until the soldier's gunfire damages the car and it finally breaks down! But least we worry because Providence has one more trick up his sleeve. After all, the car hosts a hot air balloon that lifts them to safety! The balloon floats along towards Providence's rendezvous with Pamela and her father. The vehicle is blown up in **Here We Go Again, Eh Providence?** just as it was in **Life is Tough, Eh Providence?**

And not that there was any doubt in the viewer's mind that a twist would occur at the end, and it does. Pamela is actually married to the famous bandit "Cian Ku La" (posing as her father), and they travel around the west ripping people off. All this leads to a showdown at the end with the obvious Caucasian actor Luciano Catenaci playing Chin Yu Kin, his band of kung fu fighters (Martial Arts movies were hot at that time) against Providence, The Hurricane Kid, and Ci-Hao! Like the rest of the movie, the end fight has assorted craziness going on, including Providence consuming a can of spinach ala Popeye and defeating the bunch. It ends with Providence giving The Hurricane Kid and Ci-Hao the bounty on Cian Ku La's head as he floats off alone in the hot air balloon.

Here We Go Again, Eh Providence? while technically a better-looking film than **Life is Tough, Eh Providence?** colors too far outside the lines and becomes a jumbled up stew of gags that quite honesty becomes rather tedious as it wears on. I was so frustrated with it by the time the end credits rolled that I was glad another installment of the films wasn't made. Tomas Milian again is the star of the show and he doesn't disappoint here, but his performance as Providence while good does grate on the nerves- and he again is center stage and all-consuming- the rest of the characters are rather shallowly put together. Gregg Palmer is given a bit more to do here, but his talents are wasted here as he mostly just stands back with varying dumb looking expressions on his face as the spotlight shines on Milian. Viewing the two Providence films back to back for this article was a bit redundant as much of the same formula was used in both films, sans the overuse of **The Good, The Bad and The Ugly** bit in the second film. But we have the same type of punch-ups, the chasing of the vehicle by horseback riders leading to its explosion, and the fast pace, slapstick gags. In **Here We Go Again, Eh Providence?** the trick shooting involving Rick Boyd was repeated three times and the boys attempt to secure the $500,000 was repeatedly done as was the riding in of the calvary to foil their plans.

If I must admit I enjoyed the first film slightly better as it was more structured. **Here We Go Again, Eh Providence?** flew off its tracks early and just hurried about in the middle of the film in a madcap style that left my head swirling around. While I am not a fan of Italian-western comedies, I found these two films decent enough views… but that said, I won't be revisiting either in the near future! **Here We Go Again, Eh Providence?** varies a bit here and there from the script- In the script it calls for a scene where the steam car is built by a group of workers- In the film the car is introduced built. One almost gets the feeling that the

Here We Go Again, Eh Providence?
Top to Bottom: Providence's steam car; Italian Title card; Milan with "toothbrush mustache" as Providence; Gregg Palmer and Tomas Milian; Carol Andre as Pamela

Here We Go Again, Eh Providence? Top to Bottom: Retirement home for bandits, where The Hurricane Kid retired to, until Providence lures him out; Rick Boyd (Federico Boido) Tomas Milan and Yu Ming Lun; Milian and Palmer;The ice skating scene(?)!, Providence's hot air balloon

writers of this piece tried to add some of the whimsy of films like Chitty Chitty Bang Bang (U.K., USA, 1968) and the bold colors of a Willy Wonka (USA, E. Germany, W. Germany, Belgium, U.K., 1971). Like noted above the film is bold and bright the only instances of earthy colors are during the saloon detours with Rick Boyd and the "Bandits" home where The Hurricane Kid had retired to before Providence lures him out.

Just too much is going on in Here We Go Again, Eh Providence? and that creates a problem for the viewer. The non-stop constant barrage of gags wears thin and plot and character development are sacrificed for Milian's over the top comedic shenanigans. About as vapid of a film as one could find that causes confusion in one's mind and fights its way in only for the viewer to do everything within their power to repel it. At the end of the script the film is to revert back to the turning of The Hurricane Kid in for a bounty as opposed to the filmed ending which concludes with Providence rising into the clouds in his hot air balloon.

Tomas Milian was a major star in Italy and appeared in some of the finest Italian westerns ever made, including: **The Ugly Ones** (El precio de un hombre: The Bounty Killer, Italy, Spain, 1966), **The Big Gundown** (La resa dei conti, Italy, Spain, 1966), **Django Kill… If You Live Shoot** (Se sei vivo spara, Italy, Spain, 1967), **Face to Face, Run, Man, Run** (Corri uomo corri, Italy, France, 1968), **Tepepa, Companeros,** and **Four of the Apocalypse**. Gregg Palmer, a minor star of Hollywood in the 50s; transitioning to character actor as the 1960s rolled around- he probably is best known for appearing in six John Wayne Films. The two Providence films were Palmer's only Italian westerns.

The French actress Carole Andre appears as Pamela in Here **We Go Again, Eh Providence?** she starred in three other oaters, the Mike Marshall western **Death Rides Along** (Con lui cavalca la morte, Italy, 1967), **Face to Face**, and **White Fang** (Zanna Bianca, Italy, France, Spain, 1973). The easily recognizable blonde sinister-looking Rick Boyd has a small part in the film, and he appeared in close to forty westerns, mostly as an edgy antagonist. The rest of the cast is filled out with fine character actors, including Luciano Catenacci, Rosario Borelli, Carla Mancini, Nello Pazzafini, Omero Capanna, and Goffredo Unger. Rafael Albaicín, a former bullfighter, appeared in three Alberto De Martino films as an Indian chief: **Assault on Fort Texan, One Hundred Thousand Dollars for Ringo** and **Here We Go Again, Eh Providence?** [20]

El Paso, Texas. April, 29, 1972

In **Here We Go Again, Eh Providence?** when Providence is looking through his Wanted posters, he pulls one out for *Minnesota Clay* and says, "Uhm... Minnesota Clay... I've taken care of him..." Of course, **Minnesota Clay** was directed by Sergio Corbucci, and Milian had appeared in two previous Corbucci westerns **Companeros** in 1970 and **Sonny and Jed** in 72. When **Companeros** was released in the states on some double bills, it was paired up with **Minnesota Clay**!

The cinematographer Alejandro Ulloa was born in Madrid, Spain, in 1926 and died there in 2002. Ulloa worked on one hundred and nineteen films as a cinematographer, including the westerns: **Sugar Colt** (1966), **Hate For Hate** (Odio per odio, Italy, 1967), **The Mercenary** (Il mercenario, Italy, Spain, USA, 1968), **Kill Them All and Come Back Alone** (1968), **Companeros** (1970) and **What Am I Doing in the Middle of the Revolution** (Che c'entriamo noi con la rivoluzione?, Italy, Spain, 1972). To this viewer, Ulloa's work on this film is the highlight of it, along with the outstanding score by Ennio Morricone and Bruno Nicolai.

Filmed in Almeria, Gruadix, La Calahorra, Manzanares El Real, Spain and in Rome Italy at Cincetta and Dear Studios. A Spain, Italy, and France co-production: Les Films Corona (France), Oceania Produzioni Internazional (Italy) and Producciones Cinematograficas D.I.A. (Spain). [19]

Here We Go, Eh Providence? is Alberto De Martino's last western, but he did direct seven more films: The Antichrist (1974), **Strange Shadows in an Empty Room** (1976), **The Chosen** (Holocaust 2000, Italy, U.K., 1977), **Pumaman** (L'uomo puma, Italy, 1980), **Blood Link** (Italy, W. Germany, USA, 1982), **Formula for Murder** (1985) and **Miami Golem**. De Martino had a hand in writing six of his last seven films, the only exclusion being the crime-drama **Strange Shadows in an Empty Room**! Alberto De Martino's Italian westerns were all competent and proficient, excluding the 1965 film **Assault on Fort Texan**, which can only be labeled as a mess. Alberto De Martino was a professional director, helming a near classic in **One Hundred Thousand Dollars for Ringo**, an upper-tier film in **Django Shoots First** middle-tier westerns in **Terrible Sheriff**, and **Here We Go Again Eh Providence?** and one bottom tier entry in **Assault on Fort Texan**.

End Notes

[1]. Darkening the Italian Screen, Eugenio Ercolani..McFarland Books. 2019

[2]. De Martino worked as the second unit director on **Duck You Sucker** for his good friend Sergio Leone. Leone had asked him to assist him. De Martino used the Americanized name Martin Herbert, a name he used on and off throughout his career.

[3]. In Eugenio Ercolani's brilliant book Darkening the Italian Screens, De Martino is interviewed and says he was brought in to replace the original director on **Terrible Sheriff**. Antonio Momplet is credited as co-director on some sources on both **The Invisible Gladiator** and **Terrible Sheriff**. De Martino says he did not know who Momplet was and he did not work on either film, just a Spanish name for co-production requirements. Antonio Momplet was a director/writer of some note and was born in Spain in 1899 and died there in 1974. But the director De Martino says that he replaced on **Terrible Sheriff** was not Momplet.

[4]. Giorgio Simonelli would become ill towards the end of filming of **Two Sons of Ringo** and according to Marco Giusti was replaced by Giuliano Carnimeo. Simonelli would die October 3, 1966 at sixty-four years of age.

[5]. **Perseus Against the Monsters** (1963): While it is not altogether successful, it is still an enjoyable romp! What kept going through my mind was how well executed the riding scenes were as the cavalries were attacking and how utterly disastrous, they were performed in Assault on Fort Texan (1965). The Medusa and Sea Serpent are surprisingly inventive creations, limited but still effective. Richard Harrison was born to play these types of parts. Solid cast! The painted backdrops and the use of fog causes a bit of eyestrain!

[6]. Darkening the Italian Screen, Eugenio Ercolani

[7]. El Cine Del Oeste Comunidad Madrid, Javier Ramos and Angel Castellano, La Libra, 2019.

[8]. Darkening the Italian Screen, Eugenio Ercolani. McFarland Books. 2019

[9]. Darkening the Italian Screen, Eugenio Ercolani. McFarland Books. 2019

[10]. Edmondo Amati- Some sources claim Edmondo Amati died in 1992 and not 2002.

[11]. www.giornalepop.it

[12]. Riccardo Freda. Roberto Curti

[13]. Austin Fisher's list may not be complete as a few films may have escaped its grasp. But still it is a fascinating looking into a large body of data to come away with at least a good idea of how films and directors performed at the Italian box office. Radical Frontiers in the Spaghetti Western. I.B. Tauris, 2011

[13a]. Darkening the Italian Screen, Eugenio Ercolani

[14]. **Trinity is Still My Name** (1971), was the highest-grossing Italian western in Italy in 1971 (and all-time) by far. Its box office of 5,268,718,000 Lira helped revive the genre momentarily. But if you look at the raw numbers, you see that the combined box office of **Trinity is Still My Name, Red Sun**, and **A Fistful of Dynamite** (all 1971) totaled 9,426,107,000. The box office total for the 42 films made that year was 19,099,782,000 lira. So, taking those three films out of the 42 films made that year, the total box office for the remaining 39 was 9,673,675,000 lira. And doing a bit more math, the average of those 39 was 248,042,000 (roughly). And even worse is that a couple of other 1971 oaters did reasonably well at the box office, like **Don't Turn the Other Cheek** (1,019,096,000), **Guns For Dollars** (787,555,000), **Return of Sabata** (730,592,000) and **Bad Man's River** (605,516,000). Excluding the top seven films from that year, the average was a very discouraging 186,597,000 per film. The end was no doubt there!

[15]. [From the Spaghetti Western Database: https://www.spaghetti-western.net/index.php/Petroni_on_his_westerns_(interview)].

[16]. From the Spaghetti Western Database: https://www.spaghetti-western.net/index.php/Petroni_on_his_westerns_(interview)

[17]. From the Spaghetti Western Database: https://www.spaghetti-western.net/index.php/Petroni_on_his_westerns_(interview)

[18] The actor playing the Colonel Mike Good Morning who gives Providence and The Hurricane Kid a quiz on banditry was Mike Bongiorno, an American- Italian personality, who was known in Italy as "The Quiz King" for his television hosting duties on game shows!

[19]. According to Terence Denman in his book *Fistfuls of Dollars in Almeria*- Filming took place in Almeria for a week, beginning July 9, 1973. Other locations include: Guadix, La Calahorra. Rome (exteriors and interiors for five weeks). Madrid: Madrid: Manazanares El Real, Ice Hockey stadium, railway station at Las Delicias.

[20]. Luciano Catenacci who played Count De Ortega in the film **Here We Go again, Eh Providence?,** also served as a producer/production manager on the film along with Alfonso Donati.

Shooting schedule for Here We Go Again, Eh Providence? The film did occur financial problems and some things had to be cut, including the building of the car and other scenes

29 MAG. 1973

Zaccaria Donati

OCEANIA Produzioni Internazionali Cinematografiche

"CI RISIAMO, VERO PROVVIDENZA"

Titolo inglese suggerito : "HERE WE GO AGAIN, PROVVIDENZA"

Screenplay by
CASTELLANO e PIPOLO

Final version. April 1973

LARGE SHED - (Interior Day)

                                    PROVVIDENZA REFRAIN

A wooden shed with primitive conveyer belts which carry pieces of metal, fenders, tubes. They are parts of Provvidenza's new steam carriage.
Some blacks work on the assembly line. Some screw knots, some assemble the various pieces, some paint them. The steam carriage begins to take shape. Provvidenza, wearing a bowler and carrying a purse and an umbrella supervises the work, gives orders, removes from his purse blueprints of the carriage, consults then, then approaches some of the workers directing the assembly of the various parts. (Ci-Hao) an elderly Chinese technician with slanted eyes and an Oriental goatee, stops and scratches his lead, looking concerned. Proffidenza pushes him aside and makes a very rapid calculation.

Upper- Left: A Man Called Noon on a double-bill with Lady Kung Fu (Hon Kong, South Korea, 1972). Harford Connecticut- October 10, 1973
Upper- Right: Once Upon a Time in the West (C'era una volta il West, Italy, USA, 1968). Indianapolis,,Indiana- August 11, 1969
Bottom: Tepepa (Italy, Spain, 1969) with Hester Street (USA, 1975). Boston Massachusetts- Dec 31, 1975

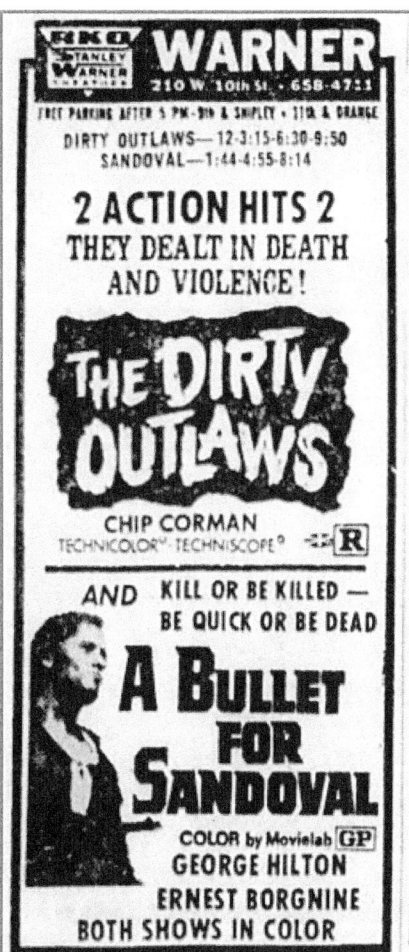

Companeros and Minnesota Clay- April 29, 1972
Dirty Outlaws and A Bullet for Sandoval- Wilmington, Delaware. October 28. 1971
The Last Tomahak. WFIL-TV6- Philadelphia, Pennsylavania- Feb 19, 1967

Roma, 21 MAG 1964

Ministero del Commercio con l'Estero
DIREZIONE GENERALE PER LE VALUTE

Div. VII
Rif. VII/171666/71 del...
Risposta al foglio N°
del

Al - UFFICIO ITALIANO DEI CAMBI
Transazioni Correnti
Conti Autorizzati
ROMA.

e, p.c.:

- MINISTERO TURISMO E SPETTACOLO
D.G. Spettacolo - Div. VI
ROMA.

- SOC. JOLLY FILM
Largo Messico, 6
ROMA.

OGGETTO

Pagamento del compenso dovuto al Sig. Clint Eastwood per le sue prestazioni artistiche nel film "IL MAGNIFICO STRANIERO".

La Società in indirizzo ha chiesto l'approvazione del contratto stipulato in data 4 marzo c.a., tramite la William Morris Organization di Roma, con il Sig. Clint Eastwood di nazionalità americana, in base al quale questi si è impegnato a prestare la sua attività artistica nel film "Il Magnifico Straniero" per un periodo di dieci settimane consecutive.

In corrispettivo delle sue prestazioni professionali il predetto attore avrà diritto a percepire i seguenti emolumenti:

- compenso forfettario di $ 13.500 (dollari tredicimilacinquecento) da pagarsi, nel controvalore in lire italiane, alla predetta William Morris Organization, Via Nomentana n.60, Roma;
- diaria settimanale di $ 400 (dollari quattrocento) da corrispondere nel controvalore in lire italiane, durante il periodo delle lavorazioni in Italia;
- pro-rata temporis di $ 215 (dollari duecentoquindici) al giorno per prestazioni artistiche eccedenti il periodo suindicato;
- rimborso delle spese di viaggio per due persone in aereo I Classe Los Angeles-Roma e ritorno.

In relazione a quanto precede, si comunica il benestare di questo Ministero all'esecuzione del contratto in questione.

Per Copia Conforme

IL MINISTRO
Per
D. Paolis

GIO/eb

INVALIDATO AI FINI VALUTARI
per $ 1.291,30 Roma 14/7/64
BANCA D'AMERICA E D'ITALIA

La Societa in indirizzo ha chiesto l'approvazione del contratto stipulato in data 4 marzo c.a., tramite la William Morris Organisation di Roma, con il Sig. Clint Eastwood di nazionalita americana, in base al quale questi si e impegnato a prestare la sua attivata artistica nel film "Il Magnifico Straniero" per un periodo di dieci settimane consecutive.

In corrispettivo delle sue prestazioni professionali il predetto attore avra diritto a percepire i seguenti emolumenti:

- compenso forfettario di $13.500 (dollari tredicimilacin-quecento) da pagarasi, nel controvalore in lire italiane, alla predetta William Morris Organisation, Via Nomentana n.60, Roma;
- diaria settimanale di $400 (dollari quattrocento) da corrispondere nel controvolare in lire italiane, durante il periodo delle lavorazioni in Italia.
- pro-rata temporis di $215 (dollari duecentoquindici) al giorno per prestazioni artistiche eccedenti il periodo suijodicato.
- rimborso delle spese di viaggio per due persone in I Classe Los Angeles-Roma e ritorno.

In relazione a quanto precede, si comunica il benestare di questo Ministero all'esecuzione de contraito in questione.

Dated 14 / 7/ 1964

The Company in address requested the approval of the contract stipulated on 4 March ca, through the William Morris Organization of Rome, with Mr. Clint Eastwood of American nationality, on the basis of which he has undertaken to lend his artistic activity in the film "Il Magnifico Straniero" for a period of ten consecutive weeks.

In consideration of his professional services, the aforementioned plaintiff will be entitled to receive the following emoluments:

- flat-rate compensation of $ 13,500 (thirteen thousand-five hundred dollars) to be paid, in the equivalent in Italian lire, to the aforementioned William Morris Organization, Via Nomentana 60, Rome;
- weekly allowance of $ 400 (four hundred dollars) to be paid in the counter-issue in Italian lire, during the period of work in Italy.
- pro-rata temporis of $ 215 (two hundred and fifteen dollars) per day for artistic performances exceeding the indicated period.
- reimbursement of travel expenses for two people in I Class Los Angeles-Rome and back.

In relation to the above, the approval of this Ministry for the execution of the contract in question is communicated.

Dated 7/14/1964

Page 208: Clint Eastwood's contract for A Fistful of Dollars. Courtesy of Steve Carver and Tom Betts
Page 209: Tom Betts printed out the terms of the contract in Italian and English for The Spaghetti Western Digest readers

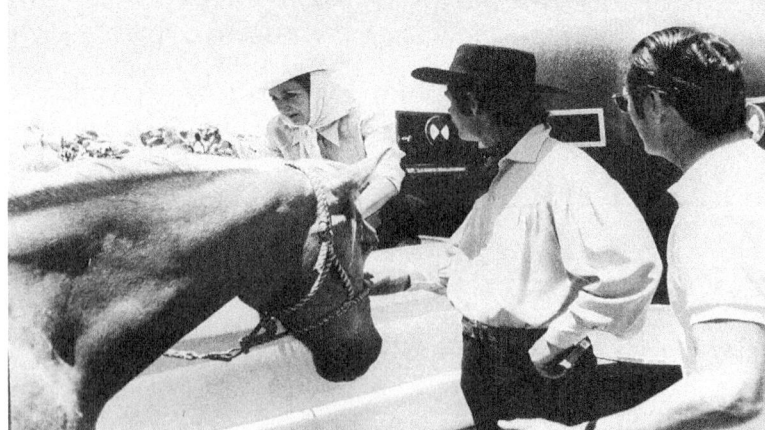

Behind the scenes of A German film crew interviewing Stephen Boyd on the set of A Man Called Noon. Thanks to Mike Siegel and Steve Mason for these rare photos

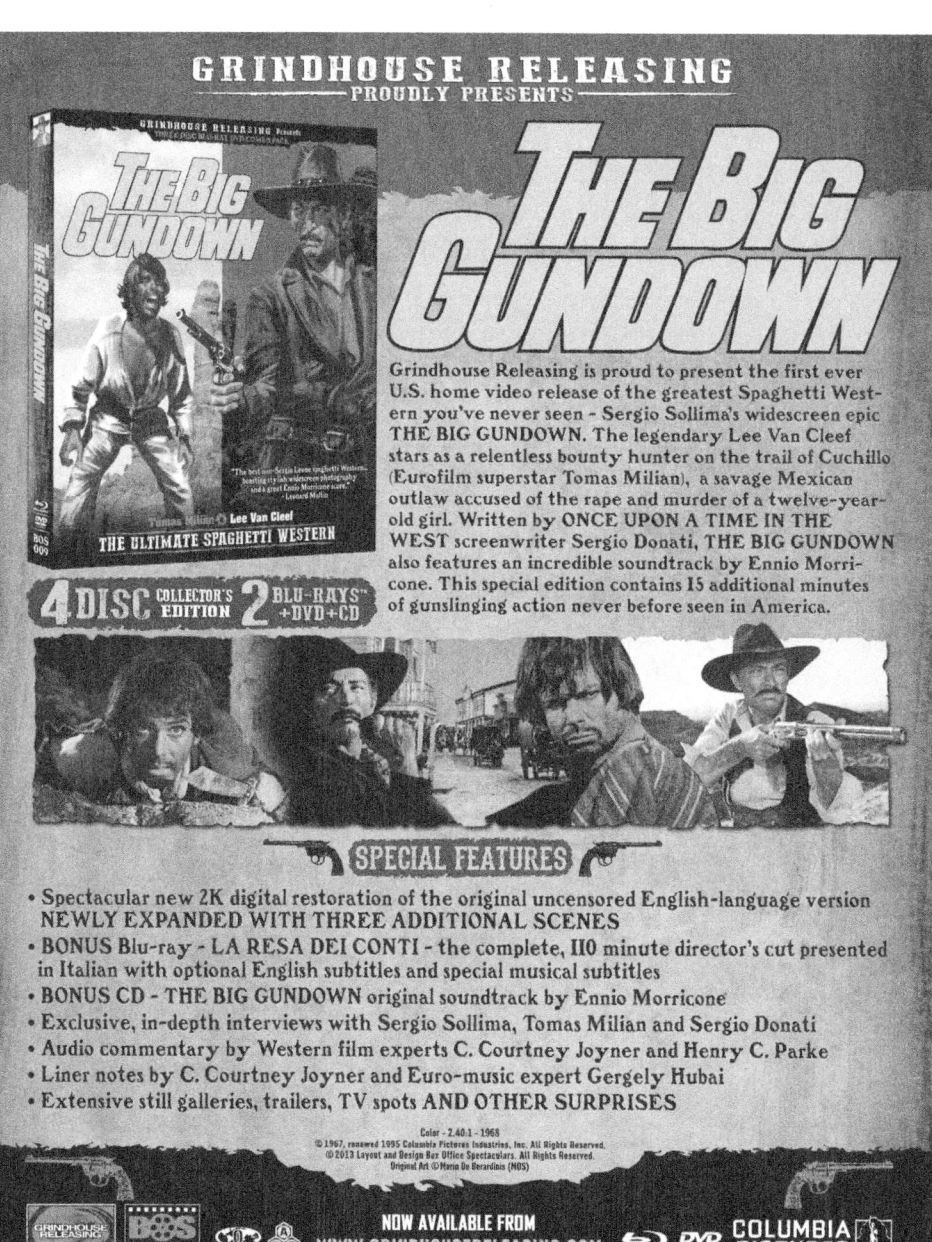

Steve Fenton Reviews.................

The Relentless Four (I quattro inesorabili, 1965)
Bullets Don't Argue (Le pistole non discutono, 1964)
Charity – The Strange Smell of Money (Sentivano... uno strano, eccitante, pericoloso puzzo di dollari, 1973)
Death Walks in Laredo (Tre pistole contro Cesare, 1967)
The Devil Was an Angel (Una colt in pugno al diavolo, 1967)
The Dirty Fifteen (Quindici forche per un assassino, 1968)
Execution (1968)
Three Dollars' Worth of Lead (Tre dollari... di piombo, 1964)
The Man from Oklahoma (Il ranch degli spietati, 1964)

Page 212: Italian Quad poster
Page 213: Top to Bottom:
Adam West (Sam Garrett) confronted by Robert Hundar (Allan) and Raf Baldassarre (Moss).
Roberto Camardiel (Anders), Adam West.
Adam West in a shootout.
Adam West and John Bartha (John).
Adam West getting an Italian Western Send-off!

The Relentless Four (I quattro inesorabili, 1965, Italy/Spain)

Synopsis (ATTN: THE FOLLOWING FOUR PARAGRAPHS CONTAIN SPOILERS!): Houston, Texas. In the desert, outlaw Rex Calhoun (José Canalejas) is hounded by Ranger Sam Garrett (Adam West). Garrett is beaten to the catch by four unscrupulous bounty-hunters, led by Allan ("Robert Hundar"/Claudio Undari), who kill Calhoun cold before Garrett can bring him back alive. To delay Garrett's return to town, one of Allan's men shoots his horse out from under him. Nonetheless, Garrett makes it to the sheriff's office in time to claim the $500 reward for the dead man.

Illicitly aided by a corrupt sheriff's deputy, the four bountymen commit murder then implicate several law-abiding citizens, for whom rewards are posted. Garrett, serving as the sheriff's aide, heads to the homestead of local cattleman Jeffrey Anders (Roberto Camardiel), only to have his visit interrupted by advent of the four bountyhunters, now wearing bandannas over their faces. Knocking Garrett unconscious and dressing in his clothes, one of their number murders old Anders in cold blood then steals his fortune, leaving the Ranger to take the rap; first pouring a whole bottle of liquor down his throat to render him hopelessly drunk.

Lack of witnesses makes it simple for the real killers to convince the cattle breeder's widow that it was actually Garrett, in a drunken daze, who had committed the heinous crime. While the sheriff gathers a jury for his trial, Garrett is tossed in a cell. By duping Deputy Vince (Cris Huerta) and his men, Garrett escapes, seeking shelter at the ranch of his old friend, John (John Bartha). Bounty is promptly offered by the newly-widowed Mrs. Anders ("Pauline Baards"/ Paola Barbara) for his recapture, with even the four actual culprits in their audacity helping search for Garrett. Following a shootout at John's place, he is caught while waiting to hop a fast train to Tucson. Allan and his surviving bountybuddy start back to claim their reward. Getting loose once again, Garrett kills Allan's partner, but, following another altercation, runs smack into the welcoming long arms of the law.

The dead cattleman's widow and their daughter Nancy (Dina Loy) are summoned for jury duty at Garrett's trial. Miss Nancy has long been in love with Garrett and wishes his life spared, while her mother wants him hanged with the greatest expediency.

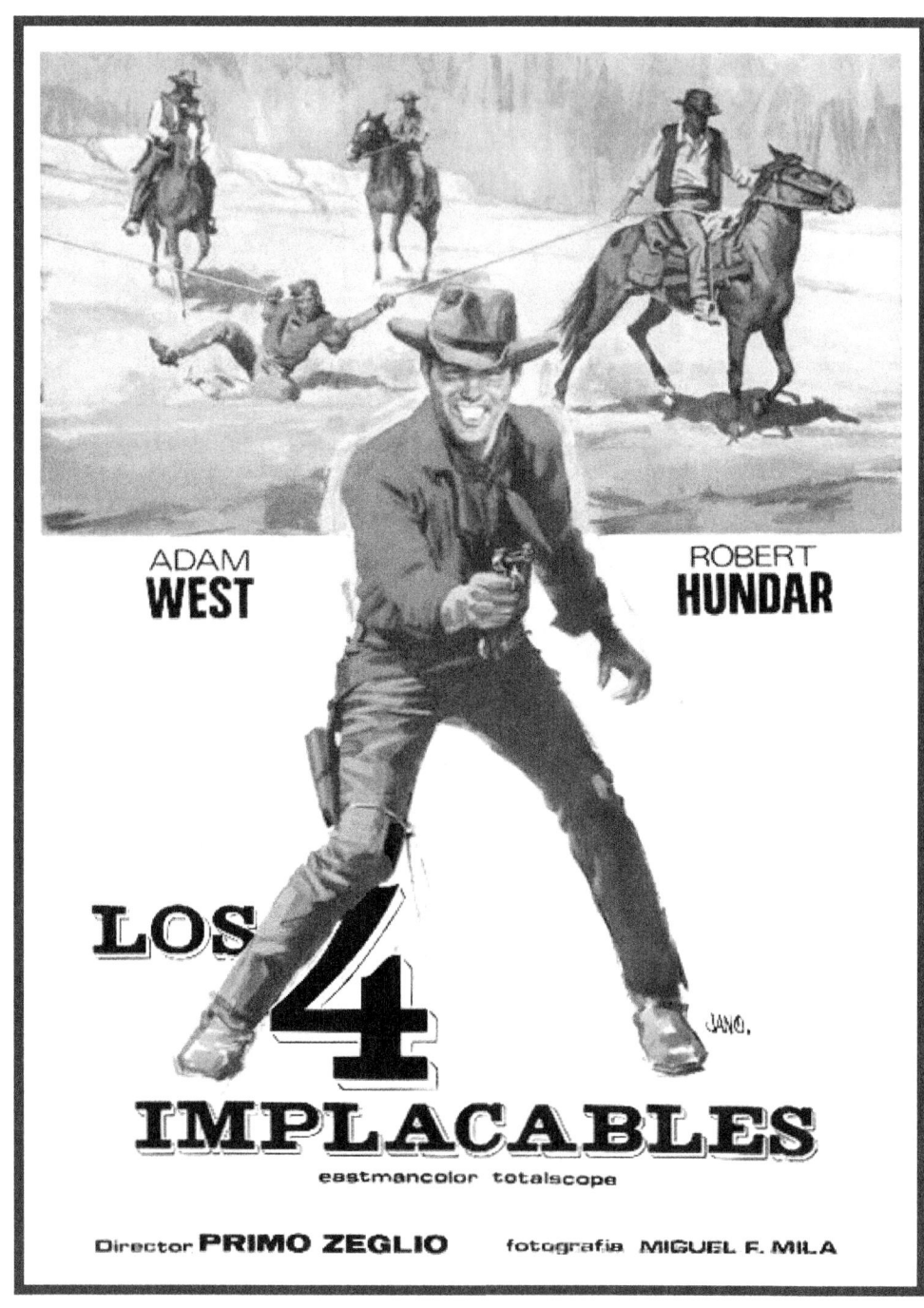

The Relentless Four - Spanish Pressbook

In short order, the jury finds Garrett guilty. He convinces honest Sheriff Luke (Luis Induni) of his innocence, and together they stage a fake 'hanging', in which Garrett apparently dies. A witness has since come forward with irrefutable evidence that the four 'honest citizens' are actually guiltier than sin. When Allan goes to collect the avails of his gang's crimes, he is caught red-handed by the sheriff, the Widow Anders... and, Garrett, still very much alive! Escaping, Allan heads to demand the bounty money from Deputy Vince, whom he must kill in 'self-defence.' After barricading himself in the sheriff's office, Allan makes a break for it, only to be shot dead by Garrett. With The Relentless Four now all duly delivered unto poetic justice, Garrett is released to rejoin Nancy, his lady love.

Comments: Theme lyrics: *"Ranger / Where you riding now? / Ranger / What is coming now?...Ride on / Ride on / Ride on..."*

In late-'65, *Continental Film Review* reported, "Now the current vogue is for westerners..." An early pre-boom western, which began shooting on May 5th of that year at Italy's Elios Film Studios, with location-work done at the increasingly-busy Tabernas western set in Almería, Spain.

This early theatrical appearance for impending cathode tube star Adam West (1928-2017)—by then already an alumnus of umpteen US TV oaters—was early on described in the Italian press as a western avventuroso-psicologico (an "adventurous psychological western"). In his autobiography, *Back to the Batcave*, West makes a passing reference to this his sole Euroater: his **Batman** producer William Dozier has a right old laugh over it, actually referring to the film as a "spaghetti western" and joking about the fad, which still had yet to take place. At that time, this so-called 'fad' was barely six months old in Europe and had yet to see export to North America. Leone's **A Fistful of Dollars** (Per un pugno di dollari, 1964, Italy/Spain/West Germany) the great-granpappy of all modern spaghetti westerns, was still a good year away from its theatrical premiere on this side of the Atlantic. The term "spaghetti western" (snicker, snicker) was yet to be coined by some smart-aleck wag on the Continent, and would not at that point have become a common euphemism (i.e., connoting 'crappy foreign shootemup'). Only examples of the genre to wash up on these shores to that point were a couple of Fish'n'Chips westerns: Raoul Walsh's **The Sheriff of Fractured Jaw** (November '58) and Michael Carreras' **The Savage Guns** (August '62); plus an equal number of Yank-backed Euroaters: Roy Rowland's **Gunfighters of Casa Grande** (May '65) and Tulio Demicheli's **Gunmen of the Rio Grande** (June '65). Other genre spaghetti/paella way-pavers such as Sergio Corbucci's **Minnesota Clay** (April '66), Lesley Selander's **The Texican** (October '66) and Burt Kennedy's **Return of the Seven** (November '66) had yet to ride into town.

As for **The Relentless Four,** it went before cameras under the direction of Primo Zeglio (sometimes known as the unlikely "Anthony Greepy") in the early spring of '65; mere months ahead of West's proposed nighttime American teleseries, **Batman** (which first aired in January of '66). It's doubtful at the time of shooting his superhero pilot that West would have been privy to an advance screening of his European western, which was not released to theaters in Italy until fully a month after **Batman** made its 'Stateside premiere. Of making a non-American western, the actor—who was still enough of an unknown commodity not to flatly turn up his nose at even a foreign-made western—took the ribbing with good humor. West then returned west to star as Batman for the next two years, whereafter, despite appearing in numerous other roles of note, he became permanently identified with the character as surely as William Shatner remains best-known as Star Trek's Capt. Kirk. Belying the biblical connotations of his Christian name, Adam West was not the first (American) man in the West (Italian-style!). The star—here often looking much like a mixture of Tab Hunter and Ty Hardin—fares well in the lead, being suitably athletic and deadpan (i.e., tongue-in-cheek) regarding his material. He downplays wisely, in some scenes even affecting a pre-Clint squint which leads you to ponder—*GASP!*—how well West might have fared in place of Eastwood had history taken an entirely different turn (that said, given his performance herein it's a cinch to picture West subbing as The Man With No Name… but perhaps a whole lot harder to imagine Eastwood as The Caped Crusader!). Due to the sheer numbers of American actors who later claimed to have been offered the lead in **A Fistful of Dollars**, it is highly feasible that West may at some point also have been up for the part. However, although he plunks two silver dollars down on dead bandido José Canalejas' wanted poster, Ranger Sam Garrett has little in common with No-Name. Herein, the bounty hunters are uniformly presented as scurrilous scum, while West stoically adheres to the staunch honor code of the Texas Rangers.

As the merciless bounty boss with the photogenically oversized face and frame, Robert Hundar plays it emotionless and motionless of expression; here at times looking oddly a lot like Lurch from **The Addams Family** (tele-version). His hideout is wall-papered with the wanted posters of prospective victims. Of course, he and his bountyboys—including genre regular Raf Baldassarre—mostly wear jet-black hats and vests, while West appears atop a white horse dressed in more suitably-heroic beige duds. In truth, the Ranger's dress code might make for much more practical camo against the sandy terrain; whereas Hundar's hunters stand out like black squirrels (or perhaps more fittingly, *skunks*) on virgin snow.

(ATTN: THIS PARAGRAPH CONTAINS SPOILERS!) Vengeful middle-aged rancher's widow—dressed all in black—is played by Dina Loy. An unusually strong distaff character for the time, she is determined to see justice done no matter how much it costs her in time…or dollars (and bullets). Ignoring her justifiable grief ("*Murderer! Murderer!!*"), the beastly Hundar thinks nothing of using Loy as a handy human shield behind which to make his getaway bid. When Hundar's corpse is finally carted past, Loy can understandably barely contain her disgust… or her saliva.

Despite its early vintage, **The Relentless Four** mostly wears a classic Spaghetti appearance: scruffier, dustier, dirtier and more unshaven than the Hollywood norm of the time. No expense was apparently spared by big-time Roman movie tycoon Alberto Grimaldi (head honcho at Produzioni Europee Associate [a.k.a. simply PEA or "EuroCoPea"] and future co-producer of the second and third films in Clint the Squint's "No-Name" trilogy) and his Spanish colleague Ricardo Sanz to bring the correct depth of ambience to their cast and settings. Sets literally teem with background extras, and the cast is far larger per capita than that in upcoming mega-hit **Fistful** (where basic under-population only augmented Leone's stark, nihilistic vision). Multiple scores of stone-slinging extras turn out in **The Relentless Four** for West's would-be necktie party and subsequent trial-by-kangaroo court, while literally dozens of fully-equipped horsemen provide escort to his impending execution.

(ATTN: THIS PARAGRAPH AND THE NEXT CONTAIN SPOILERS!) Playing his usual sober representative of justice, Luis Induni (w/ rifle, that great equalizer) acts as a level-headed mediator between West and the unruly mob (who yet again confirm that Democracy is by no means the optimal political system in a Constitutional Republic. In an imaginitive but believable scene, West employs a bar of jailhouse soap to make his break: rather than carving it into the shape of a pistol, he instead smears it all over his cell floor, soon causing disreputable deputy Cris Huerta to slip onto his sizeable ass. Resultant multi-man punchup that dismantles the jailhouse amusingly foreshadows a word-balloon brawl from a **Batman** episode (just add *POW! BIFF!* and *WHAM!*). In his position as tertiary gang-member, Giovanni Cianfriglia—himself a future masked superhero a.k.a. "Ken Wood"—later matches fists with "Batman" and goes through rather than over a saloon bannister with only a cushiony-soft collapsible pool table to break his fall (a great stunt!). West also throws himself into his fight scenes with great enthusiasm, bouncing off boulders and roughing it with admirable aplomb alongside the durable Euro stuntmen (many of whom had made their bones during the preceding Peplum cycle of Italian commercial cinema, and would go on to appear in countless Italoaters more). A good reason why West decided not to stay on in Europe might have been because he was very nearly seriously injured during the shooting of a stunt sequence (done without benefit of a double) while on location in Spain. This may have soured him on the idea of returning for spaghetti seconds (one can only wonder what kind of insurance coverage he got, if any).

Before pounding the horse-chips out of Hundar, lone ranger West first dares him to drop his Winchester to even up the odds. Even after the fists have stopped flying, Hundar staggers relentlessly on foot after his persecuted prey, who is also proceeding on foot. Another touch of pure spaghetti flavor comes when West trails Hundar by following a fresh spoor of spilled dollar bills. After getting shot from the saddle, Hundar is then ingloriously dragged down main street by his frightened mount, leaving a fluttering green wake of paper bills. As at the conclusion of Ferdinando Baldi's well-above-par **Viva Django!** a.k.a. **Django, Prepare a Coffin** (Preparati la bara!, 1968 [the first official sequel to Sergio Corbucci's founding '66 film, starring Terence Hill as a credible surrogate for originating Django-man Franco Nero]), the method behind West's earlier phony-baloney hanging is explained.

Here, wild westers enjoy their recreation as much as their killing time. At the saloon, squaredancing rowdies engage in a kooky variation of musical chairs: whenever the piano player stops plunking the keys, they target-shoot at (full) beer bottles hanging on the wall. Whether such a noisy pastime has some basis in historical fact is open to debate, but it seems a dead cert that rollicking cowpokes would at least have drained those beer bottles *dry* first before shooting them to bits! For another scene, West plays cards with Roberto Camardiel on the back of a rolling wagon.

As one of the (uncredited) theme song's few intelligible lyric lines proclaims, "Hope is a boring song." Spaghetti Western tunes could seldom be classified as boring; driven as they so often were by the sincere Italian passion of their vocalists, whose emotional delivery often overwhelmed even their correct phonetic pronunciation of the English words. Unintelligible at times, maybe; boring, rarely! Charging strings, trumpets and flutes set an appropriate 'western' mood for **The Relentless Four**; while the titles are modestly if stylishly blasted apart by animated bullet shots. Elsewhere in Franco Pisano's and Marcello Giombini's score are subtle hints at future Ennio Morricone compositions. At other times, the score takes on an irresistibly twangy, pseudo-Duane Eddy feel.

The Relentless Four possesses a convoluted (if plausible) storyline, sincere acting performances, a convincing look and enough slambang action to please. Along with **Three Dollars' Worth of Lead** (Spain/Italy, 1964, D: "Joseph Trader"/Pino Mercanti), it represents an important early step in the evolution of the 'modern' Spaghetti Western as we know and love it. [With some invaluable input from Michael "Ferg" Ferguson.]

Notes: The future Batman was then such an unknown commodity that, in their review for **The Relentless Four** (which was released in the UK as **The Magnificent Four**, shades of you-know-what [albeit minus 3!]), Britain's usually-knowledgeable *Monthly Film Bulletin* listed "Adam West" as a pseudonym for Sam Garrett, his character's name in the film! West would not return to the plains of Spain for another western role until the 1990s, when he guested on an episode of Disney's **Zorro: The Legend Continues** teleseries (namely Season 2's lead-off episode, "The Wizard"); wherein he portrayed the great-great grandfather of Batman's alter-ego, Bruce Wayne (!).

Bullets Don't Argue (1964, Italy / Spain / West Germany)

Synopsis (ATTN: THE FOLLOWING TWO PARAGRAPHS CONTAIN SPOILERS!): 1890s. Meeting at a sleepy Mexican *pueblo*, "Lonesome" Billy Clanton (Horst Frank) and his equally-no-account brother George (Ángel Aranda) plan a $30,000 bank heist 35 miles North of the border – in Rivertown, the Clantons own home turf, where fabled lawman Pat Garrett holds (Rod Cameron) sway. While Sheriff Garrett is in the midst of his marriage vows to Martha Coogan (Laly Soldevila/"Tenory"), the pair of sibling bandits rob the bank. When George's bandana slips down from over his face, one of the tellers recognizes him, necessitating that all witnesses must be 'silenced'… permanently. When George turns squeamish and cannot bring himself to murder them with his knife, Billy coldly guns-down the two clerks instead. Together the pair of perpetrators then skidaddle over the border into Mexico. From the dying teller, newlywed Garrett learns the killers' identity and leads a posse in hot pursuit. Realizing they're out of their jurisdiction, Garrett's men refuse to cross over into Mexico. Using his Winchester, Billy snipes the pursuing Garrett's horse out from under him, leaving him stranded deep in the badlands. Thinking he's one of the dangerous Santero Gang, little Mike Garry (child actor "Ludwig"/Louis Duran) takes a potshot at the sheriff, who then meets the boy's elder sister Agnes (Vivi Bach) and explains his presence. On their way to Corona, the Garrys offer Garrett a lift in their buckboard. Back at the pueblo, George and Billy are confronted by Garrett, who incapacitates and binds both, regaining possession of the 30-grand. George nurses a non-fatal shoulder wound, which is treated by Garrett. Because he has acted without proper authority in the outlaws' arrest, Garrett must elude Mexican *federales* while transporting his prisoners back to America. While they stop at a rancho to buy horses and supplies for the trip, a fat, greedy rancher named Contes (Tito García) espies the sack of stolen cash and quickly reports the news to Santero, the bandit leader ("Dick Palmer"/Mimmo Palmara).

Billy mounts an incessant psychological campaign against the middle-aged lawman, who is also harassed by the Santero Gang. When Billy succeeds in escaping while handcuffed, he is critically wounded by Santero's knife. But, instead of dollars, the *bandidos* find only worthless pebbles in the money sack. Upon finding Billy, Garrett ends his agony with a mercy bullet. Then Garrett and George, latter gone sun-crazy from thirst, enter a derelict mining town, where they must contend with Santero's *pistoleros*. Pinned-down in an old mine and gasping for water, Garrett and

Bullets Don't Argue
Top: Spanish Handbill
Bottom: German Lobby Card

George make good their escape on an ore car and ride to the Garrys' farm near Death's Valley. Come nightfall, Santero's boys besiege and set fire to the house. George uses the confusion to escape from Garrett... but returns next morning leading a squad of U.S. Cavalry. His gang duly eliminated, Santero rides for it with the money-stuffed saddlebags, chased by Garrett. Santero dies by first clumsily falling on his own knife, then over a cliff. Convinced George has been reformed, Sheriff Garrett allows him to stay on at the Garry farm to help Agnes rebuild her home. Then, taking the $28,000 remaining from the bank-job, he heads towards Rivertown.

Comments:

Theme song: *"Always lonely / Always looking / To get even with the men who did him wrong / That was Billy / Lonesome Billy / Who was quick to think / A gun could make him strong / No one's tougher or more daring / Only he and his gun sharing / The great fight to live / And his great love to fight / A rough man who played with danger / To whom trouble was no stranger / Until one day he lay dying / He'd filled his date with Destiny..."*

This serviceable lower-case western was made next door (at the Mini Hollywood western backlot in Madrid, Spain in April 1964) while the less-expensive but infinitely more famous **A Fistful of Dollars** was simultaneously in-production. Both films utilized many of the same technicians and carpenters, but this one ironically had almost double the budget at its disposal. Comparing the two all these decades later, one can well see exactly what made **Fistful** so different from all other westerns being produced at that time. **Bullets** is modeled after your typical Hollywood programmer, and those not paying too much attention might easily mistake it for one. Although quite functional and entertaining if taken on its own terms, aesthetically and stylistically speaking it pales in comparison to **Fistful**. The only conspicuous constant is that both films' scores—albeit as different from one another as night from day—were composed by Ennio Morricone (here going by his occasional "Leo Nichols" alias).

Towering (6-foot-5) Calgarian-born Saturday matinee star Rod Cameron (1910-1983) barely gets ruffled when his marriage is unceremoniously cut short and he is forced to take an unscheduled (solo) honeymoon down México way. Following this indignity, he laudably manages to keep his temper in check even when his posh wedding suit gits all mussed. Upon confronting Ángel Aranda as George Clanton however, Cameron promptly wrings his scrawny neck and dunks the spunk out of the punk in a water trough, before crashing big brother Horst Frank's hotel room to lay the wooden end of a Winchester across his chops. Seconds before, Frank instinctually sinks an accidental bullet into his panic-stricken junior sibling. Bleeding, Aranda fears he's going to die, but Cameron reassures him with wry optimism: "You're more likely to be dyin' of a sore throat... *hangin' from a tree*!" Although he had played some pretty vicious baddies in his day (e.g., his Kid Curry character in Lesley Selander's lively programmer **Dakota Lil** [USA, 1950], co-starring Marie Windsor in the title role springs to mind), it's doubtful Cameron would have been *quite* so ruthless as the hero in one of his old-time Hollywood westerns, but he adapts well here, meting-out rough justice with few qualms. A man who functions best under pressure with a mind as quick as his gun, thinking on his feet Pat Garrett uses a block-and-tackle to whisk his hog-tied captives into an attic out of sight; this a mere instant before Federales bust down the hotel door and crash into the room on the sniff for funny business. Although looking older and jowlier here than in his leaner heyday, Cameron still makes for an imposing *hombre*, whose gruff confidence is highly credible. A real stickler for details, he keeps an accurate running count of every hour he's been married, and routinely checks his sweetie's photograph for good luck.

Cameron and Frank both smoke eight-inch stogies, tempting Freudian analysis (if you believe in that sort of thing). For the oddest scene—one to again make Freud scratch his head?—while taking a siesta Aranda has a rattlesnake slither up under his bedroll; in order to smoke it out, bizarrely enough, Cameron promptly gets down on his knees and blows tobacco fumes up Aranda's inside-leg (but sometimes a cigar is just a cigar and a snake is just a snake…)! As the understandably disgusted reptile wriggles away, Cameron then proceeds to blow its head off via sixgun. In his stetson, Cameron looms a full *foot* taller than Frank. Face to face—more like eyebrow to Adam's apple!—with the lofty Cameron, Frank's macho threats seem rather out of reach for such a comparative little squirt (not that the size makes the man, of course).

German villain Horst Frank, both coldly calculating and hotly impetuous by turns, adds a Gestapo-like kink to his black leather baddie suit. He quotes from Proverbs ("Ah, you and yer *Bible*!" laughs baby bro George with tolerant contempt). Playing Frank's wide-eyed whippersnapper of a brother, Aranda engineers the Sartana-like feat of pinning the Queen of Hearts to a door by throwing-knife during a hand of "52-card pickup." An amusing sight gag occurs when Cameron, leading the brothers by a length of rope, considerately plonks matching straw sombreros on their heads to prevent them from croaking due to sunstroke out in the desert. There, on the long, dusty trail back to Justice, Frank promises "I've got 21 notches on my gun, and before we reach the border I'll have one more!" However, the only notch he does get comes from Dick Palmer's knife: not on his gun, but on his spine. George, meanwhile, just ain't man enough to pull the trigger of Vivi Bach's foot-long Buntline Special.

The film's only real lowpoint occurs during a moment's peace at Bach's family farm when she and Aranda kick out the jams on an old folk ditty set to piano and mouth-harp while the jolly fat housemaid twitters along at a caged canary. Other than that, **Bullets Don't Argue** is mighty decent indeed, pilgrim.

Notes: Production manager was "Frank Palance"/Franco Giraldi. This amounts to a loose retelling of the Pat Garrett (1850-1908) and Billy the Kid tale, with Billy's last name inexplicably changed from Bonney to "Clanton." The equivalent goodie/baddie roles were respectively played by Fausto Tozzi and Peter Lee Lawrence in Julio Buchs' Spanish-majority coproduction **A Few Bullets More** a.k.a. **I'll Kill Him and Return Alone** (El hombre que mató a Billy el Niño, Spain/Italy, 1967). Another, much more famous version of the story was told by Sam Peckinpah in **Pat Garrett and Billy the Kid** (USA/Mexico, 1973), co-starring James Coburn as Garrett and Kris Kristofferson as Billy.

Bullets Don't Argue's US trailer featured action highlights from the film backed by the Marty Robbins-styled theme song quoted off the top of this review (which equates Cameron's character with Frank's and has little to do with the main gist of the movie). In the early-1990s—presumably public domain?—clips from the film were used by a certain major Canadian beer company in a televised commercial spot that capitalized on the schlock/camp value of "spaghetti westerns" (the term was shamelessly name-dropped during the sales pitch). The same mock-Aztec ruins seen here had previously been on view in **The Savage Guns** (Tierra brutal, Spain, 1962, D: Michael Carreras). Some music heard herein was reused on Morricone's soundtrack for Franco Giraldi's rip-snortin' oatcom **Up the MacGregors** (7 donne per i Mac Gregor, Italy/Spain, 1967). [*With some invaluable input from Michael "Ferg" Ferguson.*]

Top to Bottom:
Pre-Title card.
Title Card of Charity and the Strange Smell of Money.
Robert Malcom as "Charity."
The gorgeous Rosealba Neri in a scene with the star Robert Malcom.

Charity – The Strange Smell of Money ($entivano... uno $trano, eccitante, pericolo$o puzzo di dollari, 1973, Italy)

Synopsis (ATTN: THE FOLLOWING PARAGRAPH CONTAIN SPOILERS!): Mr. Costello, an immigrant Sicilian gangster, operates the Gila Bend town bank, as well as running the local loansharking racket. While *en route* to Gila Bend, the Reverend Higglethwaite ("Peter Landers"/Piero Scheggi) is hijacked by The Bronco Kid (Piero Vida), a rotund outlaw with a $5000 reward on his head. Bronco steals not only the Reverend's horse, clothing and identity but also his pet parrot, then sets up shop in the town church. An allegedly acclaimed bountyhunter and all-round humanitarian known as "Charity" ("Robert Malcolm"/ Roberto Rossi) also hits Gila Bend on Bronco's trail. On the side, Charity has been employed by the government to ride shotgun for a $1-million shipment of federal money set to arrive by railroad at the Stratford City junction. Also arriving will be Costello's sister, Maria. Upon arrival, the cash is transferred to a stagecoach which heads back to Gila Bend. Along the road, Mexican bandits blast a narrow canyon pass, cutting off the stage. When Charity thwarts the robbery attempt, the money is sealed safely in Costello's bank vault. Costello it turns out plans to rob his own bank, with the help of his henchmen disguised as Mexican bandits so as to divert suspicion away from the real culprits. Things go awry when the real Mexicans get wise to the plot and pull off the heist themselves, only to discover the strongbox is empty and blame the Bronco Kid. Bronco and Charity unite gunhands to overthrow both sets of robbers. A Union cavalry troop intervenes in time to witness Costello accidentally push a dynamite detonator, thus destroying the cash.

Comments:

Pippo, the pesky parrot: *"It's your funeral, friend— who cares?! SQUAWK!"*

Directed by usual lowbrow commedia erotico specialist Italo Alfaro from a script by low-budget schlock/ sleazemeister Piero Regnoli, **Charity – The Strange Smell of Money** (whose original Italian title translates to "They Smelled... the Strange, Exciting, Dangerous Scent of Dollars") exposes its low-grade origins even before the titles roll, as an uncoordinated burlesque revue of saloon gals in one-piece undies shake their tushies into the camera while backed by horrible high-speed piano, hideous synth and screechy la-la-la-la female chorus. The dominant look here is very cheap, very unconvincing, and very, very ugly indeed. (But don't let that stop ya, *compañeros*!)

This dubious, unfunny comedy oozed from the prolific pen of ex-director Regnoli, and **C–TSSoM**'s director Alfaro had a similarly prolific genre background toiling deep down within the little leagues of the Roman film industry. Graced with a larger-than-usual promotional push in both its native country and in ethnic North American Italian theatres, the horrendous dubbing of the export print perhaps explains why it never made it into Anglo cinemas (although, even if the dub-job was utterly flawless, chances are the film would still never have made the cut, so far as most distributors were concerned). Examples of the surreal dialogue, which often comes across like some alternate-reality version of English: "Should I put a bullet through his *occiput*?" (look it up). And, "You're a buncha horrid oafs! About as useless as *blowfish*!" To make matters worse, it sounds as if the same two voiceover actors dubbed-in every last character's dialogue without barely even attempting to vary their speech patterns accordingly from one character to the next. English-language signs are misspelled: for instance, "Curch" (in Italian, the letter C on its own is typically pronounced with a "ch" sound). And even though draped with Stars 'n' Stripes flags and red-white-and-blue banners, an antique Italian chuff-chuff steam engine sure ain't no Iron Horse, Kemosabe. Looking as though they'd rather be anywhere else but there, self-conscious nonspeaking extras hang around the severely under-populated backlot, trying to look as though they belong there.

Alfaro attempts to replicate the zany flavor of "Anthony Ascott"/Giuliano Carnimeo's comicartoon westerns (e.g., **His Name Was Holy Ghost** [Uomo avvisato mezzo ammazzato... Parola di Spirito Santo, Italy/Spain, 1972]), but, try as he might, the laughs mainly fall flatter'n a wet flapjack under a bison's butt. Sight-gags come thick and fast: An elderly roulette player lifts off his hat, and his hair goes with it. Stinky red-socked feet poke from the end of a too-short coffin. Jean-Claude Jabes as Pablo the Mexican *bandido* is hoofed in the cajones, hops about singing soprano and subsequently reappears wearing a diaper-like groin support to cradle his literal and figurative injured manly pride. Yet another fat actor ("Landers"/Scheggi) runs around in red longjohns (see also Mario Brega in "Willy S. Regan"/Sergio Garrone's jim-dandy **No Room to Die** [Una lunga fila di croci, 1969]). Frying-pan dental surgery—an Ascott, um, 'specialty'—also figures, as when one of Costello's boys uses one of said cooking utensils to separate a Mexican bandit from his teeth. Stupidest moment arrives when Costello's bunch and Ramírez's bandits face off chin-to-chin in two parallel symmetrical lines, then a bluegrass fiddle starts up and they commence a 'squaredance,' egged-on by that dang talkin' bird. Slapstick, lackadaisical comedy often segues into unfunny attempts to be 'cute.' As the title implies, an assortment of stereotypical characters get a whiff of odoriferous lucre, converging on it like so many blue-assed flies to fresh horse-chips...

Roberto Rossi's smirky, swaggering hero is mostly unappealing. Despite blue-steel irises set into a tanned, angular face and the ability to shoot a hole dead-centre through an airborne silver dollar, he lacks much real screen presence, quite frankly. When Rossi cockily announces he's "Better known as Charity!" you wonder not just why but also where and by whom. Luigi Montini's gaudy godfather twirls his curly little moustache like Hércule Poirot, speaking broken English with a stereotypical "Italian" inflection. The actor playing Andrew, Costello's main man (who should perhaps have been called Abbott!), wears a form-fitting plush leather shirt and affects a poor-man's Gilbert Roland routine. As the spurious clergyman-by-circumstance, Piero Vida's comedy relies purely on obvious ironies. He pounds on the doors of the Elios church set, yelling, "Open up, godammit!" He swears a lot and mixes up both psalm numbers and the names of his congregation. Vida's severely-overworked predecessor had up and skedaddled due to the excessive number of burial services he was obliged to perform.

 C–TSSoM's most earitating cast-member isn't even human: namely, "Pippo," as "George Washington" (!) the smartmouth, foul-mouthed parrot ("*SQUAWK*! Up yours!" – "*SQUAWK*! Lousy sons-of-bitches!" – "*SQUAWK*! He's got you by the short hairs!" [You get the idea]). Vida's phony preacher character at one point threatens to shoot lovable Pippo dead, but unfortunately doesn't follow through with his threat. (In Giulio Questi's landmark **Django Kill... If You Live, Shoot!** [Se sei vivo spara, Italy/Spain, 1967], head baddie Roberto Camardiel had gun-blasted his own babbling birdie into pillow-stuffing.)

Salvatore Puntillo is likeable enough as the pot-bellied Mexican bandit boss, bellowing "¡Vamos, muchachos!" with the best of them and packing sloppy overgrown bangs that fall in his face just like Fernando Sancho's in **A Pistol for Ringo** *et al*. Coming off best with her composure intact is unflusterable 'Seventies sex kitten Rosalba Neri (whom her onscreen brother astutely describes as "A pulchritudinous gal... she's very *female*!"). For the moronic conclusion, she grabs a blunderbuss and abruptly demands that Charity marry her forthwith, at which he rides outta town quicker than a stereotypical Scotsman at first sight of a Salvation Army donation box. Even the sultry Ms. Neri's token bubblebath and dignified restraint can't save this prairie oyster.

Yep, there's a strange smell alright... As Pippo the Wonder Parrot squawks at one juncture, "A lot of *bull*!" ...understatement being merely another of this film's numerous weaknesses. But genre completists might want to see it for its basic obscurity value anyway, as a curio (back in the 'dark age' of the Betamax/VHS video era [the '80s], it was released on tape in Greece by Video Mercury, dubbed into English but with Greek subtitles; the version reviewed here). And, as with even the most minor, sub-mediocre movie fare, there's some entertainment value to be had here, however fleeting and fitful. Hell, who knows, it might even turn up as a Special Edition Blu-ray loaded with special features any day now… but don't hold your breath! [*With some invaluable input from Michael "Ferg" Ferguson.*]

Death Walks in Laredo a.k.a. Three Guns for Caesar (Tre pistole contro Cesare, 1967, Italy / Algeria)

Synopsis (ATTN: THE FOLLOWING THREE PARAGRAPHS CONTAIN SPOILERS!): From a lawyer name of Joshua Leacock, three young men of diverse ethnic origins receive notice of their joint inheritance: the map to a goldmine situated in Laredo, Texas, accompanied by the photograph of an unidentified young girl, their long-lost sister. The three heirs are: Whittaker "Whitty" Selby (Thomas Hunter), a former sheriff and crack gunman in Sherrin Grove, Kentucky. Étienne Devereux (Nadir Moretti), a French magician. And Lester Koto (James Shigeta), an Amerasian acrobat in Cedar Gap, Missouri. Separately but simultaneously setting-out for Laredo, the trio run into one another and each man's belief that the other two are interlopers results in a fight. Things blow-over when the three men discover they are all semi-siblings, sons (by different mothers) of their father Mr. Henry Langdon, whose death ten years earlier still remains a mystery. The three half-brothers have actually been summoned by old Stanford (Vittorio Bonos), caretaker of their pa's estate.

Arriving in Laredo, Whitty is forced to gun down seven local toughs in self-defence. He is of the opinion that the responsible party is Julius Caesar Fuller (Enrico Maria Salerno), an egocentric megalomaniac and town tyrant, whom Mr. Simpson, the town's former newspaper editor, explains killed Mr. Langdon. Fuller dwells in a mountaintop castle, where he emulates the ancient Roman emperors in his dress and lifestyle. An alcoholic academic reads to "Caesar" from classical texts. Fuller forces his will upon Tula, one of his unwilling concubines, and eagerly seeks to usurp ownership of the half-brothers' mine. His murder of Mr. Langdon has proved fruitless, as the location of the gold has been lost for a decade. When Fuller's gunmen descend on the Simpson ranch and kill their father, the Simpson brothers seek revenge.

Whitty, Lester and Étienne interfere with Fuller's plans, killing-off thirty of his best men, for which he understandably desires them killed in return. The three hide out at the Cave of the Great Spirit, an old Indian burial ground in the mountains. Bronson (Umberto D'Orsi), Caesar Fuller's 'centurion,' cannot outdraw the combined talents of Whitty's gun, Lester's gymnastics and *prestidigitateur extraordinaire* Étienne's sly sleight of hand. So, Fuller opts for the more subtle techniques of Woman. Mady (Langdon's real adopted daughter [Delia Boccardo]), then Debbie ([Gianna Serra] posing as their sister) each lead the girl-gullible brothers down false trails.

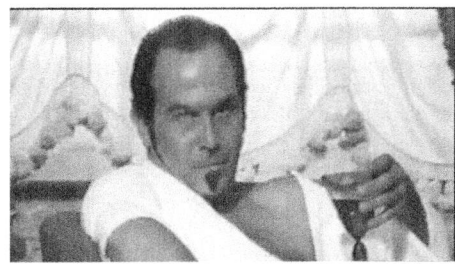

Top to Bottom:
Dino De Laurentis production.
Italian Title Card.
Enrico Maria Salerno as Cesear Fuller.
Brothers Three: James Shigeta, Thomas Hunter and Nadir Moretti.

When Whitty is captured and hung over a blazing bonfire by Fuller's men, Lester, Étienne and Stanford come to the rescue, eliminating the sadistic Bronson and his underlings. With his brothers' assistance, Whitty then takes revenge for their father's murder, killing the pseudo-Emperor in the bathhouse ("And so dies your Caesar!"). Thus unburdened of Fuller's interference, the Langdon brothers and Mady come to the ecstatic realization that their late father's old "brass" bed is actually made of solid gold!

Comments:

Theme song: *"Three riders / All heading for Laree-doh / Three strangers / Full of evil / Young riders / What brings you to Laree-doh? / Young strangers / Why Laree-doh? / There's a secret you've been told / In the mountains there is gold / Maybe Hell to pay / But we're on our way / So we're riding, riding, riding..."* Vittorio Bonos as Stanford: *"The mine. It ain't worth a plugged dollar. There ain't an ounce o' gold in the whole mine!"*

Vittorio Bonos as Stanford: *"The mine. It ain't worth a plugged dollar. There ain't an ounce o' gold in the whole mine!"*

Filmed during the 1966-'67 Italian film season (starting in August '66), on location in Algeria (rather than Almería, as per usual!) and with interiors canned at Dinocittà (De Laurentiis Studios), Rome, **DWiL** was first scheduled for release by Dear Film. However, in September of '67, a legal dispute between Dino De Laurentiis and Dear's president Robert Haggiag resulted in a premature rupturing of their five-year business contract (that was initially planned to expire in 1971). This was another film in Thomas Hunter's seven-film contract with De Laurentiis. They had previously collaborated on "Lee W. Beaver"/Carlo Lizzani's rollicking **The Hills Run Red** (Un fiume di dollari, 1966) together, but in place of his generally more cleancut visage in that film, here Hunter cultivated a hairier countenance. In direct contrast to his sullen, more-wooden earlier performance, Hunter here—no doubt due to his additional experience before cameras—is far more animated.

Another part-peplum, in **DWiL** (originally entitled "Three Guns Against Caesar") the so-called "Julius Caesar" Fuller keeps a well-stocked harem, employs dancing girls and spends his recreational time frolicking at his in-house Roman steam baths. As equated with mad Emperor Nero and played by accomplished actor Enrico Maria Salerno (a future fixture of the '70s poliziesco genre), Fuller is blind in one eye, wears a small triangular goatee under his lower lip and makes a formidable, charismatic supervillain of the scenery-masticating 007 school. Then-rising starlet Femi Benussi, playing a concubine named Tula under a giant bouffant wig, allegedly hails from "Hong Kong."

Nadir Moretti uses (quote) "magnetism" to hypnotize his foes motionless before disarming them, and later deploys a similar technique to tamper with a roulette wheel in he and James Shigeta's favour ("Put ten dollars on the red!" he boldly bets). As the Japanese halfbreed, Shigeta prefers a more direct—and painful—approach... karate! Hunter's twin pistols come equipped with derringers built into the butts. During the prologue following a poker game, Hunter blasts four disgruntled opponents dead using his four-barrel pistol ("A Royal Flush!"). In advertising artwork, star Thomas Hunter was depicted toting this fanciful mutant revolver. At first glance one might think he is merely 'fanning' a single-barrel specimen. Wrong! Hunter gets to use a ridiculous quad-barrel contraption which we're sorry to say looks downright foolish. This was a far-fetched 'highpoint' in the history of Spaghetti Western super-weaponry. At least when Marco Guglielmi came up with a four-barrel shotgun or when Van Cleef memorably used a four-barrel derringer in "Frank Kramer"/Gianfranco Parolini's **Sabata** (Ehi amico... c'è Sabata. Hai chiuso!, 1969, Italy), those weapons looked believably functional. That said, the silly 'exotic' firearm in **Death Walks in Laredo** was no doubt one of the main reasons why Yank distributors passed on releasing the film stateside. Thankfully, this witless weapon is not overused onscreen, so doesn't spoil the proceedings as a whole.

Marcello Giombini's enjoyable score is kick-started by Don Powell's passionate vocal on the excellent theme song. Musical impetus is kept going by Delia Boccardo's rambunctiously rumbustious rendition of "I Got Me a Gun" (*"I'll do it my wa-ay!"*), which she punctuates with lusty blasts from twin six-shooters. Despite her song lyrics, the Boccardo character informs Hunter, I particularly dislike men who are quick with their guns" (symbolism alert [see also Romolo Guerrieri's, er, 'phallically-loaded' **Johnny Yuma**

{1966}]). Instrumental side of the score is made up of polished, whistle-heavy '60s instro rock à la Hank Marvin & The Shadows (who, like Duane "Rebel Rouser" Eddy, were a major influence on SW score composers). Gotta love it! Set to Don Powell's sultry signature tune "Tula" and mock-Egyptian electric guitars, Benussi performs a seductive dance. In a scene played strictly for comedy (accompanied by silent movie-style piano), Ms. Boccardo and Gianna Serra gradually divest one another of their apparel during a heated catfight which gets all the hotter as it progresses.

In spite of its fanciful premise—and possibly even because of it—**Death Walks in Laredo** amounts to a highly enjoyable tongue-in-cheek romp, with fast'n'furious action, good stunt choreography (by Rinaldo Zamperla) and robust principal performances.

Caesar gives this one his personal double thumbs up! [*With some invaluable input from Michael "Ferg" Ferguson.*]

Notes: Playing the Larry Simpson character here, actor Yacef Saadi's first big break came in Gillo Pontecorvo's award-winning semi-documentary **The Battle of Algiers** (Il batalla di Algeri, Italy, 1966). Here, Saadi also co-produces. There are some superficial plot similarities to "Anthony M. Dawson"/ Antonio Margheriti's later fun 'east-meets-western' **The Stranger & the Gunfighter** a.k.a. **Blood Money** (Là dove non batte il sole, Italy/Spain/Hong Kong/USA, 1974), which likewise featured the beauteous Benussi in another teasy 'window-dressing' role.

Italain 2-F manifesto: The Devil was an Angel aka Colt in the Hand of the Devil

The Devil Was an Angel (Una colt in pugno al diavolo, 1967, Italy)

Synopsis (ATTN: THE FOLLOWING TWO PARAGRAPHS CONTAIN SPOILERS!): The mid-1860s, during the American Civil War; in and around the Mojave Desert, the shortest route to California. A wagon train of prospectors, seeking to mine rich deposits of gold in the Panamint, are attacked by Mexican bandits who dwell in a deserted town and keep scores of prisoners who toil for them as slaves. A disgraced ex-Cavalry captain, Scotty (Bob Henry), who was expelled from the Army for committing certain breaches in security, is re-recruited by the General to overthrow the bandits and rescue the townspeople, aided by a half-caste woman, Maya (Marisa Solinas). In New City, Scotty, aided by Dick Carson ("Jerry Ross"/Gerardo Rossi), a young plainclothes soldier, kills-off several of the bandit gang. Posing as a mining engineer, Scotty is taken to their hideout by the bandits, who are led by Capataz "El Condor" Muñez (George Wang) and are likewise interested in mining the Panamint's rich gold deposits. Because he claims he can guide Muñez's men to the gold veins, Scotty's life is spared, and he is commissioned by Muñez to do just that using his new-fangled prospecting gadgetry.

Dick leads an attack on a party of bandits, during which all his men are killed. Captured by Muñez and tortured, Scotty intercedes to save Dick's life without blowing his cover. Dick is revealed to be Janet's lover, to the envy of Muñez, who also desires Janet (Lucretia Love). When the Army attempts to smuggle guns hidden beneath the false bed of a wagon into the occupied village, they are discovered by Muñez, who trades Dick's release in exchange for Scotty, whom the bandit chief wishes to hang for treachery. Taking matters into their own hands to rescue Scotty, Maya and some elder villagers bump off Muñez's sentries, then Maya helps Scotty get loose. When the Confederate Cavalry bombard the bandits using artillery, Dick and Jane perish, while Muñez makes a run for the hills, followed by Scotty. They face off in a gun duel, but due to their grudging fondness, cannot kill each other. Scotty is forced to wound Muñez, whereupon he is captured and sentenced to hang. Scotty, who has since grown fond of the Capataz, interecedes on his behalf to stay the execution, which is commuted to a jail term. The bandit chief vows to reform himself behind bars.

1. Title card: The Devil was an Angel
2. Opening scene: Aftermath of a massacre
3. Scotty (Bob Henry) prospecting for gold as Munez (George Wang) and his men look on.
4. Bob Henry, George Wang.
5. Maya (Maria Solinas) and Scotty (Bob Henry).

Comments: During the opening massacre that sets the stage, director Sergio Bergonzelli refrains from dwelling on the grisly details. Rather than concentrate on falling bodies, he shows an uninterrupted montage of George Wang's gang blasting-off enough ammo to equip a John Woo shootathon. We then cut to shots of dead bodies littered amongst overturned wagons; a toddler's frightened crying is heard above the wind that blows dust and tumbleweeds across the carnage. A crude if eyecatching main title sequence—sometimes shot POV down a stylized 'gun barrel'—follows.

Lead Bob Henry was apparently cast strictly on account of his height rather than his overall suitability for the part; as he looks uncomfortably like the too-tall Siamese triplet brother of Alan Ladd and Bob Newhart, separated at birth (*sorry!*). Here boosted to the second line, usual lowly support player Wang (father of Hong Kong kung fu movie performer "Don Wong"/Wang Tao) earns his highest billing ever and has a fine time hamming it up as the hearty bandit chief. Much screentime is spent showing Henry and Wang's burgeoning mutual affection through macho comedic interplay (e.g., shooting each other in the hat). Immature male bonding turns into a violent brawl when Henry slugs Wang—the cad!—for ripping luscious Lucretia Love's shoulder strap... but this soon degenerates into more immature if harmless male bonding. Truth be told, for someone who is intended as a sympathetic character, Wang spends an inordinate amount of screentime whipping or kicking underlings and terrorizing women. Henry, meanwhile, spends much of his time playing with his surveyor's theodolite, pausing periodically only to woo the volcanic Marisa Solinas and rowdily dismantle the saloon when hassled by local rednecks and former army buddies for fraternizing with the bandits. Wang sounds the 'scramble' for his gangmembers by shooting a church bell at their hideout. In the interests of not-so-subtle anticlerical commentary, blond Gerardo Rossi is interrogated and threatened with a smoking firebrand directly beneath a badly-skewed crucifix.

Las Vegas, New Orleans, Guadalupe and Chicago are all name-dropped in passing, with familiar disregard for accurate geographic location. Giampiero Reverberi's delicate score of acoustic picking and relaxed whistling seems to have been composed for a far more subtle film than this. Facile energy is injected by having stuntmen—framed in longshot—engineer spectacular death rolls down sandy hillocks (a favorite ploy of "Miles Deem"/Demofilo Fidani when he could think of nothing better to do!). Credibility is most taxed when Solinas uses the mirror / magnifier lens of Henry's surveying instrument to burn through the noose like a laser beam from only a hundred yards away.

Production values are tolerable enough, with lots of the budget expended on all the extra extras and proper props: but, something still seems out-of-whack. Maybe it's the unconvincing recoilless artillery pieces; maybe it's Henry's spurious-looking surveyor's gear or designer bandanna, but **TDWaA** simply doesn't coalesce. Even for all its original export trailer's go-for-da-gusto energetics, it's hardly surprising this oddball concoction never secured a domestic North American release. [*With some invaluable input from Michael "Ferg" Ferguson.*]

Notes: An Anglo export trailer for this lesser-seen SW is included on Wild East Productions' now-long-OOP (?) compilation DVD, **For a Few Previews More** (2003). The present film's original Italo title should not be confused with that of "Frank G. Carrol"/Gianfranco Baldanello's **A Colt in the Hand of the Devil** (Una colt in mano al diavolo, Italy, 1973), co-starring Robert Woods and William Berger and again featuring George Wang in a major supporting part. Present film's scripter Ambrogio Molteni had earlier co-written Bergonzelli's 'naïve' prototypical SW **The Last Gun** (Jim il primo, Italy, 1964), starring Cameron Mitchell. For whatever reason, certain printed sources replace **TDWaA**'s gold prospecting angle with a hunt for sulphur. Assistant director was Aldo Lado. Unintelligible theme singer Reitano would later star in his own western, the ultra-obscure **Tara Poki, Sicilian Revenge** (Tara Pokì, Italy, 1971, D: Amasi Damiani).

Who was Bob Henry? Turn to page 243 to find out, Courtesy of Tom Betts!

The Dirty Fifteen Spanish Pressbook
**The image from the poster originally appeared on the poster for My Name is Pecos (2 once di piombo, Italy, 1966)

Top to Bottom:
Spanish and Italian co-production
The Dirty Fifteen title card
Suzy Andersen (Barabara)
George Martin (Cassel) and Craig Hill (Bill Mack)
Jose Manuel Martin (Benny) and Craig Hill

The Dirty Fifteen a.k.a. 15 Scaffolds for a Killer (Quindici forche per un assassino, 1968, Italy / Spain)

Synopsis (ATTN: THE FOLLOWING THREE PARAGRAPHS CONTAIN SPOILERS!): Cassel (George Martin) and his gang rustle a herd of horses, killing their rightful owner the rancher Mr. O'Connolly in the process. Having since unloaded the stolen horseflesh, Cassel and his boys then hole-up in the barn at the farmstead of the widow Madeleine Cook (Margarita Lozano) and her young daughters Liz (Eleonora Brown) and Ann. Along with his two accomplices – including a former preacherman named Benny (José Manuel Martín) – Cassel's old associate Bill Mack (Craig Hill) arrives to propose a deal: that the Mack and Cassel gangs should join forces to 're-sell' the stolen horses back to O'Connolly's grieving widow. Upon agreeing to do this, their plans are dashed to smithereens after Ann Cook's fiancé Steve ("Howard Ross"/ Renato Rossini) Gorman happens along to discover to his horror that all the Cook womenfolk have since been murdered by an unknown assailant. Due to their proximity to the scene of the crime being understandably – if wrongly – accused of murdering the woman and her two girls, Mack and Cassel, together with their thirteen buddies, must place their personal grudges on hold and form a shaky alliance in order to elude capture by the vengeful posse led by Sheriff Sandy (Antonio Molino Rojo).

Having lit-out for the nearby town of St. Anne, relentlessly pursued by the two-dozen strong posse, the allied gangs make hostages of old Pastor Ferguson's (Andrea Bosic) young wife Barbara (Susy Andersen) along with Juan the bartender (Ricardo Palacios) and head for the Mexican border. There they seek temporary refuge with friendly peons in the disused army stockade at Fort Tortuga. During the night under cover of a fiesta, at Mrs. Ferguson's behest captive Juan succeeds in slipping out to summon Sheriff Sandy's men, who promptly lay siege to the derelict fort. Much senseless violence follows as the posse keeps the fugitives pinned-down inside; with neither provisions nor an avenue of escape at their ready disposal. Gradually Mack's and Cassel's cohorts are either picked-off or apprehended and lynched outside the walls. As desperation mounts within, loyalties shift, with the gang leaders fighting amongst themselves like cornered rats. When the posse members launch a fiery nocturnal attack on Fort Tortuga, sole survivors Mack and Cassel shoot it out inside.

However, after the deceased Cooks' new neighbour old Mr. Bennett (Tomás Blanco) divulges certain crucial evidence involving an outstanding I.O.U. and a wanted poster offering a $10,000 reward for a certain individual, it soon becomes apparent that the man responsible for murdering the widow and her daughters is by no means the one anybody has been expecting all along... Once the true culprit has been duly dealt with, Mack and Cassel patch-up their differences and are permitted to take the long ride to freedom.

Comments:

Aldo Sambrell as Danny Boyd mouths an ideal potential SW title: "*First we hang them, then we can judge them!*"

Andrea Bosic as 'real' Pastor Ferguson (in a real fake Scotch brogue): "*An' dinna ferget: 'Thou shalt not kill'!*"

José Manuel Martín as fake minister Benny: "*Thus spake the Lord... Amen!*"

Craig Hill as Bill Mack waxes self-destructive: "*...I'm the one man I have a right to kill!*"

As if you couldn't tell, the title was of course a blatant cash-in on Robert Aldrich's international megahit WW2 actioner **The Dirty Dozen** (USA/UK, 1967), which was a huge influence on many European films of its day. In our considered opinion the present film's title would have been a good deal catchier if they had called it "The Dirty Thirteen" instead, as there are altogether far too many characters crammed into the scenario, so a couple less wouldn't have been missed much.

While the screenplay at times gets a little too convoluted for its own good, it does succeed in keeping viewer expectations forever flipping on their heads. For instance, upon first glimpsing G. Martín's character in the prologue, as was presumably genre one-timer Nunzio Malasomma's intention, we assume that Martín and his cohorts are merely honest ranchhands plying their profession. A short time later we realize that they are actually lowdown dirty rustlers in the commission of a capital offence. And while it is G. Martín who commits the lion's share of despicable deeds, he is not without his moments of merit; such as when he gives boorish Frank Braña a faceful of fist for messing with the womenfolk.

Similarly, when we are introduced to star Hill—whose character has seemingly been commissioned by the murdered rancher's widow to bring the perpetrators to justice—we presume he shall shortly be assuming 'heroic' duties as avenging angel of the piece (if not the peace). On the contrary, Hill is also set up as quite the cold-hearted bastardo (both he and G. Martín had previously co-starred in a similar amoral light in Tonino Valerii's **For the Taste of Killing** [Per il gusto di uccidere, Italy/Spain, 1966], which also featured J.M. Martín). Hill looks impressively long, lean and mean in his understated generic brown cowman's duds and week's growth of facial fuzz. In an early scene he calmly drops four challengers with five shots, then— just when we almost think he might be about to show some mercy—coldly adds one more to a wounded man squirming in the dirt. In a subsequent scene, he uses big Ricardo Palacios for a heavy-bag. Later still, conventions and conceptions go all topsy-turvy on us again when Palacios' character is revealed to have perhaps the noblest motivations in the entire film when he selflessly risks personal life and limb on heroine Susy Andersen's behalf, only to wind up propped-up dead and trotted out on a horse for his troubles. For a change, even Aldo Sambrell in his 'Black Bart'-styled wardrobe operates on the right side of the law; although is by no means such a moralist that he isn't above stretching it—along with a few necks!—via a lynching (or three, or four...) if necessary to see that justice is served (cold), albeit without the formality of a fair trial first. Outside the walls of Fort Tortuga, hanged men dangle from gibbets, which are lined-up like so many telegraph poles at roadside.

As only one of many widows within this corpse-strewn and densely-packed scenario, before winding up a corpse herself, husbandless Margarita Lozano must rely on an, uhhh, 'male substitute' for she and her daughters' protection ("The only defence we have is my Winchester. I even take it to bed at night!"). In another potentially phallic bit of innuendo, star Hill subsequently proudly announces to Andersen—herself yet another impending widow— "This gun has *never* fired on a woman." All that said, there is little intentional humour to be had in this film's largely grim storyline. Although some further unintentional humour does arise due to Ms. Andersen and Andrea Bosic as the Fergusons' decidedly wonky 'Scotch' brogues;

which wouldn't even pass muster in a MacGregors comedy!

Most of the characters—and, not even including title fifteen there are a lot, which might help to explain it—aren't much more than one-dimensional thumbnail sketches. For instance, Howard Ross as tertiary protagonist, who spends a goodly chunk of the remaining narrative laid-up in bed nursing a bullet in the back, as if scriptwriters were no longer sure quite what to do with him now that he had fulfilled his primary catalytic function by setting the wheels of justice in motion (even if they already had been rolling along quite nicely without his help). Although one of the film's more interesting personalities, J.M. Martín as a lapsed minister, a self-professed (quote) "soul in hell surviving on the memory of his old vocation," adds some color ("Rest in peace with the good Lord, and God forgive him, cuz he knew not what he did," he proclaims over one of many fallen sinners). Even if, as with widows, the film already has its fair share of preachers too! In a dented tophat and dusty black coat, J.M. Martín frequently refers to his breviary and scolds a fellow gangmember who neglects to repeat "Amen" following his prayer. No sooner has J.M. Martín's own last amen arrived than G. Martín dares to speak ill of the dead ("He was a moron!"); precipitating a punchup with Hill that not only drags José Canalejas into it but Frank Braña too, the latter pitching in with a pitchfork (putting farming implements to improper use seemed to be a Braña specialty; he did so in many films, and not just westerns either).

In some other believable touches of human nature, a compassionate youth liberates the gang's horses to save them from being eaten after the besieged fort's food supply runs out. Ironically, no sooner has he done this noble humanitarian deed than the boy is himself cut down in the crossfire that erupts as a result of his impulsive actions. Following this senseless slaying, paternal Francisco Nieto 'surrenders' to the posse under a white flag of truce; which soon proves merely a ruse for him to gun down Pastor Ferguson in revenge, kamikaze fashion.

In addition to fine locations and settings, another of **The Dirty Fifteen**'s best assets is Francesco de Masi's polished score, which succeeds in sounding eclectic even while staying strictly within those paint-by-numbers parameters recently established by Ennio Morricone (just compare de Masi's work here with the far more Hollywood-style strains he composed for the earlier **The Man From Oklahoma** a.k.a. **Ranch of the Ruthless** [Il ranch degli spietati, Spain/Italy/West Germany, 1964, D: Jaime Jesús Balcázar] to hear how far he had come in the interim). Soaring trumpetry adds extra bigness and excitement to galloping equestrian pursuit sequences, of which there are many, utilizing literally dozens of riders charging back and forth between hell and high water (a hardly surprising detail considering Spanish-end co-producer Agustín Medina was also a skilled horsemaster, and evidently emptied-out his stables for this gig). Especially rousing are early sequences showing G. Martín's bunch driving the stolen horses across rugged Almerían terrain set to de Masi's electric guitars, which at times have a pleasingly bouncy, almost Johnny Cash-like countrified twang to them. The heartfelt theme song—co-written by Alessandro Alessandroni—opens and closes the film in rousing style, even if what few lyrics can be discerned are of the decidedly generic and saccharine 'love ballad' variety. But then, when it came to Raoul's vocal performances, the level of emotion in his delivery was generally of greater importance than the mere meaning of the words anyway. Plus non-specific wording meant that the tune might conveniently be re-licenced for use on another film if necessary (as Roman music producers were prone to do on more than one occasion).

Albeit in different dress, the climactic siege of the stone-ramparted castillo sequences almost bring to mind a staple situation of the preceding peplum cycle within which director Malasomma had previously worked extensively. The ending dispenses with all plausibility by having Hill and G. Martín not only both ride away scot (or is that Scotch?) free, but—having previously repeatedly tried to murder each other—are inexplicably suddenly good buddies again! [*With some invaluable input from Michael "Ferg" Ferguson.*]

Notes: Pyrotechnical FX were handled by the "Esplosivit" company. Back in the '80s, an Anglo-dubbed export print under the present title had been available on VHS videocassette from Jamjoom Video of Algeria (fully-letterboxed, with joint Arabic/French subtitles; albeit struck from a exceedingly scratchy, choppy transfer print indeed. It was that version which served as basis for this review, although **D15** has much more recently been made available on DVD). Some original press materials identify G. Martín's character as "China" Cassel, although he was not addressed by that nickname anywhere on the print reviewed here (indeed, entire alternate synopsis descriptions differ drastically, as was often the case on other films). IMDb mentions Fernando Sancho as appearing, but he does not. (Possibly in an alternate version to the Algerian vid-print reviewed here? Which seems unlikely, unless he just happened to put in a quickie cameo for a single scene which was cut out, which seems equally as unlikely.)

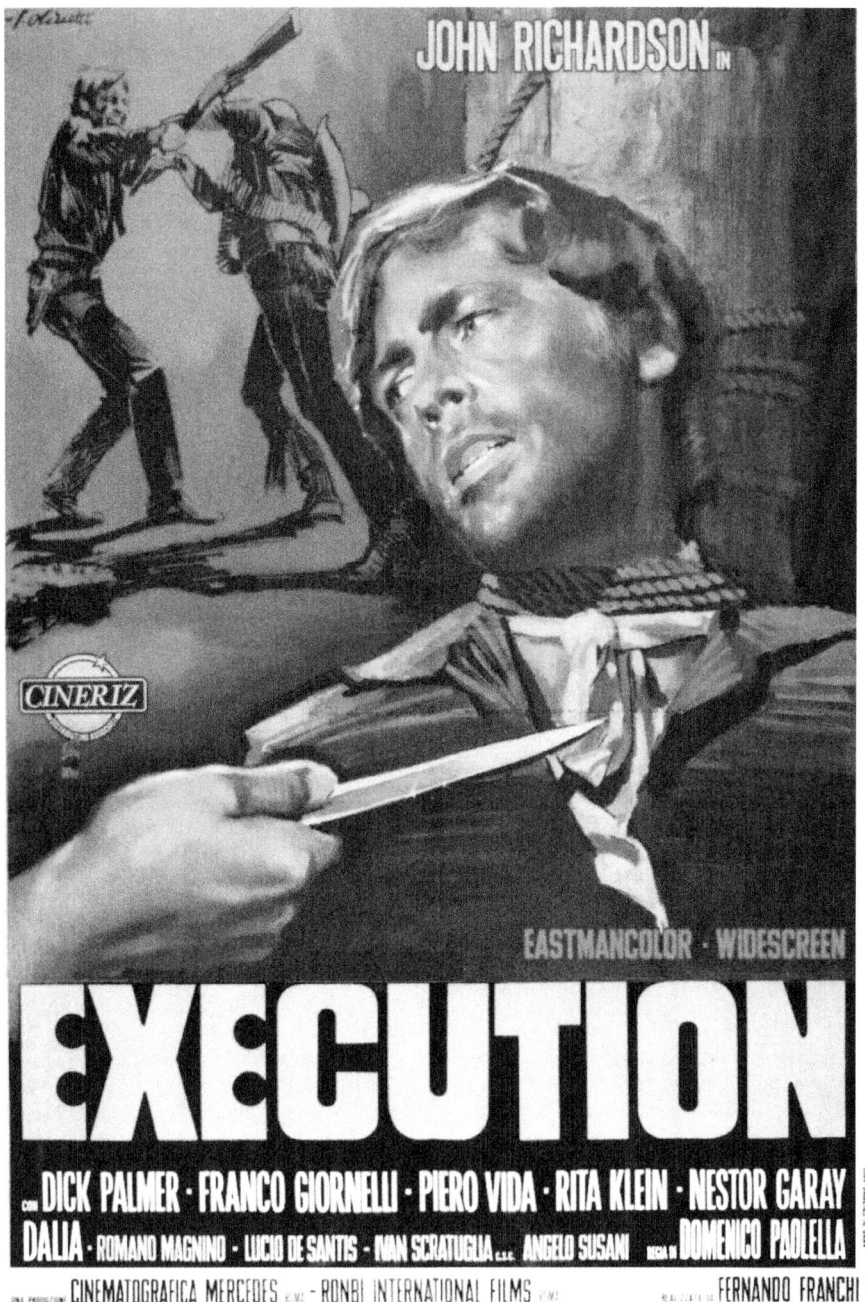

Top to Bottom: Portuguese Prssbook; Bill Cooler (John Richardson); Bill Cooler (John Richarsdon); Dick Palmer (Klint Clips)

Execution (1968, Italy / Israel)

Synopsis (ATTN: THE FOLLOWING PARAGRAPH CONTAIN SPOILERS!): 1867. Having spent many long years in prison, Klint Clips ("Dick Palmer"/ Mimmo Palmara) earns his freedom. One goal and one goal alone obsesses him: to collect the $20,000 bounty on the head of one John Cooler (John Richardson), a gold-hungry outlaw who has cheated Klint and his other cohorts out of their share of the takings; namely, a fortune in gold ingots rightfully belonging to the U.S. Army. Klint, by means of an official warrant for his arrest, plans to take John Cooler... be it dead or alive! But, Klint has competitors in his search for the outlaw, including Bill Cooler (John Richardson)—John's evil twin brother—and Sancho (Romano Magnino). The pair relieve Klint of his arrest warrant, but he manages to take it back later. Just when the price on Cooler's head is ready to be lowered due to his apparent disappearance, Klint locates his hideout. Their reunion is frought with tension, and, when John's bad twin Bill shows up, Klint is killed. The brothers discuss sharing the gold ingots amongst themselves. When John is later arrested and imprisoned in an Army stockade for theft, Bill negotiates with Captain Charlie (Franco Giornelli) that his brother be released in exchange for the gold.

Comments: Described by *Variety* as a "Holy Land western," **Execution**—director Domenico Paolella's second and final genre offering—was one of two Italoaters produced by the Mercedes-Ronbi production tandem in 1968, filmed at Eilat Studios near the Gulf of Aqaba in Israel and at Elios Film and In.Ci.R.-(Angelo) De Paolis Studios in Italy.

Producers of the day were ever on the lookout for something a little different to distinguish their films from the rest of the herd on the hoof at that time, at the very acme of Spaghetti westernmania. Other filmmakers were vacating the usual Spanish badlands in favor of such novel locales as Sardinia (for Gian Andrea Rocco's **Garter Colt** [Giarrettiera Colt, 1968, Italy]) and the Canary Islands (for Ferdinando Baldi's **The Forgotten Pistolero** a.k.a. Gunman of Ave Maria [Il pistolero dell'Ave Maria, 1969, Italy/Spain]), even ranging as far afield as The Land of the Rising Sun (for "Vance Lewis"/Luigi Vanzi's **The Silent Stranger** [Lo straniero di silenzio, 1968, Italy/Japan/USA])... and at long last making that previously-unheard-of, Bunyanesque leap to the genuine United States (for Sergio Leone's **Once Upon a Time in the West** [C'era una volta il West, 1968, Italy/USA]). For the film presently under discussion, Italian producer Fernando Franchi teamed-up with Israelite Alexander

Hachon to shoot **Execution** in the Holy Land (back-to-back with the Robert Woods starrer, **Black Jack** [1968, Italy/Israel, D: Gianfranco Baldanello]; Woods being under contract to Hacohen at the time). The arid Israeli desert and mountain ranges here make a nice change of pace from the way-overused Almerían vistas and Roman gravel pits seen in much of the competition. On the downside, horses appear rather pitiably puny in comparison to the more robust Latin breeds usually seen.

Westerns pitting good and bad twin brothers against one another were by no means new, even to Hollywood: witness "Joseph West"/George Waggner's poverty-row programmer **Black Bandit** (1938, USA), starring Bob Baker in double-vision. In **Execution**, director Paolella cast against type by having John Richardson play the sullen villain (as well as the hero). Brit actor Richardson had been a long-time resident of Italy, but at first glance might still seem an odd choice to play lead in a violent western. This quirky casting gamble pays off however, with the star portraying twin siblings: one good, the other bad (but *neither* ugly). For the film's first half he plays a boyish cowpoke who is mistaken for his evil twin brother. Later, Richardson—under spectacles and growth of beard—is virtually unrecognizable as the decidedly non-identical bad twin bro. A full hour in, the two square off via some competent over-the-shoulder stand-in camera work and Richardson's costume quick-change routine. The illusion is at times seamless. Perhaps for the better, only minimal (and costlier) split-screen special effects were utilized. A complicated, exaggerated sequence has Richardson as the 'good' brother rigging-up extra pistols and rifles on a series of ropes and pulleys to fool the gang into believing he's more than one man (in this case, he actually was). **Execution** ends with the good Richardson grieving, not over the death of his evil brother, but over his murdered friend.

Likewise cast against type—albeit in a single role—is brawny ex-peplum player Dick Palmer (a.k.a. Mimmo Palmara) as the wronged antihero, whose character bears the rather ungainly handle of "Klint Clips." Usually seen as an outright heavy, three years prior Palmer had essayed another heroic character in "Frank Kramer"/Gianfranco Parolini's minor programmer **Left-Handed Johnny West** ([Johnny West il mancino, 1965, Italy/France/Spain] which, coincidentally enough, also included twin brothers played by a single actor). For **Execution**, Palmer is an ex-con on the prowl for a former gangmember with a reward hanging over his head like a noose. Much like a scene out of the co-star's pectoraled peplum past, Palmer's meaty chest is laid bare here, though this time with a difference. During an extended torture scene, Palmer's pecs are repeatedly clawed and gored by a captor's fork in an effort to loosen his stubborn tongue. When he finally escapes from the bandits' hideout, an innocent woman who had taken pity on Palmer is accidentally shot in the back by a fellow outlaw. With knife duels and its wicked ball-and-chain torture scene, the film often has more in common with a period Sicilian bandit drama than a spaghetti western (which were, after all, heavily influenced by period Sicilian bandit dramas). As the torturer named Sancho—no relation to Fernando!—Italo actor Romano Magnino is even more gleeful in his sadism than his Spanish namesake ever was. Richardson later gives the undeserving Sancho a fair fighting chance before plugging him fully six times (just for good measure, you understand!).

A traveling theatrical troupe, that staple of the genre, appears once again. In a rare development, fleeting female nudity is glimpsed when a kidnap victim is molested by Nestor Garay as a bandit boss named Juárez (no relation to the real Juárez). [*With some invaluable input from Michael "Ferg" Ferguson.*]

Notes: Assistant director was Renzo Girolami. The main title theme was subsequently used in countless "Miles Deem"/Demofilo Fidani westerns. **Execution** became available on DVD via Germany's Koch Media, as part of that company's "Django Italo-Western Box" set.

Left: Italian Fotbusta- Three Dollars of Lead
Right: Fred Beir in Three Dollars of Lead
Page 237: Spanish Pressbook: Three Dollars of Lead

Three Dollars' Worth of Lead (Tre dollari... di piombo, 1964, Italy / Spain / France)

Synopsis (ATTN: THE FOLLOWING TWO PARAGRAPHS CONTAIN SPOILERS!): After spending some years in prison, Rudy Wallace (Fred Beir/"Blayr") escapes and returns to the ranch of his birth in order to avenge his father Ezekiel Wallace's murder. Reprehensible 'businessman' Mr. Morrison ("Oliver"/Olivier Mathot) is responsible for ordering the crime. Along with his men, led by Mark, Morrison intimidates local residents, including Ann and her father. Morrison's gang vandalize the Wallace ranch and interfere with Rudy's reopening of the place. Frightened neighbours will not come to his aid. In the local saloon, Rudy confronts his tormentors. During a brawl, he is about to be backshot by Morrison when he is saved by a stranger's disarming gun-blast. Rudy's saviour turns out to be an ex-sheriff, Raf ("Andrew Hart"/Andrea Fantasia), who has been tailing Rudy in order to escort him back to prison. Rudy pleads for just twenty-four hours in which to settle up scores with Morrison, but Raf refuses, disarms him and starts back toward jail in Santa Monica.

While crossing the prairie, Rudy and Raf are attacked by Morrison's gunmen, and are victorious. Raf breaks his leg when he falls from his horse, but refuses to set Rudy free. Wandering in the wilderness—with Raf limping along on his broken leg—they are rescued by Ann (Evy Marandi), Rudy's sweetheart, who takes them back into town. Morrison later hires a Mexican bandit to murder Sheriff Raf with a knife, but Raf instead kills his assassin. Rudy challenges Morrison to a showdown in the town square, while terrified citizens huddle inside the church, further dissuaded from violence by their preacher. When Morrison gains the upper hand, Raf's advent in a wagon draws the villain from cover, and he kills the brave former sheriff. Rudy then kills Morrison, and, their courage restored, the townsfolk band together to mop-up the remainder of Morrison's mob.

Comments:

Translated French-Canadian AGI videotape blurb: *'A Film of Adventure... Great Sensation... Transporting You Into a Violent World...'*

Three Dollars' Worth of Lead was originally due to begin shooting the same month in Yugoslavia under direction by Italo co-producer Pino Mercanti. The film ultimately wound up on Spanish locations with native castilian José María Zabalza at the reins, shot jointly at Ballesteros Studios, Spain and Bruno Cera Studios, Italy starting in July of '64.

Upon returning to the cobweb-infested old homestead, little-known American-born star Fred Beir is overwhelmed by nostalgia and 'relives' his childhood by affectionately fondling every damn western prop on the farm. Beir gives a credible enough performance and looks believable as a gunslinger; especially during the film's grand finale, for which he applies formal black leather vest and shootin' gloves. As in Cesare Canevari's quaint early euroater **Die for a Dollar in Tucson** (Per un dollaro a Tucson si muore, 1964, Italy/Yugoslavia/France/USA)—although less synthetically—cinematography stresses the quaint picture-postcard scenery greenery of European farmland. Close attention is paid to the accoutrements of everyday frontier life: dressers literally *load* sets with wagons, western saddles, etc. The general store is a veritable well-stocked supermarket of rifles, tools and water canteens (maybe there was a special ten-for-one offer on down at the property rental that day?). Backgrounds are thoroughly outfitted with all the appropriate props and extras. Production values are surprisingly high, also affording a squaredance well-attended by properly-attired celebrants and a fiddle band whose entire repertory however seems to consist of a single neverending tune (licensing even a single extra tune for them to play was evidently beyond the scope of the budget).

Although many cast members sport several days' growth of facial hair, dominant look here is checkerboard shirts and vests, à la olden days Hollywood. Typically, the main theme lyrics are absolutely unintelligible (English? Spanish? French?), swamped by bad sound production. Sometimes (on the formerly available Québec videocassette print at least), audio mix is so poorly done that sounds of punches drown out the lowing of a cattle herd and the click of Beir's empty gun muffles the hoofbeats of a half-dozen galloping horses. Gioacchino Angelo's overly sentimental score is at times way too threadbare and minimalist (i.e., amateurish), often sounding better attuned to an American comedy or drama from the '40s or '50s. Down at the Long Branch saloon, haystack-haired singer Dinah de Santis performs an insipid gals'n'guns ballad, "Silken Stockings" (dubbed in patchy English).

Some fights and stuntwork are stiff and stagey, especially Roberto Messina's systematic—but unconvincing—brutalization of an aging rancher. Beir brings far more conviction to his own action scenes, especially an extended fistfight with Messina in the saloon, where latter (who also served as stunt arranger) 'interacts' with a very sturdy-looking, non-breakaway bar table. Every time Beir and Messina meet, they come to blows... or bullets. Closing battle sees old Andrea Fantasia—may not look the part, but sure acts it—careening supine 'round town in an uncovered wagon while plugging baddies right, left and centre. Perhaps Beir should have been assigned this heroic duty, as he spends most of the final reel barricaded behind barrels with pistol in fist. Fantasia goes out clutching his tin star in a stubborn dead man's grip. Enough *kerrang!*-ing ricochet shots are heard to equip a dozen Hollywood shootemups.

Despite its naïve appearance and formula programmer status, much care was obviously lavished on **Three Dollars' Worth of Lead** in a number of departments; and for this reason it stands as an important pre-Leone example of the Spaghetti Western. *[With some invaluable input from Michael "Ferg" Ferguson.]*

Notes: Filmed in the "TotalScope" widescreen format. AGI's French-language Québecois VHS/Beta videotape release utilized artwork of Claudio Camaso (who is not in the film), chomping-down on a golden dollar (said art had originally appeared on French posters for "Sidney Lean"/Giovanni Fago's **Vengeance is Mine** a.k.a. **$100,000 for a Killing** [Per 100.000 dollari t'ammazzo, 1967, Italy], which did co-star Camaso). This film was shot back-to-back with "Joseph Trader"/José María Zabalza's **The Damned Guns of Dallas** (Le maledette pistole di Dallas, 1964, Italy/Spain), also toplining SpagWest two-timer Beir.

The Man from Oklahoma a.k.a. Ranch of the Ruthless (Il ranch degli spietati, Italy / Spain / West Germany, 1964)

Synopsis (ATTN: THE FOLLOWING THREE PARAGRAPHS CONTAIN SPOILERS!): The town of Red River, New Mexico is dominated by powerful cattleman Rod Edwards, whose swaggering bully of a ranch foreman, Hondo, uses blatant intimidation tactics to keep local residents under the fascistic boot-heel. Edwards is a voracious land-grabber out to gobble up all available—or even unavailable— local property, and rules the town by means of Hondo and (quote) "50 tough cowpokes."

Enter Dan Cross, a no-nonsense Oklahoman—hence his nickname of "Oklahoma" —who has arrived in the lawless frontier town to assume his officially appointed post as its new sheriff... whether Edwards and Hondo like it or not. It develops that, unbeknownst to his father Mr. Edwards, the rancher's no-account spoiled-rotten son Jim was complicit in not only a stagecoach robbery but also the murder of Mr. White, owner of valuable oil-bearing lands in the vicinity coveted by Mr. Edwards. This property has since fallen to the late landowner's beautiful young daughter, Georgiana White. Trustingly—if unwisely—Georgiana signs a Power of Attorney temporarily giving over the deeds of her land to her 'concerned friend' Steve Watson, proprietor of the local drinking establishment, who has both an ulterior motive and a hidden agenda.

Local old timer Ken Hogg becomes another victim of the villains' scheme to illegally acquire the oil lands. Sheriff Dan determines to bring those responsible to justice. After young Jim Edwards subsequently confesses to his father that while under the influence of alcohol he had murdered Hogg – who had borne witness to Jim's and Hondo's earlier crimes—Mr. Edwards disowns his son, leaving him to fend for himself. Jim and Hondo—the latter working in secret cahoots with shady saloonkeeper Steve Watson—shortly begin plotting to clean out the safe of the local Sandy Creek Bank. During commission of this robbery, Hondo fatally shoots a bank teller in cold blood, and as he and his accomplice the Edwards boy make good their getaway, Watson poses as an innocent bystander and administers a self-inflicted gunshot wound to his forearm so as the deflect any suspicion from him. Having fled the scene of their crime, Jim Edwards and Hondo hide out in the wilderness, while Sheriff Dan and his deputy Mike form a two-man posse and get hot on the perpetrators' trail. In the mountains, a shootout erupts between the two bank robbers, during which Hondo backshoots the fleeing Jim, mortally wounding him. After the wounded Jim rides off into the surrounding countryside, Hondo attempts to bushwhack Dan and Mike as they ride into sniping range. Upon finding himself pinned down by their return fire, dry-gulchin' polecat Hondo attempts to bargain for his life by pinning the recent crimes on Jim Edwards, denying all involvement in them.

Back in Red River, Jim's pa Mr. Edwards rides in leading a force of his hired gunmen, intent on putting paid to Sheriff Dan, believing him responsible for the killing of his son. Joined by Mike, Chuck and a number of armed townsmen, Dan prepares to hold off the cattle baron's attack. However, rather than resorting to wholesale bloodshed old Mr. Edwards determines to go one on one with the sheriff. Just as he is striding towards Dan with rifle in hand, who should ride in but Jim Edwards, close to death. With his dying breath, Jim defuses the volatile standoff by informing his father that it was actually Hondo and not Sheriff Dan who had shot him. At the saloon, acting on his suspicions Dan thereafter confronts the treacherous and conniving Watson, who has 'legally' assumed possession of Georgianna's land and remains smugly self-assured of his untouchability in any and all criminal wrongdoing. However, taking the law into his own hands, the vengeful Mr. Edwards walks in and pumps fully seven Winchester bullets into Watson's scurvy hide!

Comments:

Karl-Otto Alberty as the blustering Hondo talks tough: *"Ya better clear out, before I put my brand on yer hide! An' I don't use a brandin' iron, that's fer cattle. Fer a critter like you, I like ta use a shootin' iron!"*

Rick Horn as Oklahoma Dan: *"Do you expect me to get scared-off like the other sheriffs? Never! Not me."* – *"I'm here ta keep the peace: looks like I got plenty ta keep me busy!"*

Shot upon the newly-erected Esplugas City western set—which already appears noticeably scrappy and ramshackle herein, as though it had already been standing for decades—this was workaholic Catalán producer Francisco Balcázar's next project following his more-than-respectable Robert Woods star vehicle **Five Thousand Dollars on One Ace** (5000 dollari sull'asso, Spain/West Germany/Italy, 1965). Filmed beginning in October '64 near Fraga, Spain over a five-week shoot—you can tell it was shot in the wintertime, as star Rick Horn's frosty exhalations are plainly visible in one scene—**The Man from Oklahoma** (a crossover three-way split paella / spaghetti / sauerkraut coproduction) was Balcázar's second western venture; predating an impending mid-'60s production glut which would shortly seriously undermine the domestic Spanish film industry, very nearly ham-stringing it conclusively in the process.

Page 239: German Lobby Card
Page 240: Top: Italian Locandina
Page 240: Bottom: Dorado DVD release

Despite flourishes of more modernesque violence—for instance, the Ken Hogg character's corpse is found with a bloody bullethole in its forehead—the general tone here is wanna-be old-school Hollywood all the way. Rather than sleeker Colts, revolvers are largely of the clunkier looking Webley type. Fashion-wise, the predominant look for males is leather vests worn over check shirts. Unlike many another Spaghetti leading man, Horn's wardrobe doesn't really stand out in a crowd and as good as blends in with the scenery. Here making his one-and-only genre outing, top-billed Horn as the hero—who at times brings to mind Dan Vadis, at others a 'bigger-faced' Robert Woods—is first glimpsed as a mounted silhouette riding behind the opening titles while accompanied by Francesco de Masi's traditional orchestral theme. When asked what his name is, Horn replies, "Oklahoma Dan is what they call me. Folks shortened it up, though: 'Oklahoma' is what they call me now." Although he is clearly delivering his lines in English beneath the post-synched dialogue, only occasionally do the movements of Horn's lips actually match up with the dubbed words heard purportedly coming from his mouth.

Despite his black hat playing a more traditional incorruptible hero than any sort of antihero—although if it means anything, said hat seems a few sizes too small for his oversized head—the big-chinned Horn affects a cocky swagger, twirls his shooting iron on his finger by its trigger guard and commits himself with some zeal to the physical side of his role, even if virtually every line that leaves his mouth is a solid macho cliché (e.g., "If anybody's gonna do any shooting, *I'm* gonna have a hand in it!"). Shortly after pulling into town, he sets up shop in the disused sheriff's office. Indicative of just how long Red River has been left lawless, a thick layer of dust covers his predecessor's desk. Horn actually says "That's no way to treat a lady" when a drunken male saloon patron gets boorish with one of the fairer sex in attendance. In one of the more unintentionally amusing scenes, Horn is looking-over heroine Sabine Bethmann's sprawling spread, whereupon, having spotted a small pool of dark liquid on the ground, he kneels down to scoop up a handful of same for a taster, in the interests of identifying what it is. Fully ten seconds (perhaps more) later, he comes to the none-too-swift realization that "This is *OIL!*"—gee, talk about a delayed reaction! But he's such a man that he not only doesn't spit, but doesn't even so much as sputter in the presence of a lady, either. In mixed company or not, even such gentleman gunnies as Gary Cooper, Randolph Scott or Joel McCrea at their most prim'n'proper couldn't have maintained such perfect composure!

Easily this exceedingly minor if entertaining programmer's best scenes are those in which our hero mixes it up with the head heavy's head henchman Hondo, as played in suitably smirky, arrogant style by German actor Alberty (a typecast Aryan/Teutonic player of nasty Nazzies in war movies, whose English-language dialogue dubber here often seems to be attempting an Edward G. Robinson impression!). Right in the prologue, Alberty establishes his hateful Hondo character by putting the strong-arm on impending new lawman Horn's professional predecessor. With horseshoe designs stitched into his gunbelt and real handy with throwing knives, the smirking Hondo is a one-dimensional shit-disturber through and through, forever looking to stir up trouble wherever he can find it (or better yet, cause it). A classic case of hate at first sight, no sooner have they met than Alberty threatens to boot Horn out of town for horning-in on the baddies' turf. During another of their several—*um*—'differences of opinion,' Horn punches Alberty face-first into a mud puddle. Prior to still another altercation, Horn announces, "I think Hondo needs *another* lesson!" He and Alberty then proceed to dismantle the barroom, during which the latter not only takes a non-breakaway chair in the belly, but he then gets ploughed bodily through a breakaway table on top of it. While Alberty seems to have resorted to a stunt double for some of the more demanding rough stuff, Horn on the other hand evidently performed all his own stunts. He gets 'chaired' in return and rolls backwards over a tabletop before shoulder-slamming into the soundbox of an upright piano; this followed by a near-miss from Hondo's thrown blade which comes less than a foot shy of piercing Sheriff Dan's earlobe for him. Alberty's double apparently takes over again when he is punched through a banister off the landing of a stairway and flops to the floor below. Despite the loud smacking sounds heard on the audio track, Horn's bitch-slaps clearly miss connecting with Alberty's chops by close to a foot, but the 'recipient' crumples in an unconscious heap anyway. ("Anyone *else* like ta try?!" challenges Horn afterwards. Needless to say, there are no takers.) A total rat bastard if ever there was one, during the commission of a bank robbery, rather than simply coldcocking a captive clerk with his gunbutt to keep him quiet, Alberty much prefers to pump no less than three bullets into the prone, bound-up man instead. He later turns weasel and tries to pin all his recent misdeeds on fellow German actor George Herzig's character. Before the final reel rolls around, Alberty and Horn lock horns once again. When the former attempts to bring a Winchester to a fistfight, the latter empties his entire sixgun into the knave's wuthless carcass.

Right from the very first moment that she snubs hero Horn and he snubs her right back, we know that the heart of leading lady Sabine Bethmann ("What a lovely girl, but a temper like a cat!") shall become his by the final fade, just as surely as all the villains shall receive their comeuppance. Initially set up to be the main heel of the piece—whose hired attack dog is Alberty as the horrible Hondo—José Calvo ultimately proves to be a man of much sturdier moral fibre than we have expected; plus, he is one of the few characters in the film with a (beige) hat that is not only the right size, but actually *suits* him. Here making her one-and-only appearance in a spaghetti western, while she only appears in a couple of minor scenes, beauteous brunette second female lead "Leontine May" (née Leontida Mariotta, a passable Sophia Loren lookalike) really gives it her all while emoting over the murdered Hogg character. As sleazy Steve Watson, the dapperly-dressed but two-faced saloon owner—who virtually *reeks* of untrustworthiness right from frame one!—pencil-mustached Tom Felleghy sometimes looks a little too much like country crooner Wayne Newton for comfort! Somewhat resembling a homelier, shorter, scruffier version of apple pie western character Edgar Buchanan, Jesús Puente plays Horn's newly acquired sidekick Chuck, an ex-sarge in the U.S. Cavalry who still wears his lopsided crossed-sabers cap and misuses the sheriff's office for his personal doss-house.

For the most part, actors' performances beneath the dub-job are far more animated and competent than those of their voice dubbers; many of which might better fit an animated cartoon than a live action drama. Exaggeratedly kerranging/zinging bullet sound effects only further add to the overall cartoonishness of the audio track. Composer de Masi's music stays mostly Apple Pie in style, albeit with an occasional slight garlic flavour (one of its more ear-catching pieces is a gently-picked acoustic guitar accompanying melancholy humming). Various details of the transparent 'whodunit' subplot—including a lost spur rowel—play only passing incidental parts in the more emphasized 'town tamer vs. lawless faction' plotline.

Notes: Released stateside only to TV by them, not theatrically, Parkside Productions' Anglo-dubbed prints came equipped with only minimal onscreen cast and credits. The two above-listed directors each received credit in their respective homelands. It is quite possible (as was sometimes the practice) that they each prepared their own personal cuts of the movie for release in their respective domestic markets.

An original Anglo pressbook synopsis contained the lines: *"But all is not shooting and fighting for John and Michael. They have fallen in love with two beautiful girls..."*

While the following is by no means a verbatim transcription, at least one early Euro promotional source gave the synopsis thusly:- An officer in the US Army, operating under the alias "Oklahoma John," is dispatched to disband a gang of arms smugglers along the Mexican border. The ringleader is a wealthy land baron. John, a seasoned fighter with both guns and fists, infiltrates the gunrunners to get to their boss. Because John rises fast through the gang's ranks, he earns the animosity of envious members, who attempt to trip him up at every turn. Deciding the time is ripe to confront the smugglers, John enlists the help of an old friend and a young gunslinger named Michael who seeks vindication after a brush with the law. The three comrades erect a roadblock across the main street of the town of Rio Rojo, then shoot it out with the outlaws. Law and order returns, while John and Michael look forward to marriage with their fiancées; the former's being Gloriana White.

As you can plainly tell from the contents of the preceding paragraph, a lot more than just the names were changed in the finished film! Feasibly, some of the above-detailed events might be present in one or more foreign version of the film (?), but virtually none of them are to be found in the version reviewed here. Could it be that there are multiple versions of this minor movie in existence, or are all those discrepancies merely a consequence of a drastic script rewrite at the eleventh hour? [With some invaluable input from Michael "Ferg" Ferguson.]

Who was Bob Henry?

Bob Henry (Robert Henry Hensley)

Robert Henry Hensley was born in Artlington, Texas on April 24, 1936 to John Coleman Hensley Sr, a Pharmacist who worked for Massingill Drug Corp. as a detail man in Southern Louisiana. His mother was a math teacher and taught Math in several large high schools. Both of his parents went to Baylor - His father to Baylor Pharmacy College and mother to Mary Hardin Baylor.

After playing football, basketball and running track at Lafayette High School, Robert went to Louisiana College on a football scholarship. He went to the University of Louisiana at Lafayette for 1 year. Then he attended Baylor University for 2 quarters, and finally got his BS in Theology and Philosophy at Dallas Baptist University.

He desired to become a recording artist and hitch-hiked to Hollywood with $75 and his suitcase and guitar. He made the journey in 36 hours. He found a boarding house room for $2 bucks a night. He sat on his bed and sang with his guitar, while his landlady listened. She introduced him to a press agent Walter Compton who gave John Wayne his name. Compton listened to Robert sing and called the big band singer, Artie Wayne. Artie loved the songs and promptly moved him to his multi-million dollar home on Mandeville Canyon Road, right across from actor Robert Mitchum's home.

Hensley recorded under the alias Jericho Brown and released a single called 'Little Neva' followed by 17 other singles one of which 'Reach for a Star' reached #1 in England. In the mid-1960s he was asked to join the MGM acting school. "Some wonderful actors like Yvette Mimeo and Bill Smith were in our class of about 30. Bill Smith, Richard Chamberlain and I were brought in to MGM for a series called 'Paradise Kid'. Richard Chamberlain got the lead, but we met many good people and had some really good acting coaching."

Hensley hired an agent and manager, Bobbie Roberts and Pierre Cossett. They Managed Anna Marie Albergetti, John Rait, Elaine Dunn and Ann Margaret. They were great in everything they did. Because of their connection to Italian talent Hensley was offered a 3 million lire contract to star in an Italian western. He went to Rome in 1967 and appeared as Bob Henry in "A Colt in the Hand of the Devil" directed by Sergio Bergonzelli and co-starring George Wang.

Hensley returned to the U.S. and to the Beverly Hills Baptist Church, where he had been a member. Deeply impacted by Pastor Barry Wood who he described as "a 'man's man' loving Jesus," Bob was led to a personal encounter with Jesus Christ. This one moment would redefine the rest of his life. After 15 years of "Hollywood living," he surrendered to the call of ministry that his mom had prayed for. From street-witnessing to Hollywood's hippy runaways, he followed the call to Grand Prairie, TX, birthing True Vine Ministries where over 3,000 received the Lord Jesus Christ.

In 1973 he married actress Pamela Baird [1945-   ] who was a TV actress who appeared as Mary Ellen Rogers, Wally Cleaver's girlfriend, in the 'Leave it to Beaver' TV series. Bob and Pam were married for 43 years and had five children and six grandchildren (Alexandra, Victoria, Christian, Emory, Isaac, Danielle and Joshua).

Robert Henry Hensley died in Arlington, Texas on May 22, 2016. He was 80. Bob was buried in Bluebonnet Hills Cemetery in Colleyville, Texas.

-Tom Betts

www.diabolikdvd.com

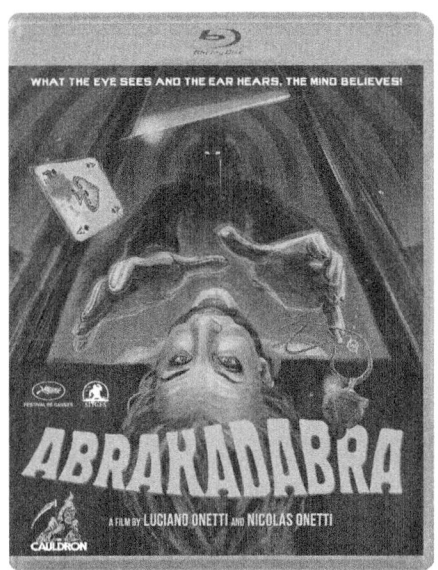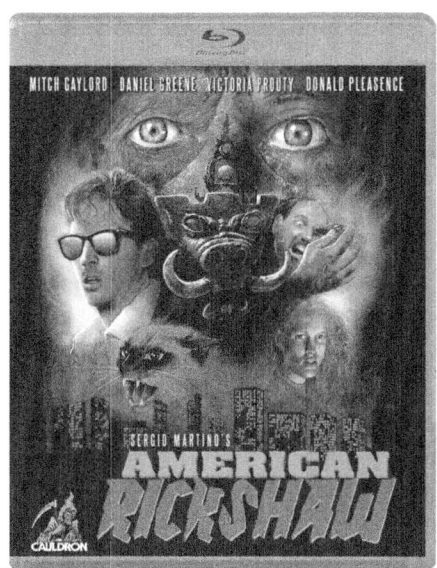

www.cauldron-films.com

Afterword

Well, here we are again, eh my friends at the end of another issue of The Spaghetti Western Digest. Thus far all of my friends and family (knock on wood), have avoided the Covid plague and here's hoping it stays that way! Hope you enjoyed the second issue of The Spaghetti Western Digest and issue #3 is slated, to be released somewhere around December 2020- January 2021. After issue #3 the digest will come to an end and then its time to ride off into the sunset... Well not really! There are lots of things going on behind the scenes at M.H. Books and 2021 looks to be an exciting year for us. And no need to worry Amigos' because whatever M.H. Books has in the pipeline, it will include (long as their willing), all the writers involved thus far in The Spaghetti Western Digest! Anyways thanks again for reading the digest and look for issue # 3- Coming later this year or early next... Oh and BTW, issue # 3 will include some films that influenced or were influenced by the Spaghetti oaters- And an interview with the Iconic Fred Williamson! Once again thanks to all the readers of this digest and the contributors!

Thanks

First off, I must thank one of the best Amigos I have ever had the pleasure of knowing in Tom Betts! Thanks to Tim Paxton, the 'Zine guru who has been a guiding force through the publishing of the digest. Thanks to Eric Mache for the amazing photos he is always so gracious to share with us here at The Spaghetti Western Digest and Ally Lamaj for sharing his knowledge. Thanks to my Amigos: Robert Woods, David Koenig, Daniel Camargo, Dennis Capicik, Anthony Thorne, Tony Nash, Artus Films, Wild East Productions, Fred Williamson, John Crummett, Keir Arts, Kevin Grant, Roberto Curti, Mike Siegel, Paul Bishop, Pete Chiarella, Rene Hogguer, Rudulf Schutz, Sarah Smith, Steve Mason, Steve Fenton, Eugenio Ercolani and Van Roberts, Sebastain Haselbeck, Phil Hardcastle, John P. Dulaney, Tom Beterams and Tom Prickette!
Thanks as always to Carl Black!

Well friends its time to mosey on out of here… Happy Trails to You… Until we meet Again! Adios Amigos!
-Michael Hauss

Printed in Great Britain
by Amazon